Kevin Wilson was born and educated in Yorkshire, lived for a time in North America and now resides in Cheshire. He spent most of his working life as a staff journalist on British national newspapers, including the *Daily Mail* and latterly the *Daily* and *Sunday Express*. He held a pilot's licence for 25 years and has had a life-long passion for personal history, particularly the experiences of Second World War Allied bomber aircrew. His previous, highly acclaimed, trilogy included *Bomber Boys* (2005), *Men of Air* (2007) and *Journey's End* (2010). He is married with three grown-up sons and a daughter.

Praise for *Blood and Fears*

'An experienced author in the World War Two field, Wilson's polished storytelling, inspired by first-hand accounts (from diaries, letters and interviews) brings the reality of the American Air Forces' bomber offensive in Europe to life – both on and off the battlefields ... honestly portraying the triumphs and tragedies of war' *Who Do You Think You Are?*

'Overpaid, oversexed and over here ... Who but the Yanks in Second World War Britain? ... Wilson's all-guns-blazing history of the USAAF (United States Army Air Forces) boys and girls covers everything from Glenn Miller dances and gifts of silk stockings to nerve-wracking daylight raids over Germany. It flies' *Sunday Express*

'Wilson has already written about the British and Commonwealth experience in a series of excellent books and this latest volume completes the picture ... A war of attrition that was every bit as grindingly bloody as the trench fighting of a generation before' *Mail on Sunday*

'A brilliant book' Robert Elms, BBC Radio London

'In the hands of a master craftsman with a keen eye for human detail the story [Wilson] has to tell is as compelling as it is comprehensive' *Eastern Daily Press*

'Abounds with arresting detail – the widespread use of Benzedrine to fight tiredness, the frustrating performance of the electric suits designed to keep flyers warm at 28,000 feet ... the role of sheer luck in determining who lived or died and the shockingly high risk of collision' *Kirkus Reviews*

KEVIN WILSON

BLOOD
AND
FEARS

How America's Bomber Boys and Girls
in England Won their War

W&N
WEIDENFELD & NICOLSON

To Macy and Austin,
who bring joy to our hearts

First published in Great Britain in 2016
First published in paperback in 2017 by Weidenfeld & Nicolson
an imprint of The Orion Publishing Group Ltd
Carmelite House, 50 Victoria Embankment
London EC4Y 0DZ

An Hachette UK Company

1 3 5 7 9 10 8 6 4 2

A CIP catalogue record for this book is
available from the British Library.

ISBN 978 1 474 60163 4

Typeset by Input Data Services Ltd, Somerset

Printed in Great Britain by CPI Group (UK) Ltd, Croydon, CR0 4YY

Contents

WINTER

SPRING

List of Illustrations

List of Maps

'I sometimes feel like a ghost.'

> Navigator Lt Andrew Vero, 306th BG, Thurleigh, Bedfordshire, who at the
> request of another officer desperate to finish his tour and go home, swopped
> planes with him then saw him die as that plane collided with another

'I think you think clearer when you're so damned near death.'

> Medal of Honor winner 2/Lt Red Morgan, blown out of his exploding
> 482nd BG bomber still clutching his parachute, finally managing to
> clip it on at 500ft as he hurtled towards burning Berlin

'Inside we found blood spatter and small scraps of meat. We
laughed about it then. We were so callous as 16-year-olds.'

> German schoolboy flak helper, describing wreckage of a B-17 blown apart on its
> bomb run, which came down near his Merseburg gun emplacement

'An Fw 190 came up between our tail and our wing so close I could
see his face. I'm sure I didn't miss.'

> Waist gunner S/Sgt Jack Laswell, recounting the disastrous Kassel
> mission from which only three of the thirty-five planes of
> his 445th BG returned safely to base at Tibenham, Norfolk

'Aircrew officers were very young, well paid, able to go wherever
on free time and had plenty of wild oats to sow.'

> Pilot Lt Howard Roth, of the 306th BG, a B-17 commander at just 21

'BOOM!!! The ship exploded. The fuselage forward of the ball
turret was gone. Everything to the rear behind the tail wheel was
also gone. I rolled out of the hatch. My chute was on upside down.
I pulled the cord, wait, wait, wait, was it going to open. POW! I got
the full impact in my face.'

> Ball turret gunner S/Sgt Calvin Brend, whose Group lost seven bombers in one
> Big Week mission

'I saw at least a dozen ships go down in flames. I was scared silly
and I am not afraid to admit it.'

> Combat diary of T/Sgt Ernest Barton, top turret gunner with the 493rd BG,
> Debach, Suffolk

'What a year! Wouldn't have missed it for anything.'

> Letter from Kay Brainard, American Red Cross assistant attached to the 486th
> BG, Sudbury, Suffolk

Introduction

The young crews of the United States Army Air Force who arrived in Britain with bright and boundless optimism in the opening months of 1944 to finally put paid to Hitler, stepped down from their Flying Fortress and Liberator bombers into an atmosphere guaranteed to dampen the enthusiasm of the most hopeful heart. England and in fact the whole of Europe was gripped in the rigours of the worst winter for nearly thirty years. The airmen's months of training in the New World's sunshine states had left them ill prepared for it.

As they groped through the blackout to their temporary billets there was the first intimation of a climate of fear. The excitement of arriving in the old world where centuries-old customs still held was quickly dissipated by the chilling cold of Quonset huts at holding bases before assignment, buildings of iron where the rumours echoed and the tabulations of chance were added up and taken away again. In the autumn, only weeks previously, sixty of the 320 US bombers which had set out to bomb the ball-bearing factories of Schweinfurt had not returned and another 120 were so badly damaged they were off the flight roster. It was the second time it had happened in short order, a similar toll being exacted in a Schweinfurt-Regensburg mission in August. US 8th Air Force (8th AF) operations had been virtually halted and Congressmen had debated whether to end altogether America's daylight partnership with Britain in the European bomber offensive.

If the youngsters got off base there was little comfort to be found by wandering into one of the English pubs they had heard so much about. A chance encounter with a fellow airman from the RAF or Dominion air forces would provide no welcoming warmth of comradeship, but more likely a taciturn stiff-upper-lip or a depressing litany of loss. Morale on the RAF bomber stations was at rock bottom as the nocturnal Battle of Berlin cut a swathe through the ranks of the boys in blue.

But in fact the college boys and high school hopefuls from America had arrived at a turning point, the hinge of a beginning, not an end. Within weeks the ebb in the Allied air war would change to flow in a suddenly more positive direction. The influx was here to at last make possible round-the-clock bombing – the Americans by day, the British by night, a desire of the Casablanca Directive encapsulated at the 1943 North African conference of the joint US/UK chiefs of staff, but so seldom achieved. Now America's men and machines would ensure Germans had no rest, just as Britons had little respite in the Luftwaffe city blitz of 1940–41. The vast resources of the United States, its armaments plants producing a total of 276,000 aircraft in the war, would overwhelm the output of German factories, preparing the way for D-Day. To win the battle of the beaches the Luftwaffe would first have to be defeated in the air and in the factories which kept it alive.

The year that mattered most to the German economy was 1944. After years of under-production as the German people enjoyed the fruits of easy victory – Great Britain alone had produced 54 per cent more war planes than the Nazis in 1942 – the Reich Armaments Minister Albert Speer had finally rationalised and dispersed manufacturing to achieve a wartime peak of aircraft production in September 1944. But by then it was too late. The world's great arsenal across the Atlantic had already poured forth an ever-gathering stream of bombers and fighters for the final *Götterdämmerung* in the skies above the Reich. The aircrew needed for those planes flew in and came ashore in ever-increasing numbers from the beginning of 1944 to make final victory inevitable.

And while all this was being achieved in the air the American boys created a social change in Britain, often by their sheer volume, which would build to a sociological revolution. They were an incomparable force of nature. One in six people in the county of Suffolk, where many of the 8th AF bases were, would be American by 1944. In the tired, war-weary villages of Suffolk, Norfolk, Cambridgeshire and north Essex where lists of sons had been building over four years to join their fathers on war memorials, the arrival of the Americans proved a shock the repercussions of which are still being felt today. Hollywood burst into the hamlet. A succession of film actors arrived to serve or entertain and British civilians and US personnel alike found themselves rubbing shoulders with stardom. It gave glamour to lives already scripted with high drama in which American flyboys had the 'Aw, shucks' charm of screen idols.

The lure of such clean-cut crusaders was not lost on village maidens, who provided solace and comfort to the young men far from home who daily returned from visions of aerial horror no training could prepare them for – fearful scenes in which friends were burned alive in stricken bombers or were seen tumbling helplessly to earth without a parachute. In fact the promise of such a warm, female welcome had even been alluded to in official USAAF training material. A movie star turned airman-documentary maker had turned to the camera, pointed to his pilot's wings and said the glittering badge's effect on girls was 'phenomenal'. That desire to cut a dashing figure when the draft came had proved a bigger draw than the words of any recruiting poster.

But there were other more serious reasons for choosing to join the air war, rather than slog through mud in the infantry or face endless stretches of ocean in the navy. In the immediate previous decades of peace the youngsters of the United States had become more air-minded perhaps than any other nation as the new travel medium shrank its vast continent. Now American boys were getting the chance to turn remote hope into reality by learning to fly at the government's expense. Seldom expressed, but buried in the psyche was also the greater knowledge that the Nazis were enslaving the old world across the Atlantic – a Europe many of the young airmen's ancestors came from. Striking from the sky at the heart of the enemy seemed an effective way of breaking those chains.

The training and the clumsy experimentation of the first two years of war were now over. American youth had come en masse to do or die in the skies of Europe. Die they would, 26,000 being killed in the 8th AF. And as suddenly as the Americans had arrived, shaking the foundations of an ancient society, the survivors disappeared back across the Atlantic. They took with them 41,000 British girls and more than 14,000 children they had fathered.

For most combat airmen of the 8th AF the stuff of nightmares they witnessed in the skies over Europe would gradually be swept into the recesses of gentle memory over the following decades. Most of them today would admit their time in the service has a dream-like quality as if it was another young man who had stood in their place and stepped through the fire to glory decades before. But fortunately for the generations that followed, the airmen wrote diaries, a vast number of them, unlike their comrades in the RAF, who in fear of security breaches were not encouraged to do so. And it was not only the men who kept journals. The women who came with them, the WACs and Red Cross girls, created records too, writing home, perhaps more assiduously, about the lost Britain they were enshrining for ever, from the glitz of 'Yank' London to the country kindness of strangers. Not all of the Americans lived to read those scribbled records to their grandchildren. It is the content of these diaries and letters, written within hours of traumatic events in the sky seventy years ago, which is the heart of this book.

WINTER

1

'He had us dead to rights'

It was a brutal way to begin the last day of your life. The torch beam in the eyes, the cold hand on the shoulder and the chilling enlightenment: 'You're flying a mission today, breakfast in half an hour, briefing at 0515', by which many of the USAAF's young airmen were wakened at their English bases was guaranteed to concentrate the mind in a moment. As the Quonset hut door banged shut behind the retreating Charge of Quarters enlisted man in the pre-dawn of 20 February 1944, all dreams of America, home and beauty vanished in a flash and were replaced by the shock of fear spreading from the stomach to the brain and back again. It wasn't just the cold of billet concrete which started limbs shaking and the mind racing as feet hit the floor, but the knowledge of what had already been witnessed happening to others. The swift departure of a crew in a flak burst, the slowly spinning fall from formation of a fighter-crippled bomber, the blast of cannon which turned comrades into pulsating bloody flesh on the flight deck were images which now easily transposed with your own face, your limbs, your aircraft at the centre of the horrifying picture.

As the trudging lines of dispirited aviators made for their

mess halls and the waiting operational fresh eggs that February morning, there was the faint prospect that the mission would be abandoned. Heavy rain at most bases was turning to snow showers and visibility extended no further than the end of runways. It was little better as the young flyers stumbled into operation blocks for briefing in hope the low clouds offered reprieve from the Luftwaffe. As they sleepily gathered on the hard benches, some not long out of high school remembered it was Sunday and cast minds back to family walks to church, Mom and apple pie before this hellish mayhem had been unleashed. Now someone else was eyeing up their best girl in the pew and they were gathered in growing apprehension to hear how accurately to ruin a German Sunday. Earlier they might have heard the sound of RAF bombers based at neighbouring bases in East Anglia returning from a maximum-effort raid to the very place where many of them would soon be heading, Leipzig. The operation had been launched against a Luftwaffe night fighter force at the peak of its powers and a total of seventy-eight British bombers and their crews were now lying broken in foreign fields as dawn stretched its frosty fingers across the Reich. At 9.5 per cent, it was the second biggest loss Sir Arthur Harris's command would suffer in one night.

For others, at the 8th Air Force bases nearer London, at Ridgewell, Essex, and Thurleigh, near Bedford, little more than twenty-four hours before the war had been brought visibly home to their billets with searchlights lancing south across the night sky to the yellow flash of anti-aircraft fire and the crimson bursts of bombs. Now the USAAF bomber boys were themselves waiting to be hurled into the maelstrom of aerial combat. It would be the first time the 8th's three bombardment divisions (BDs) had been despatched in concert on Germany since a mission to Frankfurt am Main sixteen days before, when twenty of the 748 Flying Fortresses and Liberators which took off failed to make it home.

'He had us dead to rights'

This was the big one, Mission 226 of the USAAF's campaign against German industry. The earnest Operations Staff, pool cues in hand to point to the key areas of the routes, told them more than 1,000 B-17 Flying Fortresses and B-24 Liberators from twenty-nine bomb groups (BGs) in the UK would be attacking various targets in the Reich. It would be the largest bomber force ever assembled by the USAAF to date. It would also be the longest penetration of Axis-held territory, necessitating a return trip of up to 1,150 miles. There would be another record statistic to come: more Medals of Honor, the highest award Congress could bestow, would be won that day than any other in the European air war as young airmen on both sides battled for supremacy.

Throughout East Anglia eyes were turned to the end wall of operations blocks and riveted on the map of Europe with its red marker which crawled across the North Sea. Crews of both the 1st and 2nd Bombardment Divisions saw the tape stretching over Holland almost all the way to Berlin, before splitting into abrupt course changes just west of Brunswick. The B-17s of the 1st Division would go on to hit targets at Leipzig, Heiterblick, Abtnaundorf and Bernberg, individual numbers of Groups dividing again en route. To further confuse the enemy as to American intentions the B-17s of the 3rd Division would fly in over Denmark then turn south, again indicating a raid on Berlin, but in fact splitting to strike at the Focke-Wulf 190 fighter factory at Tutow with the Heinkel 111 bomber plant at Rostock as a 'target of opportunity', a term which was often used in post-raid intelligence to cover the dumping of bombs by unsuccessful returning planes on anything which looked useful. The B-24s of the 2nd Division would at first follow the same route as the 1st BD then take on aircraft industry complexes at Brunswick and Gotha. Deputy lead on the Brunswick mission would be a pilot well known to the crews as an Oscar-winning Hollywood star, Major James Stewart of the 445th BG.

5

The largest force would come from the 1st BD, in the triangle between Peterborough, Bedford and Cambridge. It would be despatching 417 Flying Fortresses, followed by 314 from the 3rd Division, north of Ipswich, then 272 Liberators from the 2nd around Norwich. To protect the bombers almost as many fighters would be aloft, 835 Lightnings, Thunderbolts and Mustangs from fifteen USAAF fields and others from sixteen squadrons of the RAF and Dominion air forces. What united the forces was intention; all targets had been selected because of their importance to the Luftwaffe, from the Messerschmitt 109 and Junkers 88 factories at Leipzig to the Me 110 plants at Brunswick and Gotha. In all twelve centres of aircraft manufacture would be hit in one joined-up plan. This blow it was hoped would start to put the Luftwaffe out of business long before the prime targets of helpless, wallowing lines of landing craft hove into view off the D-Day beaches that summer.

It was obvious there would be no 'milk runs', as American airmen termed less-exacting missions, today. But at first the crews of the 3rd BD thought they had drawn marginally the least dangerous of the three divisional tasks – much of their route being over the sea. Then they were told none of the fighters available would be assigned to them. Lt Gen. James Doolittle, only weeks into his new job of overall controller of the 8th Air Force commands, had calculated he could risk leaving them defenceless because he estimated the Luftwaffe would be too busy dealing with what they would see first as a threat to Berlin then trying to fend off the attacks to the aircraft towns to the east and south of it. Crews were not convinced. They remembered a similar plan for Anklam, near Tutow, only a few weeks before when other – fighter-protected – divisions were attacking targets at Marienburg and in Poland. It had cost the unescorted Anklam force eighteen of its 106 bombers despatched.

What none of the combat airmen knew, in any of the three divisions, was that to a certain extent they were bait for the

Luftwaffe, for this was the first day of Operation Argument, the opening shots of Big Week, a concentrated period of intense raids on the German aviation industry which it was hoped would draw the Luftwaffe to battle so that it could be defeated both in the air and on the ground. It would thus point the way to eventual total American air supremacy and help RAF Bomber Command at the same time by reducing the number of single-engined fighters now wreaking a horrifying level of attrition among British bomber crews at night. The abundance of US fighters going along were there to achieve that; no longer would fighters be tied to the bombers. When the Luftwaffe appeared as specks in the sky they would peel off to meet them, guns blazing. But the losses among the bombers were expected to be heavy. General Frederick Anderson, Chief of Operations of the new United States Strategic and Tactical Air Forces in Europe, whose detailed plan Operation Argument essentially was, had estimated that one fifth of the force might fail to return on the first day. The crews were told meteorologists had forecast clear weather over Germany. The predictions also held good for another two days, though that wasn't revealed to the airmen themselves lest they drew the inevitable conclusion that those who returned would be going again within hours.

But to the briefed officers and enlisted men at many bases it looked unlikely they would be taking off at all as the jeeps and crew trucks drove them out to the glistening dispersal pans where their loaded Fortresses and Liberators waited to cough rudely into life. The rain was coming down hard by the time the last of the crews climbed nervously aboard and joined the line of grumbling machines edging down the perimeter path. At each base the first of the bombers turned on to its runway and momentarily sat back heavily on its tyres as brakes were applied. Then, throttles pushed to the wall, the manifold pressure on instrument panels rapidly climbed to 35 inches of mercury, the great machines bucking and vibrating as pilots tightened their grip on the control yokes, eyes riveted on the tower awaiting the Go signal.

Many crews still expected a red flare signalling abandonment of the mission. But inevitably came the green through the mist. The brakes of the bomber at the head of each queue were released with a hiss of hydraulic fluid, then it was bounding away, tail lifting from the glistening tarmac, thundering towards the distant point where concrete met grass and hedgerow, rumbling wheels lifting then settling again until finally the machine boomed up towards the overcast at the end of the runway where it disappeared from view. At thirty-second intervals the rest followed at each base and climbed out at standard airspeed, their crews peering into the cloud for signs of other aircraft as they headed for their wing assembly radio beacons known as bunchers.

Ralph Golubock was at Shipdham, Norfolk, home to the 44th Bomb Group in the 2nd BD, tasked with hitting the Messerschmitt plant at Gotha with the firm's factories at Oschersleben and Helmstedt as a last resort. The pilot watched as the first of his Group's B-24s thundered down the runway into the mist and prepared for the hazards of an instruments take-off, where the co-pilot's task would be to measure the aircraft's position relative to the runway centre line by concentrating on the blurred grass edge and calling out to the captain as it neared or receded, showing the laden, roaring aircraft was veering off the concrete and towards disaster. 'Upon leaving the ground we were immediately immersed in rain and clouds,' Golubock later recorded. 'The tail gunner was back in his position with an Aldis lamp which he blinked on and off so that following planes could see the light and keep their distance. The climb was long and grinding.'[1]

But at 17,000ft the B-24, climbing at the prescribed rate of 130 to 150mph, broke through the clouds into a deep blue sky with a golden sun shining on the cotton-wool layer Golubock had just left. Other aircraft popped up around him. Then the game to find the relevant squadron, group and wing began; lumbering, unwieldy machines, struggling to stay in contact with the assigned beacon as the buzzing, growing swarm lifted apparently haphazardly through the overcast. Soon there came the inevitable crunch and flash as a laden bomber connected with another in the cloud, a B-17 of the 385th BG which had taken off from Great Ashfield near Bury St Edmunds minutes earlier coming down at Tuttington, eleven miles south of Cromer with three doomed crew still aboard.[2]

The rest of the glittering mass gradually formed into squadrons, groups and wings, orbiting their Buncher beacons every six minutes until a whole hour had ticked away and they were able to take their final allotted place in their bombardment division, setting course into the sun, a ninety-mile-long phalanx of aircraft droning across the North Sea, each Group split into a high squadron, a middle in the lead and a third below and behind, to give the maximum spread from the Group's .50 machine guns. Once above the cloud many had found assembly easier than usual and remembered that they had been promised clear weather over the Reich where it mattered.

2/Lt John W. Howland, a 23-year-old Wyoming navigator with the 381st BG, had been awakened at around 5am in his uninsulated, cement-floored Quonset hut he shared with fifty others at Ridgewell, and found he was going to Leipzig. 'Helluva lot of planes scheduled to hit the target and weather looked good,' he later noted in his diary. 'We were assigned No 474 a new B-17G with a Gee Box. Navigation was very easy during assembly and around England. I was able to get a good wind for DR navigation.'[3]

Among the cohesive stream Lt Don Ackerson was helping with navigation as a bombardier with the 384th BG at Grafton Underwood, bound for Bernberg. Just two years before he had been finishing high school in New York. Today he and the rest of his crew had been rated experienced enough to lead their squadron, the 547th, for the first time.[4] There was little time to reflect on whether this, their thirteenth mission, would prove unlucky. As Ackerson, Howland, Golubock and their comrades entered German airspace the clouds started to thin and disappear just as they had been promised they would. Below a snow-covered landscape began to unfold.

The B-17 of Colonel Harold Bowman, CO of the 1st Division's 401st BG, was the first American bomber to cast its shadow over Reich territory, bound for Leipzig. His Group was new to the European Theatre of Operations (ETO). It had only arrived in the UK in November, but had been chosen to lead because of its already high reputation for accurate bombing. After the massive reaction by the Luftwaffe to the maximum-effort RAF raid the night before, many fighters were dispersed across Germany. But in the approaches to Leipzig where the RAF had struck, the Luftwaffe was still strong. As the feint towards Berlin ended and Col. Bowman's force turned to starboard towards Magdeburg and Leipzig, Luftwaffe Major General Max Ibel of the 2nd Fighter Division realised the city was about to suffer its second blow within twenty-four hours and ordered his Me 109s into the air. Fw 190s and Me 110s would join them.

Lt Howland had been wondering how long the aerial armada could escape. 'The trip into the target was pretty uneventful until we passed south of Magdeburg,' he later wrote in his diary. 'There the solid undercast was beginning to break up but we had no reports of enemy aircraft in the area. I was looking out of my right side window when I saw a Fw 190 climb out of a cloud and pass *under* our right wing and *over* our elevator and vertical stabiliser. He had us dead to rights, but his guns never fired a shot. Either his guns were jammed or he forgot to turn on his arming switches or he was so busy trying to avoid a mid-air collision he didn't have time to fire.'[5]

One of the Me 109 pilots, Lieutenant Dieter Petz, was the first to spot the formation at 3 o'clock and to call out 'Indianer' to alert the others to attack.[6] Col. Bowman's bomber had just left the Initial Point (IP) and turned onto its bomb run for the A.T.G. Machinenbau GmbH plant at Leipzig. Bowman's bomber escaped the fighters' flashing cannon, but the deputy lead's B-17, *Battlin' Betty*, lost an engine and when the fighters damaged another she was forced out of formation. To prevent the Luftwaffe moving in for the kill, Lt A. H. Chapman, in the command pilot seat with the deputy lead sitting alongside, put his plane into a spiral dive in the hope the fighters would think he was finished. The trick worked and at 2,000ft Chapman pulled the aircraft out of its rapid descent and started the long route home alone.[7]

The 351st BG was among the leading waves in the Leipzig force, not far behind Col. Bowman's Group. As the 351st left the target after bombing, one of the Group's B-17s, named *Ten Horsepower* and commanded by Lt Clarence Nelson, was hit by an Me 109 cannon shell which smashed through the starboard windscreen decapitating the co-pilot Ronald Bartley and badly wounding Nelson, who slipped into unconsciousness. The top turret gunner, S/Sgt Carl Moore, had been firing at the Me 109s when the B-17 seemed to stop in mid-air, before sliding off on its left wing to begin the so-familiar spin which now pinned each surviving crew member to his position. Only S/Sgt Moore was able to clamber forward from under his turret and into the gap between the pilots' seats. He gasped in horror at the scene on either side, but grabbed a yoke in each hand and by extraordinary force endowed by the need to survive gradually pulled the aircraft out of its spinning dive. The navigator, Lt Walter Truemper, was now able to crawl up from the nose hatch and Moore handed over control to him. Truemper had washed-out early in pilot training, but there was another man on board who had some experience at the flight deck controls, S/Sgt Archie Matthies the ball turret gunner, who had been born in Scotland and emigrated to Pennsylvania with his parents. Matthies struggled up from his turret and into the *Ten Horsepower* command seat. The navigator and Matthies then decided to try to fly it home. A long ordeal across enemy territory in the freezing cold, battered by a gale coming through the shattered windscreen, began.

The B-17 of Lt William Lawley was another hit as the tight-packed stream turned away from Leipzig. *Cabin In The Sky* was a brand new Fortress on its first mission, but the bombardier had been unable to release the bomb load because the rack activating mechanism had frozen at 28,000ft. A later USAAF report said:

Coming off the target he was attacked by approximately 20 enemy fighters, shot out of formation and his plane severely crippled. Eight crew members were wounded, the co-pilot was killed by a 20mm shell. One engine was on fire, the controls shot away and Lt Lawley seriously and painfully wounded about the face. Forcing the co-pilot's body off the controls, he brought the plane out of a steep dive, flying with his left hand. Blood covered the instruments and windshield and visibility was impossible.[8]

Now at 12,000ft Lawley, who had flown nine missions with the 305th BG, was sure the engine fire would soon cause the bomb-laden B-17 to explode so rang the bell to abandon aircraft. The flight engineer went out, but a waist gunner told the pilot that two crewmen were wounded so badly they could not use their parachutes. At that point Lawley decided he had no choice, but to stay with whoever wanted to remain aboard with him and like those aboard *Ten Horsepower* began his own lonely battle to try to reach England, almost five hours' flying time away. Lt Harry Mason, his bombardier, tied the co-pilot's body to the cockpit seat back with a Parka to keep the already-damaged instrument panel clear, then stood between the two flight deck seats and helped

Lawley with the controls. The conditions in the tight confines of the cockpit, which had been sprayed with blood as the co-pilot was killed by a shell exploding in his face, can only be imagined.

Only minutes before *Ten Horsepower* and *Cabin In The Sky* were hit Lt Ackerson, bombardier in the 384th BG flying in the middle of the 1st BD stream, had attacked Bernberg to the north of Leipzig. 'This was a perfect mission, even though it was eight hours and 30 minutes long,' he wrote. 'The target, a Junkers plant, was really pasted. Almost all bombs landed right on target. Flak consisted of two separate attacks by 25 Fw 190s, which made passes from astern but were scared off by our fire. Later these were dispersed by our P-47s.'[9]

Another savage air battle was taking place to the west as B-24s of the 2nd Division hit Brunswick and Gotha. Here USAAF P-47 Thunderbolt and P-51 Mustang pilots were credited together with bomber gunners with shooting down no fewer than thirty-six German fighters with another thirteen probably destroyed and a further thirteen damaged. The 2nd BD had put up the smallest number of bombers for the day, 272, yet the fact that they shot down almost twice as many as the 1st Division is testimony to the ferocity and continuity of the Luftwaffe's onslaught.

One P-51 Group, the 357th, had flown its first mission only nine days before. The start of Big Week marked the initial successful combats of its flamboyant commander, Col. Henry Russell Spicer. He spotted what would be his first claim, a Ju 88, 2,000ft below, just after he left the target at Gotha at 23,000ft still escorting the B-24s. Back at the 357th's home airfield at Leiston, Suffolk, hours later he detailed in his official encounter report what happened next. The adrenalin rush of kill-or-be-killed combat leaps from the mimeographed pages.

I pulled off and gave chase. He went down fast, losing altitude in a deep spiral. At 3,000ft I turned tight inside of him and he obligingly straightened out, allowing me to do the same, so I closed in straight down the alley and opened fire at about 600 yards in an attempt to disconcert the rear gunner. Steady fire was held until he burst into flames. I overran him rapidly (cause seeming to be excessive air speed as I was indicating 550mph at the time), so I yanked it out to the side to watch the fun. The whole airplane was coming unbuttoned. My wingman, good old Beal, had slowed down a bit and later stated he saw two men jump and their chutes open (poor shooting on my part). The ship continued straight ahead, diving at an angle of about 40 degrees until contact with Mother Earth was made, which caused the usual splendid spectacle of smoke and fire.'[10]

Col. Spicer then looked up to make sure he wasn't being followed. 'Lo and behold if there wasn't an Me 110 dashing across the horizon,' he reported.

He showed a little sense and tried to turn, so I was forced to resort to deflection shooting – opening up and spraying him up and down, round and across (I believe I was a little excited at this point). Fortunately the left engine blew up and burst into flame. As I overran him (still indicating 500mph) the pilot dumped the canopy and started to get out. He was dressed in brown and had streaming yellow hair, the handsome devil. I lost sight of him at this point (1,000ft) and again pulled out to the side. No chute was seen, but the aircraft descended impolitely into the town of Erfurt, causing rather understandable confusion as it blew up and burned merrily.

Again as I looked up (this is getting monotonous) an Fw 190 whistled up and as I began to turn with him my engine quit, embarrassing me no end. Believing I had been hit by the 110 gunner and being at a loss to the next move I opened fire (90 degree deflection) at zero lead and pulled it around clear through him until he passed out of sight below the nose (more bad shooting) intending to frighten him off more than anything else. No claim is made as I saw no more. Here the engine caught again, labouring and pounding badly ... we crossed out without further incident, going south of the Ruhr. I claim: One Ju 88 destroyed; one Me 110 destroyed; one Fw 190 scared. Ammunition expended: 533 rounds.[11]

It was the P-47 Groups who were most in evidence on 20 February, however, as the USAAF began conversion to the P-51 that winter and spring and in fact 668 of the 835 fighters despatched to cover the mighty assault by the bombers were Thunderbolts. The most famous P-47 Group of all, the 56th FG of Col. Hubert Zemke, who had a cousin flying for the Luftwaffe, were credited with fourteen enemy aircraft destroyed for no loss themselves; the similarly equipped 352nd FG with eleven, again for no loss.

At Brunswick, as the Thunderbolts dived to break up a head-on assault on the B-24s by Me 109s and Fw 190s, wings winking their familiar cannon tattoo, was Major Jimmy Stewart, and it was on that day that his reputation for keeping a cool head under fire was established. Of the eight Liberators shot down on 20 February, three were from Stewart's Group, the 445th. Stewart was later awarded the Distinguished Flying Cross for holding his formation together under the intense attacks to hit the primary target.

A third of the 2nd Division's B-24s were tasked with hitting an aviation plant at Halberstadt, but the target was obscured by cloud, so fifty-eight of them struck at Helmstedt as a last resort target, the bombs of thirteen went down on Oschersleben and ten bombed targets of opportunity.[12] Crewmen from this force reported attacks by thirty-five to forty Fw 190s and Me 109s plus Me 110s as well and Group gunners claimed five kills. Three of the 392nd BG's Liberators were so badly damaged they were lost in crashes on returning to England. The aircraft of 2/Lt R. K. Goodwin, flying his fourth mission, was hit in an attack which left his flight engineer, S/Sgt Landon Brent, with an unexploded 20mm cannon shell in his back. 2/Lt Goodwin had to feather two engines of his crippled plane.

Even further north the airmen in the 3rd BD, unescorted in their attack on the Focke-Wulf factory and airfield at Tutow and who had feared a bloodbath, found much assistance from medium bombers of the US 9th Air Force. Twin-engined Marauders had been assigned to hit German airfields and thirty-six of them from the 386th and 322nd bomb groups helped to prevent Luftwaffe fighters in Holland from mounting a coordinated attack on the 3rd BD Flying Fortresses. Instructions to the airmen of the 386th were categoric at briefing: 'The primary object for this mission is to furnish a diversionary support for the 8th Air Force operations. Airdromes which are being hit by this Ninth Air Force Command are first priority airdromes currently in operational use by the German Air Force. In hitting these airdromes it is desired not only to pin down the enemy fighters in this area, but also try to destroy fighters on the ground!'[13]

In fact six of the 314 Flying Fortresses from the 3rd BD which had set out that morning were lost and the division's air gunners were credited with shooting down fifteen fighters and probably destroying another fifteen. However, apart from confusing the enemy as to the USAAF's planned targets the bombers had little effect on Reich fighter production. The Pathfinder aircraft which had been assigned to mark the Tutow factory with pyrotechnics for following Groups failed to take off, so 105 of the bombers unloaded in the area of Tutow, Griefswald and Stralsund at estimated time of arrival. Targets at Posen (Poznań) and Kreising (Krzesiny) were assigned as primaries for the rest of the formation, but it was considered cloud would prevent accurate bombing, so seventy-six aircraft bombed Rostock and the huge total of 105 bombed targets of opportunity.[14]

The ravaged Groups of all three bombardment divisions now faced the long haul home, but the blood-letting was not over. The 392nd BG for instance was hit again by Fw 190s after leaving the last resort target of Helmstedt. Four made passes on the B-24 of 2/Lt C. E. Jones, which was named the *Dixie Dumper*. One 20mm shell knocked out the No. 2 engine and another exploded near the top turret. Three other planes in the formation had one engine feathered at the end of the twenty-minute attack. In the 392nd BG Liberator of Lt Goodwin the pilot was weighing up the fact that he faced more than 400 miles of flying on two engines and still had to get his wounded flight engineer, S/Sgt Brent, medical treatment as soon as possible.

As the battered air fleets trailed over the snow-covered western reaches of the Reich, Lt Truemper and S/Sgt Mathies aboard *Ten Horsepower* battled to keep their B-17 airborne without a conscious pilot. On board *Cabin In The Sky* the bombardier Lt Mason was standing between the two cockpit seats, helping Lt Lawley with the damaged controls, when enemy fighters closed in on the crippled bomber and renewed their attack. Lawley managed to give them the slip by sliding into cloud. 'One engine again caught on fire and was extinguished by skilful flying,' an official USAAF report said. 'Lt Lawley remained at his post, refusing first aid until he collapsed from sheer exhaustion caused by loss of blood, shock and the energy he had expended in keeping the plane under control. He was revived by the bombardier and again took over the controls.'[15] 2/Lt Mason was also finally able to jettison his bombs, lightening the load and saving fuel, as the plane approached the English Channel.

Across the glittering blue above the Reich and its occupied territory and over the seas which separated England from its enemies, smoke trailed from lifeless engines of B-17s and B-24s; in those airframes the turrets and the Perspex of windshields and side windows advertised by their bloodstains the death or wounding of crew members. Apart from the 149 men now missing, a total of twenty young lives had been snuffed out aboard the planes in the three air divisions and twenty-seven wounded.[16] Among the latter was S/Sgt Brent with an unexploded 20mm cannon shell in his back. As his damaged B-24 began to lose altitude Brent's captain Lt Goodwin could not maintain formation. Four P-47s provided cover until fuel shortage forced them to break away. Over the Channel the B-24 was down to 5,000 feet. There was talk of ditching, but Goodwin realised that Brent was probably too seriously wounded to survive immersion in the sea.

As the day wore on and the shadows lengthened across the airfields in England where the dead and now dying had lived, commanders – who knew how much had been risked on committing so many aircraft at one time – gripped the rails of control tower observation platforms and scanned the skies to the east for the first sign of those returning. On the grass below ground crew sweated out the mission no less anxiously as they stood alongside the poised ambulances and fire trucks.

The bombers began landing back in England from 3.30pm. First came the few intact and untouched Groups, joining the circuits of their airfields in strict order. In the first run to one side and into wind of the active runway, two three-plane elements of each Group peeled off one behind the other to the left, six aircraft curving round en masse to sink into the landscape again as their wheels gratefully grabbed the concrete. Remaining elements of the low squadron then split away from the Group and flew an orbit above the landing bombers, lowering their undercarriages on their second run over the field to come in and land also. And so it went on, element by element until a whole thirty-six-plane

Group was safely down, tyres rumbling as they turned off the runway to waiting hardstands.

Lt Howland's bomber arrived over its field at Ridgewell. 'Our spirits were high as we returned to base and landed, but the red flares being shot from the ship in front of us indicated "wounded on board" and he was requesting an ambulance,' Howland recorded. 'Our hardpan was right next to them and we walked over to see what had happened. The top turret gunner was dead. The top of his head had been blown off, but it wasn't enemy action that killed him. A careless gunner in our Wing had accidentally fired a round, probably while cleaning his guns. The .50 calibre bullet caught him clear in the forehead.'[17]

There then followed the parade of the damaged and the doomed as the litany of crashes which followed any raid began. Lt John Peyton's B-24 *Coral Princess* was among those mauled in the fighter attack on the Messerschmitt works at Helmstedt. Short of fuel, he attempted an emergency landing at RAF Manston on the north Kent coast, an emergency field with a long, wide runway for planes which had lost hydraulic power to brake. But during the approach the *Coral Princess* inexplicably exploded, killing all on board.[18]

Lt Goodwin, commanding the second of the three crippled 392nd BG planes, had decided to attempt a landing at the small RAF field at Southend to seek treatment for S/Sgt Brent. He managed to get in on his two good engines for a crash landing which destroyed the aircraft and injured another crew member. Brent was taken to a nearby hospital for a prompt operation and the surgeon gave him the 20mm shell that had entered his back. While Brent was recuperating the rest of the Goodwin crew was assigned to the 15th AF in Italy. Brent finished his tour flying with other crews. 'Sometimes I look at the 20mm shell that hit me and I think of Lt Goodwin and Lt McGee (the co-pilot) and other crew members and the four P-47 pilots I never knew,' Brent wrote fifty years after the war. 'I have not seen any of the crew since that day. I wish I could tell them how much I appreciate what they did for me.'[19]

The Fortress *Battlin' Betty*, which had lost the use of one engine and had another badly damaged on the bomb run at Leipzig, maintained the low height of 2,000ft it had been forced down to to avoid further attacks. It trailed the rest of the 1st BD all the way back from Leipzig, a black shadow over the frozen Reich. Expecting any moment to be caught by a flak nest, Lt Chapman flew on into Holland without being spotted by fighters again and across the North Sea. Hours later he made it back to his home base of Deenethorpe in Northamptonshire.

At Tibenham Major Jimmy Stewart's Group, the 445th, was counting the gaps in its flight line where three Liberators had stood only hours before, when the last of the 392nd BG's crippled B-24s arrived over the field. Lt Jones's *Dixie Dumper* flew past Tibenham with the fuel needles showing empty tanks and Jones realised his Liberator was unlikely to make its base at Wendling. Harry Thomas, his bombardier, recorded what happened next, as the damaged bomber circled Tibenham: 'Jack [Morris, the navigator] and I were still in the nose when the engines quit. We were a little over 500ft then. Jack had on his head set and heard Johnny [the co-pilot] call to "clear the nose and prepare for crash landing." Jack glanced at me with excitement and shock on his face and then went through the passage like a scared rabbit.' Thomas rapidly followed him to the area above the bomb bay where most of the crew were grouped.

'When we first hit it was like a normal landing then it seemed like all hell broke loose. I felt the force of the turret above me and the fuselage on my right came [with] the "force of all forces" to smash us down and together. Then we stopped. The first thing we did was have a rapid roll call. Everyone was smothering almost and had the force of a ship's part or the part of one of the other fellows on him.' Thomas was trapped by his foot which had gone through the floor of the *Dixie Dumper*. Others in the crew managed to take off his shoe. 'After a few pulls, pushes, pulls and grunts I got loose and they slid me down the left side of the fuselage into some on-looking Limey's arms ... An ambulance was on the way.'[20] Before it arrived to take away three injured crew members they were able to look back to the *Dixie Dumper*'s entry path and saw it had just missed a house thanks to its pilot's skill, then cut a smooth path through a beet field until it hit a ditch and swung round, wrecking the airframe.

Lt Lawley in *Cabin In The Sky* saw the English coast coming up just as a second engine ran out of fuel and a third engine caught fire. Lawley now had to put down quickly with only one working engine. 'He was looking for an open pasture,' Ralph Braswell, one of the plane's two waist gunners, recalled many years after the war. 'All of a sudden, there was a Canadian fighter field. He flashed the emergency signal and we went right in.'[21] All the wounded crewmen survived the crash-landing at RAF Redhill, Surrey. The flight engineer who had parachuted out near the target was captured, but also survived the war.*

It was 4.30 in the afternoon before Lt Truemper and S/Sgt Mathies brought the battered *Ten Horsepower* over their home airfield of Polebrook and at last called up for help because neither of them had any experience of how to land a bomber. They were told to bale out, but refused because Lt Nelson, though deeply unconscious, was still alive. So while the rest of the crew took to their chutes under orders, Lt Truemper and S/Sgt Mathies kept the B-17 flying as the Group Commander, Col. Eugene Romig, took off in another Fortress to fly alongside and show them how

---

* Lawley recovered from the deep cuts on his face, neck and hands, completed four more missions with the 305th BG, then in August received the Medal of Honor for his actions on 20 February and was returned to the United States for a bond tour. He retired as a Colonel from the USAF and died at 78.

to make a final approach and landing. The first two approaches in *Ten Horsepower* proved too high and Mathies and Truemper turned to make a third attempt. This time it was long and low, but *Ten Horsepower* came in too fast, bounced off a field and dropped a wing. It dug in and the big bomber cartwheeled and broke up, killing both Mathies and Truemper. Posthumous Medals of Honor were awarded for both of them weeks later. Lt Nelson, the man they had tried to save, was still alive when rescuers arrived, but died from his wounds a short time afterwards.[22]

The generals were now ready to weigh the cost of the operation in which all had been risked to strike a hammer blow at fighter plants and defeat the Luftwaffe in the air as well. Throughout the evening they waited at Bushy Park, south-west London, headquarters of the new United States Strategic and Tactical Air Forces Europe, from where General Carl Spaatz was in overall control of the 8th, 9th, 12th and 15th Air Forces. They had braced themselves for heavy losses. But as the Group reports chattered in over the teletype machines it was obvious it was the Luftwaffe which had suffered mightily in comparison to the Americans. There were total claims for 153 fighters destroyed. This was later scaled back to fifty for the bomber gunners and sixty-one for the US pursuit planes as Group claims were compared, but it was still a crushing defeat for the Luftwaffe over its own territory. A USAAF analysis of the mission regurgitated by the Air Ministry read: 'An outstanding feature of the operation is the small loss – 21 bombers and four fighters . . . it is apparent that the German Air Force was surprised and overwhelmed by the large force and its employment, particularly following the large scale RAF attack on Leipzig the previous night.'[23]

Newspapers on both sides of the Atlantic were euphoric about the round-the-clock hammer blow on Germany. The banner headline in the official US Army newspaper *Stars and Stripes*, which published an edition in England, funded by the US Government and staffed by its servicemen, read on the morning after the three-division attack: 'Greatest day raids hit Luftwaffe plants'.[24] The British edition of Stars and Stripes was printed on the presses of the more staid Times in London and that too had reacted with superlatives for once to mark what was seen as a turning point in the conflict, with its story headed: 'Nearly 3,000 aircraft attack Germany'. The reporter, trying not to be partisan, wrote:

2,000 Allied aircraft including a very large force of American heavy bombers took part yesterday in the greatest daylight air assault of the war. Their targets were fighter aircraft factories in Germany and the attack followed a night assault by the RAF in which more than 2,300 tons of bombs were dropped on Leipzig by nearly 1,000 British bombers ... Our special correspondent on a Fortress bombing Leipzig reported that one officer who was making his 26th mission over Europe said, 'In my opinion it was very successful. The fighter opposition was not bad, but the flak over the target was very heavy – close and accurate. The target was wide open to us, clear, with no cloud.'[25]

Damage to Germany's aircraft industry had indeed looked promising at first, particularly in the Leipzig area, target of most of the 1st BD. But as the strike photographs were developed there was some disappointment. Lt Ackerson, whose crew had acted as lead of the low squadron on the Junkers factory at Bernberg, later recorded: 'Photos showed our bombs off target because of poor formation.'[26]

However, the strategic bombing campaign was a joint British-American effort where many attacks, day and night, were intended to gradually bleed to death the whole monster that was Nazi Germany. The RAF Photographic Interpretation Unit at Medmenham produced its own document on the Leipzig double strike following reconnaissance flights. 'The recent raids on Leipzig have damaged some of the city's most important industries and out of the ten works listed as being of the very highest priority, five have suffered severely,' it revealed. On the west side of the city there was a heavy concentration of damage mainly from fire in a closely packed industrial area, east of Plagwitz station, most likely to have been caused by the RAF alone. 'Between 20 and 30 firms have suffered. The most important of these is the largest wool spinning and dye works in Europe, over three quarters of which was destroyed by fire. Business and residential damage was very slight compared to industrial.'[27]

What that meant to the morale of those on the ground was recorded by a young nursing student who had been studying in Westphalia and returned to her former home in Leipzig not long after the raids to pick up some belongings. After the war Ilse McKee described the acres of RAF destruction that met her eyes as her train drew into Plagwitz station. 'I was shocked at what I saw,' she wrote. 'The gigantic hall was just a mass of tumbled-down girders, grotesquely-bent metal structures and splintered glass. In order to get out of the station I had to climb over several great mounds of rubble.'[28] As she ceased clambering she was stunned by the wilderness of what had been a thriving city centre. 'I looked around and I could see nothing but ruins,' she wrote. 'The big square in front of the station, which was usually so busy, was almost deserted. There were hardly any trams or buses running . . . I went across the Bahnhofsplatz up to the Bruhl and turned to the left towards Augustplatz. I stopped and looked around, searching for the spire of the Thomaskirche which should have been quite near, but I couldn't find it . . . not a building was left intact . . . everything was still.'[29]

It was an image that would be repeated across the rest of Germany's cities before the war's end. The true meaning of round-the-clock bombing, in which the German people and their defence resources would have no rest, was about to be assessed at Reichsmarschall Goering's headquarters in Berlin. The scale of damage in Leipzig had indeed been considerable and there were those among the population, worked into a frenzy by press and radio descriptions of *'Terrorfliegers'* and *'Luftgangsters'*, who wreaked their revenge. In the days following the double strike captured aircrew saw evidence of that rage.

English flight engineer F/Sgt Bill Isaacs, who had been shot down to the north of Leipzig in the RAF raid of the night before, breaking his ankle and shoulder, and had not been found until the next morning, had then been transported with others by a horse and cart to a Leipzig hospital after the USAAF attacks. 'As we went into the city I saw six airmen strung up from lamp posts. We didn't know whether they were English or American,' he reported.[30] Another English flight engineer shot down in the night raid, Sgt Montague Clarke, of 102 Sqn, evaded capture for almost a week. After he was picked up he was eventually driven to the Reich capital, which was by now on the USAAF target list. 'As we entered Berlin I saw the body of an airman hanging from a lamp post,' he said.[31]

The fury against Allied aircrew was being fostered by the Reich Propaganda Minister Josef Goebbels, particularly now that the Americans were beginning to show what damage they also could inflict on Germany's city-bound industry. Just over a month before Big Week a Berlin newspaper had printed a picture of Lt Ken Williams, a USAAF bombardier, wearing a combat leather jacket with *'Murder Inc'* inscribed across the back. Lt Williams had had it painted on at his Polebrook base because it was the emblem on the nose of the Flying Fortress his crew had been assigned. In fact they never flew it. Because it was in the hangar being repaired they were assigned a new plane for their first mission. By the time their second raid came round in late November *'Murder Inc'* again wasn't ready, but Williams was still wearing the jacket with its emblem when he took off for Bremen in the same new B-17 he had flown on his first mission. The new plane was downed by flak and fighters near Eggese and when the English-speaking Luftwaffe *feldwebel* who captured Williams saw his jacket he made a point of taking photographs, which then ended in the hands of the Gestapo. The image of the shocked baby-faced flyer, who only moments before hitting the ground had seen his horror-stricken pilot plunge past him without a parachute, was then repeated again and again in German propaganda sheets, including a fictional serialisation of his previous life, saying he had been a Chicago hoodlum in the infamous gang known as Murder Inc – a far cry from Williams's actual history of student life in a college run by monks.

This story and others helped Goebbels persuade the German public that it was their duty to attack and kill downed flyers, even writing an editorial for the front page of Nazi Party newspapers within months which in essence ordered German troops and police not to prevent German civilians executing downed Allied airmen and encouraged German civilians to lynch them. 'American attacks over Germany are no longer warfare,' he wrote, 'but murder pure and simple . . . Fighter and bomber pilots who are shot down are not to be protected against the fury of the people. I expect from all police officers that they will refuse to lend their protection against these gangster types. Authorities acting against the popular sentiment will have to answer to me.'[32]

Between now and the coming of peace there would be many instances when American and British aircrew would be lynched by the populations of towns and cities which felt the increasing effect of their bombs. The true nature of that combined onslaught was about to begin. The attack in daylight by more than 1,000 bombers and almost as many fighters now being assessed in the Reich and in USAAF headquarters in England was only the start. Big Week would continue and within hours the young airmen who had travelled across the Atlantic to end the war would be taking off once more. They would be called again and again before the week was over and as exhaustion mounted they would pay a savage price to wrest air supremacy from the Luftwaffe.

2

'Things are going to be tough from now on'

The concerted and prolonged battle over Germany the US Army Air Force was to win over the next five days had been a long time in coming. As crewmen clambered into their bombers for a second day after a shockingly short time of rest many of them were able to reflect on how far they had travelled, both emotionally and in experience.

The few veterans now coming to the end of tours which had begun in the late summer remembered with horror the dreadful mauling the Groups had suffered in attempts to neutralise the Luftwaffe in the double-strike missions to Regensburg and Schweinfurt on 17 August, a running battle in the sun across the skies of Germany costing the USAAF sixty of the 370 aircraft it despatched and which Lt Col. Beirne Lay Jr, an observer from 8th Bomber Command headquarters, described as 'a sight that surpassed fiction'.[1] The fact that another hundred bombers had been so badly damaged they were only good enough for spare parts – this against a tally of fifty-seven fighters lost to Germany – brought the whole future of daylight bombing into question in Washington.

Confidence had not been helped by another serious incursion

into the Reich three weeks later, a raid on Stuttgart in which only one third of the 338-strong force was able to bomb the city and forty-five bombers were lost, eleven to ditching. On 10 October the 8th visited the centre of Münster on a Sunday morning and thirty out of 313 failed to return. Four days later survivors were sent back to Schweinfurt. It became known as Black Thursday among the shattered East Anglian bomber groups. Not only were another sixty bombers lost to almost continuous fighter attacks again, a further seventeen crashed in England and the damaged roster read 138 out of 320 machines which had set out. At the end of the day the USAAF Groups in Britain had been left with just one hundred effective bombers. The fact that the raid had cost the Luftwaffe a hundred fighters and the ball-bearing factories of Schweinfurt had been accurately hit (in fact temporarily reducing ball-bearing output by 67 per cent) did not stop morale plummeting to a new low in the 8th AF.[2] Briefings before the mission had been so tense that when the CO of the 385th BG, Lt Col. Elliott Vandevanter, wished his crews at Great Ashfield 'Good luck, good bombing and good hunting,' one gunner had yelled back, 'And good-bye.'[3]

It had been the fifth mission of 2/Lt Joel Punches, a navigator with the 385th BG. In his diary he recorded on his return: 'How we ever got back from this one I still don't understand! Four hours over Germany and three hours under fighter attack . . . I'm afraid things are going to be tough from now on. No milk runs.'[4] It was achingly clear after Black Thursday that neither the B-17s nor B-24s could defend themselves without fighter escorts which could reach all the way to the target.

The myth of a self-defending 'Flying Fortress' had finally and convincingly been exposed. It was a dream the USAAF overall commander General Hap Arnold had promulgated in the days of peace. The man appointed to build an American bomber force in Europe, Brigadier General Ira Eaker, believed in that myth also when he arrived in Britain in February 1942. He came with six staff officers, including Captain Frederick Castle, an early service pilot turned businessman and a godson of Arnold's who in less than three years would become a USAAF hero. The brigadier's brief was to begin cooperation with Sir Arthur Harris's RAF Bomber Command, operating at night while the 8th Air Force would fly by day. The fact that the RAF had been forced into night bombing because of huge losses on day raids did not escape Eaker, a close friend of Harris, but was weighed against the knowledge that both the B-17 and B-24 were equipped with multiple .50 machine guns compared to the shorter-range and far less hard-hitting .303s of RAF bombers. Besides, the USAAF was wedded to a precision bombing campaign, not then possible at night as the RAF had shown by pragmatically carrying out area attacks on cities.

When the fledgling 8th Air Force carried out its first B-17 raid in August 1942, successfully hitting the Luftwaffe airfield at Rouen, with Major Paul Tibbets piloting the lead plane and General Eaker flying with him as observer, the 'Flying Fortress' case seemed proved as the twelve-strong formation returned without damage by the enemy. It didn't stay that way as B-17s, eventually carrying thirteen .50 machine guns and B-24s ten, were regularly knocked out of the sky by the Luftwaffe over the following months when accompanying P-47 and P-38 fighters had to turn back for lack of fuel.

In the summer of 1943 the US Assistant Secretary of State for Air, Robert Lovett, was despatched to England to visit USAAF bases and weigh up morale at a time when the odds of surviving a tour were about one in three.

Captain Robert Morgan, commander of the Flying Fortress *Memphis Belle*, based at Bassingbourn in the 91st BG, was one of those whose tours finished while Lovett was in England and could testify to how B-17s alone were no match for the Luftwaffe. 'The worst mission we flew was to Saint-Nazaire,' he remembered.

'We were just experimenting really and the generals thought we'd go in at low level to beat the German radar. We went in at 4,000ft and we had the living H blown out of us. We lost three out of 12 in our squadron, including the squadron commander.'[5]

Throughout 1943 General Eaker still believed in the invincibility of the Flying Fortress – a title the B-17 had won shortly after its maiden flight in 1935 when its maximum speed of more than 280mph made it faster than most fighters then flying – and Hap Arnold was backing him.

But Arnold swiftly changed his mind when Lovett returned to Washington with his report that June. In days the USAAF commander, fully aware of the urgent need to subdue the Luftwaffe over Germany before D-Day approached, stressed in a memo to his chief of staff, Major General Barney Giles: 'Within the next six months you have to get a fighter that can protect our bombers.'[6] He did not mention the P-51, but that remarkable aircraft known as the Mustang was already in production by North American Aviation. In its first three months of operation over Europe its pilots shot down three times more Luftwaffe fighters than those claimed by P-47 Groups. Two British designs turned it into a war-winner.

The first was its Rolls-Royce Merlin 61 engine, which in 1942 replaced the Allison, under-powered for the kind of high-altitude flying needed for a bomber escort, and at last the USAAF, which had originally ordered only two P-51s for testing, increased that order to 2,200 by late 1942. Giles, pressurised by Arnold, now turned the heat on the plane makers, but was told the Mustang would not be available in quantity until the end of the year. It would arrive at the 8th AF airfields only just in time as final preparations for Big Week began.

The second campaign-changing adaptation of the Mustang was the addition of weight-sensitive paper-composition drop tanks which would give it the fuel duration to easily accompany bombers all the way to Berlin and back and have enough reserves to fight with. The USAAF had already designed its own metal auxiliary fuel tanks – in 1942 for ferrying fighters to Britain – and in fact added a 75-gallon metal tank to each wing of its P-47s, giving them the range into Germany needed for Big Week. But bigger tanks were needed for further incursions and extended fighting time. Continuing delay in getting 108-gallon steel tanks into production led to the 8th AF turning to a British firm, who produced paper tanks strong enough to withstand pressure at above the 25,000ft at which the US bombers and their escorts would fly. It was this 108-gallon paper tank – filled with 100-octane fuel providing greater range and acceleration – which became the standard for P-51s from May 1944 to the end of the war. With one attached to a pod on each wing the auxiliary tanks added 750 miles to the Mustang's radius of action, allowing it to fly as far as Poland. Until the paper tank came along, and in fact in Big Week, the P-51s made do with the 75-gallon metal tanks shipped in from the US.[7]

The fact that the US 8th Air Force was temporarily out of the main business of war after Black Thursday was hidden from the public both in the United States and Britain by the intervention of what had usually been seen as an enemy to operations by the 8th – traditional European winter weather. Almost continuous heavy cloud closed in over the Flying Fortress and Liberator bases in Britain and what would have been their targets deep in Germany if aircraft had been available in strength. It gave Eaker the ability to rebuild his forces as closer German targets were chosen and the 8th raided airfields and V-weapon sites in France.

In the next four months from mid-October 1943 an almost un-broken, and expanding, supply chain of new aircraft arrived from the factories of North America, the fresh crews for the air war taking their first leap into the unknown at the end of training by navigating the featureless wastes of the Atlantic in often marginal weather. There were two routes to choose from, northern or southern. The former left the United States from Bangor, Maine; took in a stopover in Goose Bay, Labrador; a second stop in Greenland, another in Iceland; then finally entered the four-hour leg to Prestwick in Scotland. The latter route, though daunting because of its length, was less treacherous. It stretched from Florida to Trinidad, then down the east coast of South America to a landing in Natal, Brazil. From there the B-17 and B-24 crews flew on to Dakar, West Africa, then often the next day went on to land at Marrakech, Morocco. Once the weather looked clear they flew out once more over the Atlantic and through the Bay of Biscay to land at St Mawgan or St Eval in Cornwall. A variation took them past neutral Ireland and into Valley in Anglesey.

The northern route, which began over the most heavily populated part of the United States, usually allowed crews to make a detour before leaving the mainland to buzz a crewman's family home or that of his girlfriend. Lt Jack Watson, whose family lived in Indianapolis, went one better. He took his B-17 low over New York City on his way north with three other crews and led them in buzzing Yankee Stadium during a World Series baseball game. It made him famous throughout the 8th Air Force, but it didn't please New York's hierarchy. Sgt Walter Peters, a correspondent for *Yank* magazine, came across Watson that winter as he and the other pilots anxiously awaited assignment to the 303rd BG at Molesworth, Cambridgeshire, and talked to them in their quarters in England. 'Mayor La Guardia raised an awful stink when that happened,' he wrote. 'The boys were hauled over the coals for it by their CO when they reported to their field in Maine. "All that looks funny now that we're going into actual combat," said one. "It's the first mission that counts . . . I'm just itching to get that first one in."'[8] In fact the mayor wanted Watson and the others court martialled, but instead they were fined several hundred dollars.

The northern route, which had so tempted Lt Watson, was used less in the colder months, but Lt Howland, the 381st BG navigator whose Flying Fortress narrowly missed a collision with an Fw 190 on the way to Leipzig, found himself navigating the north Atlantic in the heart of the winter of 1943–44. Howland's pilot, 2/Lt James Tyson, brought his brand-new B-17 into Prestwick seven days before Christmas after a hair-raising night flight in which the outside air temperature was recorded at minus 100 centigrade; the Pitot tube froze so the crew had no way of knowing their air speed and they had to orbit for half an hour because they were convinced they were over-flying Scotland in the direction of the enemy. Eventually Prestwick control identified them right over the airfield at 26,000ft. After a few hours' rest they then flew on to No. 2 Base Air Depot at Warton in Lancashire where new machines were prepared for combat in the operational Groups. It was here that crews received their first shock about service in the European theatre when they were relieved of the gleaming machine they had nursed across the Atlantic and hoped to fly in anger. On arrival at their assigned Group freshmen crews would usually find themselves flying a war-weary bomber instead.

Howland and Tyson's arrival at Warton was not auspicious, their aircraft veering off the runway and getting stuck in the mud. They were told to leave personal possessions in the plane and $50 worth of perfume, soap and candy Howland had brought over the Atlantic 'for English lasses' was stolen from it by an American AA gun crew while they were eating, Howland related in his diary. Most new crews arriving in Britain soon took the train to the vast US replacements depot consisting of three hutted camps at Stone in Staffordshire. 'Stone is an army distribution centre and they didn't seem to take to Air Corps officers too well,' Howland wrote. 'I can't say our stay was enjoyable except perhaps for the guy who stole my watch.'[9]

Tyson's crew got their orders to report to the 381st BG three days after Christmas and their first mission was to fighter factories at Oschersleben, south of Magdeburg, on 11 January. It was a rare departure from the newly recognised limitations and one of the few times missions in strength to Germany had been laid on since Black Thursday. It proved a disaster again, particularly for the 1st Bomb Division. The Liberators of the 2nd and 3rd BDs were meant to be bombing aircraft plants in the Brunswick area while the 1st BD were engaged at Oschersleben and another aviation industry target at Halberstadt. Deteriorating weather at English bases brought a recall signal, however, when leading elements were within twenty-five miles of their objective. Some continued, and the depleted force lost eighteen bombers to enemy action. But the full fury of the Luftwaffe was concentrated on the Oschersleben and Halberstadt Groups and in three and half hours the fighters shot down forty-two out of 291 bombers. The 303rd BG had sent forty crews. Eleven were lost and Lt Watson only just made it home. Enemy fighters first attacked over the Zuider Zee in Holland and replacements were there to hit the bombers again as they flew back to England. Watson's aircraft *Meat Hound* had two engines set ablaze, the left elevator shot off and damage to one wing adjoining the fuselage. The crew, with the exception of the pilot, baled out, four landing in the water and drowning. Watson flew home alone and brought his B-17 down through cloud to crash land at a fighter base at Metfield, Suffolk. After hearing what had happened Mayor La Guardia sent a telegram to the pilot at Molesworth telling him that all was forgiven for his buzzing of the World Series.

This time the buck would not stop at Eaker. He had been replaced a week before by Lt General Carl Spaatz in far-reaching changes ordered by Hap Arnold. The glory for Operation

Argument, the plan for the concerted, massive day-after-day blow against the German aviation industry Eaker had been trying to mount since late November, would belong to Spaatz, not to the man who had built up the 8th Air Force in England.

Spaatz, who had been heading air force operations in the Mediterranean, now found that from headquarters near London he would not just be in charge of the 8th, but of the 15th Air Force in Italy under the new organisation the United States Strategic Air Forces in Europe. He would coordinate the efforts of both as General Dwight D. Eisenhower and the RAF's Air Marshal Sir Arthur Tedder at Supreme Headquarters Allied Expeditionary Force (SHAEF) planned the build-up to D-Day and beyond. Eaker, who was transferred to the Mediterranean to head Allied air operations there, was told it was a promotion, but he knew he had been sacked and blamed Hap Arnold, though Eisenhower had previously worked with Spaatz in the North African operation and favoured him. Eaker had not been convinced about the need for long-range fighter escorts but Arnold had and Eaker had to go. It was also felt that Sir Arthur Harris's boys of the RAF were winning the bombing war and garnering all the publicity as such and a change needed to be made if there was ever to be a US air force independent of the army.

Lt Gen. James Doolittle, who had done much for home front morale by raiding Tokyo in retaliation for the attack on Pearl Harbor, was moved from leading the 15th to be given, under Spaatz, overall control of the 8th's commands. Major General Nathan Twining, who had been in the South Pacific, then flew to Italy to take over the 15th AF.

The tactical fighters and bombers which made up General Louis Brereton's 9th Air Force were also moved from the Mediterranean to Britain for pre-Invasion targeting, allowing Doolittle a total of 1,300 bombers alone to call on.[10] The US fighter strength in England had trebled in the final three months of 1943 as new

Groups were formed, giving Doolittle a total of 1,200 pursuit planes when he took over. And, of course, among the most important of them was the mighty Mustang. Under Doolittle's command it and all 8th AF fighters would be released from Eaker's edict that their first duty was to protect the bombers by flying close escort instead of pursuing the enemy.

General Arnold was happy to announce in Washington in January that the near future was likely to be critical for the Luftwaffe as the USAAF carried out its concept of strategic bombing by first destroying the enemy's fighter strength. 'It is now plain that for us the beginning has ended; for our enemies the end has begun,' he prophesied. Just in case the Axis didn't get the point that Armageddon was coming it was revealed that the USAAF was currently the world's largest air force with 2,385,000 officers and men.[11]

The new dawn which now shed its rays over the Army Air Force's horizon also brought the promise of better weather. Conditions at bases in England or over planned targets rendered the 8th inoperable on an average of 250 days in any year of the bomber offensive and rain, ice and snow in the winter of 1943–44 had been particularly cruel.[12] Operation Argument required a forecast of visual bombing conditions for at least three days and hopefully a week. A new weatherman was being employed, Major Irving Krick, who had developed a system of forecasting European weather by studying patterns over fifty years and guessing they would be repeated. Weeks passed without a suitable weather front to study – time in which Doolittle benefited by 600 more bombers arriving in Britain from America – but on 18 February Krick was able to alert 8th AF headquarters to a 'good-looking pattern' in the making and the next day forecast 'three days suitable for visual bombing and perhaps more'.[13]

Operation Argument, cancelled again and again because of poor forecast weather, was finally on and only just in time. The official history of the USAAF in the Second World War states: 'By February the destruction of the German fighter production had become a matter of such urgency that General Spaatz and General Anderson were willing to take more than ordinary risks in order to complete the task, including the risk of exceptional losses that might result from missions staged under conditions of adverse weather.'[14]

It was essential that this joined-up plan to wreck German fighter production be victorious if D-Day itself was to succeed. A debate within the Committee of Operations Analysts, a Washington group of business tycoons and economists, had decided almost a year before that attacks on fighter assembly plants would throttle the Luftwaffe more easily than on fighter engine production.[15] If the attacks were coordinated, for instance the Messerschmitt assembly plant at Regensburg-Obertraubling being bombed simultaneously with the component factory at Regensburg-Prufening, it would quickly cause calamitous bottlenecks. To do so would require the 15th Air Force attacking at the same time with its 900-strong force from Italy. It had been unable to join the first mission of Big Week because it was needed to bomb German positions at Anzio to support Allied ground troops. Depressingly they would not be able to join in on Day Two either.

The B-17s and B-24s which now climbed out above the fields of East Anglia in the early morning of 21 February 1944 did so in only slightly better conditions than the day before. The visibility on the ground was much improved, but at 3,000ft several bombers went through a band of ice which could be seen building up fast on wings. There was no alternative at this height but to continue climbing. Layers of unremitting grey gradually made way for trails of smoky yellow, as the sun above slowly lightened the gloom and eventually the lumbering B-17s and B-24s burst through into a burning blue above a desert of white, stretching from horizon to horizon. Hesitantly more black dots appeared above the fluffy cloud layer, wheeling to form up, then spreading in stacked layers, 924 bombers heading east for Germany.

Their targets were Me 110 component factories at Brunswick and German airfields at Hanover, at Achmer and Gutersloh near Osnabruck and at Hopsten in the same area, as was the fighter air depot at Diepholz. The overcast failed to thin out as promised and there was further icing over Germany, though this proved more of a problem for the Luftwaffe climbing up to meet the B-17s and B-24s than the crews in the bombers themselves. That same inclement weather over Europe was keeping the 15th AF bound to the ground at its bases around Foggia. Of the three bombardment divisions of the 8th Air Force now in the sky only one, the 3rd, had Pathfinder aircraft equipped with H2X radar to bomb through cloud. The result was most of that force unloaded on their briefed main target areas at Brunswick and Diepholz, but the other divisions had to seek targets of opportunity.

Lt Joel Punches, the 385th BG navigator, was on the penultimate mission of his twenty-five-mission tour in the crew of Lt Robert Taylor attacking Hanover with eighty-seven other B-17s. 'Over the target we were hit by flak which knocked two engines out,' he later wrote. 'We had to leave the formation and drop down and back. Ten minutes later two German fighters spotted us and attacked head on. They knocked one more engine out. We were then at 6,000ft and going down at 1,000ft a minute with one engine on fire. The German fighter planes were circling and getting ready for the kill, so we decided that if we kept flying we would never make it back to England and would have to ditch in the Channel, which in the Winter was suicide. We all baled out through the bomb bay.' Punches came down at Barneveld, near Apeldoorn, Holland, 'hid my parachute and opened my escape kit and got my compass and silk maps out and started walking southwest'. The air war would change greatly before Punches got home.[16]

Lt John Howland, the navigator with the 381st BG, bombed an airfield at Gutersloh with his Group. He described in his diary what happened as his Group came up to the Initial Point where the straight and level bomb run began.

The lead ship made a 360 degree turn to the left into a cloud bank and broke up the formation pretty badly. We missed the target. Then the fighters jumped us. They went after the ships that had fallen out of formation. I saw two Fw 190s shooting hell out of one B-17 which blew up a few minutes later. I was manning my MG and gave up navigation for a while since I wasn't the lead navigator. We were under sporadic attacks for about 30 minutes and Sgt Jensen, our top turret gunner, winged one Fw 190. I am now able to control my emotions much better than I did when flying missions. And I kept up my DR plot and nav. responsibilities all through the attack . . . The lead navigator screwed up again and lead [sic] us right over Osnabruck, which was hidden by clouds. They threw up a barrage of flak and a piece came through the glass window above my gun mount and missed me by a few inches. Most of the flying glass hit my steel helmet, but one piece about the size of a quarter missed my helmet and flak suit and hit me in the neck, right over my jugular vein. Fortunately it landed flat, not sharp-edge down so it made a circular cut in the skin, but bleeding wasn't serious. I was still shaking . . . The trip home was pretty uneventful, but I damn near froze in that blast of cold air coming through the broken window.

However the blast of air was nothing to what happened to a plane piloted by George McIntosh. An exploding shell shot away the entire Plexiglass [sic] nose. The bombardier was wounded and both he and the nav. baled out over enemy territory. McIntosh was able to bring it home despite that gaping hole scooping air into the cockpit at 150mph.[17]

Lt Don Ackerson, the 384th BG bombardier, was also frustrated by the confusion that day. He was in an attack on railway yards at Lingen, to the north of Osnabruck, which he tersely described in his diary as 'poor, disorganised'.[18] Weather conditions failed to improve on the journey home and as the Groups began descending through cloud to reach their bases, the 385th lost another two planes to add to that of Lt Taylor. Captain John Hutchinson and his crew were within minutes of finishing the final sortie of their twenty-five-mission tour as they let down over Reedham Marshes in Norfolk, heading for their base at Great Ashfield, when disaster struck. Lt Eugene St John, piloting the third B-17 in Hutchinson's element of three, had a horrifying view of what happened as twenty-one men in two planes died, as he later recounted.

We encountered dense undercast. Due to its depth the Group meteorologist told us to descend through the undercast in three-ship elements. Our element was made up of Captain Hutchinson leading, Lt Warren Pease on his right wing, with us on his left. As co-pilot I was flying the aircraft and I pulled in tight with my right wing tucked inside Hutchinson's left wing. Pease was flying a more loose position (further out). When we broke through the bottom of the cloud base I glanced to my right quickly and saw that Pease was missing. As I looked round for him he suddenly broke through the clouds at full power and directly behind Hutchinson who was descending at a very steep angle.

As he descended under Hutchinson he pulled upwards sharply and the rear of his aircraft wedged between the No. 3 engine and the right side of Hutchinson's fuselage. The

forward two thirds of Pease's aircraft were sheared off by
the propellor which then flew back off Hutchinson's B-17.
As Pease was under full power his plane shot straight up
and hung on its props entirely. At this time I made a steep
left turn to avoid involvement. This all took place at 800ft
altitude. My right wing being at a high angle I was unable
to see what happened next. One of my crew said Pease's
aircraft had flipped over onto Hutchinson's plane. Both aircraft ploughed straight into the ground. It occurred to me
as I thought back that as I broke through the undercast and
due to the proximity of Hutchinson's plane I saw him in the
cockpit smoking a big cigar celebrating the 25th and last of
his missions.[19]

It was now time to balance the profit and loss of the second day's
assault in the clinical ledger of war. As part of its contribution to
Big Week, RAF Bomber Command had mounted a 600-plane raid
on Stuttgart the night before with light losses of only ten aircraft;
the US Army newspaper *Stars and Stripes* took this into account
with its main headline of 22 February trumpeting '8,000 tons
on Reich in 36 hours'. *Stars and Stripes* reporters were at some
debriefings and naturally reported the more upbeat, particularly
from those who bombed the fighter centre at Diepholz under
visual conditions. 2/Lt Donald L. Ahlwardj, of Danbury, Iowa,
pilot of Fortress Romeo, was quoted as saying: 'The target was
wide open and visibility was perfect. When we left you couldn't
see the target for smoke.'[20] Diepholz apart, however, the reconnaissance photographs showed indifferent results. At Brunswick,
one of only two primary targets the bombers had been able to
attack, most of the bombs had tumbled through cloud onto the
city itself rather than the Me 110 factories. There was some solace
to be found in the casualty reports. They showed only twenty-two
bombers lost, including five over England and one in the North

Sea. Bomber gunners were claiming nineteen Luftwaffe fighters destroyed and the fighter Groups, which had lost five planes, were claiming thirty-three kills, fourteen of those by the new Mustang Groups, the 357th and the 354th.

Doolittle realised that the USAAF's biggest continuous effort so far would have to show better results than these if the week's campaign was to succeed. He was encouraged by a message from General Twining that the 15th Air Force would be able to join any assault by the 8th the following day. The weather forecast also showed improvement, with a high-pressure system moving south through Germany. It promised visual bombing conditions over two of the most important targets in the USAAF lexicon. The first, the Me 109 factories of Regensburg, was handed to the 15th Air Force, the second to the 8th. It was the ball-bearing factories of Schweinfurt.

There was some dismay as the by now exhausted crews of the 3rd Bombardment Division tumbled into operations blocks and saw the red tape stretching to the most feared of targets. Their 333 B-17s would be the only ones going to Schweinfurt while the 1st BD attacked the German aircraft industry at Ascherslben, Bernberg and Halberstadt. The Liberators of the 2nd BD were tasked with returning to the Me 110 plant at Gotha they had hit on the first day of Big Week. The forecast for all targets was clear skies for visual bombing, but as the crews left the operations blocks and prepared to collect the paraphernalia of war it was obvious the low cloud over England itself would mean instrument take-offs for many, with all the risks that entailed as pilots painstakingly tried to follow strictly designated rates of climb and airspeed in the struggle through the overcast to orbit assembly beacons. In fact failure to appreciate all vagaries of the weather would mean a day of costly blunders in which the great courage of crews would be to no avail and more than 800 living under the Nazi jackboot in occupied territory would be killed in error.

At Thurleigh in the 1st BD area where S/Sgt Calvin Brend was a ball turret gunner in the 306th BG crew of Lt J. P Toombs Jr, the mission, his fourteenth, seemed star-crossed from the beginning. On leaving the crew truck by his aircraft *Margie*, the cord of Brend's electric suit got caught and badly ripped the material. He had to go back for another suit. By the time he returned his comrades were already aboard with the engines running. In the darkness he almost walked into the spinning prop, then on taxiing *Margie* blew a tyre. A maintenance crew came out to change it. 'The others were already up and mostly formed into formation by now,' he wrote years later. 'As we rolled down the runway an unexpected snowstorm came up. The clouds were high, we were on oxygen before breaking through into sunshine. As we broke through the snow the Group came straight at us and very, very close. The pilot rolled to the right and dove, not a thing to do with a B-17 fully loaded, but necessary. We climbed back and joined our squadron.'[21]

In the same division the 384th BG from Grafton Underwood, which included Lt Ackerson, was also suffering from the weather conditions, the young bombardier recording in his diary: 'The mission started off wrong. We (our group) had a mid-air collision on the assembly and lost two ships and crews.'[22] In fact a Flying Fortress of the 384th had collided with a B-17 of the 303rd BG over Irthlingborough, nine miles away from the Northampton-shire base, and only two of twenty men escaped. In the next few hours three more bombers from each Group would be lost.

Further to the east in the assembly area of the 3rd BD, whose airfields lay in a narrow corridor between Norwich and Ipswich, solid cloud up to 26,000ft prevented six combat wings forming up over the next hour. There were more close calls by converging bombers and as the threat of a major tragedy unfolded the division's commander, Curtis LeMay, ordered a recall, the B-17s to let down at 500ft a minute on a prescribed signal.

'Things are going to be tough from now on'

The Liberators of the 2nd BD based at all the compass points around Norwich had also taken off into low cloud, but without the extreme conditions their comrades had faced further south they cleared the overcast safely. As the division's eight Groups prepared to form up, however, Flying Fortresses of the 3rd BD were still milling around, waiting for the order to start letting down, endangering the Liberators. The time for the 2nd BD to leave the east coast of England passed with several Groups still trying to form up so at 12.25 hours the 2nd BD too was recalled. However, a part of the force had been able to create its proper defensive box and by the time the recall signal came this formation was already beyond the enemy coast and some, including the 446th BG, had even crossed the border into Germany. They started orbiting to return.

That left the 1st Bombardment Division. Leading it was Brigadier General Robert F. Travis, known to his crews as an eager beaver who was prepared to take the same risks as the crews he drove on.[23] At the time the 2nd BD was recalled, following the order to the 3rd to land, he was a hundred miles from his targets. He continued on course, later claiming he had not received a recall order, and his division, every man of them, followed. With the 3rd BD and most of the 2nd now reprieved from combat that day, it left General Travis's men totally exposed to enemy fighter attacks, later established as the most numerous since the disastrous mission to Schweinfurt the previous October. For Lt Ackerson and the rest of his crew, flying high squadron in the 384th BG, it was the 'worst mission by far that we ever had, a long ride of more than eight hours of hell. Not much flak, but more fighters than I've ever seen or want to see.'[24]

Ackerson's Group was not hit in the first interception over Holland, but they did not escape for long. 'Almost half hour inside the German border about 20 Me 109s hit our squadron,' he wrote. 'They attacked for about five minutes and then left. The attack was taken up by more than 30 Fw 190s who kept on us for about 30 minutes, just going around and around . . . We lost three of our squadron, Kew, Defries and McDonald. Evasive, active and accurate shooting saved our necks. We fired about 2,000 rounds in all. Tom, Red and I claimed one apiece. From there to the target we had no more opposition and no more trouble until three minutes from the coast on the way out when two more Fw 190s made a pass. One was shot down by Red with no damage to us.'[25]

Good fighter support was provided by P-47s on the penetration and by P-51s over the target. P-47s were airborne to provide withdrawal support, but they obeyed the recall order to return to England and the bombers had to defend themselves on their return. Attacks intensified when the fighters left, the Luftwaffe boring in in groups of fifteen to thirty aircraft. Over 300 enemy fighters were observed on single occasions. Some Fw 190s carried belly tanks and showed such determination they attacked with them attached. A number fired rockets and returning crews reported a few appeared willing to ram a B-17.

The lack of fighter cover spelt disaster for the 306th BG. The Group had put up thirty-nine planes, nine of which had aborted. Now seven were to be shot down. *Margie*, in which S/Sgt Brend was the ball turret gunner, was the second to go, as he later described.

A long stream of fighters made a pass between the lead squadron and us, the low squadron. On this pass they got our left wing man. He went down. I saw several chutes open. The fighters reformed for a second attack from the same location. As they started the attack our right wing man suddenly left us and pulled up and over to join the lead squadron . . . The next thing I heard, almost immediately, were guns firing again. Suddenly there was a great jolt and we started down. I saw flames coming from the number three engine, we started our death dive. I rolled the ball turret up to get out. As I reached behind my head to unlatch the hatch, a heavy G-force held me down. The pilots although they must have been mortally hit, made a last heroic effort to straighten out the ship and allow the others to bale out.[26]

Brend finally managed to release himself into the blazing fuselage to be struck by a 'terrible smell!'

Like a mixture of an electrical fire, oil, gas and what I believed was flesh burning. Standing by the waist door was our radio operator (Paul G. Gaire). He seemed frozen. He did not jump. The ship was level now thanks to the pilots . . . I turned to grab my chute which was wired to the ball turret support column, so it would not get tossed around and lost. My thoughts were that I would take the radio operator with me, pull his chute, then pull mine. At that moment 20mm shells burst around me. One struck the turret support column just above my head. This sprayed shrapnel over me, striking my head and shoulders. No big pieces, thank God, just very small ones . . . I broke my chute loose with one hard tug and turned, snapping the chute on and took one step toward the rear. BOOM!!! The ship exploded.[27]

Brend was knocked unconscious and came to, wrapped in ammunition belts, to find only a small section of the B-17 remained. 'The fuselage forward of the ball turret was gone,' he recalled. 'Everything to the rear behind the tail wheel was also gone. I quickly realized I should not go out over these sharp openings as there was too much jagged metal. Once I removed the ammo belts I rolled out of the hatch next to me.' He intended to delay pulling the cord as airmen were instructed to do, but didn't know how long he had been knocked out and couldn't see the ground, so looked for the handle. 'Panic again! My right hand could not find the cord handle. I looked down at my chute. I had it on upside down. The cord was on the left side. Would it open upside down? I pulled it; wait, wait, wait, was it going to open. POW it opened as I was looking at it. I got the full impact in my face.' He found he was only about 200ft from the ground. 'A hard landing and roll out in a snow covered field. Even a large boulder had it in for me,' he wrote.[28] Brend had been courting a Bedfordshire girl and his first thought was that now she would wait in vain for him at the local cinema. The next day he was captured by the Gestapo and found that only he and the two waist gunners had escaped from his B-17.

The pitting of a single division against the complete resources of the Luftwaffe had brought little reward for such a high cost. Only forty-seven of the 1st BD Flying Fortresses attacked the Junkers plant at Bernburg, thirty-four were able to bomb the factory and airfield at Aschersleben and just eighteen hit the primary at Halberstadt. Another seventy-five unloaded on targets of opportunity. Of the 289 B-17s which set out thirty-eight failed to return and among those which did come back lay the bodies of thirty-five crewmen with another thirty wounded. Of the twenty-three bombers of the 306th BG which returned to Thurleigh after attacking Bernburg, all were damaged, sixteen by fighter attack.

Because the planned strike against German targets had been reduced by two divisions the Luftwaffe was also able to concentrate on the 15th Air Force coming up from Italy. A total of 183 bombers had flown over the Alps to Regensburg and 118 had hit the Messerschmitt factory at Obertraubling, but the cost had been fourteen machines. One of them was shot down by Lt Heinrich Freiherr von Podewils, of 1/JG5. His unit had just been equipped with new Me 109s at their Obertraubling base when they were scrambled to intercept the 15th AF bombers heading for the two Messerschmitt factories at Regensburg. 'The Americans came in at about 6,000m high,' he recorded later. 'They first dropped bombs on Prufening and then it was Obertraubling's turn. We attacked from behind with all guns firing and the Americans' projectiles came at us like out of a watering can. I had damaged a B-17, continued with further attacks and finally shot it down 15km south-west of Straubing. Three men bailed out. The machine crashed close to a wood.'[29]

He returned to the airfield to find barracks and hangars had been hit by bombs and had to land between craters. 'A gruesome scene greeted me close to where I parked my machine,' he wrote. 'An American had come down by parachute, he had dropped on a metal structure which had cut him open from between the legs to his head, into two halves.'[30]

Others had already died on the ground in Holland, by a tragic mistake. The 446th Bomb Group's Liberators had completed two complete orbits of the Dutch-German border area a few miles to the north-east of the flak fields of Essen, Duisburg and Krefeld looking for a target of opportunity after being recalled on the way to Gotha, when two likely towns with warehouses and railway installations came up. A barrage of flak appeared from one of them. Unaware a strong wind had drifted the formation too far west, twelve B-24s unloaded a total of 144 500lb bombs on a target at one town and twelve dropped the same total over another. But the communities were on the wrong side of the border, in fact Nijmegen and Arnhem – in seven months to become known around the world in an ill-fated Allied drive to isolate the Ruhr – and 885 Dutch civilians were killed. Captain Max Alfred, who was in one of the planes, wrote in his combat journal shortly afterwards: 'General Hodges at 2nd Air Division was plenty mad. We heard later he softened when he heard we hit a gas storage installation used by the Germans.'

Day three of Big Week had at first glance been encouraging for the Luftwaffe. A total of fifty-five Flying Fortresses and Liberators had been shot down together with eleven American fighters. But as the encounter reports were completed by P-47 and P-51 Groups safely back at their bases they showed claims of fifty-nine kills. The grinding mills of aerial attrition had stepped up a gear and the point was not lost on the commander of the Reich fighter force, Adolf Galland, that whereas the Americans could easily replace their lost machines and crews, the Germans could not. The production of Luftwaffe aircraft would also be slowed in the months to come because surprising damage had been created by the ill-fated 306th BG to the Junkers plant at Bernburg, and even more at the firm's factory at Aschersleben, bombardiers from the small force which got through cutting production by half for two months. The Obertraubling raid by the 15th AF had also been successful.

It had not been the devastating blow to the German aviation industry which had been intended, however, and at Spaatz's headquarters there was chagrin at the chaos in two whole 8th AF divisions caused by the weather. That same weather front would now bring relief for the young American flyers.

Wednesday dawned wet at the USAAF bomber bases below The Wash and the exhausted crews, both those who had battled the elements and the rest who had fought the Luftwaffe, slept late in their chilly Quonset huts. The constant calls for action were already having a debilitating effect on the airmen, whose youth was a barrier to fatigue that could only be stretched so far before they became 'flak happy'. The flight surgeons had an answer to the tiredness which killed many an airman, Benzedrine. The amphetamine, which would be known to many of the airmen's club culture children in the 1960s and '70s as Speed, was used heavily in the Second World War by the Americans to keep troops awake over lengthy periods. Its effect was that the eyelids were no longer heavy, the muscles lost their ache, thirst and the need for food were suppressed and the mind seemed more sharply focused on the job in hand. It was ideal for the army, the navy and particularly the flight surgeon's dispensary.

But the result of prolonged use was that airmen found that after the effects of Benzedrine wore off and they were back at base they became like zombies. Movements were slow and poorly coordinated, there was a yearning for deep sleep which wouldn't come, thirst and hunger returned worse than ever. The symptoms were recognisable in combatants on both sides of the conflict, Germans as well as Britons and Americans being prescribed vast amounts of amphetamines. In Britain's forces alone, it is believed the air force, army and navy consumed 80 million pills during the war.[31] Particularly in Big Week there was a reliance on pills at USAAF bases. Apart from the Benzedrine to keep airmen awake, there were pills to make them sleep for the next morning's raid and, if needed, other pills to perk them up out of their depression.

General Doolittle, who believed every man was born for a purpose and whose name belied a personality of vim and vigour, left the matter of breaking points to the doctors and had originally planned another day of action, to give the Luftwaffe no chance to recover, but the final forecast in the late evening of the 22nd proved correct and low cloud and heavy rain closed the 8th's airfields. Only the 15th was able to operate. General Twining despatched more than a hundred bombers to Austria, wrecking one fifth of the Steyr Walzlagerwerke ball-bearing plant.

The English rain was a welcome sight for the pilots of the 8th's fighter Groups also. The 20th at Kings Cliffe, Northamptonshire, was the only one able to put planes into the air that day, forty Lightnings carrying out a high-altitude familiarisation sweep over the coast of Holland, Belgium and France. Meanwhile the force of war-winning Mustangs, which would eventually equip nearly all of the 8th's fighter Groups and strike such fear in the Luftwaffe, was growing. Those of the 357th at Leiston, Suffolk, and the 354th at Boxted, Essex, which together had already shot down thirty-three Luftwaffe fighters in Big Week raids on the first two days for the loss of only six of their own, were now joined by the newly equipped 363rd at Rivenhall, Essex. The next day, 23 February, was a day to recondition and make ready, and flight lines at the three bases throbbed to the sound of Packard Merlin engines on test. A total of eighty-eight Mustangs would be ready by the morning. At the bomber Groups, too, dispersal points were busy throughout the evening with bomb loading and last-minute repairs after the damage of the past few days. There was the usual crop of accidents and at Kimbolton the night sky was lit up for an hour as one of the 379th Group's veteran Fortresses caught fire and burnt out during servicing.

The next day was dry and frosty. The good news was that clear skies were forecast for visual bombing of most of the selected targets. The bad news for the 1st BD was that it was Schweinfurt once more. It didn't help the superstitious nature of those who had survived the previous Schweinfurt mission on Black Thursday in October to remember it was a Thursday again. Doolittle had more than 800 bombers available after the repairs of the previous day and the three bombardment divisions would be divided between targets in north and central Germany. The 15th AF would also help to dilute Galland's resources by sending 115 bombers back to Steyr in Austria, this time to bomb the Daimler engine plant.

The more experienced among the 1st BD flyers were further disheartened to learn that they, like the Liberator crews of the 2nd Division who would be going to aviation industry targets at Gotha, would take off earlier than their comrades in the 3rd BD, thereby gaining the attention of German radar operators first. It was obvious that they would therefore likely be the Luftwaffe's own target for the day. This was in fact Doolittle's plan because he was risking part of the 3rd BD by sending it to bomb Focke-Wulf airframe plants as far away as Kreising/Posen in Poland, beyond the then range of his fighters, while others on the same route bombed Rostock.

In fact it was not the Schweinfurt-tasked 1st BD or the over-reaching Groups in the 3rd BD which suffered greatly that day. It was the Liberator crews with aiming points at Gotha. The force was divided into three large combat wings and the first was still eighty minutes from the Me 110 factories when the Luftwaffe swung in out of the sun, cannon flashing. The wind strength and direction had not proved to be as forecast and the spearhead wing of the B-24s was well ahead of schedule. Fighter attacks continued all the way to the target. At the Initial Point to start the final run there was further turmoil when the lead bomber in the 389th Group lost oxygen causing the bombardier to collapse over his sight with anoxia, tripping the release switch. The remainder of the Group's bombs and that of other Groups then followed his, forty-four loads falling around Eisenach miles away from the target. The 445th Group had seen the error and were left to continue to the Me 110 plant alone, but the Luftwaffe now concentrated on them and in the space of an hour on the journey homeward thirteen of the Group's twenty-five bombers were destroyed and only three of the rest escaped battle damage. Nor did the 389th, which had bombed Eisenach, escape, seven of its aircraft failing to make it home.[32]

The full and varied arsenal of the Luftwaffe was employed on 24 February in the skies above the snow-covered fields of Germany. Apart from multiple cannon fired from *sturmgruppen* of specially armoured Me 109s and Fw 190s, other Me 109s dropped bombs on the Groups, rockets were fired from twin-engined Me 110s out of range of the bomber gunners and a few other twin-engined aircraft, Ju 88s, flew over the B-24s with bombs suspended on cables. Lt Sidney Swanson and his co-pilot 2/Lt Ralph Clapps were in a 445th Group Liberator hit in the nose by a rocket. They fought to control the bomber as the rest of the crew baled out, but went down with the plane.

The second wing of B-24s, consisting of the 392nd and 44th Bomb Groups were also badly hit from crossing the Dutch coast onwards, the 392nd losing seven of its planes, but this did not effect its bombing ability. All but two per cent of the Group's bombs hit within 2,000ft of the Gotha factory aiming point. This accuracy, together with that of the 44th, meant an estimated six to seven weeks of lost production. But the total cost of the great damage to almost every one of the Me 110 plant buildings had been thirty-three of the 239 Liberators which had set out shortly after dawn.

In contrast the bombardment division which Doolitle was gambling with by sending it the furthest and with minority fighter protection, the 3rd, suffered least of all, only losing five of its 304 aircraft because the Luftwaffe was already concentrating on other Groups further south. But the gain had also been slight. On the bomb run for the Heinkel works at Rostock a Pathfinder plane accidentally released early and more than sixty following B-17s did the same, in similar fashion to the 389th Group at Gotha. And cloud cover prevented any Groups hitting the Polish Fw 190 plants at Kreising/Posen, so instead they sought targets of opportunity.

The denial of fighters to the 3rd was the 1st BD's gain as it set out for Schweinfurt, where the meteorologist's team had predicted visual bombing conditions. Lt Ackerson was the 384th BG's deputy lead bombardier on the raid and recorded after eight hours in the air:

We had fighter escort all the way. We were never out of sight of the escort – P-47s, P-51s and P-38s. We saw some of the biggest dog fights I have ever seen, but we had complete air superiority. The Fw 190s still came in on the low groups and shot down about four B-24s and two B-17s that I saw. They were engaged by our P-47s however and several were destroyed. The weather was beautiful. I did dead reckoning all the way and picked up the target without trouble. The target was obscured by bomb bursts from leading groups. We had to find its position by check points around the area. The target must have been hit partially though ... Flak over the target was moderate. Fighter opposition on our groups – none. Enemy fighters seen – over 25.[33]

Eleven of the 266 B-17s which set off for Schweinfurt were shot down, but 238 had got through to the target and the town's important ball-bearing plants had been damaged.

To support the American Big Week effort, Air Marshal Harris sent more than 700 of his crews to Schweinfurt that night. Only twenty-two brought back photographs as evidence of release over the target, proving Harris's theory that the ball-bearing plants in a smoke-obscured valley were not suitable targets for night bombing at that time.[34]

Further south the 15th Air Force was appraising what aircraft it now had available for the next day after losing seventeen of the eighty-seven planes which eventually made it to Steyr, from coordinated Luftwaffe attacks which included rocket-firing Ju 88s and even Me 109s dropping bombs on the Groups. A maximum effort had already been called.

Friday the 25th, the final day of the Big Week onslaught, promised to set a new record for American air power over Germany as the exhausted crews were woken, shivering from the tortured images of their dreams, to do or die once more. The weather was predicted to be so clear over the whole of Europe that General Doolittle could pick any target.

He chose to risk the long haul to southern Germany. The 8th AF would hit both Messerschmitt plants at Regensburg, the parent factory at Augsburg, the Bachmann-Von Blumenthal factory at Fürth, supplying parts for the Me 110, and the VFK ball-bearing works at Stuttgart. From Italy General Twining agreed the 15th would hit the Messerschmitt plant at Regensburg-Prufening with 176 bombers an hour before the 8th AF were due while another 200 of his bombers were tasked with a range of targets including the airfield at Graz-Thalerhof.

The largest force from England would be provided by the 3rd Bombardment Division, 290 B-17s heading for Regensburg. The 1st BD would divide its 268 B-17s between Augsburg and Stuttgart and the 2nd would send its 196 available Liberators to Fürth. For the first time there would be more American fighters in the air than the bombers they were there to protect, nearly 900, 139 of them the redoubtable Mustang. Adding the bombers from Italy would mean nearly 2,000 aircraft challenging the Luftwaffe on its home territory, taunting the Swastika with the white star of the USA. Overnight compilation of 8th AF encounter reports and claims from the bomber gunners the previous day showed the Luftwaffe were likely to be already short of 120 fighters.

Lt Howland and his crew, who had been to Schweinfurt the day before, were woken at 5am. 'We were so weary we didn't have much to say to each other,' he wrote. 'Briefed for the Willy Messerschmitt fighter plane factory located on the west side of Augsburg . . . 1,380 miles, longest mission flown out of Ridgewell.'

But at his aircraft's hard standing he discovered that 'We weren't carrying bombs in our plane. We were the "paper boys".' His B-17's bomb bay was full of propaganda leaflets called the *Sternenbanner* (Stars and Stripes), a miniature four-page, four-column newspaper telling the Germans in their own language of disasters of which their government had not chosen to inform them and advising them to quit. The 1st Bombardment Division was in fact taking two million leaflets to Augsburg. 'While taxying out we had a blow out,' Lt Howland recorded. 'I felt good about that but I didn't realise that everyone in the whole 8th was apparently interested in seeing that the leaflets got to the target. I think everyone on that field who knew what a wheel looked like converged on our plane. They jacked it up, put a new wheel and tire on and had it changed within an hour. We were able to climb to altitude and catch the Group before they left the assembly point over the field.'[35]

Lt Ackerson was also going to Augsburg, flying lead of the high squadron of the 384th BG on his crew's fifth mission in six days. It would be nearly ten hours later before he was back on the ground at Grafton Underwood. 'We had sporadic fighter attacks on the way in and out with no losses,' he wrote in his diary. 'Fighter escort was good, weather beautiful. We could see the Alps for hours. The bombing results were good, flak intense at the target and meager on the way out. A Me 110 jumped us out of the sun on the way in. He was shot down by a P-51 as was an Me 109 that also jumped us. We also saw a Ju 88.'[36]

The 306th BG, which so far had seen ten of its crews disappear in Big Week, lost another three of its Fortresses on the mission to Augsburg, in the vulnerable position of low Group of the 40th Combat Wing. The first, commanded by Flt Officer Ray Coleman, was shot down by a single-engined fighter not far from Saarbrucken, a little over three hours after taking off from Thurleigh. Other planes in the Group reported seeing all the crew bale out. One of them, Lt Oscar Bourn, the co-pilot, plunged through a tree. 'Just as I neared the ground, after a long fall in my chute, I remember seeing the canopy at a strange angle above me, partially collapsed, then a green blur in the tree tops,' he later recorded. 'I came to, flat on my back and blinded by the bright noon sun. After slowly testing one arm at a time and then each leg, I decided I had no broken bones, so I gathered up my chute, dragged it over a field, across a road and into the woods where I tried to dig a hole in the snow to bury it.'[37]

Lt Howland arrived at Augsburg to find:

The bombardier in the lead ship zeroed in on the hangar and shop area and released his two smoke bombs and 10 500lb demolition bombs . . . Everyone else in the wing dropped their loads as well. There was only one thing wrong. Outside of our propaganda leaflets the bomb load for the 1st was 100lb M47 oil and rubber incendiary bombs. The lead bombardier had based trajectory for the drop on the load of heavy, 500lb bombs he was carrying. His 10 bombs hit in the target area on the west side of the autobahn. But more than 2,000 lightweight oil and rubber incendiaries fell short of the target and landed in a wooded area on the east side of the autobahn. It sure seemed a hell of a long way to screw up like that.[38]

In fact twelve years later Howland met a German from Augsburg who told him the Messerschmitt factory's air raid shelter was in the trees and numbers were killed and buried. It was the plant's most damaging raid of the war.[39] There was no doubt from USAAF reconnaissance photographs that thirty of the plant's buildings had been hit, reducing production by 35 per cent. Thirteen bombers were shot down from the 1st BD force to Augsburg and Stuttgart.

In a French wood not far from Germany's border Lt Bourn had been hiding, listening to people passing on the little road he had crossed after being shot down and trying to work out by their language whether he was in Belgium, France or Germany itself. He didn't succeed. 'Late in the afternoon a couple of wings of

B-17s flew over on their return to England,' he wrote later. 'How I longed to be up there in one of those planes looking forward to a good meal and a warm place to sleep that night! As they droned out of sight a loneliness came over me that I never felt before.'[40]

Nearly all of the Liberators of the 2nd BD had made it through to their target at Fürth, six failing to return, but damage was not to the same degree as at Augsburg. The most convincing de-struction of all, however, was at Regensburg. Captured German documents showed post-war that as a result of the bombing pro-duction at the Messerschmitt assembly plant fell from 435 fighters for the month of January 1944 to 135 in March.[41] Most of it was achieved by the 3rd BD of the 8th. They were led to the factory by smoke from the 15th Air Force's raid an hour before, but the Italian-based airmen had paid a terrible price. The Luftwaffe's 7th Fighter Division headquarters near Munich had seen two forces approaching and decided to attack the one from the south. With-out escorts able to reach such a distant target to defend the 15th's bombers the Luftwaffe shot down thirty-three, approaching 20 per cent of those tasked with hitting the Messerschmitt com-ponent factory at Regensburg-Prufening. The 8th's 3rd BD lost another twelve. But the overwhelming force of fighters sent from England kept many of the Luftwaffe pilots at bay and shot down a total of twenty-six for only three of their own. Gunners in the 8th's bombers claimed another twenty-three.

That night Harris sent nearly 600 bombers to Augsburg in clear weather and destroyed its centre from where the city and its aircraft factories were administered and transport links were coordinated. A total of 85,000 people, some of them undoubtedly key workers at the aircraft plants, were bombed out. As the RAF flew home the weather was already changing, a low-pressure area moving in. Big Week was over.

By the time the RAF Lancasters passed westward though Ger-many and into the Low Countries Lt Bourn was asleep in the warm bed he had craved. Shivering with cold he had taken a chance by knocking on a farmhouse door and whispering to the surprised old man who opened it: *'Je suis aviator americain.'* He was hauled inside and met an older woman and an attractive girl in her mid-twenties with a baby. There was a table, chairs, a cot and a double bed. The old man helped him to get his flight gear off:

> ... by use of signs and drawings I conveyed to them how I had got there and they made me understand that they saw me descend in my parachute. Soon the man pointed to the cot and I needed no more persuasion to get down to my long johns and crawl in.
>
> Later in the night I woke up and much to my surprise the light was still burning. I looked about and there in the double bed lay the girl with her baby and the older woman, all sound asleep. I pondered this peculiar situation for a while and then fell asleep.[42]

In the morning he gave the girl a sixpence as a souvenir. After a bowl of broth the old man helped him along a path outside then pointed the way he should take along the track into the forest. He met up with the Resistance.

> Later I found out from an English-speaking member of the French Underground that I had become an item of extreme amusement in addition to some ribald jokes, among the Resistance movement in the nearby town. Unknown to me, until my English-speaking friend related the story, I had stayed all night with the young Czechoslovakian wife of the German military manager of the large communal farm. It was well known her loyalties were not with the Nazi regime. That day her husband had gone into town for business

reasons but had decided to stay there overnight rather than go home. The Resistance fellows were circulating the story, which may have been true in one part, that while he was in town spending the night with a lady friend his wife was home entertaining an American flier![43]

Bourn was free for about a month, being moved along an escape line as far as Paris. There he was captured by the Gestapo, along with Flt Officer Coleman, and they spent the rest of the war as PoWs.

But one of their crew did evade successfully. Lt J. Louis Rodriguez, a navigator on his fourteenth mission, made contact with Resistance men and was hidden for two months with four other Americans and two RAF flyers in a lean-to shack in the Ardennes Forest, eventually reaching Switzerland.

The Friday of Big Week had been the crushing turning point for the German fighter force. Both the USAAF and the Luftwaffe had much calculating to do in the days that followed. It was clear it had been the most concentrated period of missions to date for the 8th, contributing 3,300 bomber sorties and 6,000 tons of bombs to the 8,148 sorties and 19,177 tons total of the combined USAAF–RAF Bomber Command effort during this period.[44] Two new Groups to the ETO had joined in the final mission of the week's campaign, making the 8th a bigger bomber force than Harris's command which had literally carried the flame for four years. More American Groups still in training in the States would be coming.

The attacks of Big Week forced a desperate dispersal of the Reich's aircraft production which finally put paid to German Air Ministry dreams of 5,000 fighters a month. The splitting of production centres would eventually make the supply lines fatally fragile to the might of the Allies' later Transportation Plan campaign. Big Week by no means finished the Luftwaffe, but it was the beginning of the end for Goering's force.

The cost to the Luftwaffe in February had been 33 per cent of available aircraft. American aircrews had claimed 317 German fighters destroyed in the heat of combat.[45] The numbers were later found to have been greatly exaggerated as airmen registered hits in split seconds, not knowing that many others were firing at the same target. But the Luftwaffe did lose nearly a hundred of its Jagdwaffe fighter pilots. This was 17 per cent of its veterans whose loss was never to be replaced by pilots of similar experience. The Me 110 had been proved to be thoroughly outclassed as a day fighter, thereby removing it from future daytime defence of the Reich. By comparison the 8th Air Force lost ninety-seven B-17s and forty B-24s. The 15th lost ninety aircraft and total American fighter losses amounted to twenty-eight. It was less than 7 per cent of USAAF strength in the two air forces. Now that the American aircrew training programmes and aircraft factories were producing in top gear the gaps would be easily filled, unlike those in Germany which would eventually begin to widen.

There were other hidden benefits in England to the success of Big Week. It gave a cement of solidarity to the transatlantic alliance in the air war, more fragile at times than officialdom would admit. A report to Churchill and the rest of the British War Cabinet on Monday, 28 February made much of the fact that Big Week had included the support of the RAF. 'The week has been the most active of the whole war, 20,000 sorties having been flown, 9,058 tons of bombs dropped on Germany alone,' the Secretary of State for Air stated. 'It is believed that the German capacity for aircraft production has been considerably reduced as a result of the combined UK and US air offensive culminating in the attacks carried out the previous week.'[46]

It also gave the 8th Air Force, not known for its reticence, the confidence flowing from the top that they could lick the Germans in the air. Exactly the opposite reaction was being felt by the Luftwaffe. The 8th's commanders were now ready to take on the biggest prize of all – Berlin. The crews were less ready and they had a week to recuperate as the weather closed in. They ached for rest, mental and physical. Tail gunner S/Sgt Bill Deblasio, approaching the end of his 100th BG tour, told *Yank* magazine after the 24 February raid on Rostock: 'They better give us a rest and a few short raids. I am very tired now.'[47]

In fact what was to come for the 100th BG would cement its reputation as the 'Bloody 100th' where half or more of the men you ate breakfast with could be dead by dinnertime.

3

'A gasp of surprise and dread'

The Battle of Berlin which American youngsters would wage at great cost in March 1944 opened a new chapter for the 8th Air Force and closed another for RAF Bomber Command. On fifteen occasions between the middle of the previous November and mid-February Sir Arthur Harris had sent hundreds of bombers to the Reich capital by night in the hope of achieving the kind of cataclysmic blow which had taken out most of Hamburg's industrial capacity in the summer of 1943. He had promised Winston Churchill before the battle began that it would cost Germany the war 'if the USA will come in on it'.[1] So far the Americans had not come in on it, though crews had been all set to go as they stood by their aircraft on the morning of 23 November, the mission being eventually abandoned because of poor forecast weather over the target.

Harris's Bomber Command had continued alone at mounting cost without commensurate returns. By the end of January 1944 a total of 1,792 RAF and Commonwealth airmen who had celebrated the beginning of 1944 and had at least hoped to see the spring were dead following six Berlin raids in thirty nights. Another 464 were PoWs.[2] It was the biggest monthly loss of the war for Bomber Command and the Big Week raids which Harris had been persuaded to take part in had come only just in time to stem the bloodletting. Now it was the Americans' turn.

It was with some trepidation therefore on the morning of 3 March that crews lined up on benches in briefing rooms throughout the three bomb divisions, eyes riveted on the map cover at the end wall. At Thorpe Abbotts on the Norfolk–Suffolk border Lt Edwin A. Stern Jr, bombardier on *Eager Beaver*, recorded: 'At briefing I remember the gasp of surprise and dread that arose from the assembled airmen when the curtain was pulled back.' The choice of Berlin as the target for the first time would, he wrote, lead to 'one of the biggest fiascos I can remember'.[3]

Crews of the 100th BG considered that too often the Group had been assigned a position in the combat stream of the 3rd BD where they were at the mercy of the Luftwaffe. Sgt James F. Mack, who had arrived in England in June, noted as Big Week ended a week before that, 'of the 15 gunners that came to the 100th BG only three of us are left.' He was at the same briefing and wrote: 'When I saw the target on the map my morale hit a new low.'[4] The admissions, typical of many airmen that morning, were proof that the new confidence that the 8th could now take on Berlin's defences was felt more by its commanders than the boys on the flight line. Generals Spaatz and Doolittle were rightly convinced there was a need after Big Week to continue the attrition of the German fighter arm. It was considered the German fighter commander Adolf Galland had been reluctant to commit some of his forces to combat the bomber incursions in Big Week. Berlin would, therefore, be the bait to draw in his fighters where they could be destroyed by superior forces.

But the weather did not match the sky-high ambitions at 8th AF headquarters. A total of nearly 1,500 aircraft, evenly divided between bombers and fighters, would be taking off, their primary targets industrial areas and aviation industry plants at Berlin, Erkner and Oranienburg. Yet many bases reported scattered snow showers limiting visibility to 300 yards.

'The whole formation ran into stratocumulus clouds so dense you could not see your wingman,' Stern wrote. The wall of cloud went up to 27,000ft, and 'When the word to abort finally came turning planes began running into each other. Only with some luck and skill by pilots Massol and Granger [his own] did we avert colliding with another aircraft.'[5] Sgt Mack's experience was similar. 'We were called back when within 40 miles of Berlin,' he wrote. 'Two Forts collided and blew up at 27,000ft.'[6]

In fact deteriorating weather forced a recall for all the twenty-nine bomb groups which had taken off three hours before to turn back before 11am. As the 1st Combat Wing wheeled by 180 degrees through dense condensation trails it met the 4th Combat Wing head on. A Flying Fortress of the 94th BG and another of the 91st collided and a third B-17 was reported as going down after being hit by debris. In the confusion of the melee a 100th BG crew landed their damaged B-17 at a Schleswig airfield thinking they were in neutral Sweden then found themselves surrounded by Luftwaffe guards. Most bombed targets of opportunity and a total of eleven crews failed to make it home that day. Three of them were from the 100th BG at Thorpe Abbotts.

It was not a good start, but *Stars and Stripes* made the most of it because Lightnings with long-range tanks which had been sweeping ahead of the bomber groups did fly over the capital. They were led by Lt Col. Jack S. Jenkins, commander of the 55th FG from Nuthampstead. The army newspaper's splash headline read: 'Berliners See 1st US Planes' and the carefully phrased report went on: 'American airplanes droned through the skies over Berlin yesterday for the first time in the war. The planes were fighters making an offensive sweep over the German capital while US heavy bombers were striking targets elsewhere in NW Germany.'

Col. Jenkins, who would be a PoW within a month, told the reporter that as he looked down he could see Berlin was snow covered. 'It sure looked cold for people to be running to air raid shelters. The planes saw no fighters or ack-ack bursts at all . . . We caught some flak from other cities we passed . . . The toughest part of the trip was the stiff headwind on the way home and the intense cold which seemed to get worse on every mile of the 560-mile trip out and back. For two hours after I got back I could not even feel my feet with my fingers.'[7]

The P-38s lost none of their own and made no claims, but the 130 P-51s in the escort took eight kills for the loss of seven Mustangs. Almost one third of the Mustangs had been led by Colonel Henry Spicer of the 357th FG, who had shot down two enemy aircraft at the start of Big Week. One of the missing Mustangs belonged to his Group and it was down in the Channel, a fate Col. Spicer himself would suffer within forty-eight hours. The pilot was Lt Robert Foy, whose coolness was remarked on in a later report by the 65th Fighter Wing, at Boxted, Essex, coordinating US air-sea rescue at the time. Foy 'came through on a regular Mayday call at 1158 hours, stating that his engine had quit and was burning', the report read. 'The pilot retained his composure at all times. He gave excellent calls at intervals and at 1204 while at an altitude of 7,000ft the pilot gave his last call and baled out.'[8] A comrade from the 4th FG who had heard the distress call then dived and spotted Foy in his dinghy. One hour and twenty minutes after baling out an Air Sea Rescue boat picked up the pilot and took him to Ramsgate Naval Sick Bay, suffering from shock. Foy, whose life prospects when he hit the sea were reckoned at no more than ten minutes at that time of year, soon recovered to become an ace with his Group, being credited with fifteen victories. And before the war was over he survived another immersion in the Channel after being forced to abandon his fighter.

It was an indication of how determined the 8th Air Force commanders were to bring the Luftwaffe to battle over Berlin that within hours of returning the Flying Fortress crews of the 1st and 3rd BD found they were on alert for the morning again. The preparation, which would go on throughout the night at damp and chilly airfields all over the eastern counties, now began. It started with the field order, chattering over the teleprinters from 8th AF headquarters. What happened from then for a typical mission was described in an article published in winter 1944 by a correspondent for the army's *Yank* magazine, Sgt Walter Peters, who watched progress at the 95th BG's Horham, Suffolk base.

Deep inside a single-story building, was the Intelligence Room. Large maps of the fighting fronts adorned the walls and colored markers indicated important enemy targets and other information about them. Except for the maps the Intelligence Room might have passed for a board of directors office. In the center was a long, well-polished table, surrounded by eight comfortable leather chairs. In the corner was a radio playing soft music transmitted by a BBC station. An S2 1st Lt relaxed in one of the chairs, his legs slung over its arm. A staff sergeant walked out of the room then returned. 'The FO is in Sir,' he said. 'Okay,' replied the lieutenant. 'Call the Colonel.' Three other members of the S2 staff walked in . . . When the field order was brought in the officers began to study it.[9]

At that point, for security reasons, Peters had to leave.

The reporter visited the officers' club where the bartender, Cpl James Mohafdal told him: 'They're a swell lot of boys here. There's no rank pulling. I've seen lots of them come in from the States and I've seen lots of them go on their first mission and never come back.'[10] Sgt Peters made his way past the noise of the movie from the base theatre, which doubled as a church on Sundays, to the Aero Club, run by the Red Cross.

Enlisted men were reading home-town newspapers, playing billiards or standing in line by a long counter for an evening snack [Peters wrote]. A round-faced sergeant with a neat, black moustache, Vincent Barbella, of Brooklyn, New York, was drinking a Coca-Cola and doing a lot of talking. With him was T/Sgt Harry D. Cooper, a radio gunner, from Dayton, Ohio.

'Tomorrow's my 12-B,' Barbella said, then laughed. 'To Hell with it, I won't call it 12-B. I'm not superstitious. I'll call it straight No. 13. I certainly hope we go tomorrow though,' Barbella said. 'That will make it about the sixth time I've been trying to make my 13th.'

Cooper smiled: 'You'll make it tomorrow. I'll bet anything on that. The night is clear and the odds are that it will stay that way until morning.'

'It's not the raid that bothers me,' Barbella said. 'It's these damned abortions. People don't realise how much there is to making a raid. They figure all you have to do is jump in a Fort and up you go. They don't figure that weather over here can change within a half-hour or after that and a guy is up there for a couple of hours then something can go bang with the oxygen system and you have to turn back.'

At an adjoining table a sergeant was reading a newspaper. Barbella turned and read the headline. 'Berlin', he said. 'Boy is the RAF giving them the works now. Boy would I like to go over there. It'd be nice to say I'd been over Berlin.'[11]

Many of the men who were there that night were on the mission of 4 March to Berlin, but tail gunner Vincent Barbella was not with them. He had been killed over Brunswick three weeks before, a day when the 95th BG lost seven aircraft. This time the bomb group would lose another four as they and the 100th became the only one of the twenty Groups which had set out that actually reached Berlin. Once more the weather made a mockery of all the planning.

At Horham, where Lt Bill Owen and his Pathfinder crew from the 482nd BG had arrived the night before to target mark for Berlin, there was a fifteen-minute delay before take-off because of a snowstorm. But as they climbed up through the clouds they quickly burst through into sunshine. Other crews were not so lucky and three B-17 Groups wheeled around at the French coast because they had been unable to complete assembly. As the remaining Groups headed on into Germany they found towering cloud banks up to 29,000ft and a recall signal was issued at noon. The Groups turned back onto a westerly heading and looked for targets of opportunity. However, Lt Col. Griffin Mumford, who was leading the mission with a reduced combat wing of twenty-nine bombers from the 95th and 100th BGs, continued because it was considered the recall was a German trick.

The briefed target in Berlin was the Robert Bosch electrical factory located in Klein Machnow, producing aircraft ignition parts. As the Group headed past the Kassel area Me 109s flashed through the formation. Flt Officer Chuck Yeager of the 357th FG, who would achieve world fame after the war as he broke the sound barrier for America, claimed one at 1.05pm south-east of Kassel. 'I was flying at 26,000ft when I spotted a Me 109 to the right and behind us about 2,000ft below,' he related in his encounter report back at Leiston.

I broke to the right and down. The e/a turned right and down and went into a 50 degree dive. I closed up fast and opened fire at 200 yards. I observed strikes on fuselage and wing roots, with pieces flying off. I was overrunning so I pulled up and did an aileron roll and fell in behind again and starting shooting at 150 yards. The e/a engine was smoking and wind-milling. I over-ran again, observing strikes on fuselage and canopy. I pulled up again and did a wingover on his tail. His canopy flew off and the pilot baled out and went into the overcast at 9,000ft.[12]

It was Yeager's first victory.

There were further fighter attacks as the Group continued towards Magdeburg and to Oranienburg twenty-five miles north of Berlin and finally to the Initial Point for the bomb run. The top turret gunner of the 100th BG's *Rubber Check*, T/Sgt Harold Stearns, opened fire at 400 yards on one at 12 o'clock level and crew members confirmed it spun down in flames. When Col. Mumford had turned onto the bomb run flak bursts came up on all sides. Ahead of them were more fighters, but the crews were relieved to see they were American, Mustangs of the 4th and 357th Fighter Groups who had been told to orbit in readiness as one combat wing was continuing to the target. Mumford then realised his bomb doors were frozen shut and the Pathfinder B-17 of Lt Owen became the first American aircraft to bomb Berlin. A total of five B-17s were lost to enemy fire over the capital, one from the 100th BG joining the four lost from the 95th.

Among those from the 95th was Lt Melvin Dunham's *Slightly Dangerous II*. On the bomb run flak hit the No. 1 engine, which burst into flames. As the plane started going down still with its bombs on board the flight engineer Marvin Anderson had to hand-crank the bomb doors open due to a malfunction. 'By the time we'd dropped the bombs the German fighters were upon us and kept up relentless attacks from all directions,' Sgt Lawrence Pifer, the ball turret gunner later reported.[13] The ball turret frosted over in the rapid descent, so Pifer climbed up into the fuselage just in time to see both waist gunners killed by 20mm cannon. The fighter attacks severed the interphone lines which prevented Pifer from hearing the bale-out order. 'I kept alternating from one waist gun to the other until flames and smoke came streaming

71

past the waist window. I looked out to see the extent of the damage to the engines and saw some tree tops not too far away. It was then I knew we weren't going back to England and I had to get out – fast. After grabbing my chest chute, frantically clipping it on, I bailed out via the bomb bay. I pulled the rip cord as I went past the ball turret and after what seemed an eternity the chute snapped open,' the gunner said. Pifer soon hit the ground, breaking his ankle and several ribs. He saw smoke and flames erupt a quarter of a mile away as his B-17 went in. He was rounded up with the seven other survivors of his crew and taken by truck to Berlin, then on to prison camp.

Back at the bases newspaper reporters were waiting, ready to mark the propaganda victory of the first American bombs on Berlin. At Thorpe Abbotts T/Sgt Stearns was interviewed by *Stars and Stripes* as the first USAAF gunner to down a fighter over the spread-out area of the Reich capital. At Horham the 8th Air Force top brass were waiting with the Army newspaper. 'Going in wasn't tough [though] the weather was pretty bad,' Col. Mumford told a reporter. 'Clouds were broken and it was cold, damn cold, down to 55 degrees below zero . . . My navigator – and believe me he deserves all the credit [he was 1/Lt Malcolm D. Durr, of Altona, Illinois] – saw several good points to set us up for a visual bomb run. But then the clouds closed in the city and the bombing was done through cloud.'[14]

The *Stars and Stripes* reporter was also eager to interview 2/Lt Marshall Thixton, bombardier in the nose of Lt Owen's B-17 and therefore the first Flying Fortress airman over Berlin. Thixton revealed that for him and four others in the crew it had been Mission 12B 'and a lot of us were sweating'.[15] Four days later the newspaper ran a photograph of Col. Mumford having the Silver Star pinned on his jacket by Brigadier General Curtis LeMay for 'gallantry in action' in leading the first Army Air Force raid on the Reich capital.

'A gasp of surprise and dread'

By then the Groups were still reeling from two other Berlin raids which had brought devastation to the Luftwaffe, but had also downed a total of 106 B-17s and B-24s. The record cost of one of the missions would stand for ever as the highest price paid by the 8th Air Force in the whole of the war.

The 482nd BG, which had supplied Lt Bill Owen and his crew to target mark for Col. Mumford's 95th, was the only Group raised in the UK itself for the 8th Air Force, rather than in the US. It was a specialist unit formed to develop combat techniques but particularly to test radar devices, notably H2X – the American-made ground-scanning radar which British scientists had developed and which had allowed the RAF to carry out its campaign against Berlin in the almost constant overcast. The 482nd BG, equipped with both Flying Fortresses and Liberators, was now supplying Pathfinder crews to lead the way to targets when visual bombing was unlikely, which was an admission that the 'bombs in a pickle-barrel' boast for the Norden bombsight by its owners in company publicity was a high-level aim seldom achieved. From the start of 1944 to the end of the war many missions by the 8th would be area attacks, just like the RAF were carrying out at night. The mission to Berlin on 6 March turned out to be exactly one of these, though that was not the original intention.

The Pathfinder aircraft which would be leading the 3rd BD to Berlin would have as its co-pilot one of the most famous men in the 8th AF, Red Morgan. Morgan was one of the surprisingly large number of Americans who had transferred to the 8th in England after serving under Sir Arthur Harris in the Royal Canadian Air Force (RCAF), crossing the border into Canada before the USA entered the war. Morgan had been posted to RAF Bomber Command as a sergeant pilot in 1942 and in March 1943 transferred to the USAAF in the non-commissioned rank of flight officer. Four months later as a co-pilot on the B-17 *Ruthie II* of the 92nd BG he had been nearing the German coast when Fw 190s attacked, smashing the cockpit windshield and splitting the skull of the pilot, Lt Robert Campbell. As Campbell slumped forward sending the aircraft into a dive, Morgan fought for control and managed to bring the Fortress back into formation. The badly wounded and confused pilot continued to wrestle with the controls and hit Morgan with his fists, loosening some teeth and blackening both his eyes. At the same time the top turret gunner, seriously injured when a 20mm shell tore off his left arm at the shoulder, fell out of his position, and was found by the navigator bleeding to death. The navigator baled the gunner out the aircraft with his parachute firmly fixed and ripcord in his good hand in a successful effort to save his life. Morgan continued to the target. For two hours he held position in the formation – flying with one hand, fighting off the pilot with the other. Finally the navigator entered the flight deck and he and the bombardier managed to secure the dying pilot in the nose section. Morgan's B-17 successfully dropped its bombs on Hanover and, with his fuel gauges reading empty, the flight officer eventually landed the bomber at RAF Foulsham. Lt Campbell died shortly afterwards. The B-17 was declared irreparable. Morgan finished his tour, received news of his Medal of Honor in December and was transferred to the new Pathfinder Group where he was commissioned.

On the afternoon of 5 March Morgan and his pilot Major Fred Rabo had flown their B-17 *Chopstick-G George* to the headquarters of the 4th Combat Wing at Great Ashfield where they were told they would be taking the wing CO, Brigadier General Russ Wilson to Berlin, specifically to the VKF ball-bearing works at Erkner, an eastern suburb of Berlin. The next morning Morgan and Rabo were called earlier than other aircraft commanders at the Suffolk base for lead pilot preparation. The bomb load was different for Pathfinder aircraft. Instead of the ten standard 500lb HE or forty-two 100lb incendiaries in each B-17 bomb bay,

Morgan's plane and the other 482 BG raiders would carry four 500lb bombs, plus two smoke markers and six target indicators to fix the Initial Point for bomb runs.

At Ridgewell, Essex, Lt Howland, the 381st BG navigator who had logged four missions in Big Week, was called at 0345. His Group would take off early as they were right at the head of the main force. At Knettishall, Norfolk, in the 3rd BD area, Flt Officer Bernard Dopko of the 388th BG was woken to begin what would be the longest flight of his operational career. His fellow Group command pilot, Lt Lowell Watts, was hoping for a milk run as the Tannoy blared for briefing, it being the final sortie of his twenty-five-mission tour which had begun the previous November. But in the same bombardment division S/Sgt John Gabay, tail gunner in the 94th BG's *Sweaty Betty*, at Bury St Edmunds, Suffolk, was seeking a raid on 'Big B' to 'get one under his belt' after twenty other missions which had taken him to many of the cities in central and southern Germany.

At Thorpe Abbotts John Bennett was getting used to the fact that he was the new acting commander of the 100th BG. Bennett had been appointed the previous day from leader of the Group's 349th Sqn to the position of the 100th's Air Executive officer. Then his Group commander Col. Neil Harding had been taken to hospital for an emergency gallstones operation and suddenly the Texan found himself with the awesome responsibility of being in charge. That morning he briefed thirty-six crews for the 3rd BD's primary target of the Robert Bosch electrical works at Klein Machnow, Berlin.

Eight miles away at Bungay, 446th BG tail gunner S/Sgt Richard Denton boarded the truck after target briefing for the Daimler Benz aero engine works, Genshagen, to collect his guns from the armoury for his B-24 *Major Hoopo*, and install ready for Stations, the assigned time when crews had to be aboard their aircraft. The tension of that last hour before take-off into the unknown was described by *Yank* correspondent Sgt Walter Peters in his account of a typical raid that Winter. 'A half-ton truck was rolling along the runway. It was about 0600 but still very dark,' he wrote. 'The truck turned into a narrow road and stopped at a small shed. Then about six men jumped out and went inside. About 25 sergeants were cleaning caliber .50s on long benches. Above them were signs reading "Without armament there is no need for an air force. Lord Trenchard, Marshal of the RAF". . . . The sergeants carefully enclosed their guns in burlap bags and headed for the hardstand . . . It was five minutes before Stations.'[16]

Chaplains of the various faiths were still moving among the various planes across the scores of airfields patterning the bomber counties, screeching to a halt in their jeeps and leaping out to bring comfort to those of their flock who waited nervously to be tested by fire once more. As they sped away afterwards the crews drifted over to the mechanics' ground crew tents, pocketed their mission Mars bars handed out by their co-pilots, and talked of home but thought of the enemy preparing. Finally each crew commander performed his own good luck gesture of peeing against the aircraft tail wheel and called on his men to get in the plane. Peters wrote: 'Then No 1 engine was started, No 2 followed and 3 and 4 began to roar next. The plane taxied up to the edge of the runway and in a few minutes it was airborne. And that was the beginning of the mission.'[17] A total of 814 Flying Fortresses and Liberators from all three bombardment divisions lifted off over the next hour into the low cloud and began the ritual, hazardous dance of assembly. Thirty-eight of them were spares designed to fill gaps in formations, if possible, where aircraft aborted. Six of the 100th BG returned before long to Thorpe Abbotts with various problems including low oxygen supply, high oil temperature and reduced oil pressure. The new CO was waiting. 'When six of the lads returned early I was, naturally, upset,' he wrote in a letter home. 'When a group of bombers is weakened in strength it becomes an attractive target for the German air force. With a lonely 30 planes going into Germany I was not at all happy over the prospects.'[18]

The 262 bombers of the 1st BD formed up to lead the mission one minute behind schedule and crossed the coast at Cromer just after 10am. Eleven minutes later the leading aircraft of the 3rd BD passed Orfordness and set a converging course to meet the division ahead at the Dutch coast. The 200 or so Liberators of the 2nd BD followed the 1st BD over Cromer at 10.28. German Freya radar stations saw them coming as soon as they entered the North Sea and alerted fighter units in France, Belgium, Holland and Germany to fifteen minutes' readiness. Luftwaffe pilots made their way to the bleak dispersals. Most of the USAAF escorts had by now taken off and were heading east, 615 P-47s and 100 P-51s cruising at about 80mph more than the bombers to meet up en route or over Berlin itself. The twin bomber streams stretched for up to eighty miles across the North Sea, a purposeful, remorseless demonstration of American technology designed to wreak havoc in the Reich capital. As always it was awesome for those taking part and when the leading Groups reached the Dutch coast at 10.52 proved no less inspiring to those in occupied territory below.

Unexpected headwinds had made the point of the stream eight minutes late and in the 3rd BD the 13th Combat Wing, in which the 100th BG was contained, became separated from the 4th Combat Wing which Red Morgan was leading with General Wilson and in which S/Sgt John Gabay was flying. The gap between the two wings stretched to twenty miles. Another problem had already arisen which would now nakedly expose the 100th BG. From the Dutch coast onwards the three bombardment divisions were meant to form an unbroken, cohesive speeding arrow, the 1st BD leading and the Liberators of the 2nd BD bringing up the rear. But the aircraft of Col. Ross Milton, airborne commander of the 1st BD, lost use of its radar. The unusually high wind had now reached 45mph, blowing from the north-east, and without the means for the navigator of checking position by the H2X scanner the aircraft began to take a track 10 degrees south of that planned. The combat wings behind followed, including those of the 3rd BD. All, that is, except the 13th Combat Wing which had become separated from the 4th CBW ahead.[19] It and the other CBWs behind went straight on, following the original planned course. For a while there were now two separate forces flying towards the gathering defences of the Luftwaffe.

It had the makings of a classic weak defence the 8th had faced in its early days in England and which the now commander of the 3rd BD, Curtis LeMay, had designed the combat box method to avoid. Because the Luftwaffe had proved more than capable of picking off individual Groups, LeMay had developed the compressed arrow-shaped formation when he was CO of the 305th BG at Grafton Underwood in the winter of 1942–43. The squadrons were stacked in the sky with the middle leading the wedge, a second squadron slightly higher and the third slightly lower. It would be combined with a second or third combat box, thus making up a wing, which would allow cones of .50 MG fire in a concentration over thousands of yards from each direction of the remorseless, thundering force to spoil the Luftwaffe fighter pilots' aim.

But the defensive power available to the rear combat wings of the 3rd BD with the 13th in the lead was now halved. The most vulnerable force in that leading edge was usually the low box. There were two low boxes in two formations, A and B, introduced as the 'double Group' method in December 1943. The B formation low box was made up of seventeen B-17s of the 100th BG. They were about to be torn apart.

The Germans had assembled more than a hundred fighters

over Steinhuder Lake and at 11.40 they were directed exactly west into the path of the rear 3rd BD. The front of the division, now twenty miles to the south, had realised its error and as 12 o'clock approached had already started to change course to link the two halves.

But it was too late. High noon for the 100th BG came as they flew over the German border just to the north of Lingen. In less than a minute Me 109s and Fw 190s flashing in from the east shot down nine of the Group's bombers and one from the 390th. Lt Lowell Watts of the 388th BG was in the 45th CBW immediately behind and watched it all in horror, as he later reported.

About two or three miles ahead of us was the 13th Combat Wing. Their formation had tightened up since I last looked at it. Little dots that were German fighters were diving into those formations, circling and attacking again. Out of one high squadron a B-17 slowly climbed away from its formation, the entire right wing a mass of flames. I looked again a second later. There was a flash – then nothing but little specks drifting, tumbling down. Seconds later another bomber tipped up on a wing, rolled over and dived straight for the ground. Little white puffs of parachute began to float beneath us, then fell behind.[20]

Lt Col. Glenn Duncan, commander of the 353rd FG, was leading thirty-two P-47s and had just made rendezvous with the 3rd BD, watching eight Thunderbolts split away to protect the detached rear of the 13th CBW, when the disaster began to unfold. 'As the rest of the Group was closing up the middle box, some 12-plus Fws made a head on pass through the Fort formation,' he reported later that day. 'If we could have been one minute earlier we could have stopped the attack, but due to the time element we were only able to engage the e/a as they came out of the rear of the bomber formation. Two Forts were shot down by this pass which was not any fair trade for the four se/e/a [single-engined enemy aircraft] that I saw go down immediately after the attack. I went down with both wing tanks on, dropping one as I closed on a Fw 190.' Duncan, who would end the war with nineteen confirmed victories, narrowed the gap to 500 yards, causing the German to roll over. 'He was sucker bait then. I stayed with him through thick and thin (the wing tank was still pushing gas into the good ole engine) and finally after patient and incessant firing I managed to get enough strikes in the wing and cockpit to kill him. He went down.' Duncan then dropped his second wing tank and went to help his No. 2, who had a fighter on his tail. 'Lt Guertz was having a lot of fun out-diving the Jerry, but we weren't doing any good that way so I cut in and chased the Hun away. I was unable to kill him as the bombers were still getting attacks as we pulled back up to them. There were many P-47s in the area causing some confusion, but we managed to recognize them at the moment before shooting.'[21]

The Luftwaffe fighters which had caused such devastation in their first pass through the formation now regrouped to hit the weakened 13th CBW again, but a flight of eight P-47s headed by Lt Bob Johnson of the 56th FG had spotted the bandits from the north and dove into the attack. Before they got there two B-17s of the 95th BG, which would lose a total of eight that day, went down and others of the 100th BG were hit. The 100th's *Superstitious Aloysius*, commanded by Lt Mark Cope, which had had an engine shot out in the initial attack and was forced to leave the formation, was hit again in the next attack and two of his gunners were mortally wounded. Cope jettisoned his bombs and dived for the cloud layer, heading west alone.

As the Fw 190s and Me 109s poured cannon fire into the Fortresses they were hit by Johnson's Thunderbolts, who passed under four blazing bombers. The remainder of the 56th FG, led by Hub Zemke, had been covering the front section of the truncated 3rd BD twenty miles to the south-east, but when they heard the radio calls from the stricken B-17s sped for the scene of the massacre. P-47s of the 78th FG also came to the rescue and over the next minutes there was a whirling, thundering swarm of fighters, German and US, the confusion Col. Duncan referred to, as each tried to get on another's tail.

The battle continued for twenty minutes, until the Luftwaffe units were forced to break away to refuel and rearm. Meanwhile the front section of the bomber stream, now strung out over a hundred miles, had its own problems as it tried to get back on course, wandering over flak sites which damaged several aircraft. Lt Howland, of the 381st BG, later recorded running 'into a dense barrage of flak near Osnabruck. One plane from our Group was hit in the No. 4 engine, but the pilot feathered the prop, salvoed his bombs and a few minutes later aborted . . . We took some flak in the nose of our ship when a hunk of steel tore through the roof, hit the armour plate in front of the pilot, bounced off, hit my helmet and bounced again . . . Threw out some chaff to throw their aim off. But we were too late and those boys down there knew their stuff. They kept it right up there till we were out of range.'[22] By 12.30 the reunited stream was on course for Berlin. It was minus more than twenty bombers and three P-47s. The Germans, with twelve fighters down, were ahead at this stage in terms of lost manpower.

The next assault came to the north of Magdeburg where a mixed force of 72 Me 109s and Fw 190s plus forty-one twin-engined machines, some armed with rockets, had been assembling. They got the order to proceed en masse for the approaching bombers at 12.30pm. By now the P-47 escorts had used up their fuel and turned for home, but P-51s of the 4th and 354th FGs were approaching. The Luftwaffe controller had planned to orchestrate a head-on attack, but as the German fighters swept in for contact position the bombardment divisions made a slight turn south-east to align for the bomb run on their targets at Berlin's southern edge.

It caused a delay in the German assault and as the Luftwaffe moved in to take the bombers from the side the 357th FG arrived in their Mustangs. They had lost two of their number the day before, Chuck Yeager and their colourful leader, Col. Henry Spicer. Spicer, who had led his newly formed Group in the opening raid of Big Week, had baled out into the near-freezing waters of the Channel after being hit by flak while escorting the 2nd BD to French targets. As his Yoxford Boys now dived into attack north of Magdeburg, Spicer was facing a second day in his dinghy, his feet and hands badly frostbitten.

S/Sgt John Gabay, in the tail turret of the 94th BG's *Sweaty Betty*, was at the very head of the 3rd Division in the middle of the stream. He described in his mission diary what happened. 'We had some eager attacks by about 30 109s and 190s. We managed to keep them honest till our escort of P-51s showed up. Then the dogfights began. The sky above us was full of vapor trails in one massive dogfight. Several fighters were knocked down – mostly Jerries. Meanwhile the Group just in back of us lost eight Forts in one pass by about 60 109s and Fw 190s. Several parachutes filled the sky – couldn't keep track as fighters came at us. Then the 51s came and everybody was shooting at somebody. What a mess!'[23]

Lt Howland recalled that he was even further ahead in the leading combat wing of the 1st Division.

We passed by Brunswick and Magdeburg and then the German fighters hit us. I could see them off to our right, too far away to identify positively ... We were flying the No. 3 position, 2nd element of the low squadron commonly called 'Purple Heart Corner' ... They hit the high Group of our wing. An Me 109 whizzed by. He was so close I could distinguish features on the pilot, such as an oxygen mask and helmet. A fraction of a second later there was an explosion with flying Plexiglass [sic] all through the nose compartment. I realised that we had been hit, but couldn't seem to get my wits together to find out whether Frank [the bombardier, 2/Lt Palenik] or I were injured. I then noticed that the window above my desk was completely gone and that both hands were bleeding, apparently from superficial wounds made by the flying Plexiglass . . . I saw that there was a hole under Frank's left foot and was worried whether he had been hurt seriously or not as he seemed to roll in his seat, but Frank was OK. He was just looking for more fighters to shoot at with his twin 50s.

A few seconds before our ship was hit a B-17 just above us and to our left was hit in the No. 4 engine which immediately caught fire. He had dropped down and was passing underneath us at the time we were hit by 20mm shells. My first reaction was that he had exploded.[24]

A short time after the attack Howland saw a B-17 from his own 532 Sqn, coded VE-N. It

started smoking in the No. 4 engine and had to drop out of formation. They didn't make it back to base. Somewhere out of my line of sight above us another ship had been hit and the crew was baling out. They were free falling at our 26,000ft altitude, trying to get safely through the formation . . . Through my broken window I saw one fellow falling end to end. He wasn't more than 50ft from our wing tip.

While watching VE-N I saw a bunch of Fw 190s swing down and make a head-on attack on a wing flying to our right. One B-17 burst into a massive ball of flame that dropped like a rock. It hit another plane, knocking a wing off and they both went down . . . I searched the sky for parachutes. There were none.[25]

Howland's tail gunner, Sgt Arnold Farmer, shot down an Me 110. He then saw enemy aircraft at the rear shooting rockets. Each Dornier 217 fired four rockets, but the fuses were incorrectly set as they all exploded 500 yards behind. At the same time just before the IP for the bomb run more Me 210s attacked on the right. There were now only forty-three Fortresses left of the fifty-nine of the 1st CBW which had set course four hours before. A bank of cloud suddenly drifted over the aiming point ruining the necessary visual attack on such a small target. The leader of the 1st BD ordered his Groups to find targets of opportunity. The 381st went for Zernsdorf a few miles south-west of the primary. 'The bomb run was made with little flak or fighter opposition, but the lead ship accidentally released half his bombs and most of the planes in the formation released on him,' Howland recorded. 'The mission was a failure as far as our wing was concerned.'[26] Other Groups hit other small communities.

But while Howland's combat wing escaped the flak, the 94th CBW following behind didn't. It headed towards the centre of Berlin over several flak sites and the radar bomb run had to be abandoned when a barrage wrecked the H2X set of the Pathfinder and most of the wing's bombers were hit by flak.

The 3rd BD was also defeated by cloud as it made a southerly approach to the primary of the Bosch plant at Klein Maschow. It too now made for targets inside Berlin and was battered by the capital's fearsome defences. One aircraft of the 447th BG heading towards the Daimler Benz tank engine factory at Templehof had two shells burst beneath it. The B-17 carried on, minus its radioman who had been blasted through the hatch above his compartment, without a parachute. Some seventy bombers were battered by barrages as they headed for a cloud-free area at Steglitz. In the lead was the Pathfinder of Lt Red Morgan. Just before the release point a flak burst ignited the right main fuel tanks. The plane's commander kept on the bomb run until his markers had been released then ordered a bale-out. But within seconds as *Chopstick-G George* headed earthwards the bomber blew up. Morgan was blasted into the sky with the parachute he had been attempting to clip on tucked under his arm. 'I kept trying to get it on,' he said later. 'When I was falling feet first the pressure kept pushing it up too high, and when I was falling head first it kept pushing it past my chest. I guess I was on my back when I finally got it fastened on . . . I think you think clearer when you're so damned near dead. Three or four seconds after the chute popped open, I landed in the top of a tree. I fell out of it, about 30 feet, and landed on my feet. I felt like I'd busted every bone in me.'[27] Morgan was quickly captured by men from a flak battery and ended up in Stalag Luft III. He later found he was one of only three survivors of the twelve men aboard. General Wilson was not among them.

The 45th Combat Wing in which Lt Watts was flying *Blitzin' Betty* of the 388th BG chose a target of opportunity in Orianenburg when cloud covered Klein Maschow. The famed Berlin flak, which RAF Bomber Command had been suffering at night for months, now made itself evident to the 388th. There was no question of a few ranging shots: the batteries below had the formation immediately bracketed and at the right height. 'We could hear the metal of our plane rend and tear as each volley exploded,' Watts wrote. 'The hits weren't direct. They were just far enough away so they didn't take off a wing, the tail or blow the plane up; they would just tear a ship half apart . . . big, ragged holes appeared in the wings and fuselage.' A shell splinter severed the oxygen supply to crewmen in the rear and they grabbed portable oxygen bottles. 'Above us and to the right a string of bombs trailed out from our lead ship. Simultaneously our ship jumped upwards, relieved of its explosive load.'[28] Another of the 388th BG's aircraft, *Little Willie*, was badly damaged by a close flak burst. 'The propellor ran away on one engine and the supercharger on another went out by flak hit,' *Stars and Stripes* reported. 'The stricken ship fell out of formation.'[29] *Little Willie's* commander was Flt Officer Bernard Dopko and it was just the start of a harrowing ordeal.

The 13th Combat Wing B formation containing the 100th BG unloaded to the north of Potsdam where accurate flak now battered what the fighters had left. Harold Stearns, who had been credited with being the first American gunner to down a fighter over Berlin two days before, saw from the top turret of *Rubber Check* No. 4 engine catch fire after a close burst. The plane fell behind its formation and the crew prepared to return home alone. Bombs from the different Groups in the 1st and 3rd BDs had been scattered all over Berlin as gaps were spotted in clouds and targets quickly chosen amid the flak bursts.

Only the 2nd BD in the rear of the stream came anywhere near a primary target. The 389th BG in the high box of the 2nd CBW leading the division bombed the partly obscured Daimler Benz aero engine works at Genshagen on the south-western edge of Berlin. Other 2nd BD Groups aimed at the Genshagen suburb or other districts of the metropolis such as Zehlendorf. At least one Liberator in the division had already been forced to head for home. *Major Hoopo*, in which S/Sgt Richard Denton was the tail gunner, had been attacked by a fighter shortly before Berlin and with one engine out Lt Robert Paltz had had to abandon the mission.

The bomb Groups of all three divisions now headed for the Rally Point north-west of Berlin. The horrors were not over. Lt Jesse Pitts, co-pilot in *Penny Ante* of the 379th BG, saw that a B-17 ahead, with one engine feathered, had its bomb bay doors cracked open around the booted leg of one of its crewmen. 'That leg was now hanging limp in the slipstream,' he wrote years later.

'We learned later that the crewman, the engineer, had got his leg caught outside the doors as they closed and the pilot had not been able to order action to extricate the engineer before he died.'[30] Pitts saw the boot hanging out all the way home.

The returning air divisions set course to clear the problematic Magdeburg area lying to the south. It would take them past Celle instead. As they streamed westward leaving Berlin smoking behind them from hundreds of fires, they made a solid front, the 1st BD at the top, then the 3rd and 2nd. Ahead lay more fighters and more flak. *Rubber Check* of the 100th BG, trailing smoke from its flak-damaged engine, didn't last long. 'I was looking for bandits when I heard the radio operator, Grant Scott, call over the interphone "Fighters at 3 o'clock" and sure enough there was an Me 109 blasting away,' Sgt Stearns remembered. 'I think Scott must have been killed instantly. I fired from my turret and could see smoke coming from the enemy fighter.'[31] But the B-17 was now doomed and Lt Frank Granack rang the bale-out bell. 'We were losing altitude, smoke pouring from Nos 3 and 4 engines . . . I baled out from the bomb bay doors, waited until I had cleared the plane then pulled open my chest chute. In the distance I could see *Rubber Check* chugging along, black smoke trailing from its damaged engines.'[32] Stearns and seven others of the crew survived after baling out near Ostprignitz to the north-west of Berlin.

Some stragglers in the returning stream were rescued by the intervention of USAAF fighters in the withdrawal. Captain Glendon Davis and his wingman of the 357th FG were in the same area in their Mustangs when Davis came across a bomber in trouble. 'We had set course for home and were climbing up above the Big Friends when I noticed a B-17 straggler with an Fw 190 sitting on his tail at approximately 19,000ft,' he detailed later.

We dove down on the e/a and at that time he saw us and broke into us. We turned into him and then he started for the deck in a tight spiral. We followed him down indicating from 450–500mph. We were forcing him to keep a tight spiral by cutting on the inside of him when he tried to widen it out. At 10,000ft he dropped his belly tank. At 5,000ft his plane appeared to be stalling as he tried to pull out. His canopy flew off but the plane went right on into the ground without the pilot ever getting out. We circled the flaming wreckage taking pictures of it, then came on home without incident. I claim an Fw 190 and pilot destroyed.[33]

The crew of the unknown B-17 straggler had been lucky that a pair of Mustangs showed up at just the right moment. Flt Officer Dopko, trying to get home to Knettishall, wasn't so fortunate. Out of formation *Little Willie* was hit by two German fighters. 'The tail gunner, Sgt Robert Haydon Jr, of Madison, Wis[consin], set up such a hot stream of bullets that they broke off their attack almost as soon as it started,' *Stars and Stripes* reported. 'To keep from being attacked again Dopko pointed the ship's nose to the ground and screwed down to 50ft where he levelled off and started dodging rooftops.'[34] Dopko would have to continue at low level for the next three and a half hours as he covered 350 miles of German territory at a speed no higher than 115 miles an hour.

By now Lt Col. Bennett was discovering how bad the day had been for his 100th BG as Lt Mark Cope brought the badly damaged *Superstitious Aloysius* into Thorpe Abbotts after having to leave the formation. The medics called out to his aircraft found two of his crew had succumbed to their wounds from fighters.

Lt Watts had begun thinking, after the American fighters appeared and chased away the Luftwaffe, about the cable signalling the end of his tour that he would send after he landed at Knettishall. But near the Dutch border as the P-47s left, Fw 190s showed up again and attacked *Blitzin' Betty* head-on. From one of them 20mm rounds exploded beneath the pilot's feet among the oxygen tanks and splinters slashed through gasoline feed lines causing an explosion of fire through the front of the aircraft. Watts ordered his crew to bale out, his vision obscured by the flames as his B-17 collided with another, as he later recounted.

> It was a wild ride from that point. I could tell we had rolled upside down. My safety belt had been unbuckled. I fell away from the seat, but held myself in with the grasp I had on the control wheel. After a few weird sensations I was pinned to the seat, unable to move. Flames now swept past my face, between my legs and past my arms as though sucked by a giant vacuum. Unable to see, I could only tell that we were spinning and diving at a terrific rate. That wild eerie ride down the corridors of the sky in a flaming bomber still haunts my memory. But it wasn't just the terror of death, it was the unending confusion and pain of a hopeless fight and the worry for the nine other men that were my responsibility.[35]

The caprice of war which had so savagely selected *Blitzin' Betty* for destruction, now just as carelessly decided to save Watts. The build-up of centrifugal force as the bomber span tighter and tighter eventually hurled him towards the shattered canopy of the flight deck and just as playfully threw him, arms and legs whirling, into space. 'Something jerked heavily past my face. That was my flak jacket. Then my oxygen mask flew off, followed by my goggles and helmet. I automatically reached for my chest. Yes, there was the ripcord.' At the second attempt his chute opened and he found himself hanging in what seemed the most complete silence he had ever known. A burning engine flew by followed by a shower of winking, wrinkled metal. Then, further away, 'I caught sight of the bright yellow of the dinghy radio falling through space. What a screwy time to notice that radio, but ever since the sight of it has stayed in my mind more than anything else.'[36] An Fw 190 whizzed down past him and tensed as he had been for the impact of cannon fire he looked in the cockpit and saw the pilot was dead. Minutes later he saw four planes burning on the ground, including the Focke-Wulf. He landed in snow, just inside Holland, and started walking, but unknown to him he was in a little peninsula of the border and two days on he was caught by civilians in Germany. Later he discovered that he was one of six members of *Blitzin' Betty* to have survived.

A few miles further on *Major Hoopo*, which had had to turn back before Berlin with an engine out, also began to lose its low-altitude battle. It suffered further damage from both flak and fighters and just after crossing the Dutch coast another engine failed. Everything possible had by now been thrown out of the plane to try to keep it flying and, a hundred miles from home, Lt Robert Paltz had no alternative but to ditch immediately. Tail gunner Sgt Denton reported: 'We hit the water for the first time and bounced, the second time we hit the water the plane broke in half at the trailing edge of the wing. The front end of the plane nosed over and started to sink. I struggled out of the waist window and came out at the back end of the fuselage, then managed to scramble aboard a life raft that had inflated. One life raft came out of the airplane. I got out of the back of the plane, got to the raft, found the pilot and engineer and put them in the raft.'[37]

Sgt Denton's understated report in no way does justice to the courage of the three surviving crew members in the bitterly cold sea. The pilot had two broken legs and the engineer, Sgt A. L. Songer, cracked bones in his shoulder. 'When the life raft came out of the plane it was upside down,' Denton continued. 'I didn't want to risk taking the injured off and flipping it back over. I felt a tug on my foot and discovered the dinghy was still attached to the plane by a rope. The plane was sinking, so I hurriedly found a piece of metal and cut the rope.'[38] Fortunately the ditching had been witnessed by a P-47 pilot who alerted Air Sea Rescue and saw a launch heading for the survivors. Denton, Paltz and Songer were revived with rum and taken to hospital. Before he left the launch Denton handed over his flying boots to a member of its crew because he told him it was the first time they had picked up a survivor with his boots still on.

At Thorpe Abbotts Lt Col. Bennett now knew the full story of the disaster which had befallen his Group as the surviving aircraft arrived over the field at 4pm. 'Just exactly 50 per cent of our force which had entered Germany had been shot down,' he wrote in a letter home. 'The 349th Sqn, my old outfit, had taken the brunt of the attack losing six crews.'[39] Other Groups were also now counting the cost of the day's assault on Berlin. The 95th BG had lost eight crews, the 388th seven, the 91st six, the 458th five.

The last 8th Air Force machine to make it home was *Little Willie*. It arrived over Knettishall at 5.45pm, so long after it had been given up on that its commander Flt Officer Dopko later revealed his belongings had already been packed by administrative staff to be shipped home. An Associated Press reporter named Henry Jameson was at the Suffolk base as it came in to hear the details of the crew's incredible journey and turn them into legends.

After being reported as Missing In Action the irrepressible crew of the Fortress *Little Willie* finally showed up at their home station laughing and joking about their mad-cap trip home from Berlin – skimming chimneys, down main streets of German towns and never more than 100ft from the ground. They roared between two church steeples and went down the main drag of one place so low that the bombardier yelled out to the pilot, 'Watch out for the curb.' They whistled and waved at a German girl cycling down the street of one town and finally shot up all their ammunition at the German defences on the Dutch coast.

'We were flying along a road and came upon a man riding

a cart,' said Lt Glenn Cederstrom, of South Minneapolis, Minn[esota], the navigator. 'When he saw us he jumped and dived into a ditch. If he hadn't we would have knocked him off, we were so low.'

'*Little Willie* hobbled across the last stretch of the North Sea at the height of 10ft,' Dopko said as he reached for another beer.[40]

The story was printed in US newspapers two days later.

In total sixty-nine bombers went down in the Berlin mission of 6 March, one bomber in ten. It was the worst loss the 8th had ever suffered and in fact would remain a record for the rest of the war. Eleven fighters were also missing. Purely as an attempt to reduce production at all three primary targets the attack was a failure. But the plus side of war's ledger was encouraging. The 8th's fighter groups claimed no fewer than eighty-one kills, forty-three of them by the three Mustang Groups, Col. Henry Spicer's 357th among them. The man who had led them for just three weeks had another twenty-four hours to suffer in his dinghy in the Channel. Col. Spicer's hands and feet were badly frostbitten when he was finally washed ashore near Cherbourg on 7 March. He was found lying on the beach by some German soldiers and spent the rest of the war in Stalag Luft I. His 357th subordinate Chuck Yeager had evaded capture in France and made it back to England in May via Spain.

As the last hours of Col. Spicer's ordeal drifted by the aircrews of the 8th rested fitfully and desperately tried to make sense of what they had seen. Orders went out for new batches of apprehensive, replacement airmen to report at squadron offices and for gleaming new planes to fly in to fill the gaps at dispersals. The Groups were being fattened up for war once more.

4

'What are those fools trying to do, kill all of us'

It was at Thorpe Abbotts that the fatigue of continued combat against an enemy determined to defend his capital was most evident. The 100th's reputation as a hard-luck outfit was now firmly established. It had lost nine crews on the disastrous Schweinfurt-Regensburg mission in August 1943. It lost seven over Bremen seven weeks later and another twelve over Münster two days after that with only one plane returning.

Those lucky enough to survive the mission of 6 March stumbled from debriefing and crew rooms to their Nissen huts and tumbled into beds they had last seen in what seemed another lifetime. But for many, sleep would not come. As their eyes closed their imaginations snapped wide open and they saw again the fighters boring in, wings flashing cannon fire, then the Fortresses of men they had called friends falling away, obscenely graceful in their death dives as black curled-up figures fell out, parachutes streaming white against the icy blue. Both those able to snatch a few hours' sleep and those who hadn't, found it achingly easy to find a seat in the mess hall that night. The gaps created by fifteen missing crews were apparent for all to see. The logic now was that no one would finish a tour to go home to girls and family in the States.

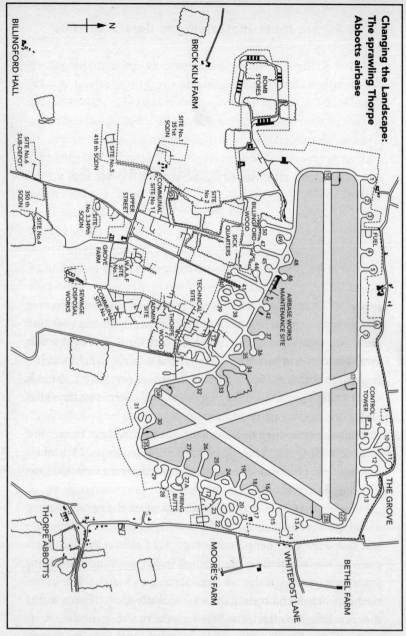

The detailed outline of the 100th BG's airfield. There were forty-two such USAAF heavy-bomber bases in England, each costing nearly £1 million to build, just part of the total of 250 USAAF stations in the UK. Not only did construction at Thorpe Abbotts require the building of three runways, each more than half a mile long, but dispersals, technical sites and living quarters for up 2,500 people. Thatched cottages and ancient woodland disappeared under the bulldozers' blades, creating a complex practically swamping the village the airfield was named after.

'What are those fools trying to do, kill all of us'

At debriefing Col. Bennett had seen the crews curse 8th AF headquarters after returning from the Reich capital on the Monday afternoon and he was now deeply worried. There is little doubt that General Spaatz would have called another Berlin mission the following day to keep the pressure on the enemy, but the weather intervened. A solid overcast covered the bases as night fell and it continued into Tuesday. Col. Bennett was grateful for the 'day off to lick our wounds' and his men hoped the stand-down would continue. After such a heavy loss on the Monday there would normally have been a chance to send a particularly exhausted crew to a flak farm, one of the series of manor houses taken over by the 8th where airmen could lounge around in civilian clothes, play tennis, eat sumptuous meals with the family silver on starched linen and generally pretend there was no war to return to. Combe House, near Shaftesbury in Dorset, was one such rest home and Lt Don Ackerson, the 384th BG bombardier who had seen so many Fortresses go down in Big Week, was billeted there with the other three officers in his crew from 3 March to the 11th, missing all the early Berlin raids. 'We had a cocktail bar before dinner,' he remembered. 'You could only go through the line at the bar one time, so all four of us would get in line and get four drinks each. The drinks were gin and orange. This was a nice rest with tea every afternoon. Tea was an event with all kinds of nice cake and cookies.'[1]

But there was no chance of a rest for the much-depleted crews at Thorpe Abbotts, if the 100th was to continue at all in the next few days. Col. Bennett talked to 3rd Division headquarters at Elveden Hall about replacements; however, they would not arrive until the end of the week. At 10pm on 7 March the teletype machines began chattering again for the attention of operations staff. A maximum effort was called for the morning. It was Berlin again. 'It's hard to describe the feeling that came over the few of us who knew that the boys were going back over the same route,'

Bennett wrote in a letter to his father. 'The operation officer was enraged. He cursed the higher command for what he said was their folly. "What are those fools trying to do, kill all of us."'[2]

The new commander of the 100th BG, gnawed by anxiety about how his survivors would react when they knew the Reich capital was the target again and that many might abort, called wing headquarters, explained the situation and asked if he himself could lead the wing of which the 100th was part. He was given permission to do so. The 100th could only scratch together enough crews to man fifteen planes and the first test of morale would be the briefing. Cheers would normally greet the evidence of a short-range target as the red thread on the map was revealed, a more ribald reaction the demand for a penetration into Germany itself.

'On the morning of March 8th when the curtain was opened there was not a sound. I was petrified,' Col. Bennett recorded. 'I had a mental picture of all kinds of personnel failures and abortions.'[3] A total of 623 aircraft from all three bomb divisions would be setting out with one united aim, to destroy the VKF ball-bearing factory at Erkner, eastern Berlin. The 45th Combat Wing would lead the 8th Air Force, followed by the 13th CBW. The 100th BG would head that wing, the second over the target with the by-then alerted Berlin flak battalions ranged against them.

Many of the men of the 8th Air Force who had survived Big Week found themselves frankly terrified by the prospect of Berlin. S/Sgt Lee Eli Baar, a ball turret gunner with the 306th BG more than two months into his tour, admitted in a post-war interview he was stunned when he heard the target announced in the Thurleigh briefing room on 8 March. 'When they said, "Berlin" everybody was scared stiff because we knew Berlin is a top city of Germany. [We knew] it's got to be the most well-guarded city in Germany with anti-aircraft flak and fighter pilots surrounding and that's what it was.'[4] The gunner would be called to the Reich capital again the following day.

Lt Howland, the 81st BG navigator, recorded that when Berlin was unveiled at briefing at Ridgewell, 'We were all nervous about going back into the same stuff we hit Monday, but we were told that every available long-range fighter in the British Isles would be over the target area to help us.'[5] In fact 891 would be aloft to meet the bombers at various points en route to provide escort. It meant there would be more than three fighters for every two bombers.

The assembly over East Anglia took place without incident in clear weather. Two other Groups formed up on the 100th BG and the 13th CBW it was leading fell in behind the 45th wing. The 8th headed out over the English coast climbing to 24,000ft. It was at that point that Col. Bennett called up the formation control officer in the rear turret of the rear plane to ask about the 100th's ships. 'Surely someone had aborted by this time,' he wrote. 'When he reported that we still had 15 planes I was strongly moved. These fine young men were following me in spite of what had happened on their last trip to Berlin.'[6] Leading the high squadron was a very brave airman indeed, Lt 'Rosie' Rosenthal. The lawyer from Brooklyn had experienced the loss of seven of his Group's B-17s on his first mission, the ill-fated Bremen raid, and had captained the only one to return on his third combat trip, the Münster mission. Now he was carrying out the final mission of his twenty-five-trip tour, determined to prove the odds could be beaten.

Above the seventy-mile-long stream of aircraft heading east over Holland fighter pilots wheeled and soared in their P-47s, searching the sky for bandits. At Dummer Lake near Lingen, where the 100th had been mauled on Monday, they turned back, low on fuel, for part of the 174-strong Mustang force to take over and ride along to Berlin. But the P-51s failed to make contact. Unescorted the bombers flew on. At Nienburg, north-east of

Hanover, the Luftwaffe struck. They flew head on into the 45th Combat Wing. Col. Bennett, leading the wing behind, had a ringside seat as Fortresses under attack by 150 fighters started to go down, some with wing tanks burning to the point of explosion, leaving nothing but four orange balls of fire; others spinning in ever-tighter circles, chutes popping out as the tail broke away. The aircraft of both the wing leader and his deputy were lost. The 8th AF official report would later read: 'All squadrons and groups in this wing were attacked savagely by enemy pilots described as the most skilful yet encountered. Attacks were virtually continuous from the vicinity of Nienburg to the target areas. Attacks by single enemy aircraft were few in number and these were concentrated principally on stragglers.'[7]

The 45th CBW was hacked to pieces. Of the three Groups in the wing, the 96th BG lost six aircraft, the 452nd lost five and the 388th, which had lost seven the day before, had another five of its Fortresses shot down. The force was now forty-five miles to the south of Berlin ready to make a left turn into the target. The 100th BG took over the lead and the enemy fighters then concentrated on it. But only one plane was badly hit, dropping into the low Group. As Col. Bennett turned onto the bomb run and the vast metropolis of Berlin neared and widened, he was able to look to the rear. 'I could see the other wings and divisions behind us,' he later wrote to his father. 'This was a wonderful and terrible sight. As far as one could see, nothing but bombers.'[8] Unlike previous raids on the capital, conditions were perfect for visual bombing and the Erkner plant was severely damaged as the bomb loads of nearly 500 aircraft went down. The thirty-three remaining planes of the 45th CBW attacked a target of opportunity at Wildau to avoid collision with the 13th and another thirty-three from the 2nd Bomb Division unloaded on the city itself to avoid a B-17 unit approaching the primary target. Meanwhile Mustangs which had gathered over the capital dropped the long-range tanks which had brought them 600 miles from England, and also slowed them down by 47mph, and went after the Fw 190s and Me 109s. Lt Bud Anderson, who would become one of the leading aces of the 357th, had his first victory that day, one of fifty-nine the Yoxford Boys would total by 11 March in their first month of operations.

Lt Howland in the 1st BD, way behind the 3rd Division which the 100th BG were leading, wrote later that the promises of the 381st BG briefing were confirmed. 'We had an umbrella of P-47s and P-51s over us all the way into the target area and didn't have a single fighter attack on our Wing today . . . The weather was absolutely perfect and we dropped our load of M47 oil and rubber incendiary bombs right on the target.'[9] As the bomber fleets turned for England, attacks which the front of the stream had suffered, died away. But as the Groups descended approaching the English coast they hit a solid undercast and many found themselves groping for their bases at low level.

At Thorpe Abbotts, after the shock and sorrow of Monday's disaster, there was now a more confident mood. Only one of the fifteen Fortresses which set out had failed to return and the dice had rolled in Lt Rosenthal's favour again, allowing him to complete his tour in his familiar B-17 *Rosie's Riveters* and prove to newer crews that it could be done. A writer for *Yank* magazine, Sgt Paul Levitt – who had himself carried out several missions with the 100th as a top turret gunner before returning to his old trade of reporter – had returned to Thorpe Abbotts to write about his former comrades in that crucial week, recording their losses and their victories.

He wrote that as Rosenthal's plane came in, swinging low over the tower in the late afternoon the 'sky was filled with flares' from the ship.

The armament men had given them two extra boxes before take-off that morning. They threw the 4th of July up at the cold, grey sky, and the control tower, which is a grave and dignified institution at an airfield – something like the Supreme Court – came back with more flares. The crew's request to the pilot that morning, when they learned it was to be Berlin, had been for a 'beautiful buzz job' coming in. The pilot gave it to them with his low swoop over the tower. It is said – though J. E. Woodward, the husky crew chief denies it – that big tears rolled down his face when *Rosie's Riveters* showed at last.[10]

But Rosenthal did not go home. The Jewish-American, who considered he had to do what he could to fight National Socialism as long as he was able, volunteered for a second tour and, after a week's leave in Scotland, came back to Thorpe Abbotts for further glory.

As the returned figures slowly trickled in from the Groups it was found that thirty-seven bombers had been lost on the mission, including another B-24 down in the North Sea, and a 390th BG aircraft *Phyllis Marie* had crash-landed in a Danish field. The Luftwaffe would later repair and fly it. Comparing the latest statistic with the sixty-nine missing after Monday's raid, Lt Howland wrote, perhaps ironically: 'It seems we are making progress.'[11] And the success of the now-mighty fighter force the 8th could put up as Mustangs and Thunderbolts flooded into Britain had been astonishing. Between them nineteen Groups claimed seventy-nine destroyed for only eighteen of their own. The attrition was undoubtedly favouring the attackers.

Stars and Stripes was triumphant the next day, splashing across its front page: 'Heavies Rain 360,000 Bombs on Berlin'. The story, not entirely accurately, continued: 'Berlin got its second major daylight bombing yesterday ... Returning airmen said smoke from the burning capital could be seen 100 miles away. USAAF headquarters said Erkner, which "produces half the minimum requirement in ball bearings needed by the Luftwaffe" was heavily hit among other targets. It is second only in importance to Schweinfurt ... Berlin radio said 60 bombers were shot down. One Thunderbolt squadron in Col. Hubert Zemke's Group claimed 20 planes destroyed. A Mustang Group claimed 28.'[12] The aircrew of the 8th did not have time to read it. By the time it appeared they were already on their way to Berlin once more.

The mission of 9 March was relatively small in comparison to what had taken place earlier in the week. Only the 1st and 3rd BDs participated while the Liberators of the 2nd BD unloaded over Hanover, Brunswick and Nienburg where the Luftwaffe had begun its attacks on the 45th CBW the day before. Many bombers were still undergoing repairs from flak and fighter damage and only 361 were deployed to the Reich capital. A total of seventeen aborted. Lt Howland found himself wearily following the familiar path. 'Up early and again the target was Berlin. This time we were briefed for a Heinkel factory and assembly plant 15 miles north and west of the city. Most of us are getting a little tired of going back to the same target.'[13]

The assembly was carried out without incident, but solid undercast all the way to Berlin made navigation difficult, again resulting in an area attack. What was remarkable was that the Luftwaffe failed to show. The 8th Fighter Groups now had so many pilots that four of the nineteen Groups despatched on escort that day flew double missions. But not one encounter report was made. One B-17 of the Berlin force had its tail knocked off by a bomb over the capital and five others were claimed by flak. One of them was *Little Willie*. It crashed near Försterei Prötze, twelve miles north-east of Orianenburg, but Flt Officer Dopko and his crew all survived to become PoWs.

The assault on Berlin ended temporarily as the weather closed in. In four days of warfare the 8th had 127 bombers missing in action. Its fighter arm lost sixty-one against what the American pursuit pilots claimed were 176 Germans shot down. The bomber crewmen filed reports of 164 kills. Claims could be inaccurate, bomber gunners' notoriously so because many fired at the same target in the heat of battle; but the fact remained that both sides had suffered mightily.* The difference was that the Luftwaffe had lost aircraft and crews it could not replace. American losses were made good within hours from the unstoppable US war machine and the number of Groups available was still growing. In March alone 20 per cent of Adolf Galland's pilots were killed or severely wounded. The Luftwaffe's leaders claimed that it was the poor weather which forced them to leave the 8th's bomber fleets unmolested as they bombed the heart of National Socialism. But the truth was that after two days of crippling losses they could not afford to take on the Americans again on 9 March.

Within weeks Galland was to report to his superiors: 'Between January and April 1944 our day fighter arm lost more than 1,000 pilots. They included our best *Staffel*, *Gruppe* and *Geschwader* commanders . . . The time has come when our force is within sight of collapse.'[14]

The evidence of how depleted the Luftwaffe had become was revealed again on 22 March when 657 USAAF bombers went to Berlin and only thirteen failed to return, three from the 446th BG flying its first mission which had two of its bombers collide over Holland and a third land in neutral Sweden. Lt Ackerson had now finished his flak leave where 'the food was good, the beds soft and we biked around to all the local pubs for hard cider' and taken the train 'back to the war, scared to death or not'. He

* The difficulty of keeping an accurate analysis of what damage your own air force was inflicting on the enemy's first became obvious in the Battle of Britain where the high-speed confusion of dog fighting led to wild claims on both sides. On 15 September 1940 the Dornier which crashed on London's Victoria Station, part of its bomb load falling on Buckingham Palace, was claimed by no less than nine pilots. (See Stephen Bungay, *The Most Dangerous Enemy*, p. 190.)

was on the mission of 22 March tasked with bombing an airfield close to the city by Pathfinder Force aided by visual check point. 'We flew deputy lead and took over the lead bombing when the lead ship had the bombs hung up,' he recorded in his diary. 'We dropped on PFF smoke bombs and the rest of the group dropped on us. The flak was intense over the target and all the way out. No fighter attacks at all.'[15] But two nights later Sir Arthur Harris's heavy bombers staged one more raid against Berlin. And this time the Luftwaffe showed it could still achieve in darkness if it couldn't always retaliate sufficiently by day. A total of seventy-two Lancasters failed to make it back, the third biggest loss in one night suffered by Bomber Command in the whole war. Harris's heavies would never return to the Reich capital; the closest they would come would be a nocturnal raid on Potsdam in April 1945. Apart from Mosquito operations by the RAF's Light Night Striking Force, Berlin – which had cost Harris the equivalent of the entire front-line strength of his command – was now an 8th Air Force battleground.

General Carl Spaatz's B-17s and B-24s would return many times and in the haphazard resistance of the Luftwaffe by day the USAAF too sometimes paid a terrible price. On 29 April the 8th lost sixty-three aircraft on a Berlin mission. Then there were the occasions just one Group became the focus of pity, the unlucky 100th BG for instance, which seemed cursed when the German capital was the target, losing nine on 24 May. Berlin and attrition were synonymous for both the RAF and USAAF. But once the daylight raids of the 8th against Berlin began it became clear which side was getting stronger as the struggle for air superiority wore down the defenders. It marked the road to final defeat for the Luftwaffe, knocked out of the sky by boys from Brooklyn to Buffalo.

Secretary of War Henry Stimpson told a press conference in Washington on 9 March as the Flying Fortresses were landing after the final raid on the Reich capital that week: 'Neither flak, fighter defences, clouds, nor fog can stop the Allied air blitz of Berlin.' Then he added: 'No target is safe by day or night.'[16] They were not and would become increasingly less safe as the war went on.

In achieving that supremacy thousands of American airmen would die. In April for instance the 8th Air Force would lose 403 heavy bombers, both shot down or wrecked beyond repair, while the 15th's losses would more than double to 214. But for the moment the thoughts of young airmen were turning elsewhere. The grip of winter had been loosened and a new season of hope was about to begin. For those youngsters from the New World the possibilities of relationships in the Old Country were blooming in apple blossom time.

SPRING

SPRING

5

'Hiya Baby! Lovely day, isn't it?'

The American airman was truly a glamorous figure in drab wartime Britain. From his neat little 'overseas' side cap to his shiny brown shoes he spoke of a different world, a land of plenty where confidence came with the territory. The closest most girls had been to American manhood in their conservative pre-war existence was the silver screen, where the macho charm of actors such as James Stewart and Clark Gable had stolen their hearts. Now here were the stars in person, walking down the street in AAF uniform.

It was an incredible shock to girls in the country, where Hollywood usually came via a travelling cinema show put on once a week at the village hall. Many of them had scarcely been as far as the nearest city before the Americans moved in to build their airbases, virtual hutted towns springing up in weeks and thatched cottages being bulldozed overnight to make way for concrete runways. The landscape of rural Britain was being changed in many directions, not least in the dating prospects for village maidens.

And it wasn't only the personnel in the USAAF radiating glamour to village girls who had dreamt nightly of their screen heroes. There was the Hollywood-style art painted on the noses of gleaming B-17s and B-24s glimpsed over hedgerows, from cartoon characters to the bold and beautiful. The girls were desperate to meet the men who came with the silver machines and the men on the bases, who only had the occasional Red Cross girls to talk to, were just as anxious to meet them too.

Lt Howland, now at Chelveston assigned to a Pathfinder school to become a lead navigator, took a weapons carrier with other airmen to Ridgewell in early April 1944 and noted: 'Saw lots of pretty girls in the towns we passed through. With Spring in the air I could really feel the hormones buzzing.'[1]

But for the most part it was airfield permanent staff, those with jobs that kept them on the ground, who got to know the locals and visited the village pub. There were up to 2,500 on each station, swamping a village, which for generations had numbered its population in hundreds, with brown uniforms. Aircrew, who were only in the area for the length of their tour, which sadly was often very short, tended to seek their off-base entertainment on a three-day pass to London.

In the villages locals found the USAAF men they met to be predominantly friendly, polite and generous. It became routine after a while for an Englishman to ask an American he had just met in the pub for a cigarette. After all, the serviceman could buy a pack of Lucky Strike or Camels for 3d (about 1p) from his base Post Exchange, the equivalent of the British NAAFI. The airmen in that pub came with the variety of accents according to their home states and backgrounds, typified by the long, slow 'Y'arll' greeting of the Southern youngster; the nasal 'moidering' of English words by the tenement boy from the Bronx; or the clipped, almost patrician, vowels of a New Englander who sounded not so unlike an English gentleman. But to the British who met them in their off-duty hours they were simply 'Yank' and this they called them to their faces, not considering it would offend the same Englishman to be addressed as 'Limey'. Sometimes the American's accent could be a complete puzzle. Lt Howland's favourite pub while he was stationed at Ridgewell was the sixteenth-century White Hart at Great Yeldham. Here, the navigator recalls, a young New York gunner 'could speak with an absolutely perfect Cockney accent', fooling visitors that he was English, but had switched to the USAAF because in the RAF 'the food was bad, the uniforms were scratchy and the pay awful'. Howland remembered that the 'middle-aged owner of the inn seemed to love him like her son'. The landlady was bereft when he failed to return from a mission. 'She tearfully informed us that she was terribly tired of war and it would be best for all concerned if we Yanks stayed on the base.'[2]

It had taken only a little time for Americans newly arrived in England to break down that famous British reserve they had been warned about. S/Sgt Robert Arbib, who came to Britain with an engineering battalion to build the USAAF base at Debach, Suffolk, described the summer night he and comrades wandered down verdant country lanes to become the first American visitors to the Dog in Grundisburgh, a pub beside the common which had served yeoman farmers and village lads for centuries and awed the GIs with its antiquity.

'When we entered the little pub, it was almost empty,' Arbib wrote. 'We found three or four small, plain rooms with wooden benches and bare wooden tables. Each room connected somehow with a central bar – either across a counter or through a tiny window. One of the rooms had a dart board and another an antique upright piano.'[3] The pub wasn't empty for long. 'The word was swiftly passed around, "The Yanks have arrived,"' Arbib wrote. 'People came in from all the farms and cottages and they filled the old public house with a carnival spirit. By eight o'clock there was standing room only and by nine o'clock even the dark narrow hall between the rooms was full and you could hardly turn around. The smoke was thick and the conversation excited . . . We started to sing and a girl named Molly tried to play the piano.'⁴ That piano at the Dog would be much used from then on, a local man called Carl Giles, who would find fame during the war and after as a cartoonist for the *Daily Express*, being photographed playing for black airmen.

Americans in England for the duration would often strike up a friendship with a particular village family, usually because the mother agreed to do the airman's weekly washing for a few shillings. Sometimes fruit canned in California for the air force would be exchanged for a simple meal home-cooked from English rations. But the servicemen almost universally tussled with the slower pace of life in English rural communities and many accounts by ex-USAAF personnel returned to the other side of the Atlantic show general puzzlement over the English tea breaks.

Mervyn Caldwell, from St Louis, Missouri, was a twenty-year-old GI teleprinter operator, first with the 92nd BG at Podington, Bedfordshire. Within months he moved to the 40th Combat Wing at nearby Thurleigh. He later recalled his life in small-town England.

I used to take my clothes to an English lady for the laundry and I used to talk to her quite a bit. England was very different to America. Little towns in America weren't anything great, but in England it seemed they had been there for ever. They were like something from a story book, sleepy little towns with no rush or hurry. One time I had a flat tyre in a town called Willesden. I stopped by a shop and asked an old man if he had anything to repair a tyre and he said he had to have tea. I had to wait until he came back. I enjoyed these places very much because we used to ride in at night on our bicycles. Every little town had its character. Service in England was like a dream-like thing, your life was suspended . . . I loved the pubs. They seemed much more friendly than bars in America. They had separate rooms and a lot of the time they had entertainment, perhaps an English soldier would be able to play the piano and we had a real good time.[5]

It was the ubiquitous bicycle, so necessary for getting around the flat acres of airbases, which often gave the airman social mobility too. T/Sgt Gordon Klehamer, a flight engineer in the 100th BG, recalls: 'My memories of off-duty time in England are of repairing an old bicycle then riding round the Thorpe Abbotts area. The bicycle was bought from an enterprising staff sergeant who had developed a bicycle business on base. He sold old, used bikes to new arrivals and then bought them back when we finished our tours and transferred out. We used them to ride around the base and to go to the mess hall and get laundry done and so on.'[6] Then there were the budding civilian entrepreneurs in the villages, who had filled a need by buying bikes from their neighbours and selling them on to the local airmen. The going rate was £6, which at that time was $30.

For the now bikeless village girls that spring of 1944 it was the fortnightly or monthly Saturday night dances at the American bases that gave them their best opportunity for meeting the boy from the other side of the ocean who sounded, and sometimes looked, like their matinee idols. Trucks would go out in the afternoon, calling at several rural communities and willing girls would be hoisted aboard for a night out transported to America. Once at the dance there would be no shortage of partners. Suffolk and neighbouring Norfolk, Cambridgeshire and Bedfordshire, where crowded bases almost overlapped each other, became known as Little America. A number of Cinderellas from the hamlets were whirled away into billets before the clock struck and the waiting trucks ticked over to take them back to a more mundane world. A few were persuaded to miss the trip home altogether.

S/Sgt Lee Eli Baar, the 306th BG airman shocked by Berlin, remembers being dropped off at his Nissen hut on arrival at

Thurleigh. 'We go in, open up and there's all kinds of twin bunks and the place is empty except there's a young lady sitting on the edge of one of the beds wearing a slip. We come running out and we tell the driver, we said, "Hey, there's somebody in there, somebody in there." "Who's in there?" I said, "A young lady, she's not fully dressed." "Oh," he said, "don't worry about it, she'll be out of there soon." That's what we found out.'[7] At Kimbolton, Cambridgeshire, the 379th BG CO issued a written order: 'All ladies attending Saturday night dances at the Officers' Club, MUST be off the base by 0800 the following morning.'[8]

The girls of the East Anglian towns rather than villages got their chance to meet a Yank by way of the 'liberty runs' for the men on the rural airfields to the nearest sizeable community. Cpl Robert Stine wrote an article for the army newspaper *Stars and Stripes* that spring about what a few hours' relaxation away from his airfield usually meant. 'Soldiers say it means run like hell for liberty,' he wrote. 'A Liberty Run is actually a convoy of 15 trucks, built to carry 240 soldiers, but which carries 360 soldiers and one disgruntled officer – the convoy officer – to any British town close to an army base . . . Rip off your clothes when the army work day is finished, take a fast shower, an even faster shave . . . borrow a GI blouse, another guy's overcoat, run to the mess.' After bolting down some food it was a dash to climb a tailgate, often as the trucks were already moving, then the start of a journey of twenty miles or so, standing all the way as the vehicles lurched down country lanes, just for four hours of freedom. They finally squealed to a halt in the parking lot at the nearest town. '"Got any gum, any sweets". It's the Liberty Run official greeters, English kids from 3 to 10,' the GI wrote. 'They like American gum and candy. They even know the day when you get your candy ration. These kids are professionals by now. Don't be a sucker, pal. Save it for your girl or some kid who doesn't hassle you for it. Talking about girls, did you see that line up near the trucks. Sure the English girls and the Americans are pairing off. Most GIs met their steadies by the trucks.' Those still footloose tended to head for the town hall dance to remedy the situation, Cpl Stine wrote, where the dance craze sweeping America had also now reached England thanks to the Yank invasion.

'So you didn't think the English could jitterbug,' Stine went on. 'Look at 'em go. Thought you'd see a dignified jitterbug coming out of the English? Next dance will be a waltz. Let's sit this one out, Yankees take a back seat when it comes to waltzing. Next one will be a slow step. Here's your chance. Get a girl in uniform or a girl in civvies. Take your pick of girls and approaches. "Wanta jump, baby?" "May I take this dance?" "How about it, Sister?" They all get results. Sit down again. Here comes one of those "excuse me jobs". The girls do the cutting.'

Duty called all too soon. 'It's the 11pm rush back to the trucks,' Stine continued. Then the long ride back standing up again in the lurching vehicle as the liberty man listened to the conversation around him in the dark. 'Boy was she a honey . . . What I wouldn't do for a hamburger . . . I'd swop my right leg for a sirloin medium, with French fries, with onions, with good hot coffee, with white bread, with chocolate pie.' Stine ended: 'You'll soon be home, you call a Nissen hut home now.'[9]

It took all types to fight the air war and many young men in US uniform simply missed their homes and familiar American life. There were incidences of suicide, including one of a young member of an anti-aircraft unit 'homesick beyond anyone's comprehension' whose friends hid his 30mm ammunition and vowed not to leave him alone. One day their guard slipped during mess call and with the sound of an exploding bullet to the head he 'went home before any of us', a comrade revealed.[10]

Mervyn Caldwell, who spent two years in England, also remembers missing home: 'Yes I was homesick at the beginning, but you didn't like to tell anyone in case they would think you were a wimp. It kind of toughened my life up when I came to England. It was like an adventure, every place I went.'[11] The homesickness felt by many young men could also spur braggadocio to hide such feelings of insecurity. Locals naturally resented the apparent backwardness of Britain being insensitively compared with life in America. Occasionally there were fights and small-town insularity and xenophobia took over. Service authorities did their best to explain Allied differences to servicemen and civilians and stress that all in uniform in Britain were engaged in a common cause.

Sometimes civilians were officially asked to form friendships with Americans. Lt Andrew Vero, a bombardier with the 306th BG at Thurleigh, remembers: 'There was a "welcome" at Cambridge station with greeting desks manned by pretty girls. No one was willing to house Americans, but a girl called us over and said "Ma" Gordon was thankful Americans were fighting for them. That's how I got Ma Gordon . . . I spent any and all my three-day passes in Cambridge, with my "adopted" family or rather who had adopted me. "Ma" Gordon was a widow whose oldest son had been killed by flak in RAF bombers.'[12]

The invitation to spend time with an English family was extended to many American flyers, who remember such contacts with gratitude. Lt Edward Logan, a newly arrived B-17 pilot in 1944 who was temporarily stationed in Newquay awaiting assignment, met an English family while walking by the sea. They invited him to dinner on the spur of the moment. He went, laden with food from the base PX including a bottle of white wine and for the couple's two children orange crush. 'Dinner was very enjoyable and they were very appreciative of the things I brought with me. It was a fine evening. I have often wondered what happened to that little family,' he wrote decades later.[13]

There would often be simple acts of kindness airmen would remember all their lives. S/Sgt William 'Ike' Adamson, a tail gunner with the 390th BG at Parham, found a long, slow wartime journey from London to Ipswich passing easily because the civilians in his compartment wanted to hear first-hand of bombing missions over Germany and occupied Europe and all about his life in America. However, there was an old lady knitting a scarf in a corner who would not be drawn into the conversation. At Ipswich S/Sgt Adamson's exit was blocked by the pensioner who reached up and wound the blue scarf around his neck. 'I knitted this for you, Yank,' she said. 'I hope it brings you good luck.' Then she added, 'Give 'em hell.' The gunner wore the scarf as a talisman on all his remaining missions.[14]

Others in Britain could find the behaviour of some American airmen downright puzzling, just as the US flyers occasionally found their English allies. F/Lt George Millington, a Beaufighter navigator at RAF Coltishall in Norfolk, described an incident in a café in Norwich one afternoon in 1944 with his pilot, George Irving, and other officers, one of whom, S/Ldr Irving, had a patch over his eye because of an inflamation and his arm in a sling due to a boil on his wrist.

There was a party of American airmen at a nearby table – some seven or eight of them. They were drunk and completely demoralised. They were sprawled across their table or draped over their chairs and talking in loud voices and we kept hearing the phrase, 'This Goddam war'. One of them came swaying across the room towards us and spoke to me. They had had enough of this Goddam war and were not going to fly any more. I was invited to join their mutiny. I was absolutely horrified at the thought of what punishment the American Air Force might inflict on American airmen who were not only mutinous, but had invited British officers to join them. I decided the best thing was not to hear what was said, so I sat still and didn't let on . . . George Irving now turned round and showed him his left side. The American was suddenly struck dumb at the appearance of a wounded hero all bandaged up. He ceased his diatribe and one of his friends came over and led him back to his own table. Thereafter they continued with their mutinous plots in very subdued voices and with many a backward glance at us.[15]

Some American flyers in Britain were embarrassed by their comrades' arrogance. T/Sgt Dan Brennan, who successfully finished a tour as a Halifax gunner with the RCAF in England in the spring of 1944 before transferring to the USAAF, completed a novel based on his experiences which was published later that year. Brennan wrote in the first person and in this excerpt, in which the protaganist is at a dance at the De Grey Rooms in York, popular with aircrew, he captures one such awkward situation:

You went downstairs and had some coffee and sandwiches in the dining room. You were sitting there when one of the Americans came in and sat down at your table. He was a big young pilot. You asked him what he was doing around York. 'Just looking at the stupid English,' he said, and laughed. 'Why, what're you doing?' You did not say anything. You saw him looking at the USA flashes on the shoulder of your uniform. 'You ought to be fighting with your own people,' he said. 'Yes I suppose so.' 'What do you think of the English?' 'I think they're all right.' 'They're terribly behind the times though, don't you feel?'

You had met other Americans in England before, and when you did you were often embarrassed for your country. There were always a few Americans who wanted to cause friction, who entered an English pub, or any gathering, seeming always to feel that because their uniform was a different colour they were something more than blood and bone, and that as a reward for their beaming presence all English within the vicinity must respond to them like filings to a magnet. Somehow they made you disgusted. They are your own people, and you should understand them, but you did not find that tendency among the English, for the Englishman may feel just as superior, but he never intrudes his superior composure on anyone's feelings. It is difficult to explain.[16]

In most cases of inter-Allied friction alcohol was the cause. It was a ready panacea for youngsters trying to forget the horror of what they had seen in the sky hours before and it could have a dramatic effect on those too young to drink in many States of their own country where bars were only open to the over-21s.

In a well-meaning effort to avoid conflict, British military authorities wrote a somewhat prissy pamphlet for female personnel, particularly NAAFI staff, advising them not to take umbrage at what might be seen as over-familiar behaviour by Americans. 'The first time that an American soldier approaches the counter and says "Hiya Baby!" you will probably think he is being impudent,' it read. 'By the time several dozen men have said it, you may come to the conclusion that all Americans are "fresh". Yet to them it will be merely the normal conversational opening, just as you might say "Lovely day isn't it?"'[17] What the NAAFI staff, who were well used to over-familiarity, having dealt with British soldiery for the past five years, thought about the pamphlet isn't recorded.

The GIs and USAAF flyers arriving in the ETO were also issued with a pamphlet. It was entitled *A Short Guide to Great Britain* and among the gems of delightfully understated information and advice to be found there was: 'You will naturally be interested in getting to know your opposite number, the British soldier, the Tommy you have heard and read about. You can understand that two actions on your part will slow up this friendship – swiping his girl and not appreciating what his army has been up against.'[18] Asking a girl he had just met whether she had a boyfriend in the British army was the last thing a let-loose flyer had on his mind and Tommy simmered while cousin Yank waltzed off with all the best girls at the dances, perhaps boasting that he had come to save British womanhood at the same time.

Those wearing wings of *any* air force were however regarded as a major prize by women and aircrew in the RAF did not usually see the USAAF as competition for wartime romance. British airmen generally had great respect for their comrades in the 8th, considering them brave beyond belief to take on the Luftwaffe by day. Conversely American flyers thought Harris's Bomber Boys intrepid indeed to risk the terrors of the night. The great majority of the British public also were glad to welcome American boys, who had travelled far to fight Europe's war.

But apart from nubile girls the section of the population who appreciated the American invasion most were the village children. Even the *Short Guide* had advised that British children, who were aware much of their food was coming from the USA, would see the American serviceman as 'something special'. Life became a daily adventure once the USAAF arrived and the new-found comrades were generous beyond belief.

Brian Hopgood was seven by the time the war ended and lived at the town of Harleston, not far from the 100th BG's Thorpe Abbotts base. 'I can remember seeing the convoys of trucks and you would put your thumb up to the Americans and out of the back of the trucks would come a shower of sweets and gum with shouts of "Give that to your Mom" or "Give that to your Dad",' he recalls.[19]

But it wasn't just candy the warm-hearted Americans could provide. Gerry Green's family were publicans during the war, not far from the 56th FG base at Boxted, and when Gerry left school at fourteen and got an offer of a job as an apprentice mechanic a few miles away, an American staff sergeant from the base made it possible for him to take it by supplying him with a bike from the base for five shillings (25p). 'My dad kept the Blue Boar pub in Kendal Road, Colchester,' Gerry remembers.

He was friendly with these American staff sergeants and they used to come round the back door on a Sunday and have dinner with us. They would share what little we had and bring tins with them. One of them was also friendly with my aunt and uncle who had the Ardleigh Crown Inn right outside the 56th FG base at Boxted, four miles from Colchester. He said he would show me round the airfield. The family used to call him 'Papa Denny'. He took me round the P-47s and then he took me in the mess hall and I had a metal divided tray on which was put bits and pieces, fried chicken and things I hadn't seen before. He piled my tray up and we sat down and I tucked in and ate most of it but there was one thing that puzzled me. I looked at it and it was a piece of white bread. We didn't have white bread during the war because we couldn't get the grain from Canada or America and had to use our own grain, which gave bread a grey tint. There was some stuff on this white bread I had never seen before in my life. 'Go on boy, you eat that and you'll love it,' the sergeant said. In the end he talked me into it. I picked it up and bit it and found it was a thing called peanut butter. I did love it and even eat it today. When I left the mess hall to go home the airmen threw me their Hershey chocolate bars and chewing gum to take back to my brothers and sisters. I went home and told them all, 'I had peanut butter.' I thought more about that peanut butter than all the other food put together.[20]

In 1944 Douglas Brett was eight and his brother Dennis two years older. They lived at Steeple Bumpstead, Essex, in the heart of 381st BG country. 'At the time my mother was in hospital and I was staying with my Auntie Eva at Toppesfield, which was near the Ridgewell base,' Douglas recalls.

I loved seeing the Americans and the bombers. It was so exciting. The Americans used to come to the Red Lion in Steeple Bumpstead. I was a scruffy little urchin then from a family of eight and we used to shout out, 'Got any gum, chum' and they would throw us chewing gum and little bags of Lifeboy Sweets. The Red Lion would be full of the Americans, chasing the girls and the girls chasing them. The Americans at Ridgewell gave some nice parties for us kids. We'd never seen food or candies like it before. There was ice cream and everything. There were liquorice sticks and Sharp's toffees and dark chocolate. It was very welcome because it was hard for everybody at home then with the rationing. You couldn't say, 'Dad, I can't eat this meat,' – you had to eat it. I must have gone to parties three times at Ridgewell. The word used to go round that they were giving a party for the kids and then they would come to the village with a truck and take us into the base.

My brother and I and my cousin George used to skip school to see the bombers. We would go to the edge of the perimeter at Ridgewell and knew where to hide in some bushes. On one particular day we saw this aircraft land in a very shot-up state. It stopped near to us and the blood wagon, as they called it, came out and the medics got this wounded man out of the plane and laid him on the ground. His flying jacket was all burned down one sleeve from the fire on board and there was blood inside. They took it off, together with his flying helmet and threw them on the bank near where we were hiding. Then they went off with him in the ambulance and they never came back for the clothing. We waited until dark and then, being naughty boys, we stole it. The next day we wore it at school in Haverhill. My brother had the jacket and I had the leather helmet. We were pretty popular with the other lads at school that day. They couldn't believe where we got them from, but we got told off by the teacher.'[21]

On 24 March 1944 the Pathfinder crew of a B-17 of the 305th BG, assigned to lead a mission to Schweinfurt, crashed close to Ridgewell, coming down near the village of Great Yeldham. The blast killed the crew, eight US servicemen in an off-base barracks and two sleeping children. 'There was a terrific explosion,' Douglas Brett remembers. 'It landed on the railway from Haverhill to Marks Tey near some lands settlement houses. It demolished about three houses and knocked some of the windows out of my Auntie Eva's house two or three miles away.'[22] It was even a shock to the American flyers, who lived with death every day. Lt Howland, who had moved from Ridgewell to Chelveston, wrote in his diary: 'About 0130 William Sellers, the red-headed pilot in the room next to ours, crashed while taking off killing himself and his entire crew.'[23]

Douglas and Dennis Brett couldn't resist skipping school to view the crash site. 'American and British police were around but we knew of a ditch where we could get close without being seen. There was an engine here and a piece there, all burning. As we walked down the ditch my brother found an American boot with the foot still in it. We had to take this to the police and they took our names and addresses. I got a real telling-off from my father, but we couldn't let anything like that go, we had to report it. My brother also found some American coins in the wreckage.'[24]

The 8th Air Force extended more than just compassion to those

British civilians who suffered loss because of air accidents. War orphans could often expect to be adopted by a bomber base, under a fund launched by *Stars and Stripes* in association with the Red Cross, whereby servicemen contributed from their pay to raise $400 per child to give them a start in education or get them past the critical first year after losing one or both parents, where it was felt public assistance might not adequately care for them. One case in 1944 was particularly heartbreaking. The newspaper showed a picture of four-year-old Tony Everitt, holding spring chicks in his hands, unaware of what had just happened to him. His mother Betty had died trying to rescue a gunner from a burning Havoc of the 409th Light Bomb Group from nearby Little Walden airfield. It had crashed and exploded at her farm near Saffron Walden after hitting a Mustang on take-off. The *Stars and Stripes* story revealed that the men at the crashed plane's base raised $500 in one day for Tony, whose father had died the year before.

Traditional British newspapers, anxious to illustrate Allied cooperation, also carried the story in some detail. The *Daily Telegraph* quoted Mrs Mary Baldwin, the twenty-seven-year-old wife of a missing airman from the village, who saw the Havoc come down, as did an American staff sergeant passing by: 'As I raced towards the spot where I guessed where the plane had fallen the sergeant asked me where it was and I said, "Follow me",' Mrs Baldwin related. When they reached the wreck they saw an injured and trapped gunner. 'Just then Mrs Everitt came up. I knew her to be a trained nurse and she gave me the order, "Get along to the farmhouse at once and bring a sheet and some first-aid equipment; there are other men here to be got to safety."' The report continued: 'While the sergeant and Mrs Everitt helped the injured airman to safety Mrs Baldwin did as she was told. She had nearly reached the farmhouse when there was an explosion. Mrs Everitt had been killed outright as she tried to drag a second man from the wreckage.' The sergeant assisting also died as did the crewman they were trying to help, but the American gunner they had helped to safety survived.[25]

Earlier the 367th squadron of the 306th BG at Thurleigh had adopted a three-year-old girl. A book about the Group published during the war revealed that three enlisted men had gone to London with £101 (over $400), 'mostly in silver and oversize British pennies'.

> The money was the contribution of the enlisted men to the newspaper-backed British Orphans Fund. It was money enough to supply the extras for one orphan for nearly five years. Corporal Irvin W. Coombs led the detail as chief foster father because his contribution had been the largest. Spending their brief leave they had come to see our baby. Secretly they hoped it would be a boy. Then they'd call the new mascot Butch. But it wasn't a boy. Red Cross workers produced for their startled eyes chubby-faced Maureen.
>
> Maureen was taken on a visit to the base by a Red Cross worker and had a B-17 named Sweet Pea in her honour. Maureen had a real Army suit with pants and the pants had pockets. Never once did she get her chubby little hands out of those pockets, except when a heaping plate of GI rations was put at her place of honor in the enlisted men's mess of the 367th.[26]

Forty years later the 306th BG veterans association decided to track down Maureen for a reunion at Thurleigh, enrolling the Salvation Army and the Red Cross. The *Sun* newspaper found her in April 1982, revealing in its story: 'She is Mrs Maureen Eason, of Link Lane, Wallington, Surrey . . . Maureen [by then a happily married mother of two] said: "They were always buying me presents and sweets . . . I'd love to see them all again."'[27]

The Orphans Fund advocated in *Stars and Stripes* underwent a change in the weeks following D-Day. About one in twenty-five letters accompanying contributions to the charity read: 'For our $400 we would like to select a redheaded, good-looking, feminine little French war orphan about twenty years of age.'[28] The fund's administrators had a clause inserted in the conditions of sponsorship specifying that no orphan would be more than twelve.

The American invasion of Britain had a different, sometimes more commercial, aspect in London. USAAF bomber crews got a three-day pass to the capital on average every three weeks as a means of relieving the tensions of missions where each one was likely to be their last. The London girls, who had seen the Poles arrive, followed by the Free French, airmen from Holland and Belgium, and the Canadians en masse, at first tried to be nonchalant about the new influx. But like their country cousins they rapidly succumbed to the sheer appeal of healthy young men who sounded and looked the same as their screen heroes. The Oscar-winning movie of one such star, Clark Gable, was in fact enjoying a revival at the Ritz Cinema in Leicester Square in the spring of 1944. *Gone With The Wind*, released in 1939, was again playing to packed houses. Gable, who had been making a documentary about 8th Air Force gunners entitled *Combat America*, had flown five missions with the 351st BG at Polebrook, Northamptonshire, and had just returned to the States after being seen by many of his fans on the streets of the capital. On trips to London Cptn Robert Morgan, as pilot of the *Memphis Belle* familiar with the ways of Hollywood, sometimes had Cptn Gable with him and his fellow officers. 'Everywhere we went we were mobbed by women,' Morgan remembered.[29]

Film star or simply Sgt Sad Sack from Hackensack, the USAAF flyer at least beat his Allied soldier competitors hollow. His well-fitting, tailored, Class A beltless jacket and snug trousers, which came in far more sizes than did the British Tommy's heavy wool khaki battledress, gave him an immediate edge with the girls, as did his lack of blancoed webbing belt and gaiters and neat shoes compared to the British steel-studded, heavy black boots. The visible shirt and tie, unlike the buttoned-up British jacket, was another sartorial advantage. As a result many girls thought all Americans they met must be officers.

In fact officers of the USAAF were even more exotic. The first distinctive item of uniform to catch the eye was the devil-may-care floppy appearance of the peaked service cap. Only officers of the Air Force were allowed to take the spring stiffener from their caps, because it then allowed the bomber pilot's R/T headset to go over it.[30] Taking the rigidity out was often the first action of a flyer after being introduced to combat and the transformed head-gear quickly became known as a '50-mission crusher'.

The jacket was similar to the British officer's, but in a distinctive chocolate brown with rank bars in silver or gold on the shoulder and brass 'US' collar badges over separate winged propellers. Then there were the trousers. They were deliberately designed not to match at all and were made of a buff cavalry twill. The airmen called them 'pinks'. The flyer couldn't fail to stand out in a crowd, even more so if he wore his short leather, casual-looking A2 jacket rather than formal officer's barathea.

Both officers and enlisted men sported colourful unit shoulder patches, the yellow winged '8' on a deep-blue background, immediately identifying an American as being part of the now-huge 8th Air Force. The silver wings above the left top pocket identified him as someone who was risking his life for the old country; whether pilot, engineer or gunner the wings looked the same at first glance, unlike RAF ones where anyone but a pilot on a bomber crew got a half wing.

As if this wasn't enough there was one astounding distinction which drew many London girls to date Americans with enthusiasm, not to say abandon. It was their rate of pay. A staff sergeant gunner in the USAAF in Britain would receive $96 a month, plus 50 per cent flight pay and 20 per cent overseas allowance. At $4 to the pound that was worth £10 a week. His equivalent in the RAF got less than £3 on pay day. Among the officers, a lowly 2/Lt in the 8th was paid approximately £15 a week after all allowances. It compared to just over £5 a week for the equivalent Pilot Officer rank for aircrew in the RAF. As a stay for up to a week at a central London hotel at that time only cost approximately £5 the possibilities were endless.

Many US aircrew breezed into London with only one thing on their mind. Some were merely content to see the sights and catch a show. Either way there was an army of prostitutes ready and waiting. As soon as the US serviceman arrived at Piccadilly Underground station and came up the stairs, heading for the American Red Cross club at Rainbow Corner across the road, there would be the sound of high heels clicking behind them. Then came the greeting, 'Hello Yank. Looking for a good time?'[31] Even a year before, so brazen was the situation in central London that a US correspondent felt moved to tell families back home about it. He described the area around Piccadilly, Leicester Square and Park Lane as 'a veritable open market . . . moreover in Shepherd Market, between Piccadilly and Mayfair there is a courtyard where the atmosphere can be compared only to the red light districts of Genoa and Marseilles.'[32]

Some of them were enthusiastic amateurs. 'There swarmed out of the slums and across the bridges multitudes of drab, ill-favoured adolescent girls and their aunts and mothers, never before seen in the squares of Mayfair and Belgravia,' wrote the novelist Evelyn Waugh, whose witty chronicling of wartime society could be matched by his snobbery. 'There they passionately and publicly embraced, in blackout and at high noon and were rewarded with chewing gum, razor blades and other rare trade goods.'[33] *Tit Bits*, a magazine popular with British airmen and distributed free to camps, carried an article in late February headed: 'The Truth About Britain's Good Time Girls' and reading: 'Many mothers find it impossible to control their 16-year-old daughters who stay out till all hours of the night and will brook no interference with their liberty.' It continued: 'The Bishop of Chelmsford has said the home life's very foundation is crumbling before our eyes.'[34] The bishop's Essex diocese alone contained sixteen USAAF bases, including the first to be built in Britain, at Great Sayling. Americans flocked to dances at Chelmsford Corn Exchange and for any girl willing to make the journey London was within easy reach by rail.

In the uniformed crowds bustling through the capital on any day many nations were represented, and so it was among the battalions of patrolling prostitutes. Duke Street, leading off Grosvenor Square where the American Embassy clattered and hummed night and day, was the territory of French girls, many making a living in the oldest profession after becoming refugees from their now occupied homeland.

For those servicemen who came to London looking for sexual adventure there was no shortage from a variety of partners. It quickly led to jokes on the air bases that the only thing cheap in Britain was the women and among the British themselves that there was a new type of Utility knickers, 'One Yank and they're off'. A USAAF medical survey of combat stress among bomber crews judged hypersexuality was a symptom of battle fatigue. 'Several men reported they had seduced women in quantity, not for sexual satisfaction but for the sake of subduing and conquering their defences,' read the report of the Office of the Air Surgeon.[35]

Not surprisingly there was now an epidemic of venereal disease in Britain. In spring 1944 an instructive cartoon in the US army newspaper showed a highly made-up blonde under the headline 'Chemical Warfare'. The caption read: 'Five and tenner, it takes five minutes to get acquainted and ten years to get rid of her. Flank it, Yank!'[36] In fact Americans were getting the blame, though they were issued with condoms to prevent disease as well as pregnancy. On moral grounds the British and Commonwealth airmen who formed RAF Bomber Command were not. Figures for January 1944 showed Harris's aircrew were showing an incidence of 43.9 cases per 1,000 men compared to an average of 11.2 per 1,000 ground personnel. The high incidence was also almost double that of any other RAF command, a reflection perhaps of the here-today-gone-tomorrow attitude which ruled the bomber boys' brief lives.[37]

However, the enthusiasm with which American troops had been received by the same British girls almost from their arrival in Britain was proving a headache for the generals who needed all the fit troops they could muster for the coming Invasion and the bombing war which would make it possible. Even as early as December 1942 the number of cases of VD among US troops in Britain was 58 per 1,000 men.[38] The figures sparked a campaign to bring sexually transmitted disease under control and US-made condoms became available in PXs from early 1943, though there had been reluctance to issue them – just as the RAF had debated and decided against – because it was feared they would promote promiscuity. In fact by the spring of 1944 they were even available in American Red Cross clubs for those on pass. And they were always available in Piccadilly Circus where the 'Piccadilly Commandos' cruised, a newspaper vendor who had the build of Alfred Hitchcock whispering 'Condoms?' to any serviceman who bought a paper.[39] Regular statistics charting the ebb and flow of venereal disease were released by USAAF headquarters in Britain and Group commanders were encouraged to display them. On 10 February the Daily Digest of the 446th BG on Station 125, at Bungay, Suffolk noted with regret that the station 'led the 8th Air Force in the VD Parade'.[40]

It wasn't just in London that a flyer, briefly trying to forget the ordeal of combat, might contract VD. A notice on the Base Bulletin Board of the 486th BG at Sudbury in the spring of 1944 read: 'All personnel of this command are warned to avoid contact with a woman residing in Sudbury, Suffolk.' It gave her specific address and went on, 'She is of medium height, blond, blue eyes, weighs about 135 pounds, and is about 30 years of age. Four cases of gonorrhea have been traced to her at this station and more from other stations. She is not co-operating with British authorities in undergoing treatment and is considered highly infectious.'[41]

The issue of condoms it was hoped might reduce the spread of VD both locally and in the capital. Certainly the scene in the Circus any day or night was a persuasive one as girls shone torches on their ankles as they swayed along – to signify the slave bracelets many prostitutes used as identification. In the side streets stood more elegantly clad older women, hunting the officer class.

The US military police, whose white-helmeted personnel were known as 'Snow Drops', set up a base at 101 Piccadilly and a military policeman later said there was never a dull moment in the aptly named Circus, 'the hub of GI affairs'. He said each prostitute had her own territory and 'woe betide any girl who tried to poach – almost certainly a fight would ensue. We often pulled them apart, pointing out that while they were pulling each other's hair they were losing customers . . . Those girls worked hard for their money. They took terrible risks, often they were beaten up, they were robbed and several were stabbed.'[42] The prostitutes featured so prominently in the US airman's view of London that one B-17 of the 306th BG at nearby Thurleigh in Bedfordshire was named *Piccadilly Commando*, with a cartoon on its nose of a naked girl clutching a bomb.

It was because of what was on offer in the doorways around the Circus that Rainbow Corner was established as a healthy alternative. The biggest American Red Cross (ARC) club in London opened at 23 Shaftesbury Avenue, just off Piccadilly, in November

1942 and closed in January 1946. It was housed on the site of the old Del Monico's restaurant and a Lyons Corner House and it was designed as a haven for boys far from home where they were guaranteed to find a complete American atmosphere and most things wholesome from a haircut to a newly pressed uniform. A motherly volunteer at Rainbow Corner sewed on more than 10,000 stripes, inserting a lucky farthing coin underneath for every combat airman. By way of reward a B-17, *Lady Irene*, was named after her. The staff of 450 would also provide bed and breakfast for 2s 6d (approximately 12p) and lunch or dinner for 1s (5p). The club served 7,000 meals a day over twenty-four hours. In the basement was a specially built drugstore just like the ones in the men's home towns, offering Coca-Cola and milkshakes. The airman or soldier could play pinball machines which had been collected from the piers of British seaside resorts, closed for the duration. Just across from the drugstore was a writing desk where women volunteers waited to help the servicemen compose letters to the folks back in the States.

In the upstairs lounge home-town newspapers were available and in the lobby visitors – up to 70,000 a day – were invited to stick a flag on a map of the United States, cleared weekly, showing where they were from, so that others in the club might find them that day. The army newspaper ran a picture of General Eisenhower sticking in a flag marked 'Ike, Abilene' into the Kansas section.[43] He was among a host of celebrity visitors including Irving Berlin, George Raft, James Stewart and his fellow film personality, Kim Hunter, who would go on to star in the post-war classic *A Matter of Life and Death*, about an RAF bomber pilot guided back over Britain by a WAC air controller. The famous also helped to staff the club, among them Fred Astaire's sister Adele, who had married into the family of the Duke of Devonshire and was now known as Lady Charles Cavendish. She wasn't the only American connected to the Devonshires now serving in

Britain. Katherine Kennedy, sister to a future US President, had been in the country since late 1943 with the American Red Cross and would soon marry the Duke's son and heir the Marquis of Hartington.

Rainbow Corner provided a library, a room for board and card games, and a classroom for lectures. And there was a fine ballroom from its days as Del Monico's. Only American service personnel were allowed in the club except by specific invitation. The names of British female guests invited for special dances, such as for Thanksgiving, had to be submitted for vetting forty-eight hours before. Glenn Miller and his orchestra played there as did Artie Shaw's Navy Band.

So many USAAF personnel were now flooding into London on short passes that it was difficult to find accommodation, whether hotel or ARC club, 400 of which had now been set up in England. Major Ward Walker, Base Section Special Service Officer, had the army newspaper run a story in March 1944, warning that hundreds of US personnel were having to sleep in air raid shelters and on chairs and floors in London because too many were coming to London for the ARC clubs to cope. 'He says US base administration officers in the UK should make sure all men leaving for London have Form TPM No 3 (pink paper), or the white furlough certificate (WD Form 31) and designate a club to which the man must go,' the story ran.[44] But Major Walker's advice could not stop the tide and neither could recently renewed raids by the Luftwaffe. What was known as the Little Blitz began in January 1944 and lasted until April, killing 279 people in London. The human traffic around Piccadilly Circus barely broke its stride.

But for every airman tempted by the prostitutes of London's wartime West End, hundreds of others just wanted to dance with an English girl or visit the sights. The statistics of fifty-eight VD cases in every thousand GIs were shocking enough, but told a story of celibacy for the majority and unless an airman hooked up with a professional, many went back to his base with similar memories to when he left.

Lt Richard Turner, a twenty-three-year-old Mustang pilot with the 354th FG at Boxted, Essex, got his first three-day pass to London in February. He and a fellow pilot, Cptn Frank O'Connor, booked in at a hotel recommended by a friend.

[There] we were politely informed that for £5 apiece we would have the second floor suite with breakfast for ourselves and our guests. Up in the suite Frank wondered what they had meant by guests? I told him that the word meant the same here as it did in the US, and Frank pointed out the fact that we didn't know anyone in London to invite as friends for breakfast. I ventured that the English had ample confidence in the gregarious nature of American pilots since there had evidently been a few here before us. At any rate, freshly scrubbed and armed with hope Frank and I set out for the pubs. We investigated every female available in every spot we hit, with a date for the evening's festivities in mind, but our every tactic was expertly countered. We ended the evening congregating with other luckless pilots, trying hard to drink the pubs dry . . .

Returning to their hotel they slept too late for breakfast each day. 'In the train back to base Frank made the astute observation that, "If this war lasts long enough those people are going to become millionaires on unserved breakfasts!"'[45]

Lt Turner's experience was typical, though there is no doubt Americans had many advantages over their British comrades, not least that coming from a co-educational system they were more used to women. American anthropologist Margaret Mead, who worked for both the British Ministry of Information and the US Office of War Information in the Second World War, delivering speeches and writing articles to help American soldiers and British civilians understand each other better, observed that in the flirtations between American airmen and British women there was a misunderstanding about who was supposed to take which initiative. 'The [American] boy learns to make advances and rely upon the girl to repulse them whenever they are inappropriate to the state of feeling between the pair,' she wrote. This contrasted with British mores where 'the girl is reared to depend upon a slight barrier of chilliness ... which the boys learn to respect, and for the rest to rely upon the men to approach or advance, as warranted by the situation.' She claimed this resulted in British women interpreting an American soldier's gregariousness as something more intimate or serious than he had intended. She described as 'astonishing' to the American eye the lack of an early flirting culture between British girls and boys.[46]

Whatever the cause there was considerable resentment towards Americans, in particular prior to D-Day, by British soldiers who did not give the USAAF bomber crews the credit they deserved for the enormous sacrifices they were making to win the European war. Among the more visible manifestations of British chagrin was a somewhat disparaging, anonymous poem, entitled *Lament of a Limey Lass*, which began:

> Dear old England's not the same
> We dreaded invasion – well it came
> But no, it's not the beastly Hun
> The Goddam Yankee Army's Come

The rhyme went on to denigrate Americans for among other things taking up much-needed transport and stated stingingly: 'We walk to let them have our seats and then get run over by their Jeeps.' As the well-circulated verse also jeered at the transatlantic allies for comparing British beer to water – 'but after drinking two or more you'll find them lying on the floor' – it is most likely it was written by an English man not a woman and probably one disappointed in love at that.[47]

Those unappreciative of the friendly invasion as it later came to be called tended to describe Americans as 'Overpaid, oversexed and over here'. From early April the self-same Americans could riposte, 'And you're *under* Eisenhower.' SHAEF had been born to prepare for D-Day and apart from the Allied armies Ike now commanded he also had total control of all strategic bombing operations in Europe – including those of the RAF. Both Harris's men and the USAAF 8th Air Force would shortly be engaged in new campaigns which would signal the end for the Luftwaffe and Nazi Germany.

6

'Up and down the streets people jeered and spat at me'

The missions the young men of the 8th Air Force flew in the spring of 1944 were both varied and exacting. In the nine weeks of battle between the beginning of April and D-Day the tally of trips down flak alley that crews thankfully ticked off towards a ticket home ranged from oil complexes and transportation targets to V-weapon sites, Luftwaffe targets – both rural and urban – and even repeatedly to Berlin again. The cost could be staggering. In April alone 361 bombers were shot down and another forty-two were brought back so damaged they were rated as wrecked beyond repair. Together, they added up to the 8th's highest monthly total of the war.[1]

But by now so many new Groups had arrived in England with their flight lines fed to capacity with fresh aircraft that the rate of loss across the command was just 3.6 per cent. Eight months before – thirty-one days of which had included the disastrous second Schweinfurt raid – lossses amounted to 9.2 per cent of all sorties. The increased chances of an individual crew surviving its tour were not lost on the high command. General Doolittle, who had been reminded by 'Hap' Arnold that crews were going home at what was probably their peak of efficiency, now raised the number of missions his men had to fly from twenty-five to thirty and soon afterwards to thirty-five.

It caused great resentment among the Groups, mindful that an overall loss reduction by almost two-thirds still meant thousands of telegrams to homes across America informing mothers and wives that they could now not expect to see Johnny come marching home again, ever. The April loss percentage of 3.6 was also only two points less than the average figure for Sir Arthur Harris's night bomber boys in the four-month period of the Battle of Berlin, a loss rate so debilitating it had made the Chief of the Air Staff, Sir Charles Portal, force him to call off his campaign.[2]

Lt Don Ackerson, the 384th BG bombardier who had begun his tour the previous December and gone right through Big Week, remembers: 'If you already had a certain number of missions your new tour total was pro-rated between 25 and 30. I had to do 28 under the new system. We were all highly pissed off, but went ahead anyway. It sure increased our chances of getting shot down.'[3]

What was particularly worrying for crews at that time, dependent for their defence on flying in close formation, was that the flak fields they had to fly through seemed to be getting thicker. In fact one third of the bombers lost in April were brought down by ground gunfire, almost twice the number in March. The Luftwaffe began employing new gun-laying techniques including greater use of radar, and drafting in more flak helpers from schoolboys to women and Russian PoWs to handle the 88mm weapons being churned out by Krupps in the Ruhr and Skoda in Czechoslovakia. Flak protection of its cities and the industry within was by 1944 costing the Reich two million soldiers and civilians who could have been employed elsewhere.

It was calculated after the war that 8,500 shells of the heavy 88mm calibre were fired for every bomber brought down, an astonishing figure, which shows that flak was a more psychologically

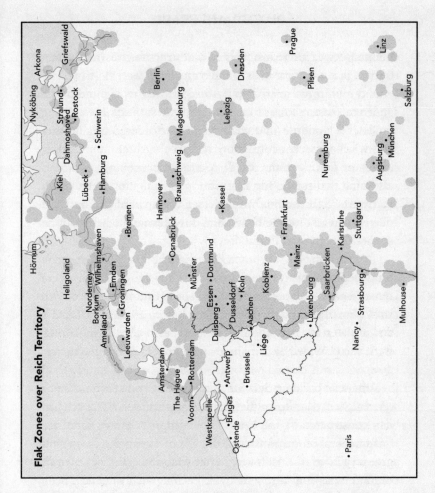

The USAAF produced regularly updated maps of known flak areas to aid route planners and navigators, particularly after the savage losses to flak in April 1944. In this map, marked 'Confidential', service cartographers have coloured in grey flak zones over Reich territory still posing a savage threat months after the Invasion of Europe.

debilitating weapon than a physically destructive one. But the fact remains that a total of 5,400 American planes were destroyed by ground gunfire compared to 4,300 destroyed by fighters.[4] The sudden increase in losses to flak in April was sufficiently worrying to General Doolittle that trials were now ordered in adjusting the 8th's close-packed formations to lessen the literally spreading success of flak, without paying a price in bombing accuracy. It was found that staggering the position of each unit in the standard twelve-squadron box would lessen the upward and outward effective spread of a shell burst and this became the new routine as more Groups took to the sky.

The final airfield to accommodate those bombers had just been completed at Debach, near Ipswich. Like the other forty-one USAAF heavy bomber bases in Britain it had cost £990,000 to build, a small part of the £645 million bill to set up the USAAF's total of 250 stations in the United Kingdom, only £40 million of which was provided by the American taxpayer.[5] At first the majority of work was carried out by Irish labour, but so extensive had the American build-up become that US army construction teams were enlisted to lay down the final seventeen airfields; Debach had been constructed by the 820th US Engineer Aviation Battalion. It had been an enormous task, the job of laying three runways alone – each up to 3,000ft long, 150ft wide and eight inches thick pointing straight as a speeding shell across what once had been dips and hills – the mightiest of all.

S/Sgt Arbib, a Yale graduate who had failed his officers' course for insufficient parade ground skills, witnessed as part of the battalion what turning ancient farmland into a fully equipped modern aerodrome entailed. He wrote only months later: 'All day long a constant stream of trucks, driven by civilians, and loaded with gravel, sand, cement, rubble from bombed cities, and cinders, rumbled along the narrow lanes and deposited their loads in the stockpiles that rose like small hills on the landscape.'[6]

At the same time other convoys of trucks, this time in US Army olive drab, would be arriving and leaving to transfer those loads to other teams of soldiers, making billets, offices and runways. It was an enterprise involving many hands and a multitude of skills. But the dirtiest job of all was that of the cement gang. 'All day long they stood on their platform and emptied hundred-pound sacks of cement into the trucks that rolled up to them, one a minute,' Arbib wrote. 'They worked in a cloud of powdery cement – it blew into their eyes, their nostrils, filtered into their clothes, got under their skin. It transformed the men into grey-green, ghostly automatons. It was the *bête noire* of the battalion. It stood as a constant threat to miscreants.'[7]

Some of the ground echelon to staff the airfield built by the 820th US engineer unit, and all of the 493rd BG's flyers who would use it, wouldn't leave the USA until the beginning of May. There had been a mix-up in orders and wrong dispersal of some personnel in the chaos of turning an army air force of only 340,000 officers and enlisted men and nearly 3,000 combat planes in December 1941 into one of 2.4 million flyers and support personnel and 80,000 planes little more than two years later.[8]

Cpl Jack Feller was one of the earlier arrivals at Debach. He and his older brother Charles had decided they wanted to be in the air force even before America entered the war. 'My brother was taking flying lessons when he was in college and then he joined the aviation cadets,' he remembers. 'I followed him at 19 and did some civilian pilot training, but didn't qualify to be an air force pilot. I decided I wanted to go to control tower school, which was in Miami, Florida, very good duty.'[9]

Captain Charles Feller had been in England for some time by the time Cpl Feller arrived at Debach on 27 March and was based at Bottisham, near Cambridge, flying Thunderbolts with the 361st FG. Cpl Feller's assignment at Debach was as clerk/typist in the control tower, to write up the subject-to-change aircraft status board for transmission to headquarters, but when he arrived not only were there no aircraft, the tower had no equipment. 'It had no radios, no desks, no chairs, no light control panels, no status board and no maps,' he recalls. 'In other words it was just a bare room with windows on the second floor facing the runways and with a narrow balcony around three sides.'[10]

At the first opportunity Cpl Feller left the cold Nissen hut billet he shared with fifteen other enlisted men stacked in double-deck bunks to go to see his pilot brother in only slightly more comfortable officers' quarters at Bottisham. It involved a journey of fifty-five miles under uncertain wartime railway scheduling, giving them little time together. 'It was three or four in the afternoon when I got there,' Cpl Feller remembers. 'He came to the main gate and said, "Go into town and I'll meet you at 6 o'clock." I went into Cambridge and looked around and then we had dinner together in a hotel. I went back to the train station and he went back to his base.'[11] Later the twenty-one-year-old corporal was able to write to his parents in the small timber and coal mining town of Mullens, West Virginia that he had been reunited with their other son in the ETO, now battling the elements as well as the enemy over Europe.

The month of April did not begin well for the 8th Air Force as it tackled uncertain weather conditions. On the very first day crews of 38 B-24s of the 392nd and 44th Groups who had been briefed for Ludwigshafen became disoriented in cloud after PFF equipment failed. A tail wind also proved stronger than forecast and the Liberators wandered dramatically off course, eventually entering Swiss air space. They then bombed the centre of Schaffhausen in error, 140 miles south of the intended target, killing forty Swiss civilians and injuring a hundred others. Less than two weeks later the 44th BG crew of Lt R. Griffith got shot up bombing a Luftwaffe airfield at Lechfeld, near Augsburg, at

20,000ft and had to steer south for Switzerland because they had lost so much fuel from punctured tanks. They were hit by flak again by the border, wounding a waist gunner, and made a rapid descent into a Swiss Air Force base at Dubendorf, near Zurich. 'We went in with no fuel at all, practically, and crashed,' the radio operator T/Sgt Forrest Clark later related. 'We cut the trees right off with our wings, rolled into a big ball on a grass field. They were flying Me 109s out of there . . . We didn't know whether we were in Germany.' Clark flipped the detonator to destroy the IFF transmitter and was walking away from the plane when he felt a gun in his back. He looked round to see a teenage Swiss soldier. 'They took us in to interrogation and asked us about [the] bombing of Schaffhausen, which was the big controversy at that time,' Clark remembered. 'We had bombed some Swiss cities, the Eighth Air Force had . . . they were very uptight about that, the Swiss were, and they interrogated us [for] about eight hours, held us in this operations center, and then, they put us in a van, took us to the schoolyard, where we slept on the ground for three nights, and then, they put us in a train, took us up to Adelboden.'[12]

Adelboden, in the Swiss Alps, was one of three internment camps which would hold up to 1,000 US flyers by the time the Allies had overrun France and 168 battle-damaged American aircraft had tried to reach safety in Switzerland. Some bombers, both RAF and USAAF, were shot down by the Swiss, at least twenty RAF and sixteen American airmen dying. One of those shot down was the B-17 *Little Chub* which flew over neutral Switzerland later in April with two engines out and one wheel down. Six crew members were killed.[13] The difficulties of trying to navigate accurately in Europe's problematic weather would cause other Swiss communities to be bombed by mistake by Americans before the war was over. The USAAF was not the only force to be deceived by the strength of the prevailing tail wind as March closed and April opened. It caused 120 Lancasters of RAF Bomber Command to mistakenly bomb Schweinfurt instead of Nurem-burg on 31 March in a raid which caused Harris's men their largest attrition of the war, ninety-six aircraft failing to return of the 950 that set out.

Ludwigshafen on 1 April had been an industrial target, the IG Farben chemical works, but the main thrust of attacks by the 8th in the first few days of the month was aimed at Luftwaffe supplies of aircraft. There had been a refinement in March of the Pointblank Directive of the previous June, ordering a combined bomber offensive. It had called for both the USAAF and RAF to give priority to the German aircraft industry to make way for the Invasion. A new diktat listed six towns or cities considered vital to the Luftwaffe: Schweinfurt, Leipzig, Brunswick, Regens-burg, Gotha and Augsburg. When the USAAF and RAF mounted attacks on Brunswick and Schweinfurt in April, both sustained considerable losses, the USAAF 2nd BD for instance losing thirty Liberators over Brunswick on 8 April, the RAF losing twenty-one Lancasters, 9.3 per cent, over Schweinfurt on 26 April and the 8th Air Force, for whom the ball-bearing city had special dread, fourteen of the 172 B-17s of the 1st BD raiding those factories on the 13th. No fewer than nine were from Lt Don Ackerson's 384th BG, his own bomber among them. The 1st BD had tried to attack Schweinfurt the day before but had turned back before the French coast because of poor weather, as Lt Ackerson recorded after the war.

We were flying group lead with Cptn C. G. Stearns and 1/Lt Bedsole and Bob Hock as navigator and Ed Hill as radio op-erator. Bob, Ed and I were the only ones from our own crew. The weather was pretty bad on the assembly. In fact Stearns said he hoped they would call the whole thing off. However, as we got over the coast it cleared up and visibility was good despite some haze at our altitude, which was 22,000ft. Bob Hock did a good job of navigation and we only got scattered flak, not close enough to do any damage.

Somewhere in the Luxembourg area, we had our first fighter attacks on the lead group. There were about 20 Me 109s who made a pass and then went over to the other side and played around for a while. A few minutes after we were hit by about 30 Fw 190s from 12 and 11 o'clock almost level. Our ship was hit on the first pass and No. 3 engine caught fire. The engine was feathered at once, but the fire spread through the wing and into the bomb bay, melting the bulk-head away. The radio operator informed the pilot and he gave the order to bale out. The navigator, after making sure I had heard the order, baled out, followed by the engineer. I was behind the engineer as the bombs were still in and I was trying to get them out.

I left immediately after the bombs were away. I pulled a partially delayed jump, delaying for a few thousand feet, lost consciousness from lack of oxygen on the jerk of the para-chute opening and came to at about 18,000ft and watched our P-51 escort, which was late that day, circle around me. I floated quietly down. I could see some home guard soldiers running up the road and they took me into custody, kicking me because I said '*Nein*' when they said, 'For you the war is over'. They kicked me all the way into a nearby town where we were searched and put in a youth camp guardhouse for a few hours. We had three others in the guardhouse including a gunner with a big piece of flak in his ankle. We couldn't get any medical help for him. That night we were taken in a truck around the country picking up other boys. We spent the rest of the night and most of the next day at an airport, also in a guardhouse. We were loosely guarded and could have jumped out the window, but we thought this is what they wanted. Late on the afternoon of the 14th we went to *Dulag Luft*.[14]

The losses on aviation industry targets had been savage indeed. But worse was to come at the end of the month. Berlin was now an 8th AF priority after RAF Bomber Command had been ordered by the Chief of the Air Staff to withdraw from its crippling winter campaign against the Reich capital. In the five weeks before D-Day the 8th would attack Berlin another four times in force and although it was evident the Luftwaffe was now in gradual decline in defence, its flak battalions were as fearsome as ever and around Berlin there were three rings of flak to enter and then exit after bombing. The first of the new round of Berlin raids, on 29 April, would prove that although the Luftwaffe could not show up in force every time to defend its capital, like a boxer on the ropes it could still swing a killer punch when it did.

Many new crews now arriving in England in the build-up for the Invasion would never see that day. Others were luckier, 2/Lt Leonard Coleman among them. The young co-pilot joined the 100th BG in mid-April to begin an intensive tour which would end in a way he could never have contemplated. Like so many he began a combat diary. He recorded that in the span of three days he was briefed for an oil target near Leipzig then found the mission scrubbed at short notice; took part in an exhausting nine-hour mission to an aircraft-industry target at Friedrichshafen; and bombed a Junkers repair plant at Dijon.

Coleman's crew was allowed a brief rest. 'It felt good to get to sleep most of the day,' he wrote. But as the pace quickened he was roused at 3am on 27 April and wouldn't see his bed again until the early hours of the 28th. 'We did something today that the Eighth Air Force hasn't done before,' he recorded. 'We made one raid and then landed the plane and made the second raid this afternoon. Our first mission was a short run over the Channel to bomb a secret on the French coast. It is believed to be a rocket installation. The flak was pretty heavy and very accurate. We didn't get any hits. The second mission we took off at 1500 hrs and bombed an airfield in France . . . I saw two B-17s go down on this trip, one was from our Group.'[15] To prepare them for the next onslaught Coleman's crew got a three-day pass to London. 'Had a very good time. That town is really something,' he wrote. What Coleman had not appreciated then was that being off base from 28 to 30 April he had missed the Berlin raid which had downed sixty-three B-17s and B-24s of the 629 which had taken off, a loss rate of 10 per cent. The 447th BG alone had lost eleven of its twenty-seven aircraft, among them that of 2/Lt William David-son, a twenty-two-year-old married pilot from Texas.

'When they had raised the map at the briefing to where you could see how far you had to go, everyone moaned and groaned because it was one of the longest missions and one of the hard-est missions,' Davidson remembered.[16] The 447th BG made up the 4A Combat Wing with the 385th BG, in the first of three bombardment divisions tasked with striking Berlin that day, the Friedrichstrasse railway station – where rail lines from north to south and east to west crossed – being the aiming point. At briefing crews had been told the purpose of the mission was 'dislocation to employees of war industries by disruption of these facilities'.

Two Pathfinder aircraft were assigned to each combat wing to guide them to the target by radar, but the 'Mickey' H2X equipment in one Pathfinder of the 4A Combat Wing failed and the set in the other only worked intermittently. The result was the wing drifted to the south away from the rest of the 3rd BD and in their isolated position were hit again and again for more than half an hour by up to 125 enemy fighters. As flaming Fortresses plummeted from the sky, trapped airmen being gradually immolated, the 4A CBW was forced to seek a target of opportunity in Magdeburg. But the attacks continued even after bombing, as Davidson remembered.

Our men were calling out, 'Fighter planes at four o'clock! Fighter planes at twelve o'clock! Fighter planes below!' and, 'Fighter planes above!' They really started hitting our Group. We had one engine knocked out and we had another engine set on fire . . . I called the radio operator and told him to watch very closely in the wing because if the fire got into the wing, we would have to bail out . . . During this time, too, we had an explosion down in the forward catwalk, just before you get to the bombardier-navigator's compartment. I asked our engineer, whose name was Murphy, to go down and check our oxygen tanks.[17]

As T/Sgt Murphy crawled down the catwalk toward the bombardier's position the radio operator reported that the fire was now spreading fast along the wing and Davidson gave the bale-out order, knowing he had only minutes before the B-17 exploded. 'I lean back in the pilot's seat where I can see Murphy down in this catwalk and I ask him, I said, "Murphy, did you get my message about baling out?" He gave me a little okay sign with his forefinger and thumb. As I'm watching him, I see him kick off the door to the escape hatch.' T/Sgt Murphy checked in that he was leaving the plane, as did the rest of the crew. Davidson then put the doomed bomber on automatic pilot although it was already in a spiral descent and left his controls to pick up his seat-type parachute pack in the catwalk to the forward escape door. He discovered it had gone. As the burning aircraft tightened the spin in its final plunge Davidson now had only seconds to find one of the spare chutes stored at the back of the top turret.

I knew that I didn't have a whole lot of time to get another chute. In my haste and hurry (and I was in a hurry!) I grabbed a chest chute. They have two handles on them, a rip cord handle and a handle to carry them by. As I grabbed my chute, I grabbed the wrong handle . . . The chute spilled out all over the plane. The air caught it and pulled it, and by luck, and a lot of help from the Lord, I went ahead and snapped the chute into my harness, which was a very quick and easy thing to do. I started gathering up the chute in my arms to try to roll it up enough, thinking I could get out of the aircraft if I could roll it up. Of course, it was catching on everything. The wind was tugging and pulling and I just kept on pulling at the chute. I tore it in several places and as I got what I felt like was enough of it in my arms, well, I walked into the hatch. And then as I rolled toward the door, I didn't jump out, but the chute went on out of the plane and naturally jerked me out.

We had been through a lot of excitement, I guess you'd call it, and then all of a sudden, there I was floating behind a chute. It was very, very quiet, but I was coming down pretty fast. I could tell that. I didn't know how fast because my chute was torn in several places. I knew it was going to be dangerous to land, but I still felt like I was very fortunate to be out of the plane.[18]

Davidson even tried to light a cigarette then found a Hershey chocolate bar in the pocket of his flight suit and had time to eat it as he saw his B-17 explode below. 'As I came on toward the ground, a fighter plane flew past me a couple or three times. I was hoping that he wouldn't strafe me. It looked like he could have. I waved at him that I was a friend. He made two or three passes at me and one time came very close, but he did not strafe. I could see people gathering, watching me descend.' Davidson, whose leg had been injured in the plane, hit the ground first with his feet, then his face and quickly found himself surrounded by angry civilians – some women, and men carrying rifles. One old man started beating him with a walking stick. 'I was tempted to grab the stick. Then

I thought, "Well, if I do, they will shoot me with their rifles. And, what he is doing is beating me because I've been bombing some of their cities." So I just stood there and took it. There were some pretty hard licks, but they didn't seem to hurt too much. I'm sure I was in a state of shock. Finally, some of the other people made him quit hitting me.'

The young pilot was then taken to a nearby town.

They paraded me up and down the streets, and of course, people jeered at me, spat at me, looked like they were making fun of me. This went on for about thirty minutes, up and down the streets, where everybody could see me. And, of course, they could see they had captured some American flyers and they were very proud of it. After this they took me to the city hall and my first experience with a *bürgomeister*. They searched me and took what few things I had. They put me in a little cell which was down in the basement of this city hall. There was another man they had captured there. He was not a member of my crew, but evidently had had an explosion in his plane and he had parachuted out all right. He had glass, bits of glass all in his face and eyes and couldn't see. When I asked him, he told me that he had been there about 45 minutes before I got there. I tried to pick some of the glass out of his cuts and got some out of his eyes with his shirt sleeve and stuff. He was in pretty bad shape. I was there with a crippled knee, but I could look at him and see how fortunate I had been.

We stayed there for about two hours. Evidently, they had notified the air force, the army, or something, because they came just to get us and took us to an airfield. There were several more men that had been shot down and they sent some of the pilots to look at us and kind of gloat over us a little bit. They were some of the pilots that were flying the fighter planes that had shot us down. We spent the night in this airfield – no doctors or anything to look at the men who had been injured. They didn't give us anything to eat. They had collected and brought to that field about 40 American prisoners.[19]

The next day all the PoWs were taken to the Luftwaffe *Dulag Luft* interrogation centre at Oberursel near Frankfurt and 2/Lt Davidson was eventually incarcerated in the American compound at Stalag Luft III. He later discovered all his crew had survived except inexplicably T/Sgt Murphy.[20]

As 2/Lt Davidson had tended the wounds of his fellow airman in the town hall basement, the remains of the battered Groups were landing back at their bases. There was a sense of shock at many of the subsequent debriefings as the details of fighter attacks and lost comrades were related. Nowhere was it more keenly felt than at the fields which made up the 4A CBW. The 385th BG in that wing had lost seven of its aircraft that had set out in the dawn from Great Ashfield. At Rattlesden almost half the hard-standings of the 447th BG now stood empty.

The final toll of sixty-three bombers missing, five down in the sea, was the 8th's second highest loss on a single mission for the whole war, only six less than on the 6 March operation, again to the Reich capital. The small loss of thirteen aircraft on the Berlin mission of 22 March when the Luftwaffe failed to show up had provided false hope for many. Nor had there been a lack of fighter protection for the great majority of the force, a total of 814 USAAF pursuit planes taking off to cover the penetration and withdrawal. However, the radar navigation problems of the 4A CBW had taken them away from their intended cover and the final division on target, the Liberator-equipped 2nd BD, also suffered from a lack of protection. Up to eighty enemy aircraft attacked them on the route in, for half an hour. A total of eighteen B-24s went down, the 392nd and 448th BGs each losing six aircraft. Then there was Berlin's awesome flak. Six of the twenty-eight losses in the 3rd BD were caused by flak as were nine of the ten losses in the 1st BD and seven in the 2nd.

It was with considerable relief as April closed that American crews, as had their English counterparts a few weeks earlier, greeted shorter-distance routes to railway targets in France and Belgium under what became known as the Transportation Plan. It was a campaign entered into with great reluctance initially by the two bomber barons, Harris and Spaatz, who considered it a waste of ordnance. There was also the worry of killing large numbers of French civilians whose loyalty to the Allied cause would be needed after D-Day. Eisenhower himself was greatly concerned about this, with some justification, and Churchill – who had been told that up to 160,000 French men, women and children might die when the concentrated urban areas which contained marshalling yards were blitzed – also had grave reservations of a French backlash.

The strategy was designed to create what was later described as a Railway Desert. Its prime mover was a British zoology professor, Solly Zuckermann. He had been scientific adviser in the Italian Campaign to Air Marshal Sir Arthur Tedder, who now as Deputy Supreme Commander to Eisenhower had recently taken control of the air planning for D-Day. Zuckerman was a key part of the Allied Expeditionary Force Bombing Committee. The committee's plan was firstly for bombing to reduce the capacity of the French and Belgian railway system to carry traffic and then, as D-Day neared, for both Spaatz's and Harris's heavy bombers to join forces with the lighter machines of the 9th USAAF and the 2nd TAF in a tactical phase, hitting railway and road junctions, bridges and rolling stock, to paralyse movement of the German army to the Invasion area and also within it. A list was prepared of seventy-five targets comprising the major railway servicing and repair centres in northern France and Belgium.

It was a compelling argument that the winners of the Transportation Plan would ultimately be the winners of the Invasion. If the Germans were able to constantly resupply their armies they would be able to fling the Allies back into the sea. But Harris, focused on area bombing where the results could be clearly seen and against panacea targets per se, was still unconvinced. He eventually lost the argument because of an RAF success. Intelligence revealed that an initial RAF deluge of 1,258 tons of bombs on the railway centre of Trappes, south-west of Paris, putting it out of action for days, had cost the lives of only sixty Frenchmen, not the thousands expected. Eisenhower's fears of heavy French casualties were assuaged and President Roosevelt too added his weight to the debate with a letter to Churchill in early May that military considerations must be paramount in deciding what to bomb before D-Day.

The accuracy of the Trappes raid also swayed Churchill and his Cabinet and it became useless for Harris and Spaatz to protest further. It was clear to the military in Britain there was a need to switch the might of both the 8th and RAF bomber commands to sealing off Normandy both before and after the Invasion. For instance, at Trappes alone six Wehrmacht trains a day went through before Bomber Command started attacking it. On 15 April Tedder gave Harris a scaled-down list of thirty-seven railways targets where it was thought French casualties would not exceed 150 each time and told him to get on with it.[21] Then Harris demonstrated yet again his great strength. Given his task he went to it with a will to make it a success. By D-Day Bomber Command – despite Harris's initial reluctance – had dropped 54,589 tons of bombs on transportation targets.[22] The USAAF had been handed more targets, forty-five, but were slower to act. Just one had been bombed by the end of April. But Spaatz did bomb marshalling yards in Germany as part of the campaign to defeat the German fighter arm in the air and keep the remainder in defence within the borders of the Reich. On 22 April he sent the majority of all three bomb divisions to the giant Hamm rail complex in the Ruhr, but the planning proved a disaster for the final bombardment division on target, the 2nd. Its Liberators returned to their bases in the dark, conditions pilots engaged in a daylight campaign were not adequately trained for. To compound the situation, Luftwaffe intruder aircraft infiltrated the stream. A total of fourteen B-24s were either shot down over England or crashed on landing and another fifty-nine were damaged. One was brought down on the runway at Seething and two more Liberators ran into it. Another crash-landed at Hethel and hit the signals hut, killing all the men inside.

'Eighth Air Force heavies conducted their first mission under the transportation programme on 27th April,' the post-war official history of the Army Air Forces admits, 'dropping 342 tons on Blainville and 230 tons on Chalons-sur-Marne with good results in both cases.'[23] 'As for the RAF its 2nd TAF was out almost every day attacking marshalling yards near the Channel and Bomber Command was piling up a notable series of victories in wiping out rail centres during heavy night attacks . . . By the end of April it was evident that enormous damage was being done. Some 33,000 tons had fallen on the rail centres and at least 12 important targets were already in Category A (destroyed).'[24]

As April turned to May the bombing of transportation centres was intensified by both the USAAF and RAF, cleverly focusing on routes which led into Normandy, while apparently concentrated on those serving other areas, such as the Pas de Calais, where Hitler expected the Allies to invade. 'On May 1st the 8th carried out its first major mission against rail centers, dispatching 328 heavy bombers and 16 Groups of fighters to drop more than 1,000 tons on the Troyes, Reims, Brussels, Liege, Sarreguemines and Metz marshalling yards,' the official record states. Several days of bad weather then followed, but on 11 May 'B-17s dropped 600 tons on Saarbrucken, Luxembourg, Ehrang, Konz-Karthaus, Bettemburg, Thionville and Volklingen while B-24s bombed Mulhouse, Belfort, Epinal and Chaumont with 440 tons. And the British air forces were equally active, Bomber Command proved so successful in fact, that it was assigned 12 targets originally allotted to the tactical air forces.'[25]

Not only were heavy bombers engaged in hitting rail centres, but also P-47s and P-51s of the 8th Air Force Fighter Groups, now that they had been released from close escort to the bombers from take-off to touchdown. Returning from escort missions they were free to shoot up anything military on the ground, from trains to planes. Cpl Jack Feller's fighter pilot brother had been so engaged and on 27 April the young Debach airman found his second opportunity to visit him at Bottisham, as he described years later.

The P-47s were just taking off on a mission when I got to the gate. I was told they would be about four hours, so I went into Cambridge and came back later as the mission was returning. I mentioned at the gate that Captain Charles Feller was my brother and I was taken to the briefing room. A lieutenant came in and said: 'I have some bad news for you. Your brother is missing in action.' He said they had been strafing an enemy airfield and made a second pass. OK one time, but a second time is bad news. He said, 'Your brother's plane was hit, but they say he had parachuted out and he might be a prisoner of war or he might be with the Underground.' He probably knew he had crashed in. I left and went back to my base. I didn't tell my parents about it and the army notified them.[26]

Within weeks came confirmation that Cptn Feller had in fact been killed, shot down while attacking the former French air force base of Etampes-Mondesir, thirty miles south of Paris and under the control of the Luftwaffe.

For the keen and the anxious in the new, untested Groups that had recently taken over bases in England in which the cement was still dusty and the paint hardly dry, it seemed they would never experience combat as training mission followed training mission and marginal weather conditions often caused a carefully planned operation to be scrubbed even after take-off. S/Sgt Irving Saarima, a Wisconsin flight engineer in the 486th BG crew of 2/ Lt William Hilfinger at Sudbury, was alerted for his first mission on 6 May, to bomb rail yards in Liege. There then followed what would become a familiar routine of hardly tasted breakfast, briefing, checking of equipment, fumbling with straps and zips as flight clothing was donned and finally take-off just as dawn was breaking. But hours later and over Holland the whole formation made a 180-degree turn homewards because of cloud cover over the target. 'We were disappointed because it didn't count as a mission and all those hours of preparation were wasted,' Saarima wrote later. 'The bombs were brought back home, everything was undone and put away.'[27]

Even when a mission did eventually go ahead, the new Groups now being committed to battle sometimes discovered in the build-up that all the training that had led them to that moment counted for little when a briefed plan started to unravel. The 486th joined the 487th BG, newly arrived at Lavenham, in a Transportation Plan mission on 11 May. Lt Robert O'Boyle, twenty-one-year-old senior navigator in the lead crew of Lt William Munroe at Sudbury, found himself being briefed for a route to the railway station at Chaumont sur Loire, south-east of Caen and in the châteaux country of the picturesque Loire

Valley. Sharing the task of target finding with him was a pilotage navigator, looking for pinpoints from the nose. He recalls:

We were a Wing with the 487th BG which was led by a gentleman named Beirne Lay, who wrote *I Wanted Wings* and to his credit he flew on the Regensburg-Schweinfurt mission in 1943 which was a hell of a rough go. Our Group, representing at the time say thirty-six airplanes, was to lead his Group. He was the leader of the Wing and Beirne and his boys missed the assembly which right from the very beginning makes it tough on you. You can't go faster, their fate is in your hands.

At any rate we did get the thing strung together in a gaggle and we flew in the general direction of Caen. We weren't to bomb Caen, in fact it was a reasonably well-defended target. We were flying at 12,000ft so the idea was not to get over major cities like that at low altitude. Unfortunately as this was an early mission we had no idea of the protocol that existed between our commander and Beirne Lay. We just knew that we should tell this guy, 'Hey you're going to lose this one, you're going wrong.' They flew over Caen and some got shot at and I don't believe they lost any airplanes, but as we went in it was pretty obvious to us these guys were way off course and getting worse all the time. If we knew then what we knew later we would have said, 'Look, you are going to correct to a certain course or we are going to leave you. But we are not going to stay with you if you fly over Châteaudun,' which is what happened. These people went over the German airfield at Châteaudun at 12,000ft. It was defended by anti-aircraft guns, though there were no fighters up in what was clear weather, a beautiful day. In the time it takes to tell this they lost three airplanes. There were some fellows started baling out. All we could do was move ourselves out of the fire. We took a few flak hits to our airplanes, but the bulk of the damage was done to the 487th BG.

However, in our ship we had one man wounded and got a hole in one engine, but it still functioned. The pilotage navigator, 2/Lt Alvin Malmer, got a miracle wound because he was hit in the head, but wasn't badly hurt. We weren't wearing any flak helmets, we just had the conventional head band with the earphones and a piece of flak hit his metal band about a quarter-inch wide and rolled into his skull. If it wasn't for that head band he would have been killed. He was in the front turret and you could see the turret almost disappear with the blast. The bombardier took him back to the rest station and patched him up.

As the 487th started to scatter over Châteaudun our choice was to complete the direction and fly over Châteaudun, or go over towards Rouen, where there was no anti-aircraft fire so we could circle and decide what to do. In the meantime some of the 487th people just decided to go home. At the time while we were pondering we knew that the standard operating procedure was that anything less than a Wing was not an operable force over enemy territory, so we turned around and went back and anyone who was in the 487th who was still around did the same and we went back to our base and they went back to theirs.

We still had our bombs on board. We fired red flares as we came into land to show we had wounded aboard and they gave us a priority. But we had had the nose wheel shot up with flak which we didn't know about. As the plane settled down and came to rest on the ground the nose wheel tyre shook like hell but we kept straight down the runway. Malmer was in the hospital probably ten days or so.[28]

Among the three aircraft shot down over Châteaudun was that of the mission leader, Colonel Lay, who had taken over the 487th only days before. Lay came down in his parachute at Coulonges-les-Sablons and with the aircraft's co-pilot, Lt Walter Duer, made contact with the Resistance and was liberated by American troops in August. After the war Lay, who in the 1930s wrote a screenplay from his book *I Wanted Wings*, returned to Hollywood and penned the novel-screenplay with Sy Bartlett, another 8th veteran, for the classic film of the USAAF bomber war *Twelve O'Clock High*. Lay and Duer had been among thirty-one men missing or killed because the formation went off course and flew over a Luftwaffe base in error.

There was a tragic postscript to the raid. Another damaged 487th BG Liberator made it back over England's south coast where the crew baled out seconds after turning the bomber on a course out to sea. But the B-24 swung round in a semi-circle and headed for the centre of Chichester. Schoolboy Peter Gardner was cycling home from classes with a friend when the war arrived in his home town with a rush. He later wrote: 'We heard and saw a large low flying aircraft pass over our heads. There was a huge explosion and pieces of debris clattered down from the sky. I rushed to pick up a piece of metal as a souvenir and dropped it immediately, it was red hot!'[29]

In fact the Liberator came down on the site of the Roman amphitheatre which had been opened up for use as wartime allotment gardens. It fatally injured one man who had been digging for victory, then slid into the rear of a laundry, its fuel tanks exploding at the same time. Two women were killed in the washhouse as well as a fourteen-year-old girl nearby. Within days a unit of US Army engineers arrived to rebuild the laundry.

The presence of the USAAF bomber boys in England was now being rivalled in number by the high-spirited, dashing figures of their nation's fighter pilots. The total of single-engine Groups in the ETO reached a peak of fifteen before D-Day, eventually able to put up 1,400 planes. Many then unknown fighter pilots began tours which would end in ace status for five or more enemy 'kills'; *Stars and Stripes* regularly listed the scores of such personalities in their aces table. But there was nothing glamorous about the way they lived between missions, cold Nissen huts in flat Suffolk farmland shrouded by mist from the nearby North Sea being the routine.

Cptn Bud Anderson was one of those who had begun combat with the 357th FG when it became operational in February and shared a hut at Leiston with other Flight leaders. For them, making toasted cheese sandwiches over a smoking coke stove ranked as a treat in the Spartan conditions. Anderson remembers those days both in and below crowded skies: 'We used to call England the biggest aircraft carrier in the world. Off-duty I didn't go to the local pubs much. We flew and then when we had regular time off we always went to London. We went over to Saxmundham, jumped on a train and "flew" into town where all the hotels had dance bands.'[30]

Ten days before D-Day he shot down two enemy aircraft while part of the escort for a 1st BD mission to targets in Ludwigshafen and Mannheim and recorded it in a gripping account years later. He described how just after picking up the bombers at 27,000ft and taking a position on their right 'all hell began breaking loose up ahead of us'.

You maintained radio silence until you engaged the enemy, and after that it didn't much matter since they knew you were there, and so people would chatter. They were chattering now, up ahead, and my earphones were crackling with loud, frantic calls: 'Bandits, eleven o'clock low! . . . Two o'clock high, pick him up! . . . Blue leader break left!' It sounded as though the Messerschmitts and Focke-Wulfs were everywhere.

'Up and down the streets people jeered and spat at me'

You knew how it was up ahead, and you knew it would be like that for you any minute now, the German single-seat Fw 190s and Me 109s coming straight through the bombers, mixing it up with the Mustangs, the hundreds of four-engined heavies and the hundreds of fighters scoring the crystal blue sky with their persistent white contrails.[31]

It wasn't the fighters the Germans were looking for, but the bombers, roaring remorselessly through the Groups head-on, then diving away to reassemble and circle ahead to come in again. 'It seemed we were always outnumbered,' Cptn Anderson remembers. 'We had more fighters than they did, but what mattered was how many they could put up in one area. They would concentrate in huge numbers.' As the Me 109s finished destroying bombers ahead on the 27 May mission, Anderson's 357th FG found the blood and guts of combat rushing towards them. 'We get rid of our drop tanks, slam the power up, and make a sweeping left turn to engage. My flight of four Mustangs is on the outside of the turn, a wingman close behind to my left, my element leader and his wingman behind to my right, all in finger formation.'[32]

A gaggle of Messerschmitts tried to bounce them from five o'clock high and Anderson led his Mustangs in a tight turn to try to hit the Germans head on.

[The enemy planes] charge past, and continue on down, and we wheel and give chase. There are four of them, single-seat fighters, and they pull up, turn hard, and we begin turning with them. We are circling now, tighter and tighter, chasing each other's tails, and I'm sitting there wondering what the hell's happening. These guys want to hang around. Curious. I'm wondering why they aren't after the bombers, why they're messing with us, whether they're simply creating some kind of a diversion or what. I would fly 116 combat missions, engage the enemy perhaps 40 times, shoot down 16 fighters, share in the destruction of a bomber, destroy another fighter on the ground, have a couple of aerial probables, and over that span it would be us bouncing them far more often than not. This was a switch.[33]

Suddenly the Me 109s, slightly slower and less nimble than the Mustangs, banked and streaked eastwards. 'We roll out and go after them. They're flying full power, the black smoke pouring out their exhaust stacks . . . I close to within 250 yards of the nearest Messerschmitt – dead astern, 6 o'clock, no manoeuvring, no nothing – and squeeze the trigger on the control stick between my knees gently. Bambambambambam! . . . I can see the bullets tearing at the Messerschmitt's wing root and fuselage.' Again Anderson fired and the 109 plummeted in a spin, the twenty-two-year-old American's sixth kill.

Anderson and his wingman then went after the remaining two. One got on Anderson's tail after the powerful Mustang swept past, but the American beat the Messerschmitt in the climb and as it stalled roles were reversed. As Anderson gave chase, yet again the Luftwaffe pilot managed to come round onto his tail, but eventually the P-51 pilot, steering furiously with right hand and feet, left hand working the throttle and all the time keeping the aircraft in trim, closed again in the climb, 'and from less than 300 yards I trigger a long, merciless burst from my Brownings . . . The tracers race upward and find him. The bullets chew at the wing root, the cockpit, the engine, making bright little flashes . . . The 109 shakes like a retriever coming out of the water, throwing off pieces. He slows, almost stops.' Anderson pulled alongside to see a cockpit full of smoke, then the Me 109 fell away, 'almost straight down, leaking coolant and trailing flame and smoke so black and thick that it has to be oil smoke . . . Straight down he plunges, from as high as 35,000 feet, through this beautiful, crystal clear May morning toward the green-on-green checkerboard fields, leaving a wake of black smoke. From four miles straight up I watch as the Messerschmitt and the shadow it makes on the ground rush toward one another . . . and then, finally, silently, merge.'

The other three Mustangs in his flight joined up with him. His wingman had shot down another of the 109s. 'We'd bagged three of the four. We were very excited. It had been a good day,' Anderson wrote. That night, back at Leiston, he stoked the stove in his quarters 'and afterward, after twirling the poker through the coals until it glowed, we ceremonially burned two more little swastikas beneath my name on the hut's wooden door.'[34] That day the 8th AF's P-51 Groups had claimed thirty-five enemy aircraft in the air and seven on the ground for the loss of six of their own. A total of twenty-four bombers had gone down.[35]

The attrition went on as the gap narrowed to D-Day and the 8th began hitting targets in Germany far and wide. In the twenty-four hours after Cptn Anderson shot down two Me 109s, Gen. Doolittle despatched 1,341 B-17s and B-24s to thirty-one oil industry targets, losing thirty-two. The next day it was the Reich's aviation industry which was hit, thirty-four bombers failing to return from 993 which had taken off. 2/Lt Andy Beasley, of the 467th BG at Rackheath, near Norwich, was in one of them. The Group, part of the 2nd BD, were tasked with hitting the Fw 190 assembly plant at Tutow, the fourth time the 8th had set out to bomb the plant, not far from the Baltic coast in north-eastern Germany. In the same way as oil plants, aviation targets were always heavily defended and by now the Germans had added 108mm anti-aircraft guns to the 88mm batteries in the area. It was flak that brought down the aircraft of Lt Rufus Stephens that Beasley was co-piloting and only five of the nine-man crew escaped. Counting off the seconds on the bomb run, in a thin-skinned machine loaded with volatile fuel and fused ordnance, as the black bursts of furious flak marched across the sky towards you was an experience few could ever forget. 'The 88mm stuff did provide more misery than we needed, but the real problem came with 108mm guns, radar controlled. You knew when they were being used,' Beasley remembers.

You'd see one burst, right at your altitude, then a second at about the same place in front of you. They always had your altitude on the money and were tracking you, but if you saw the bursts you knew they didn't quite have the azimuth locked in. These 108s were deployed in four gun batteries controlled by the same radar – and as their larger size indicates, had considerably more bang for the buck.

On that infamous day, we were under fire from 108s, saw the first four rounds detonate and then all hell broke with the next firing sequence. On the starboard wing, the outboard engine was blasted away, and the inboard engine was hanging maybe 45 degrees downward and sheeting fire over the wing back to the tail assembly. The two waist gunners baled out at that time. They landed in the Baltic and with the cold water, died of hypothermia before the Germans could pick them up.

The aircraft was now in a wind-up tight spiral and came back to the Baltic shore. The pilot, Rufus Stephens, appeared wounded, seriously. We had a very loud bell system and it was here I punched the ten-ring abandon ship sequence. Meanwhile, S/Sgt. Peacock, crew chief and top turret operator, anticipating the move, moved onto the narrow catwalk of the bomb bay and hand-cranked the bomb bay doors open – the only route of exit except through the waist gunners' windows. With hydraulics shot out, hand-cranking was the only alternative. All of us working in the nose section had chest packs needing to be snapped on to the harness. When I went out, Peacock was still on the catwalk and I can only surmise he tried to help Stephens. Another factor could explain why neither Stephens nor Peacock got out. With time the aircraft, now in a spin, created crushing centrifugal force which may have pinned either or both to the degree they couldn't make it. What Peacock did always seemed heroic to me. He could have retrieved his chest pack and got out with the rest of us. I always presumed he went to see if Stephens needed help and got caught by the centrifugal forces. Even though wounded, Stephens must have known the aircraft was a goner and had he been able, made it out. He was a good ol' Georgia boy and had a touch of stubbornness in his bones that may have led him to believe he could fly out of the situation – but that's not logical, and he couldn't see all the damage very well from his left seat. It was all clearly visible to me from my right seat.

We had both been putting a maximum effort on the yoke and rudders to hold level flight, the hanging engine was 'running away', meaning the RPM controls weren't at work and the engine speed would soon destroy it even if it hadn't been on fire. With a section of the outside end of that wing also shot away, the likelihood of regaining control of the aircraft was zero. Even with three operating engines, but with a good part of the right wing gone and the fire under control, unlikely here, descent to a lower altitude was mandated, leaving one lonely bird prey to fighters, and high fuel usage – not enough at that rate to make it home, especially with the wing fuel cells ruptured feeding that all-consuming fire. The aircraft was mortally wounded.[36]

The five men who were able to bale out were quickly captured and despatched to interrogation at *Dulag Luft*, then on to prison camp.

While Lt Beasley and his comrades were on their way to the

PoW processing centre the 8th Air Force turned with new energy to the Transportation Plan as May hazed into June, bombing marshalling yards and road bridges in France and Belgium together with airfields and coastal defences. By D-Day it was estimated at Allied headquarters that fifty-one of the eighty rail centres needed to supply the Normandy battle area were in a Category A state of destruction. Twenty-two were credited to RAF Bomber Command, fourteen to the Allied Expeditionary Air Force and fifteen to the 8th Air Force. The AEAF included the US 9th Air Force, whose P-47s ranged across the Channel shooting up ground targets beyond the beaches.

The battle for air supremacy in the five months preceding D-Day cost the 8th AF 2,600 B-17s and B-24s and 980 fighters. In those aircraft 18,400 young airmen had become casualties, 10,000 making the ultimate sacrifice. This was half as many men as the 8th lost in the whole of 1942 and 1943, which had seen some horrendous raids.[37] The day was now about to dawn in a new battleground which would eventually make the United States the most powerful nation in the world. American and British Forces alike leaned, poised, facing the English Channel, waiting to be unleashed. On the airbases too across England the machines of war were lined up in coiled expectancy. The tension would burst in a thunder which would echo around the world.

SUMMER

7

'Invasion! No longer just a gleam in the General's eye'

The sound of liberation began not over the besieged Continent of Europe itself, but in the skies of England. In the lightness of a double summertime night as the clock ticked away the eve of D-Day, the rumble of multi-engined aircraft orbiting then setting course eastward rose to a crescendo. It was heard across the towns and villages of East Anglia, it rolled across the airbases themselves and it alerted the men of the 8th Air Force to the news Invasion was here at last.

Cpl Jack Feller, whose pilot brother had been lost preparing for that day of days, had finished his shift in the control tower at Debach near Ipswich where the 493rd BG had just completed training, when he heard the sound and fury approaching. 'Several hundred airplanes were seen to form up before it was dark, at about 11pm,' he remembers. 'We could see all those British planes towing gliders and DC3s carrying paratroopers as it was dark only from about 11.30. Our Group of B-24 Liberator bombers would be in combat operations for the first time. The time of the take-off was at 6.37am.'[1]

In fact this was the day for which the whole of the 8th Air Force had been brought into being. The RAF had begun its bombing campaign as a desperate means of keeping the war going – and Britain free from tyranny – until help could arrive. That help had been provided by Hitler himself with the invasion of Russia in July 1941, thus easing the pressure on Britain and her Dominions, and then by compounding his military ineptitude with a declaration of war on the United States, the day after the Japanese attack on Pearl Harbor. For America's air generals the route had been less complicated than that of their RAF colleagues. The 8th was there to pound Germany into a state where the Invasion of France could be launched and today was the day it was happening. A total of four separate missions would be flown by General Doolittle's bomber boys on D-Day and most Groups would fly at least two.

A few combat airmen had known for hours that the moment for which they had travelled across the Atlantic was here at last. They were the Pathfinders, among them Lt John Howland of the 324th Sqn, 91st BG.

> During the evening of June 5th at about 2000 hours we were alerted by the 324th squadron commander, Lt Col. Robert Weitzenfeld and informed in the classic manner 'This is it'. We knew 'it' meant Invasion, but we didn't know when 'it' was taking place.
>
> We took off from Bassingbourn with about 17 other PFF crews, flying to various Groups in the 1st BD. Three of us, Clark, Tyson and the other PFF team which served as deputy lead, headed for the 381st BG at Ridgewell. We didn't get any sleep and received our final briefing at 0130 hours. Security was extremely tight. Only pilots, navigators and bombardiers were allowed in the briefing room. All persons briefed were pledged to secrecy until the planes were in the air and the mission was underway. Only then could location of the target be released to the crew.[2]

To the west, at Thurleigh, Bedfordshire, home to the 306th BG and 40th BW, diarist S/Sgt Arthur Bove recorded: 'Bombers, fighters and gliders streamed over the station hour after hour, in a never-ending procession.'[3]

The 306th, one of the nearest to the Invasion coast, would be one of the busiest Groups on D-Day, flying three separate missions in all – to Arromanches, Caen and Thury-Harcourt. In the first, to take out a 105mm gun a mile inland from Arromanches and a defended area near Anselles, a total of forty-two B-17s would lift off at 0430 from Thurleigh. 'This was the mission that everyone wanted and had waited for,' Lt William Leatherman, diarist for the Group's 367th Sqn, wrote: 'Today we were to operate in direct support of ground troops on French soil. From this day forward the second front is a reality and not just a gleam in the General's eye.'[4]

At Ridgewell Lt Howland now realised why he had been training intensively for two days at the end of May using the British invention Gee to find a small target – in his case Skegness pier in Lincolnshire – combined with H2X, to practise bombing through cloud. He did not know he was perfecting technique for all possible weather situations in the eventual Invasion, but that experience would now pay off as D-Day dawned with heavy overcast both at the bases and the Normandy beaches.

The 381st BG Lt Howland flew with on 6 June had an official diarist for each of its three squadrons and that of the 535th Sqn, Cptn Joseph M. Marray, recorded: 'Weather continued miserable, thickening gradually.' But it did not dampen enthusiasm. Marray wrote: 'This is what we came over for last June; this is what every heavy bomber group in the ETO has been paving the way for. Some, of necessity, knew as early as 22.00 hrs last night that the invasion of Europe was scheduled for early this morning. But even those who didn't know for certain were tense. Guards were doubled all over the line and through the living sites. Combat crews were issued with .45 automatic pistols against the possibility of their having to bale out over what was to be their first battlefield.'[5]

Despite the security clampdown, personnel on some bases had advance warning even weeks not hours before of exactly what was coming and they did not necessarily carry exalted rank. Mervyn Caldwell, teleprinter operator to the 40th Bomb Wing at Thurleigh, remembers: 'A month or two before D-Day we were given a blind field order about how it was going to happen, who was going to participate, the whole scheme for the invasion of Normandy, the 8th and 9th Air Forces. We couldn't disclose it. In getting that information you really felt great.'[6]

As combat crews in the alphabet of airfields from Alconbury to Wendling were alerted in the pre-dawn it was clear nobody in the 8th who could fly was going to be left out. Pilot John W. McCollum had recently finished a tour with the 306th BG and had got a transfer to the 482nd BG at Alconbury, flying with 'Mickey' instructors and trainees on three or four training flights a week. The Huntingdonshire base was a very relaxed posting without a parade ground.

'My impression was that, at most any time of day, without a pass and dressed in a casual way, one could walk through the main gate, cross the Great North Road and visit the pubs,' he wrote after the war. 'On the afternoon of June 5th I had decided to visit a pub in the village to have a few beers and play darts before supper. I was bewildered when an MP at the gate refused passage.'[7] McCollum went to the orderly room immediately, sure that he could sort it out. But there he found that curiously he was scheduled for a briefing at the strange hour of 3am. No one could explain why a tour-expired pilot like himself had been listed for what looked like a combat mission. 'It was a mistake I told all that would listen – but to no avail,' he wrote. He turned up at the briefing with his crew and three or four others, which included gunners, 'implying that where we were going there could be some shooting'. Then the CO and his staff arrived:

> [The aircrew were told that] this day we would be privileged and honoured to see at first hand the landing of Allied troops on the Continent. The Invasion was on. We were stunned! The blanket was pulled off the map. A ribbon stretched about in the middle of the Channel from, as I recall, somewhere south of Harwich to a point near Brighton. We were to fly the Channel. I recall that four aircraft were assigned to the mission. Vertical visibility at our altitude was expected to be fair, but air to ground less so; hence the radar aircraft. Our assignment was to fly the route designated on the map and provide periodic reports, based on radar, or if possible, visible sightings. I, in a somewhat timid manner, approached the CO, reminding him that I was a 'happy warrior' and was not supposed to fly combat missions. There is no need to mention his comments. I went on the mission.[8]

S/Sgt Lee Eli Baar, the 306th BG gunner, who admitted being 'scared stiff' by being briefed for two of the March Berlin raids, was another who found himself dragooned into flying combat on D-Day even after he had finished his quota of thirty missions. 'My next to last mission I had a problem with my ears coming down, coming out of the airplane. So, I was grounded and the rest of my crew finished their missions and I'm left alone,' he recorded for a university research project.

> I am a fill-in; someone who is short [of] a ball-turret gunner, I'm it . . . I'm getting tired of waiting to get called as a fill-in, so I figured I wasn't going to celebrate until I got my last missions finished. [But] I got tired of hanging around playing cards, went into town with a couple of guys

and I fell under the influence of alcohol . . . When I came back [to] the post, it was about six o'clock in the morning and they're looking for me. Somebody needs a ball-turret gunner; 'Oh, that's me'. I went over to the pilot, I knew the guy, and I'm standing in front him, weaving a bit, and I said, 'Lieutenant, I'm not feeling too well. As you could see I went in [to town]'. 'Oh, don't worry about it,' he tells me. 'Get into the ship, as soon as the wheels are off the ground get in the turret and put on your oxygen mask and you'll be surprised.'[9]

It wasn't the only time he would be gathered up in the urgency of D-Day.

At Sudbury S/Sgt Irving Saarima, the flight engineer in the Hilfinger crew of the 486th BG, remembers: 'We were hustled to briefing very early. The weather looked so terrible I had my doubts about taking off. We were given all the latest information, including the admonition that any airplane with three white stripes painted across the root of the wing meant it was one of our boys, don't shoot.'[10]

T/Sgt John D. Ayres, a twenty-year-old radio operator in the B-24 *Andy's Angels* of Lt Louis Andrews, in the same Group, recorded that his crew were to bomb the Norman city of Caen, crossing the enemy coast at 24,000ft as troops stormed ashore.[11] They would be part of a six-plane element led by the Group commander, Col. 'Jeep' Overing. It was a short-range target but marshalling such a huge aerial force would keep them in the air for nearly eight hours and cause problems on the return.

Lt Charles Huff, a command pilot in the Group, wrote in his combat diary about D-Day: 'The Group will fly two missions that day and I will go on the first one. Our targets will be railroads, bridges, crossroads and anything related to transportation that will keep the Germans from bringing in reinforcements.

Everything for a hundred miles inland will be bombed and our fighters will take out the enemy airfields.'[12]

At Debach T/Sgt Bill Toombs, flight engineeer on the B-24 *Baby Doll,* captained by Lt W. W. 'Woody' Bowden, remembers it as 'a day of feverish activity' as the 493rd BG became operational for the first time.[13] At Thorpe Abbotts further north, Lt Leonard Coleman was preparing to fly his fourteenth mission on D-Day. He had made up for missing the costly Berlin raid at the end of April while on pass by finding himself on the battle order for the Reich capital twice in forty-eight hours in May and had faced a 'solid wall of flak' on the first mission.[14] Now the weather alone promised to escalate the risk in the crowded sky above Normandy.

But almost without exception crews were desperately keen to go, to say they had taken part in the greatest Invasion in history and had helped to liberate the first hectares of European soil. S/ Sgt Arthur Bove, the 306th BG diarist summed it up: 'The air was charged with something electric.'[15]

The size of the huge aerial assault surprised even the top brass. Estimates in April indicated that the combined forces of the USAAF in the UK and the home-based RAF would equal 1,407 US heavy bombers, 1,180 British heavy bombers, 835 light and medium bombers, 565 fighter-bombers, 2,250 day fighters, 170 night fighters, 175 tactical and photo reconnaissance aircraft, 1,000 troop carriers and 120 transports.[16]

But in fact by the evening of 5 June British and American air strength amounted to 3,467 heavy bombers alone and in medium, light and torpedo bombers 1,645, twice as much as had been es-timated. Then there were 5,409 fighters and 2,316 transports and troop carriers – all lined up on hard standings or runways through-out Britain from Yorkshire to the south Midlands, across to East Anglia, down to the Home Counties of London and inland from the sweeping miles of the Channel coast itself.[17] Available to the Germans were 3,222 fighters and bombers.[18] However, because of the round-the clock bombing raids by the USAAF and the RAF nearly all were in the Reich iself, defending its cities and the industry within. The first evidence of how successful the combined bomber offensive had been in containing and then depleting the Luftwaffe fighter arm, both by day and in darkness, was discovered by Bomber Command of the RAF. As the Invasion fleet set sail in the evening of 5 June the RAF bomber boys flew 1,211 sorties – the greatest total so far in one night of war – bombing German gun batteries and troop emplacements facing the five Normandy beaches and beyond, but only eight aircraft were lost as the Luftwaffe was barely seen. The crews who had taken off with that 5,267-ton bomb load had been totally unaware the Invasion was on, many being shocked as they returned across the Channel to see through gaps in the clouds the greatest armada ever assembled.

Now it was the Americans' turn. The first bombers of the 8th Air Force lifted away in darkness. They came from Bungay, due west of Lowestoft and home to the 446th BG. The 2nd BD, equipped with Liberator aircraft which had a 10-mph faster cruising speed than the Flying Fortress, had been chosen to lead the USAAF bomber assault on the Invasion beach defences, with the 20th Combat Wing at the forefront. Col. Jacob Blogger's Group, known as the Bungay Buckeroos, was the spearhead of that wing. Many on the base had been up all night after crew chiefs had been ordered to supplement dispersal areas to guard their planes as they were loaded with 1,000 and 500lb bombs. Briefing had confirmed the Invasion was on and the target of the 446th was an enemy installation at Vierville on the French coast. It overlooked Omaha Beach.

The Group required not much more than two hours to assemble and fly the 240 miles to Normandy. Crews had hoped to see the Invasion craft going across, but there was cloud all the way and the

446th had to bomb through overcast at 0556 on PFF leadership, with unobserved results. Franz Gockel, a teenage infantryman in the German 352nd Infantry Division, had been on alert for hours in the strung-out defence positions below Vierville overlooking the six-mile-long beach and was sheltering in a bunker along the shoreline when there came a sound he had become familiar with in the nightly raids by the RAF on German cities. 'The American bombers flew over, although they didn't bomb us because they didn't want to endanger their own boats,' he recalled sixty years later.[19] As the Liberators turned away the defenders emerged from their unaffected trench and pillbox system, eyes searching the sea. 'During the wait I was concentrating very hard on my weapon, checking it over and over again,' Gockel remembered. 'I was also saying lots of short prayers, the ones I had said with my family while in the cellar when the bombs were dropped, kind of getting myself into a trance.'[20]

The GIs shivering and vomiting with fear and sea-sickness in their tossing landing craft were now nearing the end of their journey across the grey, white-flecked Channel. They were due to begin landing on Omaha and Utah beaches from 0630 and the first units of British I and XXX Corps, no less afflicted in their own pitching vessels, at Gold, Juno and Sword an hour later. The defenders overlooking Omaha were able to pour withering fire on the forward units of the 1st Infantry Division as they landed 30 minutes after the bombers had left. The twenty-seven DD swimming tanks which might have saved them were lying at the bottom of the Channel, the result of being launched too far out in rough seas. It would be the evening of D-Day before Vierville was captured, by which time in excess of 2,000 GIs were dead.

Other 8th AF bombers were tasked with taking out the defences facing British and Canadian troops north of Arromanches. S/Sgt Saarima, flying with the 486th BG, remembered:

While circling to gain altitude in the dim light of daybreak I could see airplanes of every size and shape through openings in the clouds. How they avoided mid-air collisions is a miracle . . . After breaking out over the clouds we continued circling because we were to be over the target at exactly 7.25 . . . Our primary target was Thory-Harcourt, but we could not see any ground at all, so we turned towards the secondary which was Caen. It was likewise under cloud cover, so our journey was for nothing. It was extremely discouraging to spend 7½ hours in the air then return with our bombs.[21]

Lt Howland later described being in the forefront of the aerial attack by the 381st BG on the defences of the British Gold Beach next to Omaha.

The weather looked bad and we were given strict orders to make certain our bombs didn't fall short. In maximum strength effort the 381st put up two 'Groups' of 18 planes, with a PFF team leading each Group. Jim Tyson and I led the first Group in an attack on the enemy defenders of Gold Beach. The second team of 18 planes was led by Carl Clark and Clem Obler . . .

The assembly went off smoothly and on time. Our months of practice and training in formation assembly paid off. We left Beachy Head on time and headed south and west across the English Channel to pick up a Gee line that would guide us to the target. Mickey operator John Spierling said that his radar scope was full of reflections from hundreds of boats in the Channel. Until he said that I didn't believe it was the real thing. I thought it was a big practice mission. At our 1,500ft bombing altitude we had a solid undercast and were forced to use the Gee-H2X procedure practised at

Skegness. I had my eyes glued to the blips of the Gee box, keeping us on course. John Spierling gave range and ground speed data to the bombardier who cranked the info into the Norden bombsight. Charlie Euger, our bombardier from the 381st BG, looked for a break in the clouds so he could take over visually. But it never came. Nevertheless our training paid off. We had confidence the Gee box course line was reasonably accurate and our practice bombing sessions had proved the Mickey operator and bombardier could hit the beach line with good accuracy. We did what we were trained to do and did it to the best of our ability with full confidence in our equipment and procedure.* Bombs were dropped at 0704. Zero hour for landing on the British–Canadian sector Gold Beach below us was 0725. At 'Bombs Away' I left the scope of my Gee box and came up for air and to look out my window. But all I could see was a solid undercast.

The target of Carl Clark and Clem Obler was an airport near Saint-Lô. While making his attack at Saint-Lô Clem started the approach with Gee. Like our formation they were not bothered by German flak. As they flew into the target area Carl brought the formation down to 10,000ft. They gained contact with the ground and the bombardier took over visually. Clem abandoned the Gee box and leaned over the bomb sight watching the aiming point hangar area of the airport with binoculars. Clem describes what followed: 'A German truck or weapons carrier came roaring across the tarmac at high speed. I could see the faces of two men clearly as they looked up at us. They came to a screeching halt at the hangar and one man jumped out to open a door.

---

* Later evidence showed that the PFF mission on Gold Beach led by Howland's crew smashed the communications network of the German 716th Division, preventing contact between its elements and destroying it as a cohesive fighting force.

He jumped back into the truck and they drove inside. Just then our bombs struck the hangar and blew it to pieces.' As Clem put it, 'The air war becomes quite personal at lower altitudes.'[22]

The attack led by Lt Howland's crew of the 381st BG on Gold Beach was only one of the D-Day missions assigned to the Group that morning. Pvt John Haggerty, who kept the war diary of the Group's 533rd Sqn, wrote at the time: 'Formation after formation made its way to one of the various objectives and dropped bombs. None reported flak and none saw enemy fighters.'[23] The story of little or no flak and a surprising absence of aerial defenders would be repeated by most of the 8th Air Force Groups, together with a feeling of frustration that after all the planning they could see precious little below. But S/Sgt Barr, hanging beneath his B-17 in the ball turret and now sober after breathing pure oxygen, was one of the few who got a grandstand view. 'As soon as we got to the Channel and I could see that line of ships, it was unreal,' he recorded. 'I couldn't believe it and then you see the battleships and cruisers off shore, muzzle flashes; they're bombing like hell inland.'[24]

Even before the first Groups had returned, succeeding missions were on their way, tasked with attacking choke points further back to prevent the Germans bringing reinforcements forward, and this was when S/Sgt Barr got a shock. 'We landed and there was this colonel, comes over, he tells the pilot, he says, "I'm putting more gas into your ship, more bombs, you're going out again."' But with the first D-Day mission the ball turret gunner had by now completed his tour quota of thirty. He told the colonel, '"Sir, that was my last mission. I should be finished by now". He says, "Get in the ship". Then I realized that a staff sergeant does not argue with a bird colonel and I went and I flew an extra mission. Nobody got hurt.'[25] Within days Barr would learn he had been awarded a Distinguished Flying Cross and was off the base, heading States-side.

The follow-up raids on D-Day were as disappointing for several of the keyed-up crews who had been desperate to see something on the ground as they were for most in the first waves. Lt Joseph Brashares was the 423rd Sqn diarist of the 306th BG. 'At 0730 a second mission to attack an important crossroads inland from the beachhead area in France was launched,' he wrote. 'A 10/10s undercast prevailed over this region and it was impossible to attack the assigned target. The aircraft returned without dropping any bombs.'[26] In fact nearly all of the 528 heavy bombers assigned to bottling up the German army in Normandy returned with their loads.

But 2/Lt Leonard Coleman did bomb as the 100th BG flew its second mission of the day. 'Our target was the town of Falaise, France,' he recorded just afterwards. 'The weather was very poor. Only got one look at the Channel on the way over. There were sure a lot of boats at the beachhead. We didn't encounter any enemy opposition.'[27]

T/Sgt Kirk Varner was engineer in the crew of 2/Lt George Leroy Jr in the Group that had opened the bombing on the Normandy beaches, the 446th, but Varner flew the second aerial assault of the Invasion, aimed at containing the Germans. He and other combat airmen had waited by the aircraft for half an hour at Bungay before getting the 'Go' signal to climb aboard as the situation in Normandy developed. 'We bombed road bridges at Caen,' he wrote in his diary. 'When we crossed the Channel I never saw so many boats in my life. It made me very proud of myself to be there and doing my part in the Invasion.'[28]

T/Sgt Bill Toombs, flight engineeer on the B-24 *Baby Doll*, of the 493rd BG, began – like nearly all the combat crews at Debach – his tour of operations on 6 June. 'I was in the top turret and didn't have the advantage to look down into the Channel, but I could hear the tail gunner and the waist gunner talking about seeing all those ships,' he remembers. 'The comment between them was, "I never saw so many ships in my life." When the bomb bay doors were open I could look down, but I could just see the planes below. It was an easy mission. We had no opposition from anti-aircraft fire or fighters.'[29]

As further waves of troops stormed ashore to build a bridge-head from the beaches and the US 5th Rangers finally began to break the deadlock at Omaha, Groups of the 8th despatched their last missions. The busy 306th BG sent off its final bombers at 5.30pm, notching up a total of three separate D-Day raids. They were briefed for a bridge over the Orne at Thury-Harcourt. By now the weather front was moving back across the Channel to the UK and although it caused problems of assembly for the thirty-three bombers forming a composite group of the 306th with two PFF aircraft, the cloud cleared halfway across the water. 'The lead and low groups bombed visually and with good results,' squadron diarist Cptn Sam McNeely wrote. 'No flak or e/a were seen – P-38s, P-47s and P-51s and Typhoons were seen covering landing craft and strafing good targets. Intense activity noted along beachhead and the sea approach.'[30] Other Groups bombed transportation targets at Vire, Saint-Lô, Coutances, Falaise, Lisieux, Thury-Harcourt, Pont-l'Évêque and Argentan.

The tour-expired John McCollum, hurriedly drafted to fly the Channel at low level to observe the progress of the Invasion, was out for the whole morning and into the afternoon. He wrote later:

Above us, at perhaps 15,000ft, the B-17s and B-24s were formed up and headed east. At the levels of these aircraft the contrails must have been a mile wide and so dense one could hardly make out the aircraft. Below them by several thousand feet were the medium bombers. And on the deck were fighters heading for the beaches . . . And below, on occasion, we could make out on the water the vast armada . . . The Navy was there pounding the coast with big guns and the Channel was covered with boats so thick it appeared one could walk on them . . . And this went on all day. I came away from the experience humbled and proud and it occurred to me for the first time that we really were going to win the war.[31]

As crews returned to their airfields from the final missions they compared notes with those who had taken off earlier. At Sudbury, home to the 486th BG, radio operator T/Sgt John Ayres wrote up his combat diary after attempting to bomb Caen in the six-plane element led by the Group commander, Col. Overing: 'On return we ran out of gas and landed at an emergency field to refuel.'[32] They were not alone. The aerial armada which matched that in the Channel was so vast it involved previously-unforeseen problems of assembly and routing. All 8th AF bombers had to exit the Invasion area in a specific traffic pattern south across the Cherbourg Peninsula, then right for a seventy-five-mile leg, then making another right turn flying due north past the islands of Jersey and Guernsey and finally back to their bases. For crews who had been unable to bomb for fear of hitting their own troops through the overcast, the return in heavily weighted machines rapidly ate into fuel reserves.

Lt Wilcox, the navigator on Lt Tom Pearson's crew of the 486th BG, was in the same element as T/Sgt Ayres. 'We could not drop our bombs because of the undercast,' he wrote. 'So we turned west and back out to sea, then northward to England . . . After crossing into southern England, Col. Overing radioed that his plane was low on gas and would be making an emergency landing at an English airbase.' Lt Pearson decided not to risk unforeseen eventualities threatening his dwindling fuel supply and followed the Colonel in. 'It was a long, grassy strip that we put down on – used to train RAF radio operators using light planes. Landing was an experience, especially with a full load of bombs and ammo,' Lt Wilcox recorded. 'The Brits graciously sent several small cars to haul us off to their mess hall for something to eat. Then their armourers (WAAFs) began to remove the bombs. Much excitement followed when our own bombardiers interrupted the operation in order to keep them from blowing us up and insisted that our men did the job.'[33]

Then followed the problem of lifting off heavy bombers from such a short grass runway. 'Picture a long, grass, bumpy field that sloped downward toward an immense English mansion with tall, stone chimneys. That was it. The pilots gunned up the engines for max. power, released the brakes and away we went. We just barely cleared those chimneys.'[34]

Lt Howland had spent much of the day trying to sleep following his return at 10.30am to the 381st BG base at Ridgwell as rumours abounded that in the event of the Invasion going badly, B-17s would be used at low level to drop fragmentation bombs and strafe. 'The rumours really didn't bother us,' he wrote. 'However, the lack of sleep for more than 30 hours was wearing us down. We made pallets of flak vests and sheepskin-lined flight suits. Using partially inflated Mae West life vests for pillows, we went to sleep on the floor of the equipment room. A squadron commander awakened us at 1600 hours. The afternoon mission had been scrubbed.'[35]

The men of the 8th could rest easy, knowing that the massive demonstration of air power had kept the enemy infantry and tanks from massing in the beachhead. Overcaution by the US-AAF's leaders, both military and political, however, caused most of the intended beach-line bomb loads to fall anywhere from a few hundred yards to up to three miles inland because of fears of short-bombing. The enemy lines on the eastern edge of Omaha, for instance, were left untouched. Earlier air bombardment had also caused the Germans to withdraw some of their Channel heavy artillery batteries, including the one at Pointe du Hoc, overlooking Omaha.

In retrospect some combat airmen thought that attacking targets at right angles through cloud had, if not actually wasted bomb loads, certainly made them less effective. John Howland, whose navigation had led eighteen B-17s to Gold Beach where they bombed in line astern through cloud, recorded several years after the war that bombing through cloud using radar (BTC) was the air generals' first mistake and the bombers should have been brought below 10,000ft to aim visually. He added:

> The second mistake was bombing at right angles to the beach line. That placed us over the prime target area at our 180mph speed for just a few seconds. We should have made a right 146 degree turn in six ship squadron formations at the beach line and attacked the grass line just above the sands of Omaha Beach. The maximum range of a 50 cal. machine gun is four miles. At 10,000ft, the .50 caliber can inflict severe flesh wounds. Every downward firing gun on the B-17s except the right waist gun should have been firing into the grass and the grass line. The primary bomb targets should have been the visible concrete gun emplacements. Further, I feel we should have smothered them with oil and rubber incendiary bombs, to create an effective smoke screen. This would effectively blind the German gunners.[36]

As dawn rose again over the beaches the message would soon spread eastwards through Europe that the long night of occupation was coming to an end. It would reach those of the 8th who had baled out in earlier air battles of 1943 and 1944 and were either in prison camp or still in hiding. Lt Joel Punches, the 385th BG navigator downed on the penultimate mission of his tour during Big Week, had been helped by the Dutch Underground to try to make his way to Spain. He wrote after the war:

> I had many interesting experiences while travelling around. At one train station I ate dinner with two German soldiers and I never said a word. Crossing river bridges was always an experience. They had German guard houses on both sides and every 10th–15th person was pulled in and interrogated. I finally figured it out so I was always the first or second to go to the guard house. I stayed in many towns in Holland – Roermond, Venlo, Eindhoven, Ermelo. In Roermond I stayed one month in a house without looking out of a window for the whole time.[37]

By D-Day he had got as far as Liège. 'They told me to stay put and wait for the US Army to arrive,' he wrote. It would be two months before the US 1st Army rolled into town, then he was free.

The progress of the US 1st Army would be aided mightily by air power. That marshalling of aerial forces had been superbly demonstrated on D-Day and it was clear as the tally was counted on both sides that from 6 June the writing on the wall spelled out eventual total defeat for the Luftwaffe. In showing they could keep Hitler's airmen at bay twenty-five USAAF fighters were lost to various causes of the 1,719 mounting escort and continuous patrols throughout Day One. 'Three Fw 190s, chased off by convoy cover were the only enemy aircraft sighted by covering formations during the day,' the official army air force history commented.[38] But among the bombers, out of a total of 3,587 sorties of 8th AF bombers on 6 June, only four aircraft went down and only one, a 487th BG Liberator, was lost due to enemy action. A second B-24, of the 490th BG, crashed on Chesil Beach. The others were two Liberators which collided after bombing. They came from the Group which had gone into action for the first time that day, the 493rd from Debach.

The young clerk/orderly in the base control tower, Cpl Feller, had two fewer planes to check off as the returning aircraft landed, one minute apart. He remembers: 'While the Group was over France and after turning to return to our base in clear skies at 11,000ft, two Liberators were flying straight and level in close formation when the left wing of one struck the tail of another. The two planes disappeared into the overcast. Only one man baled out and survived. The loss of nineteen crew in the first day of action, on D-Day, dampened the spirits of the Group. All of the men realised that war was a serious business.'[39]

8

'An Me 109 came at me head on. I was terrified'

The bomber battle over Normandy would continue for the next ten weeks and air power would finally determine the outcome of the campaign. It was a frenetic and sometimes chaotic period in which missions were planned, often swiftly cancelled then as quickly switched to new targets as the 8th Air Force reacted to the needs of the Allied armies.

Many of those who took part were fresh crews, replacing the tour-expired – their duty done in the demanding preparation to turn the tide against the Luftwaffe before the Invasion. The crew of Lt Daniel Treece were part of the new breed, joining the 486th BG the day after D-Day and becoming operational in the turmoil of mid-June. The flight engineer, T/Sgt Ernest Barton, kept a journal and summed up the frenzy he was experiencing: 'It seems as if we never get any sleep any more. From ½ an hour to four hours at a time is the most sleep I have had in a week.'[1]

The Reich was now being squeezed from the west, from the east by the Russians, from the south by the Allied armies in Italy and from the air, by night and by day. So far the Nazi homeland had faced heavy bombers from two directions, England and from Italy, where Major General Nathan Twining had enough B-17s and B-24s with the range to strike southern cities of the Reich. In the weeks following the Invasion the 8th Air Force tried hard to succeed with a tactical experiment, to split the Reich's defenders in a new direction, tackling aerial might from the east. Such dilution of the Luftwaffe's strength would be achieved by an operation aptly codenamed Frantic in the scramble for supremacy after D-Day. It consisted of seven shuttle bombing missions by American aircraft based in England or Italy which then put down at three Soviet airfields in the Ukraine, where they were refuelled and rearmed and bombed another target on the way home. The operation, which ran from June to September 1944, had long been desired by the USAAF high command, but did not get Stalin's final approval until the February. In all twenty-four targets in German-held territory were attacked. The first, four days before D-Day itself, was a considerable success, 130 heavily escorted B-17s from Italy successfully bombing the marshalling yard at Debrecen, Hungary, then landing at Poltava and Mirograd. Some took off to bomb an airfield in Romania on 6 June, returning to their USSR bases, others flew back to Italy on the 11th, bombing a second Romanian aerodrome. Unfortunately such a surprising demonstration of efficient cooperation between Western and Eastern Allies proved a false dawn.

When the 8th Air Force was called upon to play its part in Operation Frantic from England the Germans showed they would not be caught napping twice, particularly as Soviet airfields were so poorly defended. On 21 June a total of 163 B-17s from two combat wings of the 3rd BD set out from their airfields midway between Norwich and Ipswich to attack synthetic oil facilities south of Berlin. They would be heavily escorted by Lightnings, Thunderbolts and Mustangs, but instead of returning to England they would fly on to the Ukraine. All of the junior airmen briefed in the early hours were downright amazed to see what their final destination was to be, not least 2/Lt Coleman of the 100th BG, who could not believe what was being expected from his sixteenth mission.

Among the astonished was tail gunner S/Sgt Ralph Greenwood, whose own tour at Thorpe Abbotts had begun only seventeen days before but who had already carried out seven missions with the crew of 2/Lt James D. Williams in the Fortress *Shilaylee*. It was clear to Williams and all his men that they would need every ounce of gasoline to reach Poltava.

At Deopham Green, near Attleborough in Norfolk, home to the 452nd BG, twenty-seven crews were just as stunned that the air force now expected them to make the 1,450-mile one-way journey to the Soviet Union. A few of the more experienced among them already considered themselves very lucky to be alive. The 452nd had finished training and completed its move to England in January, combat crews quickly establishing themselves in the rows of hastily constructed Quonset huts planted with machine-age precision over centuries of pasture. The Group's first combat mission had proved a bloody introduction to the European theatre of operations, five of its B-17s failing to return from an attack on aircraft assembly plants at Brunswick, then on 12 May fourteen had been lost in a multi-tasked mission by all three air divisions on oil targets. Now as bleary-eyed survivors and novices alike stared at the map on the end wall of the briefing room shortly after 4am on 21 June, there was no denying another rough mission.

Among those aircraft commanders weighing up their chances that morning was twenty-two-year-old Lt Louis Hernandez. He had joined with his crew as replacements in early March and by now had completed fifteen missions. As he leaned forward on the rough bench seating with his navigator 2/Lt Alfred Lea and other comrades, he discovered the Group was being split between two different targets. A total of twenty B-17s would join a force of more than 200 planes heading for Berlin, but the other twenty-seven in the Group would be going on to the Ukraine, the majority after attacking the oil refinery at Ruhland, a few after bombing Elsterwerda, both north of Dresden. Lt Hernandez was in the Ruhland force, assigned to the aircraft *BTO in the ETO*, its first initials standing for Big Time Operator and contracted because there was another *Big Time Operator* already in the 452nd.

He learned he would be carrying an extra crew member. General Spaatz had lately begun a policy of reducing the number of waist gunners in his heavy bombers from two to one, to answer infantry demands to boost boots on the ground in Normandy. But as the 8th AF's contribution to Frantic was hastily planned it was at once obvious that to fly more than 1,000 miles exposed to any number of attacks the Luftwaffe could bring to bear would require a full complement of gunners again. The result was a call for wingless volunteers throughout USAAF bases in the UK to man .50 machine guns in the 8th's bomber fleets. The 4th FG alone supplied thirty-three personnel, transported overnight to B-17 fields. Among them was S/Sgt Robert L. Gilbert. Gilbert – ground crew chief to a leading fighter ace, Major James Goodson, at Debden – had suddenly found himself with no P-51 to service and therefore an ideal candidate when Goodson became a PoW on 20 June after belly-landing while ground-strafing. Within hours Gilbert discovered he had been temporarily assigned to Lt Louis Hernandez as a waist gunner for the Poltava mission.

As *BTO in the ETO* turned onto the active runway at Deopham Green at 0525 and waited for the green flare to send it bouncing along the concrete bound for history, Gilbert's fellow waist gunner, S/Sgt Herschell Wise, and other gunners of the Hernandez crew such as T/Sgt Arthur Hutchinson who manned the top turret, knew Gilbert only as 'the P-51 mechanic' – and so he would remain to many of them through the decades. Lt Hernandez's co-pilot, 2/Lt Thomas Madden, sitting to his right, saw the green signal arcing skyward and Hernandez released the brakes for *BTO in the ETO* to roar along the concrete, climbing into the thick cloud layer for an instrument assembly at 4,000ft. The Berlin-bound force had taken off from Deopham Green twenty-five minutes before and their yellow-tails carrying the Group's insignia of a white L in a black square were visible to one another as these bombers orbited at 10,000ft. Five thousand feet below, over the same radio beacon, Buncher 20, a force of seven B-17s of the 452nd, were also already circling, having taken off at 0515. Assembly in such conditions could be among the most dangerous moments in a mission and crewmen in all of the forty-seven bombers swivelled their heads back and forth as planes popped in and out of the overcast. But the formations gathered without incident and the spare aircraft required in case of turn-backs by faulty B-17s left the formation as it finally strung itself out for the North Sea and Germany. Lt Hernandez's plane was among those in the low position of the 45th Combat Wing formation.

Over Cuxhaven light to moderate flak burst in well-spaced rows, destruction made to order it seemed as shells briefly opened and closed their red explosive hearts then bled into careless, flimsy black clouds of spent anger, drifting across the sky when sharp, flying splinters failed to find a target. Short of Berlin the 452nd force split, twenty heading for the Reich capital with another 207 aircraft of the 3rd BD to reinforce an attack by the whole of the 1st BD. It was now that death's scythe would reach for the men from Deopham Green. On the approach to Berlin one aircraft was hit by flak and its crew had to turn away for neutral Sweden and internment; then, beyond the target, as the Group banked for home flak-damaged aircraft began to collide. The 452nd BG aircraft of 2/Lt Lemm ran into the tail of that commanded by 2/Lt Edward Arm and blew up, sending Arm's plane into a tight, downward spiral imprisoning the doomed crew by centrifugal force. Eventually the rear broke off, throwing out tail gunner S/Sgt Edward Koster, who became the sole survivor. Another of the

Group's planes was also lost to collision and two more damaged planes had to make for Sweden.

The twenty-seven in the Ruhland-Elsterwerda force flew on eastwards, crews bombing their oil refinery targets successfully with those of the 100th BG such as 2/Lt Coleman's and S/Sgt Greenwood's. Ahead lay Poland and finally the Ukraine where the epoch-making mission, which had begun with 163 B-17s assembling in the skies of East Anglia after dawn, would end. Overhead wheeled and soared Mustangs of the 4th FG, commanded by Col. Don Blakeslee, who would lead his men all the way to land at a Red Air Force airfield after a seven-hour flight, the kind of endurance for man and machine which was establishing the Mustang and its aces as war winners.

Those Mustangs shepherding the final stretch of the Frantic bombers now proved their worth over Poland as the Luftwaffe showed up with twenty Me 109s. Six of them had time for one head-on pass before they were overwhelmed by the P-51s, swooping in a glittering shower out of towering thunder clouds in the aching blue, darting like silver fish, yellow cannon fire rippling from their wings. The Luftwaffe attack lasted seconds, but it was enough to down another of the 452nd BG's planes, that of Lt Hernandez, as he remembered.

An Me 109 came right at my airplane. All of a sudden there it was right in front of me. We had heard so much about our pilots being killed in head-on attacks. I was terrified. He was aiming at me and in a split second he hit our No. 2 engine. It exploded and caused such a drag it threw us into a spin and out of formation. We were on fire and if you are ever on fire in a plane you had better get out, so I rang the bell for everybody to leave and everybody was gone except my co-pilot. He helped me put my chute on and said, 'I'll see you on the ground' then he left. I was the commander, there was nobody else around and we were pretty close to the ground, so I went. I was glad I had been able to get everybody out.[2]

The co-pilot, 2/Lt Madden, later reported to the US escape and evasion debriefing unit once back in England that when he baled out at 14,000ft, 'No. 2 engine was on fire and No. 3 disabled. There was a 3 feet diameter hole between No. 1 and No. 2 engines, the chin turret was disabled and aileron control shot away.'[3]

As the parachutes of Lt Hernandez and his crew floated down near Biała Podlaska a race began below between partisans of the Polish Home Army and soldiers of the Wehrmacht to decide who would reach the flyers first. The drone of the Ukraine-bound bombers was already fading as Lt Hernandez hit the ground. He and S/Sgt Wise hid in a wheat field at first, listening to the sound of German troops. To the east their comrades above in the B-17s were anxiously calculating fuel reserves.

2/Lt Coleman, who would later record in his combat diary: 'Russia, this was a pretty big day for me', had also found himself under fire in the Luftwaffe ambush. 'We were attacked by fighters just south of Warsaw. We lost an engine and flew the rest of the way in on three,' he wrote after the 100th BG landed at the Soviet base of Mirograd. 'Our P-51s knocked down nine out of 12 Me 109s that made the attack.'[4]

Captain Lyle Scott was flying the lead bomber of the 95th BG, based at Horham, close to Coleman's base at Thorpe Abbotts. He reported more enemy fighters downed than Coleman in the attack which had burst on the formation and in the confusion of combat did not apparently realise that *BTO in the ETO* had gone for ever. 'P-51 Mustangs of the 4th FG shot down 14 enemy aircraft in as many minutes with no American losses,' he recorded. 'One of our B-17s had a starboard engine fire and dived out of formation, but it managed to rejoin us when the fire was successfully extinguished.'[5]

'An Me 109 came at me head on. I was terrified'

For 2/Lt Williams in the Fortress *Shilaylee* of the 100th BG the battle would shortly be lost. His tail gunner S/Sgt Greenwood remembered: 'After bombing the crew dropped the plane down to a lower altitude, but ran into a thunderstorm and had to fly over it. The plane was running low on fuel, couldn't make it to any base and we force landed the plane in a wheat field. It was supposed to be a wheels up landing, but the pilot decided to put the wheels down . . . Russian peasants were around when the plane landed and the ball turret operator could speak a little bit of Russian. The people were happy we were Americans.'[6] *Shilaylee* had come down about fifteen miles from Poltava. It began to rain as Americans from the base arrived to check out the aircraft and Russians were positioned on guard around it. When Williams was ready to take off again, one of the Poltava-based Americans told the pilot that someone needed to have a drink with the Russians, as was the custom. Williams told Greenwood to take the offer. A large canteen of vodka was poured and the gunner looked for a chaser. 'The chaser happened to be a green onion and a can of butter,' he recalled.[7]

By now Lt Hernandez and S/Sgt Wise were in the hands of friends. 'I landed close to some people in the Polish Underground,' Hernandez remembered. 'I had hurt my shoulder a bit and they picked me up and took me to a house.'[8] Some time afterwards men of the Polish Home Army appeared and Lt Madden was later able to report he saw his 'pilot, navigator, bombardier, engineer [T/Sgt Hutchinson], waist gunner and the P-51 mechanic', reunited by the Partisans.[9] Three others in the crew had become prisoners of the Germans. 'I stayed in the Resistance house awhile keeping out of everybody's way, then I was given civilian clothes and moved around, never staying in the same place long,' Hernandez recalled. 'They were mostly farm houses, sometimes just a place in the woods. The Germans wouldn't come in the woods because they knew there were guerrilla fighters in there.'[10]

As the rescued flyers were being taken care of, their comrades in the other B-17s and P-51s were now safely down in the Ukraine. The 13th CBW had made it to the airfield at Mirograd without loss and the Mustangs of the 4th FG landed at Piryatin. The other combat wing, the 45th, of which the 452nd and 100th BGs were part, landed at Poltava. Each base presented a bleak aspect to the US flyers. Much of the equipment at the airfields had travelled all the way across the Atlantic to England and then on by convoy to Murmansk and by rail to the southern reaches of the USSR. There had obviously been a heavy financial investment in setting up Operation Frantic, but it was soon to come to naught.

Shortly after the 13th CBW landed a German reconnaissance aircraft which had followed the air fleet was seen circling Mirograd. Col. Joseph Moller, who had led the 95th BG, asked if some of Don Blakeslee's Mustangs could take off to shoot it down, but the Russian commanders – fearful that it would look as if the Red Air Force could not defend its Allies – refused. Moller, expecting the Luftwaffe to send a much more lethal force soon, started redistribution of the combat wing to other landing strips. The 45th CBW at Poltava nearby was not dispersed. Not long after midnight a single German flare lit up the sky at Poltava and over the next two hours the Luftwaffe bombed the neat lines of B-17s without one Russian fighter plane rising in defence. A total of fifty B-17s were destroyed and twenty-nine others badly damaged. Eighteen of those totally wrecked were from the 452nd BG, including *Big Time Operator*. Their crews watched from slit trenches as bomber after bomber exploded. Only nine Fortresses were left intact. Two American pilots were killed.

The next night the Luftwaffe arrived in force over Mirograd, from which most bombers had been dispersed by Col. Moller. 2/Lt Coleman saw the attack unfold. 'Last night the Germans bombed our field,' he recorded succinctly in his diary on 23 June. 'All the airplanes left about 8:00 last night and went to Konkof so there were only five ships left. One of them was ours because it had one engine off. Our plane wasn't hit. What a fireworks. Sure was glad I was in that slit trench.'[11] The Germans sowed the airfield with butterfly bombs which Russian soldiers cleared the next day by close-range rifle fire, suffering several casualties. Three days later Coleman was able to write: 'Today we left Russia and bombed an oil refinery in northern Poland and then continued to land in Foggia, Italy. There was quite a lot of flak over the target but nobody got hurt. (Promoted to 1st Lieutenant on this day).'[12] The hot coffee and American food provided at Foggia was never more welcome for the 8th Air Force crews, many of whom had completed their nine-hour flight from the Ukraine suffering from food poisoning.

The last of the remaining 8th AF shuttle bombers were back at their English bases by 5 July, a raid having been carried out on marshalling yards at Arad, Romania, and the secret of the giant experiment in the Allied air war could be revealed, but the equally enormous losses in expensive machinery were kept hidden. *Stars and Stripes* confined itself to stories of a lighter side by the men who had been to the Ukraine, after its reporter visited the 95th BG at Horham. 'All the little Ivans and Tanyas running barefoot around a certain Russian village now call each other just plain Mac,' the story ran, claiming the children had been so puzzled that the Americans only seemed to call each other by one name, they had taken up the New World address. '"All I hope" said radio-operator Frank Sieracki, of Buffalo, New York, "is that they didn't copy some of the other names we occasionally call each other."' Lt Randolph Johnson, pilot of the thirty-one-mission *Worrybird*, carried on, 'The Russians have got guts and they've got big hearts. Everything they had was ours and we won't forget it.'[13] Others noted that what the people of the USSR had to offer didn't amount to much, usually flowers – which as always made a good shot for propaganda newsreels.

Further, fighter-only shuttle missions and just by the 15th Air

Force, continued into August, then in September the 8th carried out other shuttle raids from England, partly in an attempt to aid Resistance fighters in the Warsaw uprising. But as autumn beckoned the great experiment was over, sunk as simply a grand gesture, by Red Air Force inability to defend its airfields and political suspicion which only showed to the Axis the divisions between the Allies rather than what united them. A range of targets from oil refineries to airfields and marshalling yards were attacked in German-held territory, but extermination camps, such as Auschwitz, easily within range from the Ukraine, were not bombed to release prisoners as Jewish agencies had requested in May 1944. To have done so might have supported the case for heavy bombing in the Allied soul-searching that followed the peace but the opportunity was lost by the air chiefs.

By the time Operation Frantic ended Lt Hernandez and the members of his crew who had remained free, including S/Sgt Gilbert, were back in England.

> The Russians eventually pushed the Germans out of the area and I was taken into Poltava. I was flown from Poltava to Teheran, to Tripoli and then to Casablanca where there was an American base. Some of our people picked me up there and flew me to Land's End in England. After we landed I had to be debriefed and first of all because I had been in civilian clothes for so long they didn't know who I was and I had to tell them. They had someone come down from my Group to identify me. I had been missing for forty-one days. They told me I could not fly over enemy territory again because I had been in the hands of the Resistance. They told me I would be going back to the States.[14]

Lt Hernandez was posted to a training base in Texas where he learned to fly the B-29 and remained an instructor for the rest of the war. However, he and his comrades who took part in shuttle raids were not forgotten by the Polish people. In the year 2000 a memorial of a full-size B-17 outline commemorating all USAAF airmen who died over Europe in the Second World War was unveiled near Biała Podlaska. The Fortress tail bears the markings of *BTO in the ETO* and the names of Lt Hernandez and his crew.

But in late June and early July as the 8th took part in Operation Frantic the battle of Normandy still hung in the balance. The heavy bombers were called upon to add their weight right up to the front line and the consequences could sometimes be disastrous. On 28 July *Stars and Stripes* reported SHAEF's announcement of the 'death of Lt General Lesley J. McNair . . . killed by enemy action in Normandy'.[15] It wasn't an Axis bullet or shell which had done for the sixty-one-year-old Great War veteran, however. It was a bomb from an 8th AF Flying Fortress, one of several that had killed a total of 102 US troops just beyond Saint-Lô and wounded at least 380 others.

The plan to use more than 1,000 heavy bombers to saturate a mile-and-a-half wide area of enemy front line immediately south of the Saint-Lô–Perriers road had been conceived by General Omar Bradley, in command of all US ground forces in Normandy. If successful it would allow his troops, exhausted by weeks of hedgerow fighting in the bocage, to break out into open country and get the German army on the run into Brittany. Bradley had been encouraged by the mass RAF bombing of Caen only a few days before, which had at last pointed towards an end of the British and Canadian stalemate and allowed General Montgomery to take nearly all the city he had rashly predicted would in fact fall on D-Day. However, the now heavily cratered ground to the south of Caen was still being held by the Germans, preventing British armour from dashing forward themselves for Falaise.

Even more reason for the Americans to take the initiative.

Bradley flew to England to consult the bomber barons and asked for an east–west approach to avoid hitting his own troops. But 8th AF leaders said a north–south approach would be necessary as otherwise too many planes would be exposed for long periods to flak, as the hour-long bomb train passed over such a small area. To avoid hitting their own troops on this long approach over US lines the air leaders asked Bradley to pull his men back by 3,000 yards from the strike zone. Bradley suggested 800 yards, so that his troops could quickly seize the initiative by overwhelming Germans still emotionally shattered by the bombardment. Eventually a compromise of 1,250 yards was reached. But Bradley, not an airman, did not realise how the vagaries of weather could wreck a carefully prepared mission and he was warned he was taking a big risk.

The 8th and 9th Air Forces were alerted for the morning of 24 July, but the Normandy campaign air supremo Sir Trafford Leigh Mallory attempted to call it off as the weather worsened. However, several Groups were already near the target and dropped 700 tons of bombs, individual crew errors killing twenty-seven members of the US 30th Infantry Division and wounding another 130. It was the twenty-sixth mission for Lt Coleman of the 100th BG. He wrote in his diary: 'Today we started out to drop bombs on the German lines in Normandy (ST. LO). The target was overcast so didn't drop the bombs. Didn't want to drop them on our own troops.'[16]

The next day 1,500 heavy bombers headed again for the same area. On the battlefield below was the veteran American reporter Ernie Pyle. He was enormously impressed by the relentless progression of the bombers towards their target, the sound of their approach shaking the foxhole in which he stood, entranced, lost in admiration for the flyboys, whose own courage he knew would shortly be saving the lives of other, ground-bound Americans. Then the ordnance began to tumble from gaping bomb bays, hitting dug-in Germans – and marching back towards the point company of his battalion, which was meant to lead the ground assault on the German positions. One of the Americans so randomly killed was General McNair who had come out from England under great secrecy as an observer because he was to succeed Patton as commander of the 'ghost' 1st US Army Group, still fooling Hitler with a radio net in the UK that the Pas de Calais was to be the site of an even heavier Invasion area. Pyle reported the army's response to the disaster:

> The company had been hit directly by our bombs. Their casualties, including casualties in shock, were heavy. Men went to pieces and had to be sent back. The company was shattered.
>
> And yet Company B attacked on time to the minute. They attacked and within an hour they sent word back that they had advanced 800 yards through German territory and were still going. And our farmyard men with stars on their shoulders almost wept when word came over the portable radio. The American soldier can be majestic when he needs to be.

Pyle ended with the thought that the bomber crews themselves were probably weeping in England that night in 'the awful knowledge that they had killed our own American troops'.[17]

The story of the Saint-Lô massacre spread, British soldiers used to the gallows humour of war repeating that, 'When the RAF come over the Germans take cover, when the Luftwaffe come over the British take cover and when the Americans come over *everybody* takes cover.' But the RAF also bombed their allies in Normandy: seventy-seven of 800 aircraft taking part in front-line support unloaded on Canadian troops waiting to attack on 14 August, killing sixty-five of them.[18] In fact the plan, the overwhelming use of available air power and the weather were to blame for what happened at Saint-Lô. Cptn 'Rosie' Rosenthal, now into his second tour with the 100th BG, had led most of the 3rd Air Division on the Saint-Lô mission and ran into scattered clouds, the whole force having to lose height just before the target, forcing bombardiers to hurriedly readjust their sights. When they arrived over the target, less than 8,000 yards wide, smoke from bomb bursts by 9th AF Thunderbolts who had arrived immediately before, added to the confusion.

Lt Coleman was also on the raid, but merely noted in his diary: 'St Lo (Ground Support).' T/Sgt Barton, who had found so little rest after beginning his tour in mid-June, missed it. The 486th BG, converting from Liberators to Flying Fortresses, was one of only two Groups to be stood down from both the Saint-Lô missions. Barton was still struggling with fatigue, recording on 27 June: 'Decided not to spend my pass in London, but in bed to catch up on my sleep. Got in about 15 hours so far.'[19] Two days before the Saint-Lô disaster Barton wrote: 'This afternoon they told us we were to be transferred to the 493rd BG and we are quite happy about it because we will be back on B-24s.' Then later: 'Arrived at the 493rd [Debach] and was assigned to 860th Bomb Squadron. Field is plenty chicken but hope we get our tour completed fast.'[20]

Many of those missions he was now asked to fly would be to oil targets. General Spaatz considered that denying the enemy his oil would win the war in Europe. He was right and the diversion to Saint-Lô had irritated him, particularly as his heavy bombers were being asked to carry out a role he considered was not theirs, being tactical rather than strategic. Now he was itching to demonstrate what his B-17s and B-24s could actually achieve, in parching the enemy machines of their lifeblood.

9

'Couldn't sleep. Kept seeing ships exploding'

The battle to drain the enemy of his oil supplies was the longest and bloodiest campaign of General Carl Spaatz's all-encompassing US Strategic and Tactical Air Forces. It had already begun three weeks before the Invasion, with five combined attacks in one day on separate German refineries, but would escalate throughout the summer and autumn then on through the winter until the following March. Even in August 1944, however, it was obvious it was already having a crucial effect on the quality of the Luftwaffe opposition. The Nazi *Experten* shot down by the American Fighter Groups and bomber gunners from Big Week onwards were clearly being replaced by under-trained novices, their instruction curtailed by lack of fuel, the young Luftwaffe cannon-fodder no match for the confident and well-drilled Mustang jockeys from the US.

On 7 August Major George Preddy was leading the 352nd FG towards a rendezvous with AAF bombers south of Hamburg when he spotted thirty Me 109s who obviously had the same plan. 'These Me 109s were flying a tight formation at about 28,000ft and though they saw me coming they did not take evasive action since they figured that their top cover – which I never saw – would take care of me,' Preddy reported when he got home. 'I went right in for the pack and shot down five, starting with the tail-end Charlie. Only one of the five managed to parachute out, the rest of them went down in flames.'[1] Preddy then went after a sixth, who turned out to be the only experienced pilot of the *Gruppen*. 'I chased him down to 5,000ft. This was the best part of the mission for me. The first five never had a chance – not one of them fired a shot at me – but the sixth gave me a real dog fight.'[2] Nevertheless Preddy shot him down too.

The idea of selecting oil as a key means of turning enemy dreams to ashes had been initiated even before America came into the war. In the summer of 1941 the USAAF Air War Plans Division had pinpointed three primary objectives for crippling Germany: the electricity supply system, transportation and the petroleum industry. By early 1943 the Committee of Operations Analysts, commissioned by General Arnold from leading business, political and legal brains of the nation, had decided that the far-reaching extent of the numerous small plants in the German power industry placed it beyond the capability of a US bomber force to destroy. Transportation also was seen as less of a priority and had moved down the desirable destruction list to bottom place of six. The lure of oil as a target strategy was easy to see. Germany had few natural oil supplies of its own, only 3.8 million barrels out of 44 million needed being produced in the full year before the start of the Second World War, another nine million barrels being made synthetically.[3]

In fact in the topsy-turvy logic of the Third Reich it was *essential* Germany continued a policy of conquest merely to keep the fuel lines of its war machine surging to pursue that self-same master plan. A major aim of the invasion of Russia had been to seize its oil supplies, necessary to fill a 26 per cent shortfall if Germany was going to be able to continue the war. In 1944, as Stalin's forces began their offensive which would eventually end in Berlin and the Romanian oilfields were wrecked and overrun, Germany became totally dependent on its own small domestic production and the larger synthetic supplies, vital for high-octane aviation fuel, from its coal hydrogenation plants. A plan to improve production to yield 60 million barrels a year of synthetic fuel was begun towards the end of 1943, but the start of Allied air attacks on the hydrogenation plants in the summer of 1944 made it inevitable that Germany would eventually lose the war unless its scientists could perhaps produce and use a weapon so terrible it would persuade the Allies to negotiate, such as an atomic bomb.

The pre-war facts about German fuel supplies being known, and with intelligent supposition following the series of defeats on the Eastern Front, it is surprising that when Spaatz proposed the Oil Plan for Bombing to General Dwight Eisenhower three months before the Invasion he did not at first find a willing ear. Spaatz had already had his orders under the Pointblank Directive of the Allied Combined Bomber Offensive, promulgated in June 1943 and still valid, to make attacks on the German fighter force his first priority before the Invasion, often by drawing it to battle. In his papers released after victory Spaatz said he told Eisenhower at an Invasion planning meeting on 25 March, in which the Normandy Transportation Plan was being discussed: 'We believe attacks on transportation will not force the German fighters into action. We believe they will defend oil to their last fighter plane.'[4] But Eisenhower decided that 'apart from the attack on the GAF [German Air Force] the Transportation Plan was the only one which offered a reasonable chance of the air forces making an important contribution to the land battle during the first vital weeks of Overlord'.[5]

In the post-Invasion period, however, the Transportation Plan having proved a great success, Eisenhower was fortunately willing to now allow Spaatz to turn in earnest to the Reich's fuel supplies. It was not before time that this key strategy which would eventually prove the single most effective means of victory became the new dogma. In fact up to May 1944, only 1.1 per cent of Allied bombs had been used on oil targets, including those of the RAF who also had originally surmised that burning a path of destruction through Nazi fuel was the road to victory and had several times bombed oil installations – but with inadequate and too few aircraft – as far back as 1940.

Once Eisenhower was convinced of the necessity of parting the Luftwaffe from its fuel sources, RAF Bomber Command's leader, Sir Arthur Harris, was also now ordered to add the weight of his aircraft and crews to a combined oil campaign. He was handed a list by the Deputy Supreme Allied Commander and ordered to eradicate ten synthetic oil plants in the Ruhr. Harris had his own ideas about how the war would be won and prevaricated with Air Marshal Sir Arthur Tedder, claiming that the heavily defended targets would have to be hit by the RAF in darkness because his bombers, armed only with .303 ammunition, would be heavily at risk from fighter attack and night meant poor bomb patterns inevitably resulting in a lengthy campaign.

But the clue to the necessity of targeting oil lay in Harris's very objections. Refineries were heavily defended because they were vital to the enemy's ability to fight on. In fact Harris would be forced by ultimatums to play a full part in the oil campaign and it was the 4,000lb bomb his Lancasters could carry that would wreak much of the lasting destruction against the Reich's oil industry. The maximum-sized bomb the USAAF Fortresses and Liberators could deliver – 2,000lb, but more usually 500lb – too often caused only pipework severance which could be repaired.

It was US bomber boys who would carry out the overwhelming number of missions to fuel targets, however, and their very persistence which would wear away German ability to recover. Those who had arrived in the late winter and spring, for Big Week and after and had so far survived, were now coming towards the end of their tours. Oil installations would feature heavily in their target records towards the end.

Lt Coleman of the 100th BG took part in his first oil mission on 28 May, an operation in which thirty-two bombers were downed by Luftwaffe fighters and his twelfth time in combat. 'Had a pretty rough day today,' he recorded in his quarters later.

The target was a synthetic oil plant at Magdeburg, Germany. I guess the Germans didn't want it bombed very bad. They sure as hell tried to keep us from hitting it. German fighters hit us just before we got to the target. Those boys really come in on us. They made about four passes one wave after another all in less than three minutes. The lead ship we were flying off from went down. We got one engine hit and had to feather it. We flew all the way back on three engines. This 17 flies pretty good on three engines. That's the first time I have had to fly one on three. The group ahead of us lost about eight planes. Guess we were pretty lucky. Our ball turret gunner got one Me 109. The tail gunner got a probable.[6]

Just a few hours' fitful sleep, then it was mission 13, another fuel installation. 'Our target today was an oil refinery and storage plant in Leipzig, Germany, another pretty trip,' wrote Coleman. 'The flak was pretty bad. We only lost one ship. Picked up a couple of flak holes in our plane.'[7]

Coleman's varied tour continued with missions to other targets, then on 20 July he found himself on the battle order for what would become one of the most feared destinations in the Reich, the synthetic oil complex known as the *Ammoniakwerk Merseburg* plant at Leuna, fifteen miles from Leipzig, which crews would eventually condemn simply as Murderous Merseburg. 'There was really some flak at the target,' Coleman recorded in his diary. 'Our squadron CO got his at the target and didn't get home. I was flying his right wing when he got hit. He dropped out of formation and came along behind for a long time but couldn't make it. He made a crash landing somewhere in Belgium. Everybody got out of the plane OK. They had a good chance of getting away in Belgium. We got a few more holes in our ship.'[8]

In fact the 3rd Bombardment Division of which Coleman's aircraft was part suffered surprisingly little from Merseburg's flak that day, only two aircraft going down, but a 1st BD aircraft-industry mission only a few miles away on Leipzig itself at the same time cost fifteen bombers, no fewer than eight of them from the 91st BG, part of an eventual war total of 197 which would be the highest attrition rate of any bomb group in the ETO. Intelligence reports were sent to Division headquarters for analysis on a regular basis and the file from the Group's 324th Sqn for the 20 July mission reads:

At 1100 hours just before IP, after calls of bandits from Wings ahead, 55 to 60 single-engine E/A hit our low Gp in two waves of equal strength from 6 o'clock level to slightly high. The attacks came from cloud and E/A were stacked up to 4 high. Massed attack lasted about 5 & ½ minutes. Individual attacks continued thereafter on stragglers. E/A were Me 109s and Fw 190s about equal in number . . . Low group was out of position and in loose formation at time of attack and fighter support had evidently been drawn to front of the Division. They came in later to take care of E/A, which used the old rolling tactics as they attacked. A/A fire was moderate and accurate.[9]

Lt Coleman went back to the Leuna complex eight days later: 'Flew my first one as a First Pilot today,' he wrote. 'Got along fine . . . Picked up a few flak holes again but nothing very bad. My crew is going on a seven day flak leave before we fly again.'[10]

The anti-aircraft battalions were now being moved from all over Germany to protect the oil refineries, evidence that Spaatz's plan was working. 14 *Flakdivision* was responsible for the defence of industry all round Leipzig, including the fuel plants at Rositz and Böhlen as well as Leuna-Merseburg. Its new commander as the oil offensive began, *Generalmajor* Adolf Gerlach, had just over a hundred heavy flak guns to defend Leuna-Merseburg alone, but Reich Armaments Minister Albert Speer – who knew that if he lost his refineries Germany would lose the war – paid Gerlach a visit and told him he would be receiving many more.[11]

'The oil refinery at Ludwigshaven was our target today,' Coleman wrote on 14 August, his tour now drawing to a close. 'Not a bad mission at all. There was a lot of flak at the target but not much damage just a few holes.' The next day he bombed the refinery at Ruhland. 'This is the same target we bombed on the way to Russia,' he recorded. 'There was quite a lot of flak but no damage.'[12]

Then ten days later, with Lt Charles J. Gutekunst as his co-pilot, he saw evidence at close quarters of the increasing protection for oil targets on the final sortie of his thirty-five-mission tour, in the erotically-named Fortress *Lay or Bust*. 'Got a nice one for the last one,' he recorded for 25 August. 'An oil Refinery at Politz, Germany. There was some real good flak and we got some pretty close hits. We got about 16 holes in our Plane.'[13]

The tour which had taken Coleman through the flak-smeared skies of Berlin to targets in France on D-Day, to Russia, to Italy and into the maelstrom of the oil campaign was over at last. Now he could rest and go home to Oregon. But there was another surprise in store. He was about to join the movie business.

The film *The Way to the Stars* which was released in the US as *Johnny in the Clouds* was meant to show audiences on both sides of the Atlantic how well British and American flyers got on with one another at a rural airfield and off-duty in an archetypal English small town – actually Bedale, North Yorkshire – redolent of a more peaceful age. Much of the action takes place in a country house-style pub/hotel – in fact the Golden Lion at Northallerton – and the location was chosen to inform American audiences about the way of life Britain was fighting to maintain. The playwright Terence Rattigan, whose drama about RAF Bomber Command, *Flare Path*, had proved so popular it had run for eighteen months in the West End, was recruited to write the screenplay and the famous Anthony Asquith to direct. The cast included the rising British star John Mills and the sixteen-year-old Jean Simmons made her debut as an unnamed singer. The American flyers included Bonar Colleano, portrayed as a loudmouth – this was after all a British-made picture. Casting complete, all that was needed were a few people who could fly B-17s.

Lts Coleman and Gutekunst were among those selected. Gutekunst, who remained in the air force after the war, retiring as a Colonel, was tracked down by Coleman's nephew sixty years later and revealed by letter how the invitation to end their time in England in a spectacular fashion came about. They were ready to leave for the United States, he wrote, when they were asked to fly a B-17 along with two other crews to RAF Catterick and were told they could go home or spend a few weeks at the Yorkshire base.

We elected to take the trip to the RAF station and as it turned out we were glad we did. Upon arrival we found we were to fly the B-17s for a British film being made called *This Side of the Ocean* (renamed *The Way to the Stars* on release in 1945). It was to be a story about an AAF bomb group that was to operate from an RAF base and bomb Germany. Using the B-17s we were to simulate bombing missions, take-offs, fly-bys and landings. When we were flying we always had RAF men and women along on the flight. They had never flown in a bomber and were eager to fly in the famous Flying Fortress they had heard so much about. We enjoyed having them with us.

Those flights included low level around sleepy Bedale, captured in the film, as young men from the New World passed over the old, the pre-Norman fortified tower of the market town's St Gregory's Church appearing to port on approach to the circuit at Catterick, roaring Wright Cyclone engines vibrating thirteenth-century knights' tombs below. Lt Gutenkunst continued:

Every day was a fun day as were the evenings when everyone congregated in the RAF mess for a fair amount of drinking, dancing and sing-along sessions. One day the Americans and RAF men played baseball for the camera crew. It was a fiasco to say the least. Towards the end of the shooting we B-17 pilots including Leonard [Coleman] and several RAF pilots had our picture taken under the wing of our B-17 with the entire filming crew. The camera crew gave me a copy of the picture I have kept for 60 years. With the weight of our combat tour off our back and the carefree flying we had at Catterick RAF station Leonard and I thoroughly enjoyed our time together for several memorable weeks during the war.[14]

The different lifestyle and society an American airman could find himself introduced to in the ETO were diverse to an incredible degree for many of the farm boys or former students of small-town America. That summer several of them at the US base of Thurleigh, Bedfordshire, found democracy in action as royalty came strolling round the corner.

The USAAF teleprinter operator Melvyn Caldwell, who had spent his early years in small towns in Missouri before his father moved the family to St Louis in the Great Depression, met King George VI, Queen Elizabeth and the future Queen when they visited the 40th Combat Wing headquarters at Thurleigh. 'I just happened to be on duty when they came,' he recalled. 'They rolled up with a motorcycle escort and I remember the Rolls-Royce. Major General Turner led our bomb wing and they came in the office and he presented the base officers and he showed them the whole base operation and took them into my teletype room. The then Queen was a very pleasant lady. King George seemed quiet, but not unpleasant. The present Queen was a pretty nice-looking girl. They had me explain all about the tele-typing and everything.'[15]

The visit was considered such a success the USAAF's top brass decided it would be wonderful publicity if the future Queen christened a B-17 at the base, as so many from film stars to pol-iticians' daughters were doing at this time. Mary Churchill, the ATS-officer offspring of the Prime Minister, had joined the Eng-lish star of the current hit film *Gone With the Wind*, Vivien Leigh, two months previously in christening a B-17 of the 381st BG *Stage Door Canteen*, another movie. But the naming of USAAF bombers by celebrities reached the risible when the film actor Edward G. Robinson visited the 381st BG's base at Ridgewell. Instead of his own name or a film he was appearing in he insisted on the title *Happy Bottom*, explaining in his distinctive vowels to drawn-up VIPs that it was for his wife 'Glad-Ass'.

The carefully orchestrated publicity plan for the eighteen-year-old Princess's visit to Thurleigh and three other USAAF bases on the same day didn't quite go as intended. First the initial name of *Princess Elizabeth* was rejected because of the propaganda value to the Nazis if they brought the bomber down in Germany and it was hurriedly changed to the less identifiable *Rose of York*; and secondly a lowly Press Relations Pfc got more friendly than senior officers liked to see with the young and attractive Princess. Gene

'Couldn't sleep. Kept seeing ships exploding'

Graff was asked to write about his experience in the *Stars and Stripes* issue of 8 July.

> Princess Elizabeth and I inspected some US bomber stations yesterday – and some other people were there too, including her mother and father and a general or so and innumerable aides and custodians. The last part is important because somehow they seemed to put a crimp on a conversation between a princess and a private . . . Shortly after the royal party arrived Princess Elizabeth was standing in front of a fireplace looking at pictures on the wall and occasionally glancing round to study faces in the room. 'Is this your first visit to an American camp,' I began. 'Yes it is,' she replied, 'and I'm enjoying it very much.' 'Do you have American guests at your hou . . . er, palace?' 'Not unless they attend State parties, or are being decorated by Daddy,' the pretty, but aloof young lady replied. 'If you mean at my parties and dances Americans never have attended – probably only because I haven't met any.' Further conversation was interrupted when a British General edged protectively between us.[16]

But there was no end to the determination of a young reporter on the trail of a royal scoop.

> Three hours and two Fortress stations later Princess Elizabeth was eating ice cream with three American Red Cross girls while the rest of the party was off discussing aeronautic engineering or something. 'Does a trip like this tire you', was the open shot. One eye noticed that Elizabeth was a pretty girl with effervescent expression. The other, of course, was peeled for interrupting officials. 'I've been enjoying myself too much to think of being tired,' the Princess said with

a pleasant smile. 'You know, I don't get to meet so many people very often. Those hats [canvas caps with jockey-like brims worn by ground crews] certainly are funny. And I never realized a pilot has to wear so much equipment.' She seemed to grow more cordial at this point and was about to volunteer further information about the mental ponderings of a princess when an RAF uniform, housing a wing commander, loomed.[17]

Pfc Graff's brief brush with Royalty was over.

Bombardier Lt Andrew Vero, based at Thurleigh, remembers another occasion in that summer of hot sunshine interspersed with sudden showers when both Princess Elizabeth and her sister Princess Margaret arrived on a 'surprise' unofficial visit to the Bedfordshire airfield. 'It was a beautiful day and the airdrome was empty, practically all the airplanes were out on a mission and there was just us stood down. The two princesses, dressed in pink and blue chiffon, arrived alone and we were at the standby plane. Margaret stood by the car with the chauffeur while Elizabeth walked by the crew.'[18]

GI William Butler, who worked in the bomb dump at Thurleigh from October 1942 until the end of the war, also never forgot seeing Royalty. 'I got all dressed up for the christening of the *Rose of York*,' he recorded. 'The visit by the Royal Family was something of a highlight. I was impressed. First, because all those GIs were on their best-dressed behaviour (which was always a proud moment) and second, there was something about the Royal Family that made you feel good.'[19] Flying in *Rose of York* made airmen at Thurleigh feel good too because it became known as a lucky aircraft. One crew finished its tour in her in July and it would take others to German targets for many months more and bring them back.

*

Those crews were now arriving at Thurleigh and other USAAF airfields in England to continue Spaatz's oil campaign. They represented a new generation of flyers. The college boys who had made up the first of the pilots, navigators and bombardiers, officers all, on hand to take part in the battles of Schweinfurt in 1943 and many of them the battles of Big Week, had now departed either back to the States or into the growing ranks of the missing. They had been replaced by the new boys of early 1944, most from much the same educational background.

But now a third generation was arriving to fight alongside the second in the remaining missions of the oil campaign and then by themselves to take Spaatz's Groups into raw battles and hardships which would include curbing the menace of the Luftwaffe's untried jet fighters in the autumn of 1944 and coping with bomb-through-cloud targets in a particularly dreadful winter. They were the high school graduates, keen teenagers inspired to fly who had been trained under a special exemption of the Aviation Cadet programme when it was realised there were too few college students to fill the extraordinary boost needed in flight-training courses. The minimum age requirement for putative officers had been dropped from twenty to eighteen and the need for two years' college education had been waived in favour of a tough written exam. The film-star pilot James Stewart, a States-side instructor with the USAAF in mid-1942, made a short propaganda movie produced by the US Army Air Force First Motion Picture Unit entitled *Winning Your Wings*. In it the then Lt Stewart made an appeal to high school and college students to sign up for the air force as requirements were lowered. He demonstrated what training they would get and also showed newly qualified pilots at a dance. In an aside he advised: 'You find out what effect those shiny little wings have on a girl – it's phenomenal!' By 1944, 65,700 pilots a year were graduating, together with 16,000 bombardiers and 15,900 navigators.

Howard Roth was one of them. He was a teenager riding in a car with a friend in his home town of Lockport, New York State, when he heard the news of the Japanese attack on Pearl Harbor which brought America into the global war.

We realised then that before long we would be in the service. I always wanted to be a pilot. I was always interested in planes. But at that time you needed to be at least going to college to be accepted for cadet training. Then the following summer they started the program where you could sign up as an aviation student cadet and take college training . . . So myself and three other buddies, Dick O'Connor, Joe Neden and Howard McIntyre went to Buffalo to take the test and see if we qualified. We all did and shortly after we were on our way to Atlantic City for the standard Army basic training, living in wooden firetrap resort hotels.[20]

Roth's progress to flying combat missions had already shown him what a dangerous world he was in. After primary flight training he went on to fly Stearmans at a base in Missouri, where an instructor totally wrecked the plane with him in it, but he got away with a gash on the head and hand. Just before Christmas 1943 Roth was presented with his wings and got time off to visit his family before starting B-17 conversion. Fate intervened again. 'Going through Ashtabula, Ohio, I was involved in a train wreck. The engine, I don't know what happened, but it was rolled over on its side and killed the engineer. Most of the passenger cars were at different angles of the track,' he recalls. He got another train to Buffalo, being delayed by about twelve hours. 'Dick O'Connor graduated as a fighter pilot and was home at the same time. He stopped at the house and we had a few beers,' Roth remembers. After his furlough it was on to Tyndall Field, Florida, for conversion to the Flying Fortress. 'It was a beautiful aircraft the B-17,' he says. 'Here I was, still 20 years old, a couple of months from 21 and I had to laugh thinking that two years ago my dad wouldn't trust me with his car.'[21]

His B-17 training over Roth was posted as a co-pilot to Salt Lake City where he met up with his pilot, 'Hoot' Gibson, and navigator and bombardier. It was now that the US Government, like all governments, showed how cheap it could be despite the sacrifices its young men were making for the nation. Until the exemption to the Aviation Cadet programme came along to draw in those just out of high school, all pilots, navigators and bombardiers in the USAAF had been commissioned as 2/Lts on graduation unless they had previously served as sergeant pilots in the RAF and RCAF before Pearl Harbor when they were made Flight Officers, a non-commissioned warrant rank, introduced in September 1942. Now the particularly young graduates from US flight schools in 1944 and 1945 were usually given that rank, thus saving several hundred dollars on commissioned-grade pay rates, which for a 2/Lt flying combat amounted to $3,060 a year, £765 in the ETO at the then exchange rate of $4 to the pound. Howard Roth, his pilot and the navigator were all made Flight Officers, only the bombardier reaching 2/Lt. The rest of the crew, the gunners, radioman and engineer were sergeants of various grades as they always had been in US bombers and where they would remain. Roth had met the noncoms at Ardmore, Oklahoma, where the whole crew undertook final operational training. From Ardmore, Gibson and Roth's crew were posted to Kearney, Nebraska to pick up a new B-17 to fly the Atlantic via Boston and Iceland. 'We went by way of Buffalo and of course I deviated a little bit and buzzed Lockport,' Roth remembers. 'I went up Main St for a final farewell and a couple of low passes and then back on route again to Boston.'[22] Now in the late summer of 1944 Flt Officer Roth was part of the 306th BG at Thurleigh about to join in the oil campaign.

'When we arrived at the base we went through indoctrination to bring us up to date on what they expected from us,' he recalls. His first mission was to bomb an oil refinery at Dollbergen, Germany on 5 August. 'We really didn't get too much damage to our planes, the flak was moderate and you could say I got my baptism of fire I guess.'[23] It would not stay that way and while the 306th BG escaped at that time, others were suffering.

The day before, Lt Robert O'Boyle, whose fellow navigator in his crew had been wounded by fighters over Châteaudun in May, took part in a raid on an oil refinery at Hamburg. 'It was a perfectly organised mission, but we had a hell of a lot of opposition,' he remembers. 'There was a lot of flak coming up. We flew in three squadrons. The other parts of the Group were attacked by fighters and anti-aircraft fire also. They were off course to be kind of brutal about it, so we just moved over and up so they took the brunt of the fire and fighter attack.'[24] O'Boyle's 486th BG lost three aircraft that day, two to collision over the target.

2/Lt Walter Douglas was a co-pilot just beginning his tour with the 305th BG at Chelveston, Northamptonshire, in August. He had made it to the right-hand seat of a B-17 by an unusual route. Douglas had originally joined the USAAF in 1942 and was sent to the UK as a sergeant telephone communications maintenance supervisor at Bushy Park. The results of bombing in London decided him to try for the aviation cadet programme and he was sent back to the States for training in January 1943, after becoming engaged to an English girl.

On 16 August he flew a mission to bomb an oil refinery at Böhlen, near Chemnitz. 'The flak was real bad and we were flying in the slot behind the leader,' he remembered.

The leader had to make three runs on the target before dropping the bombs because of clouds and smoke covering the target. We had used more fuel than we usually would and there were many holes in the aircraft. When we reached the UK we had to find the nearest base to land and as we circled the airfield the low fuel light came on, which means *get down fast*. On final approach one engine quit, so we transferred fuel and restarted it. On touchdown we lost all engines. One of our gunners started having mental problems after this experience and was grounded by the flight surgeon. Just afterwards the flight surgeon went on leave and left the assistant in charge. On the following mission the gunner that was having mental problems was cleared by the assistant flight surgeon to fly. We were in the ready tent waiting for the word to go and I noticed that the gunner was shaking all over. I told the pilot that I thought he should be replaced, but was over-ruled.[25]

Once airborne at 15,000ft the radioman called up to say the gunner was trying to leave the aircraft without a parachute. Douglas had to restrain him with difficulty and the crew had to abort the mission and land with bombs aboard. The crew was given a three-day pass and the gunner was remustered to a non-flying role.[26]

The oil campaign ground on, but there were other targets. Denying the Luftwaffe its fuel was only one part of the Allied Chiefs of Staff Pointblank Directive which had applied for a year now and called for the USAAF and RAF to hit the Reich's aircraft factories too, the main purpose of Big Week, thus drawing the Luftwaffe into defence. In August the new breed of American flyboys found themselves taking part in ground-support missions over France, bombing transport hubs, targeting remaining sites of V1 'Doodlebugs' – 2,579 of which had landed on London and the Home Counties in one four-week period alone – and hitting aircraft factories and other industrial targets as well as fuel installations.

Flight engineer T/Sgt Barton flew five missions over France

and Belgium in fifteen days from 3 August after being transferred to the 493rd BG. In that period he had also got off base for a trip into nearby Ipswich and into London as well, but had been disappointed to find the 493rd too were now converting to Fortresses from the B-24 he was more familiar with and had spent 'days trying to get checked out on B-17s'. Then on 24 August he recorded in his diary: 'Hurrah! Briefed at 4.30 and bombed Kiel, Germany. Boy, what flak! The sky was full of it, but then it wasn't too accurate. Saw three ships explode. The sky was full of planes. Germany really caught it today. No. 21 completed.'[27]

But the strain of facing fourteen more missions before he could go home, together with the knowledge he had been lucky to survive so far when so many hadn't, now surfaced. Barton's next two entries read:

August 25th. Couldn't sleep last night. Lay awake smoking until 5am when all the boys had to get up to fly 17s on a practice hop. Had breakfast with them. Came back. Still couldn't sleep. Kept seeing flak and ships exploding. Took a shower and a shave. Shined my shoes and belt buckle. Going on a pass soon. Flying B-17 transition this afternoon. Going to the movies on Post tonight.

August 26th. Flew four hours of B-17 transition this morning. For the past two days a rumour has been spreading that Treece and crew are going home. It could be because the Group is sending quite a few crews home that have 20 missions or more in. Here's hoping anyway. We sure could use a rest from this Group. It would be the first break we've had.[28]

The new breed being introduced to the medley of mayhem that summer soon understood how little they knew, compared to the veterans such as Barton. Lt Alfeo Brusetti, a bombardier from Vermont, arrived in the UK a year after his sister Dee, who was posted to the 120th Station Hospital near Bristol as an army nurse. He hoped to meet up with her soon, but on 14 August he was introduced to combat with a trip to Mannheim, and appreciated it might be better if he made that date sooner rather than later. 'On return from our first mission we saw people pointing to our plane as we taxied by,' he wrote afterwards. 'We wondered what was up. When we got out and took a look we saw a long gash right under the pilot's window that peeled the metal skin back for several inches wide and many feet long. The wings and fuselage also had many holes. I had to ask an old timer if it had been a rough mission. He laughed at how green I was and said, "One of the roughest".'[29]

Others also were realising how much there was to learn. 2/Lt Terry Messing had arrived at Chelveston, Northamptonshire, as navigator in the 305th BG crew of Lt Doug (Hank) Schmidt. 'To us in America the war wasn't a big thing at first,' he says. 'We knew who Hitler was, but we didn't know how bad he was. We knew he had invaded these countries and he started bombing England and I guess we realised he was real bad at that point.'[30] Now there was no doubt for Messing he was in a war zone, hearing 'buzz bombs coming over' as well as experiencing flak over Germany.

The tail gunner on the crew, S/Sgt Keith Hereford, had the optimism of youth that his crew would not be harmed, however. 'I was 19 and I was sure I would survive my tour and within a month I was going to be home,' he says.[31]

There was time for one short pass to London for 2/Lt Messing and a chance to see a music legend. 'The big thing for me was to hear the Glenn Miller Band,' he remembers.[32] Major Miller's Army Air Force Orchestra, with its unique music, created by replacing trumpets with clarinets and getting the clarinet players and tenor saxophonists to play an octave apart, was *the* sound of the Second World War. The orchestra had arrived in June, mostly appearing from then on at airbases and camps throughout the UK, but there was a central London venue, the Queensberry All-Services Club in Old Compton Street, Soho, now the Prince Edward Theatre. Miller soon moved out of the capital with his band because of the danger of flying bombs. There were thousands of flyers in the 8th Air Force who heard him play, however, then had time to reflect on it in PoW camps in months to come. And across London and eastern England Miller's music helped to promote the social revolution the presence of so many Americans had created, youngsters who had access to the family radio twiddling out the BBC and tuning in to the new American Forces Network.

AFN provided a virtual non-stop evening programme of the sounds of Miller, Artie Shaw, Woody Herman and Benny Goodman. 'We listened nightly to American Forces Network,' remembered one typically Yank-struck English teenage girl living near Polebrook.[33] Luckier were those who heard and saw Miller conducting his AAF orchestra, such as at the concert at Great Ashfield, home to the 385th BG, where the band played for four hours. 'I have only got to hear one of his records on the radio and I'm right back in that hangar amid all the smells of men, oil and petrol etc.,' recorded one woman.[34]

The bloom of lush summer as girls twirled in soft dresses to the new swing music at airbase dances and wild flowers created an explosion of colour in the beckoning meadows were rare diversions indeed for combat airmen. The oil campaign was now increasing in tempo and combination with other raids by the USAAF as the Luftwaffe in the air and on the ground fought bitterly to defend such key targets. Western Union telegrams were arriving like showers of arrows into mail boxes across America from big city to small farm as the air war cut a swathe through the United States' young citizens serving in the 8th Air Force and in the 15th as well, flying in growing numbers from Italy to attack southern Germany and to Austria, where Wiener Neustadt, with its well-defended Me 109 aircraft factory, was a feared target.

One such cable pierced the heart of the Brainard family in West Palm Beach, Florida. It read: 'The Secretary of War desires me to express his deep regret that your son, William Brainard, has been reported missing in action since 23 July over Germany. If other details or other information are received, you will be promptly notified.' The telegram arrived just before the twenty-sixth birthday of T/Sgt Brainard's sister, Kay. There were four siblings in the family, in descending age Betty, Kay, Newell and then Bill. Newell had also joined the USAAF. Bill had been serving as a 15th AF radioman when he was shot down over Wiener Neustadt while Newell, eighteen months younger than Kay, was logging missions of his own as an 8th AF 2/Lt co-pilot with the 445th BG at Tibenham, Norfolk.

The Brainards had originally lived in Connecticut, moving south because of the father's multiple sclerosis which eventually killed him in 1932. The mother had then raised the four children on her own throughout the Great Depression and they were a close family. Now Kay, a vivacious and intelligent young woman, began thinking what contribution she could make to the war effort that might come close to that of her brothers. It started her on a journey which would bring her to England in the closing stages of the oil campaign.

10

'Some were blazing and some were blown to bits'

It was no less than a fight to the death. To America's bomber barons the crusade against the Luftwaffe's lifeblood must inevitably mean its fighter arm would be *kaput* in trying to defend it. Equally ruthlessly and in desperate attempts to postpone the final aerial *Götterdämmerung*, the Reich's leaders were prepared to throw at the Fortresses and Liberators the new jet and rocket aircraft still in their experimental stage. The advent of strange, propellerless aircraft in the air war proved a shock to American boys if not their commanders. For months reconnaissance aircraft of the RAF, which had first flown its own prototype jet – the Meteor – in 1941, had been recording on their camera film the clear marks of scorching along the runways at some airfields in the Reich signifying jet activity, and as June turned to July thirty airfields were categorised as having special servicing buildings which signified jets. On 25 July an RAF reconnaissance Mosquito was attacked by an Me 262 at 29,000ft near Munich.[1] Three days later Mustang pilots of the 8th Air Force spotted an experimental flight of rocket-engined Me163s near Merseburg.[2] And forty-eight hours after that the RAF felt it was now time to introduce three of its own jet pilots to operations, trying to shoot down V1 flying bombs over Kent. But throughout the whole conflict the Allies' only propellerless aircraft were never allowed to fly over enemy territory, in case of capture – a technological advantage in the air war thrown away by government inertia.

Fortunately the Nazis proved even more inept. It was 16 August before the Me 163s were hurled into combat, five unsuccessfully attacking 1st BD bombers near the Böhlen refineries. Sporadic ambushes by both the rocket fighter and the twin jet-engined Me 262 continued from then on, but never in large enough numbers in 1944 to make them a big threat to the B-17s and B-24s. Hitler had at first insisted that the new aircraft be employed as fighter bombers.

Hauptmann Heinz Knoke, *Gruppenkommandeur* of III/JG 1, which had been pulled back from France to the Rhineland in the retreat with few of its Me 109s remaining, wrote in his diary for 10 September:

> We fighter pilots in particular are anxiously awaiting the appearance of jet aircraft on operations. Following an idiotic order given by Hitler a few weeks ago the first jets to come off the assembly line are to be used only for purposes of 'reprisal' [*Vergeltungswaffe*] ... The German Fighter Command is slowly bleeding to death in defence of the Reich; our cities and factories are being razed to the ground practically without opposition with deadly precision by the British and Americans. And the only idea Hitler can think of is 'reprisal'. If only we could have one or two Wings operating with the new Me 262, there would still be a good chance for the German Fighter Command to save the situation. Otherwise the war in the air will be lost.[3]

There was certainly no shortage in September of replacement piston-engined fighters for the Luftwaffe, now the German aircraft industry had been reorganized and somewhat dispersed to underground factories by Albert Speer. That month 3,821 new aircraft were delivered, the greatest number since May, but only 144 were jet- or rocket-propelled.[4] Approaching four-fifths of the new machines were Me 109s and Fw 190s. The Luftwaffe day fighter force, which stood at 1,900 aircraft at the beginning of September, would number 3,300 by the middle of November – and rapidly decline from there.

But it was apparent there was already a lack of fuel to power the fighters and the replacement pilots to fly them were desperately under-trained. 'Almost every hydrogenation factory has been destroyed, and the fuel shortage has become a matter of very great concern,' Knoke recorded. 'Furthermore a major stumbling block to the rebuilding of my squadron seems to be the personnel problem. The vast majority of experienced fighter pilots have been either killed or wounded.'[5]

The scene was now set for a change in tactics, a new means of offensive defence in which the skill of the rank and file would not be so essential – mass attacks from heavily armed and armoured Fw 190s where only the leader was required to have learned the lessons of war. It was hoped that the surprise switch would cost the 8th Air Force so many planes and men it would have to suspend operations as had happened after both Schweinfurt missions the previous year. The unit IV/JG3 was chosen as the first to employ the new tactics in which instead of flying in pairs or in fours a single force of thirty aircraft, protected by high cover of patrolling Me 109s, would sweep down at a single point on the side of the bomber stream, which usually extended for a hundred miles. At that period in the war the stream was well protected by Mustangs at the rear and the front, but at the flanks only by fighters making random sweeps. And in individual bombers themselves it was at the sides they were at that time becoming the most vulnerable since the advent of the policy to reduce crew size

Navigator John Howland (front row, second left) with his crew after the much-feared second Big Week mission to Schweinfurt on 24 February. In fact more B-17s than 2/Lt Howland could count had just 'blown the stuffing' out of the target by visual bombing. His skipper James Tyson is far right and bombardier Frank Palenik, who with Howland would experience their combat position being shot up by Me 109s on a March Berlin mission, is far left. The aircraft they took to Schweinfurt was a war-weary example given to them as an unwelcome replacement for the brand new B-17 they flew across the Atlantic to start their tour only weeks before. (Courtesy of John Howland)

The crew of the 493rd BG's B-24 *Baby Doll*. They were each presented with signed copies of the photograph, but later *Baby Doll* was lost to another Group when the 493rd switched to Flying Fortresses. *Baby Doll*'s commander Lt 'Woody' Bowden is top left and engineer T/Sgt Bill Toombs top right. (USAAF; courtesy of Bill Toombs)

Above left Debach airman Jack Feller on pass in England. Jack and his brother Charles decided they wanted to be in the air force even before America entered the war. Jack was assigned as a clerk/typist in the control tower of the 493rd BG and his pilot brother flew Thunderbolts from Bottisham near Cambridge. (Courtesy of Jack Feller)

Above right Medal of Honor winner 2/Lt John 'Red' Morgan found himself at the forefront of action again as co-pilot in the Pathfinder aircraft leading the whole of the 3rd BD on the second raid to Berlin in March 1944. (USAAF)

Middle left Lt John Welch's crew outside Sack Time Hovel, the enlisted men's quarters, at Glatton. S/Sgt John Briol (bottom right) saw a Fortress crewman blasted through the aircraft fuselage in the savage Leuna-Merseburg air battle of 2 November. A total of forty USAAF bombers failed to return. (Courtesy of Marcella Briol and John Briol Jnr)

Bottom left Lt George Murasco of the 100th BG, with his ball turret gunner S/Sgt John Day (bottom left) and flight engineer T/Sgt Gordon Klehamer (bottom right). (USAAF)

The 486th BG's American Red Cross girls in their Aero Club at Sudbury. From left: Kay Brainard, Jean St Claire and Mary Jo Wymond. ARC girls had many reasons for volunteering to serve in England but none better than Kay Brainard, who set sail in the hope of finding out what had happened to her missing co-pilot brother. (USAAF)

Lt Robert O'Boyle (back row, far left) lines up with his crew outside their B-24 at Sudbury. The 486th BG navigator saw his fellow navigator wounded in the head on a pre-Invasion transportation-target mission in which raid leader Col. Beirne Lay Jnr, only days after taking over the accompanying 487th BG, was shot down with thirty other airmen. O'Boyle's skipper, Lt William Munroe, is second from left in the top row. (Courtesy of Robert O'Boyle)

Howard Roth joined the USAAF from high school and completed a harrowing tour with the 306th BG at Thurleigh from August 1944 to February 1945. The winter in hutted quarters at Thurleigh he remembers as bitter in the extreme for all aircrew. 2/Lt Roth (second left) had just been persuaded not to ask for Glenn Miller's autograph when he saw him in the American Red Cross Club at Bedford the night before he died. 2/Lt Doug Schrack (far left) is the buddy who talked him out of it. (Courtesy of Howard Roth)

Bombardier Lt Alfeo Brusetti began his tour with the 486th BG with a mission to Mannheim in August in which a flak hit opened the front fuselage for several feet. Brusetti's sister Dee was an Army nurse in England, and within weeks they had met up and later had this photograph taken together in London. (Courtesy of the Second World War Experience Centre, Wetherby)

Above Lt Leonard Coleman of the 100th BG is pictured with the film crew of *The Way to the Stars* at RAF Catterick in the summer of 1944. Coleman, whose tour had included tough oil targets and Berlin, was told after his thirty-five missions he could either go straight home to the States or wait and make a movie. Not surprisingly he and his co-pilot Lt Charles Gutenkunst chose to join the film business. Coleman is top left in the picture with Gutenkunst alongside him. (Courtesy of Leonard Aubert)

Right The 493rd BG crew of Lt Daniel R. Treece (third left), including engineer T/Sgt Ernest Barton, who kept a journal on his base at Debach, recording his fears. He had trouble sleeping because of combat stress. (USAAF; courtesy of Larry Johnson)

Fighter ace Bud Anderson, a major at twenty-two with sixteen and a quarter confirmed air kills and two probables. He is pictured with his Mustang *Old Crow* on the flight line of the 357th FG at Leiston just after completing his second tour. (Courtesy of Col Anderson, www.cebudanderson.com)

Left The 357th FG scored fifty-six victories over the Luftwaffe in an encounter near Brandenburg on 14 January 1945 after seven B-17s of the 390th BG had been shot down. Cptn James Browning (second left) claimed three of the Me 109s. Far right is Cptn Chuck Yeager, another of the Leiston Group's aces, who had had to bale out the previous March, but evaded the enemy to return to the Group and shoot down another seven Luftwaffe aircraft. (USAAF)

Right Lt Duncan McDuffie, of the 78th FG at Duxford, fixes a rabbit's foot on his flying helmet for luck after shooting down four Me 109s in quick succession near Ruhland on 2 March 1945. (USAAF)

Above Lt Louis Hernandez (right), shot down on the USSR shuttle mission of 21 June 1944, with to his left engineer T/Sgt Arthur Hutchinson and navigator 2/Lt Alfred Lea after Polish freedom fighters returned them to England. (USAAF and *Saturday Evening Post*)

Right Bombardier and navigator Lt Andrew Vero, who met the royal princesses when they made a surprise visit to the 306th BG base at Thurleigh. On Vero's penultimate mission a fellow bombardier asked him to exchange crews and that officer was then killed in a tragic collision. (Courtesy of Andrew Vero)

The 305th BG crew of Lt Hank Schmidt, in which twenty-year-old Terry Messing was the navigator. The 2/Lt was shot down by flak near the oil target of Misburg in November. It was his tenth mission and Messing, a big-band fan, had had only one short pass to London – just enough time to catch a Glenn Miller concert. Messing is second from the right in the front row, Lt Schmidt is second from the left and directly behind him is nineteen-year-old S/Sgt Keith Hereford, the tail gunner. (Courtesy of Terry Messing)

Visitors' day aboard Royal Navy Rescue Launch RML 512. The sailors rescued the crew of *Mizry Merchant* in July while acting as part of the British Air Sea Rescue screen in the North Sea for the USAAF mission to a flying bomb plant at Russelheim. Stoker Arthur Hickingbottom, who saw an airman desperately clinging to floating wreckage, is top left. (493rd Bomb Group Museum, Suffolk)

from ten to nine, by removing one waist gunner to supplement hard-hit combat troops on the ground.

On 7 July IV/JG3 swept down on a formation of B-24s from the 492nd BG, part of a stream of 1,100 USAAF bombers heading for a series of oil plants and aircraft factories in the Lutzkendorf and Leipzig area. Taking advantage of a gap in the USAAF fighter cover, IV/JG3 shot down twelve Liberators near Oschersleben within minutes. Only six bombers of the 492nd BG made it back to North Pickenham. Since introduction to combat on 11 May the 492nd had suffered a total loss of fifty-one aircraft in sixty-four missions – a greater attrition than any other unit in the 8th. Six had also been written off from other causes. On 5 August it was withdrawn from the bomber offensive. Another sixteen of the 2nd BD's Liberators were lost from other Groups on 7 July. A total of twelve Luftwaffe fighters also went down, but it was considered the blow to the USAAF was a vindication of the new tactics and now II/JG 300 and II/JG 4 were immediately ordered to convert to the *Sturmgruppe* role as well.

The 100th BG at Thorpe Abbotts, which had endured much in Big Week and on the subsequent Berlin raids, hardened its reputation for being in the wrong place at the right time once more on 11 September as the *Sturmgruppe* of II/JG 4 found the bomber stream, heading – more than 1,000 strong – for several oil plants and refineries. It hit the 100th BG as it was about to start its bomb run on a refinery near Berlin, and eleven bombers went down, a twelfth from the Group being damaged so badly it had to crash-land in France. A total of twenty-nine other bombers from different Groups were lost as various air battles raged.

2/Lt Warren Soden, navigator in the crew of Lt Orville Everett, was in one of the Thorpe Abbotts bombers which was lost. 'At briefing [we] were informed that we would encounter strong enemy fighter opposition, however, we would have heavy fighter cover,' he recalled. When the crew received their formation sheet before briefing they found their squadron was flying top position in the Group and their aircraft on the right wing was the highest of all, therefore highly likely to be picked out if the Luftwaffe attacked. 2/Lt Soden takes up the story:

> Southwest of Ruhland we were jumped by Fw 190s. I did not see any of our promised fighter cover and I had no confirmation from our gunners that they saw any P-51s or P-47s. From my window I did see one B-17 start down and one crippled Fw 190 go through our lead squadron on the way down. After several passes by the 190s 20mm fire knocked out our tail controls, both rudder and elevator. We started down and I could see the pilot's [Everett's] feet on the rudder pedals trying to get control. I baled out and on the way down I saw our plane almost directly below me.[6]

It seemed to be under control and 2/Lt Soden concluded Everett was trying to get below the 5,000ft cloud layer before baling out.

> However the plane exploded shortly before reaching cloud cover and I saw only pieces of aluminum floating down. I landed in a forest and was picked up by Germans soldiers and put in a panel truck with Manniello [the co-pilot]. We were taken to a building where cuts on my head [and Manniello's] were closed. My major injury was in my lower back, the chest straps on the chute opening had taken most of my weight with the result that I almost had a spinal separation. Ed Minton, the nose gunner, was paralyzed from the waist down due to his chute opening while falling at high velocity.[7]

The only other survivor was S/Sgt William Kenney, the tail gunner, unconscious from lack of oxygen when the plane exploded, tipping him into the air and ripping open his chute. Sgt Edward Minton was later reported by the Germans to have died in captivity.

2/Lt Frank Gerard, a Mustang pilot with the 339th FG, was credited with destroying one of the Fw 190s and no less than three of the Me 109s meant to protect them, in the attack. He was another of the high school graduates who enlisted in the Aviation Cadet programme, just out of his teens when he arrived at Fowlmere, Cambridgeshire, and remembers 'playing a lot of golf between missions'.[8] On 11 September he was flying Red 3 in Major John Aitken's twelve-strong 503rd Sqn when the *Sturmgruppe* pounced to hit the 100th BG in the side. At the time the two other squadrons of the 339th FG were elsewhere on the mission. The *Sturmgruppe* flew straight towards the bombers at a 90-degree angle, taking no evasive action even when Aitken, Gerard and their comrades began to close with them. 'I took their tail-end Charlie and he exploded after a short burst,' Gerard related back at Fowlmere.

My wingman, Lt Mayer, saw him in a spin with wheels down and pieces flying off. Just after we reached the bombers I got on the tail of a 190 and he also exploded after a short burst. Capt. Robinson confirms this kill. I then damaged an Me 109, but in the confusion of diving through the bomber formation, dodging chutes and debris, I didn't see what happened to him. I started after another 109, but had two more coming on my tail so pulled up in a tight turn. Soon after I was on their tail and gave the nearest one three bursts. He blew up and started down and I followed to see him spin into the ground. While going down Major Aitken passed me on the tail of another 109. He was getting strikes all over it. I pulled up and bounced another 109 and chased him awhile. When I did close he blew up on the first burst and went into a crazy spin. I claim 1 Fw 190 and three Me 109s destroyed and another 109 damaged.[9]

Gerard, who had shot down an Me 109 on 16 August, was now officially an ace with five victories, less than two months after his twentieth birthday.*

The next day it was the turn of another bomb group to suffer crippling losses near the Ruhland refinery in the second round of a major forty-eight-hour assault on the German synthetic oil industry. The Group was the 306th, which the equally young Howard Roth had joined just a month before. In the fast-changing world of combat flying where pilots usually either died or got promoted, the twenty-one-year-old was now an aircraft commander because his pilot 'Hoot' Gibson had been hospitalised with a serious virus.

Roth had flown the 11 September mission to an oil industry target at Lützkendorf, but had escaped attack because the Luftwaffe assault had been well behind him in the stream. Now he was heading near the Reich capital, for Ruhland, as he later recorded.

This was the roughest mission that I flew. When we made the turn north towards Berlin, three or four jet-propelled aircraft leaving contrails far above and travelling very fast were seen to sweep down on the column of combat planes from front to rear. There was a group straggling quite badly behind our Group, the 306th. As the jets were above this Group they described a kind of wide circle and their contrails being very distinctive it was as if they were trying to mark the spot. Combat wings in front were observed

---

* Gerard would shoot down three more fighters before the war's end, claiming two Me 109s on one day in March 1945 and going on to become a Major General in the peacetime Air National Guard.

to be turning too close to Berlin and the 306th BG leader began sliding off to the left when anti-aircraft fire broke out in the middle of the combat wing to the head and on the right.

Before our Group got entirely clear one aircraft in the lead Group and the leader of the high Group were hard hit. The lead Group held together pretty good, but the high Group lost altitude following the crippled leader. Low Group, trying to get clear of the anti-aircraft fire, was run into by another Group with a red diagonal across the tail, which was the 351st Group, and they came barging up on the right, directly through the formations, breaking up both of our Groups. At this moment about another 25 Fw 190s jumped the disorganised planes and I remember that I was trying to evade a plane that I was in a collision course with and almost in a vertical bank and still all the guns on the ships were firing away. The entire task didn't last more than five or six minutes, but accounted for seven 306th BG planes, one of which crash landed in England. And the 351st, the Group that ran into us, lost five planes, so there were 12 planes that were lost.

The P-51s went after the 190s and 109s with a vengeance. There were numerous dog fights and I don't know the number of German fighters shot down or vice versa. During the battle a black parachute whizzed by and as it was a black chute I knew at least we got one of the German fighters. I don't know whether you would call it a screw-up or what, but it lasted about six minutes and then all of a sudden I was all alone, deep in Germany and not too far from Berlin . . . I thought I was a sitting duck, so I figured I wasn't going to start letting down until I hit the North Sea. If they wanted to get me they would have to climb up to 30,000ft. I've got to give credit to the navigator. He was the same navigator who brought us across the Atlantic and he got us round the flak areas and we didn't draw any flak whatsoever and got back and landed safely. Then we found out that our Group lost nine aircraft, seven to fighters and two to flak.[10]

There was another Group, of a different bombardment division, which suffered the same horrendous loss rate that day. It was that of T/Sgt Ernest Barton, who had admitted towards the end of August he had trouble sleeping because of combat stress. On 12 September Barton's was among 217 crews of the 3rd BD despatched to Magdeburg, as he recorded in his diary.

Briefed at 3am. Took off at 7.30 to bomb an ordnance depot. The flak was heavy and accurate. We got a direct hit on No. 1. We are lucky still to be here. Capt. Coulter and crew went down over target. They have been with us since we first started training back in the States. It doesn't seem possible that they aren't here and yet I helped pack their belongings. Stiffler, their RO, missed the ride this morning and he feels like —. Doubt if he'll ever fly again. Our number was almost up. We flew alone over Germany. Fighters attacked after the target. I saw at least a dozen ships go down in flame. I was scared silly and I am not afraid to admit it. Hope I never have to pull another one like that. No. 24 completed.[11]

A total of nine of the 493rd BG's Fortressses failed to return that day.

Barton's fellow flight engineer at Debach T/Sgt Bill Toombs had missed the Magdeburg mission because the crew of Lt 'Woody' Bowden was on a stand-down in this period of double crews for every aircraft. But they were on the battle order the next day for Ludwigshafen, where synthetic fuel for the Me 163 was made. T/Sgt Toombs was now fully conversant on how the B-17 worked after the Group's switch from B-24s in August. Today, he remembers, that knowledge would pay off.

No doubt in my mind the worst mission we flew was to Ludwigshafen. The flak I didn't think was so intense, but as we went over the target we had No. 3 engine shot out and No. 4 fuel tank shot out. The waist gunner said No. 4 is on fire. I got out of the turret and went back to the bomb bay catwalk and I could smell that fuel siphoning out. It looked like smoke which is why the waist gunner thought it was on fire. We had lost the two engines, No. 3 and No. 4. We tried to keep up with the Group by putting full power on the remaining engines, but they overheated and we dropped out of formation. Paris had been liberated by that time and also a lot of Belgium and the navigator asked the pilot, 'Should we set a course for Paris or are we going to try to get back to England?' . . . The pilot said, 'If we can hold altitude we will be all right', but we kept losing height. We had started off at about 26,000ft and by then we were somewhere in the teens. I got to the bombardier and said, 'We'll drop the flak suits and all the guns', and then I said, 'We'll drop the ball turret'. I had had a little tool pouch, but someone had stolen the tools so I got the fire axe and started trying to beat the bolts off the ball turret. The pilot said, 'We are not going to make it back to the base.' They chose Brussels. I was still working on the turret. I could see we were getting closer to the ground. We made it to the airfield at Brussels and got the landing gear down.

The co-pilot told me later he got in contact with the tower and told them, 'We are coming in for a landing', and they said, 'You can't come in. We've got C-47s taking off. You've got to go around.' The co-pilot told them, 'Hell, we can't go around.' The pilot told me, 'Stop what you are doing on the ball turret and get in the ditching position.' The ball turret gunner was already out and practically everybody squeezed into the radio room. We were almost on the ground then and the Brussels tower kept saying, 'You can't land, you can't land.' The words the co-pilot used were, 'Come Hell or high water we are going to land.' We went over the back of the field for about a mile and put it down in a turnip field with the gear down. There was a fence at the end and instead of going through the fence we went right down it clipping the posts off. The dust was flying and when it came to a stop we all got out. The plane looked OK on the good-engine side, but on the other side it was all shot up. A Canadian jeep came and picked us up.[12]

The crew were promised a week's flak leave, but had to make do with a three-day pass to London.

Those crews at USAAF bomber bases laden with harrowing experience were beginning to feel they were living in a land of strangers as replacements arrived for the friends and the familiar who had gone missing. Howard Roth remembers how welcome the pubs near his base were to help airmen forget the stress of combat. 'We would always go into a pub in Bedford, either the Swan Lake Hotel or the Silver Bar,' he recalls. 'There were a lot of times we'd drink right up until midnight and then get back to the base about 12.30 or 1 o'clock and then we'd get called at 4 o'clock in the morning for a mission and we'd still have a bun on or feel a little bit whoosy or whatever, but once we got on the plane with maybe about 10 minutes of oxygen our heads were as clear as a bell. . . The air crew officers were very young, well paid, able to go wherever on free time and had plenty of their wild oats to sow.'[13]

After losing eleven crews near Berlin, the 100th BG was

preparing to mark its 200th mission of the war with a party to take place at the end of September. It would help to restore the shattered psyche of those who had survived the *Sturmgruppe* ambush, and it would raise the spirits of the replacements who after hearing why they had been posted to Thorpe Abbotts were wondering how long they had to live.

Major Harry Crosby was the Group navigator: 'The 100th could really throw parties,' he wrote in a memoir. 'For the 200th Mission Party, we signed up a whole carnival with Ferris wheel and rides. We invited almost a thousand English girls. In fact, whether she knew it or not, every girl in England was invited. Wars being what they are, and soldiers being what they are, we began to accumulate all the alcoholic beverages we could acquire.'[14]

T/Sgt Toombs enjoyed his time in London. He had been advised by another crew to visit a mother who had lost her son, flying Spitfires. 'She had a big apartment close to Selfridge's department store,' he recalls. 'She said: "Young men, you are welcome to stay here, but you will have no women and no drinking in your rooms" . . . We made the pubs. One I remember well, was a kind of unique place, Dirty Dick's. We drank our beer, but we weren't a crew that couldn't make their way home.'[15]

Toombs' Debach comrade T/Sgt Barton got his lucky break at last. On 15 September he wrote in his diary: 'Miracles have happened. The squadron has decided to give us a 7-day leave to the flak home. Scotland, here we come!'[16] In fact the rest home the crew was sent to was in Southport, Lancashire. Barton had several English relatives nearby and took his chance to see them. Within hours of arriving for R&R he was able to record: 'Left for Blackpool and arrived there in time for supper. Went out with Joyce to the movies. Stayed overnight.' The next day he 'went to Stanley Park in the morning, a beautiful place. In the afternoon Joyce, Joan, Doris and I went to St Anne's on the Sea, Pier A. Lovely orchestra. Missed the last train.' The following day he still hadn't spent any time in Southport and wrote: 'Joan and I went to North Pier and heard another good orchestra play some very beautiful music. Took Joyce to the show. Spent the evening at home.' Finally he went back to the Southport R&R facility the next day to get his pass renewed, then returned to Blackpool. On 20 September he recorded: 'Took Joan and Doris out. Went to Mdm Tussaud's Wax Museum. Spent the afternoon raising the devil with the girls and Aunt Lilly. Auntie Gertie came at 6pm and spent the rest of the evening'. And finally: 'Sept 21st. Left Blackpool at 8.30am. Aunt Gertie, Doris rode as far as Lytham with me. Played golf with Scotty [co-pilot 2/Lt James Welch]. Went to the movies.' By 24 September he had returned to Debach and recorded: 'Tonight a flying bomb just cleared our barracks by about 100ft. Boy, we could see it clearly.'[17]

S/Sgt Irving Saarima, the Wisconsin flight engineer whose missions had begun a month before D-Day, had acquired a bicycle and in the late summer got to know the countryside around the 486th BG airfield at Sudbury. 'One of my favourite routes took me to an air base near Lavenham, about five miles to the North,' he wrote after the war. 'Somehow I had learned that a buddy I had known in gunnery school was [there]. I had the opportunity to visit him two or three times and discuss topics of mutual interest. On my next visit I went to the hut where his crew lived and found a strange crew occupying it. My inquiry at headquarters confirmed my deepest suspicion, Sgt Gilbert E. Rodgers' crew and bomber were "missing in action".'[18]

Saarima used to pass a farmhouse on the road to Lavenham. 'I must have become a familiar sight to the family living there because I struck up an acquaintance with them,' he remembered. 'The English people were such gracious hosts. The farmer always offered me a bottle of home-brewed beer which I thoroughly enjoyed and in turn I gave my candy ration to two young London girls boarding there to escape the Blitz.'[19]

'Some were blazing and some were blown to bits'

Lt Robert O'Boyle, the navigator in the same Group who had met a 'hell of a lot of opposition' bombing a Hamburg oil target in August, also enjoyed meeting and talking to undemanding civilians off station in the ancient hamlet of Great Waldingfield beside the airfield. 'Where we were based wasn't actually a village, there was a church, a parish house and an intersection that's all, so I was never in the pubs,' he remembers. 'We got a local woman to do our laundry and we got friendly with a fellow who was down the road. He was the brother in law I think of the laundry woman and had a blacksmith's shop. I lived in the country before joining the service so knew something about horses and I would go down sometimes and chat with him and got to be pretty good friends.'[20]

On 17 September O'Boyle flew his last mission. It was to support the British paratroop landing at Arnhem and it was an easy one to finish on. He remembers:

We were bombing anti-aircraft gun positions. We weren't right on top of the British positions and there were no fighters up to meet us. We just bombed and flew home. At that time we were qualified to return to the States at 30 missions. But when the thing started over in England, and this may surprise, they were selling US War Bonds and we were offered a credit for a mission if we would buy a war bond, so we thought, 'Hell, we will.' There was another time when I had a sinus infection and as an individual couldn't fly, so I missed the mission and I ended up with 28 and they said, 'What the hell, you've been over here long enough.'[21]

Sheer luck decided who lived and died in the air war. For instance two days after O'Boyle, S/Sgt Saarima flew his own final mission from Sudbury – a transportation attack on rail yards at Munster – and narrowly survived to tell the tale.

The flak was about the most vicious that I had ever experienced. Our No. 2 engine was hit by flak so we had to shut it off and feather the propellor. I levelled my machine guns and kept my head down to get as much protection from them as possible. It appeared as though our bomber was flying in a giant popcorn machine, on high heat . . . Those ugly black bursts were to be seen flitting by in any direction that I looked. When we landed it was determined that we suffered 18 flak holes. Our weariness and relief overwhelmed our joy.'[22]

By now bombardier Lt Alfeo Brusetti had met up with his sister serving in England as an army nurse. 'We both received a 48-hour pass so I made arrangements to meet her half way at Oxford,' he recalls. 'I asked my pilot, Lt Bereman, to go with me. We left the base late afternoon and walked to Sudbury to catch a train that evening. We didn't realize that trains did not run at night, so we had to wait for the first train in the morning. We tried to rent a room in town, but to our dismay couldn't find one.'[23]

An ex-soldier in the Canadian army in the First World War heard their accents and offered to help. Eventually, Brusetti was able to report: 'He had made arrangements for us to stay in a private home if we didn't mind sleeping on sofas. We certainly didn't . . . and were made comfortable in the living room. Since it was quite late we almost immediately retired. The next morning at daybreak we left to catch the train before anyone was up. I've often thought how kind it was for this family in Sudbury to take us, total strangers, into their home.'[24] The bombardier could now report back to his relatives in Vermont that he and his sister had met.

In the States the families of those serving in the USAAF watched nervously whenever they saw *Western Union* appear on the street, on tenterhooks that the cable arriving might be for them. 'They tell me my mother had so many candles burning she almost burned the house down,' Howard Roth recalled.[25]

The Brainard family in Florida were aware by this time that Bill, the 15th AF son missing on a mission to Weiner Neustadt, was a PoW in Stalag IVB, thirty miles north of Dresden. Now the focus of worry was on Newell, flying with the 8th AF from England. His sister Kay, who had experience working in a West Palm Beach travel bureau and in a local military hospital, had begun getting the paperwork together to see what it took to train as a Red Cross volunteer.

Across the Atlantic the yellow fields of East Anglia had turned to lemon as the wheat and hay were harvested, the big Suffolk Punch horses hauling the creaking wooden wagons farmward. The leafy tunnels of narrow country lanes leading to airbase after airbase had begun to lose their sheen after wilting in the summer heat. Cooler days were here and soon the leaves would brown and begin to fall, spinning slowly earthwards like the Fortresses and Liberators wearily dropping away over oil targets as marching flak advanced and cut them down in a deadly harvest. If the young airmen considered it at all most would judge it a strange way to fight a war, being asked to face unbelievable horrors over Germany at high noon where their lives could end in an instant, then in the early evening returning to the utter peace and bucolic charm of a landscape which seemed locked in a different age.

Every village had its thatched cottages along what was often the only street, hollyhocks proud in each garden and the Norman tower of the village church standing tall at the end. There was the occasional glimpse of a stately home, such as Gissing Hall. Within five miles of it lay Thorpe Abbotts – itself built on a nobleman's land, that of Sir Rupert Mann – and three miles away was Tibenham. The eighteenth-century calm of rose-clad Gissing Hall was a world away from the flak and fighters of furious combat at the other side of the North Sea. Yet on most days as the shadows lengthened over Norfolk could be heard the Wright Cyclone engines of the Fortresses returning to Thorpe Abbotts, or the boom of Pratt and Whitneys from battered Liberators coming home to Tibenham, both types beating a haunting message of pain across the landscape.

Tibenham was the home of the 445th BG and Kay Brainard's co-pilot brother Newell. It was also the former base of Hollywood's James Stewart, who had acted as deputy lead for the 2nd BD when it went to Brunswick on the first day of Big Week. Stewart had finished his tour, but instead of going back to the States stayed on with the 445th as Group Operations Officer in the rank of major. He recalled in an interview after the war that before a mission, 'I always went out to the hardstands of the airplanes that were going whether I was on the mission or not. As I look back at it it wasn't so much a morale thing as checking equipment . . . It seemed you couldn't check these things, chutes, flak vests, electric suits etc., enough. Someone would forget something every time.'[26] Later he became the 453rd BG Operations Officer at Old Buckenham. In July Stewart had been transferred to 2nd Combat Wing HQ at Hethel and promoted to Lt Colonel, but he still kept an eye on what was happening with the 453rd and the 445th as well, sometimes flying missions with them. The 445th's mechanics had recently had much extra to do, removing the ball turret from each B-24 in common with all 2nd BD aircraft, to reduce drag and weight, thus allowing more bombs. The 445th had a good reputation in the 2nd BD. It had received a distinguished unit citation for accurately attacking an aircraft assembly plant at Gotha on 24 February during Big Week when the lead bombardier's anoxia had led many other bomb loads astray and since then had established an above-average bombing record. The Group hadn't lost a crew since 16 August.

In the late afternoon of 26 September the red 'mission alert' flag went up at Tibenham once more to prevent personnel leaving the base. The highly detailed process now began of preparing men and machines for combat. The minutiae of war required more clerks than heroes. They were not even counted among the thirty-eight different trades of GI it was calculated were needed to put each bomber into the air. The clerks were part of a chain of labour that began with the typing of weather reports by which the actual target was chosen; worked through to supplying maps for Group Navigators to plan the routes; accessed ordnance calculations to establish what bomb load would cause maximum damage to a specific target and supplied these to Bombardier leaders at Group; and even instructed the cooks how much grapefruit juice and coffee would be needed for each flyer's breakfast. It was a clerk who typed up the Mission Field Order from Division to Wing, from Wing to Group, and a clerk in myriad sections at individual bases who then produced each list which put an armed Group into the air – from bomb load to radio codes and call signs. Clearly the war ran itself on paper. Such a cacophony of typists' key clacking and ringing of carriage shift ended with the prosaic, but perhaps single most important piece of paper of all – the typed list issued to the Charge of Quarters which he employed when he knocked on a Quonset hut door and yelled out a name.

The crews of the 445th selected in this way had their dreams shattered at 3am. There would follow four hours of work, instruction, dressing, eating, checking, praying and recalculating before they would take off to bomb the Henschel engine and vehicle plant at Kassel, target for the day for more than 250 aircraft. Later at Bottisham, sixty miles to the south near Cambridge, the men of the 361st FG were called and told they would be among the 200-plus fighter pilots escorting the aircraft of the 2nd BD into the target and out again. There was a shortage of chairs and other equipment in the rude hut used for briefing – the 361st was transferring to Little Walden, in Essex, and some men and much furniture had already left. The move would be completed the next day and by that time the pilots of the 361st in their yellow-nosed Mustangs would have established an ETO record for shooting down eighteen enemy aircraft in one mission – five of them by one pilot and three by another – damaging seven more and destroying three on the ground. All for the loss of just two of their own.

The crews of the 445th were also about to establish a record, one they could not have contemplated as they tucked into their breakfast cereal, eggs and toast in the combat mess. There was no suspicion as they were trucked to the briefing room near the technical site, to listen to their CO and his staff leaders describe the target, the flak nests, the routes in and out of the Reich, that this mission would be extraordinary. And there was no knowledge as one by one each pilot started engines, inboard starboard power plant first, with that familiar Pratt and Whitney whine, cough and splutter, that what would happen within hours would soon become a legend in the aircrew pubs of East Anglia.

The lead, 700 Bomb Squadron, was the first to fire up, its ten Liberators nosing out from their dispersals and cautiously feeling their way onto the perimeter track to form a snaking line, barking like wheezy, waddling rustics in the early mist. 2/Lt Brainard was in this squadron. As a co-pilot he had entered his B-24 through the open bomb bay bowing down with all but two of the crew as if in homage then climbing on the ten-inch-wide catwalk to go forward to the flight deck. The exceptions were the bombardier and navigator who went aboard via the nose wheel hatch. Having checked everybody aboard 2/Lt Brainard was now sitting alongside the pilot Lt Ray Carron as the squadron moved slowly along the concrete followed by the twenty laden Liberators of 701 and 702 squadrons. The nine of 703 squadron, which would be the low-left unit in formation, were moving out when one ran its starboard wheel off the track into the mud, cutting a tyre. There would be a bomber short for Kassel.

The remaining thirty-eight lurched round in turn to wait at the head of the active runway and individually, as a green flare arced skyward from the control caravan to the left, bounced away, truly flying machines now, powerful engines booming and echoing across the field. Climbing and orbiting in the uncertain dawn light, pilots peered ahead to find the Group's distinctive assembly ship gaily painted in bright orange with thick black stripes, then gradually slotted into their places in the formation plan. Groups joined Groups, Wings joined Wings and the assembly ships, from the yellow and green check of the 453rd Group to the red polka dot on yellow of the 491st BG, wheeled away. So did three B-24s of the 445th BG, returning to base with mechanical problems. The run across the North Sea by the thirty-five remaining Liberators of the Tibenham force and the rest of the Groups in the bombardment division was uneventful, but as the bombers entered Germany from Holland the Luftwaffe was alerted and this time prepared for battle. The Mustangs swept back and forth along the column, scores of eyes peeled for the enemy.

It was not until the bomb run itself, however, that the carefully orchestrated plan of attack began to unravel for the 445th BG. There were two layers of cloud covering Kassel and the Group leader deviated to the left, as the rest of the bomber stream carried on course. Lt Frank Bertram, navigator to Lt Reginald Miner of the Group's 702 Sqn, realised what had happened: 'We went further left than we were supposed to,' he recorded in a post-war interview. 'I immediately called the pilot, Reg Miner, and said, "Hey we're going the wrong way! We're going too far left. Call the lead plane and find out what's going on." And he came back and said, "They said, Hold it in, hold it in." We kept turning further left and I thought, "We're going to miss the target completely."'[27] By this time Fw 190s of II Sturm/JG4 were already airborne from

239

Welzow and those of II Sturm/JG 300 from Finsterwalde, both of them south of Berlin. They were being guided west by ground radio stations and would soon meet IV Sturm/JG3. Me 109 *Gruppen* had also been alerted to fly top cover.

The Liberators which had taken off from Tibenham three hours before unloaded on what they had assumed was the target but was in fact a field at Göttingen. They then headed for the rally point and executed one left turn and three right turns according to the withdrawal procedure to make it back towards the west and safety. But the manoeuvring had expanded their loose formation and they stood out alone against the overcast. They were an ideal target for the *Sturmgruppen* which had approached using the cloud cover. At 10.10am two *staffel* of II Sturm/JG4 swooped down together in extended order. 'Within minutes the bombers stood in bright flame, ablaze, burning, bursting apart, losing wings, debris and entire engines with which some of our fighters collided,' Oblt Werner Vorberg, leading one of the *staffeln* reported.[28] He had waited until all four engines of a Liberator filled his sight so that he and his men following his lead couldn't miss.

S/Sgt Paul Dickerson, waist gunner in Lt Cecil Isom's *Patsy Girl*, described the scene from inside one of the 445th Liberators. 'Raymond Phillips, our tail gunner, called out fighters at six o'clock high ... In waves of ten and fifteen, Fw 190s poured in on us. Machine guns were firing ... everywhere B-24s, Me 109s and Fw 190s were falling. Some were blazing, some were smoking and some were blown to bits ... A German with a black parachute drifted by our right waist window.'[29]

Lt Miner's Liberator was among the first to fall, at Gnebeneau, thirteen miles south-east of Bad Hersfeld. 'More than a hundred German fighters pounced on our Group, flying about ten abreast. They rained destruction upon all our ships practically at once,' his navigator Lt Bertram later reported. 'Our gunners did what they could and many inflicted losses on their attackers but by then many of our ships were blowing up and roaring earthwards in flames.'[30] Only a few of Lt Miner's crew were able to bale out as the aircraft went down.

A twelve-year-old boy, Walter Hassenpflug, saw Lt Miner's B-24 plummeting, as he later related.

That morning the sound of the alarm sirens had meant that the children were sent home from school. It was a dreary day with clouds completely covering the sky. We were outside and suddenly heard the sound of cannon fire. Seconds later the debris of an exploding aircraft dropped through the clouds into a wooded area. Because of the double rudder assembly we knew it was a B-24. Several airmen were floating to the ground. I learned later that these were the crew members of J-5 FO 42-50961 [Lt Reginald R. Miner crew]. Five airmen were captured in this area immediately after landing.[31]

But while the five survivors of the Miner crew were floating down, other bombers were still falling, many of them in the area of Walter Hassenpflug's town of Bad Hersfeld to the south-east of Kassel. A total of twenty-five of the thirty-five Liberators of the 445th BG which had made it to the target area, including 2/Lt Brainard's, were shot down in less than six minutes.

S/Sgt Jack Laswell, left waist gunner in the Liberator of Lt Don Smith of 701BS, the highest-right position in the formation, remembers looking across to the right waist window and watching what appeared to be P-51s approaching in barrel rolls from the rear.

On looking closer, I could see that they were Me 109s with enlarged scoops underneath. At the same time, we saw red balls exploding in front of the attacking fighters. Then all hell broke loose. Following the Me 109s were a large number of Fw 190s. They were coming in from our rear and below.

It just happened that the ball turrets had recently been removed from our planes. The fighters would come in, fire, roll over and then head for another target. One Fw 190 came up on the left, between our tail and our wing, so close I could see his face. [Laswell fired.] I'm sure I didn't miss, his windshield was completely shattered . . . planes were going down everywhere . . . During the fight I saw a flight of four P-51s dive in to about 25 Fw 190s.[32]

The flight was led by Lt William Beyer, of the 361st FG and what was now about to happen turned the cataclysm of bloody chaos which had befallen the 445th BG into a disaster for the *Sturmgruppen* also. Beyer reported back at Bottisham:

I saw about 40 e/a as they broke through the bombers and headed for the deck, so I told my flight to drop their tanks. I picked a gaggle of about eight Fw 190s and attacked them from above and to the rear. I lined up with the last one and opened fire at about 400 yards closing to about 100 yards. I got hits all over the fuselage and wings, knocking pieces off and he started smoking then he ducked into the cloud layer. I throttled back to see what he was going to do and he came back up so I opened fire again getting more hits. He jettisoned his canopy and disappeared into cloud in a spiral to the right. I made a 360 degree turn to the right above clouds and told my flight I was going through the cloud layer. As I broke through I saw his parachute off to my right. I then flew up to a little town [Eisenach, near Bad Hersfeld] where I saw another Fw 190. By then I only had my wing man with me. I got on the 190's tail and he did his most to lose me, doing split esses and tight turns.[33]

The lieutenant's Mustang was equipped with the K-14 gunsight, an adaptation of the British gyroscopic Mk IIC sight which had only been introduced to the USAAF weeks before and allowed for accurate deflection shooting where the attacker effectively aimed at a point for his victim to fly into. Beyer continued:

I followed him through all his manoeuvres until he started to climb. I opened fire on him at about 100 yards getting hits. He jettisoned his canopy and baled out. I made a turn to the right and took pictures of the crash and also watched the pilot float to the ground. I pulled up to 1,000ft and spotted another one and made a pass at him giving him a short burst and he immediately jettisoned his canopy and baled out. I followed him down and took a picture of the crash. While I was chasing this one my wing man, Titus Red Two, saw one that passed underneath him and he followed it, getting hits on it. I then saw another Fw 190 and gave chase. I got on his tail and he gave me a good race for a while. This one chopped his throttle and threw down flaps to make me over-shoot and I saw what he had done and did the same. I had to fish-tail to keep from overrunning him. He pulled up in a gentle turn to the left and I opened fire, getting hits on fuselage and wings. He also jettisoned his canopy and baled out while I was still firing. I followed his plane down and got pictures of the crash. While I was chasing this plane Titus White Four, Lt Robert R. Volkman, had joined me. When another 190 made a pass at me Titus White Four got on his tail and before he could open fire this pilot baled out. I was flying south after I shot the fourth one down and saw another 190 approaching me from the south. I immediately pulled up into a steep climb and did a wing-over coming down on his tail, but he went into a turn to the left pulling heavy streamers. I had to put heavy flap down to keep inside of him.[34]

Beyer was finding it difficult to lay his gunsight, but gave the 190 two short bursts. His account, related within hours, of what happened next in this battle for supremacy at low level by one experienced fighter pilot against another is taut with tension.

He nearly hit the grass with his prop. I took several shots at him, but I got in his prop wash and he was skidding from side to side. We almost hit a tree, then he led me towards some power lines. I saw the pole sticking up, so I pulled up over them in a crab so I could keep him in sight and he went under the wire. I came down behind him again right on the deck and opened fire at about 75 yards. I saw hits around [the] engine. It was on fire. He went on into the ground and went into a house and blew up.[35]

Beyer, who had had one previous victory in his tour, was now an ace in a day, claiming five Fw 190s destroyed. The new ace also put his finger on what starving the Luftwaffe of its oil supplies for training had now resulted in. 'The enemy wasn't any too eager,' he said, 'when he found out his attacker could stay on his tail so most of them baled out.'[36] A total of twenty-nine German fighters were shot down within half an hour, eighteen of them by the 361st FG, the rest brought down by the B-24 gunners or collision among the whirling aircraft.

The Germans had accounted for twenty-two Liberators of the 445th BG over Eisenach alone. The battered survivors now fought to make it home to base. By the time the English coastline came up there were only six. Three had to crash-land at the RAF emergency airfield at Manston in Kent. That left only three more, of an original 445th BG force of thirty-five which had set out eastward across the North Sea less than seven hours before, to finally enter the circuit at Tibenham.

Lt Cecil Isom's *Patsy Girl* was one of the trio. 'We found the plane in front of us firing red flares for an emergency landing, there were injured aboard,' his waist gunner S/Sgt Dickerson remembers. 'The tower wanted to know where the rest of the group was . . . We told them that we were the group. By the time we landed and were getting our gear from the plane, we were surrounded by MPs. We were told not to talk to anyone. They whisked us off to a de-briefing room and locked us up.'[37]

In the Bad Hersfeld area young Walter Hassenpflug was investigating the crash site of one of the B-24s, that of the Tibenham-based Captain John H. Chilton crew. 'The debris* was scattered in the woods over an area of one kilometre,' he remembered. 'Four bodies were rescued from the front section of the wreckage.'[38]

Lt Colonel Jimmy Stewart had been alerted at 2nd Combat Wing HQ at Hethel to the disaster that had befallen his former Group. He was now speeding along the mockingly-peaceful country lanes in a jeep, past the same thatched roofs, cottage gardens and Norman churches only a few hours ago so familiar to airmen who were now dead. When he arrived at the Tibenham debriefing room he found some flyers so shocked they were temporarily struck dumb. 'Since he was a veteran of many combat missions and had led us on missions, he was aware of what could happen and seemed to understand as he calmed the meeting and listened intently,' S/Sgt Dickerson recalled.[39]

The shock of what had happened over Eisenach two weeks

---

* The section of Hesse Forest where Cptn Chilton's B-24 crashed now carries a stone monument in a clearing, describing the great air battle and listing all the American and German airmen killed. The cost of preparing the site was funded by local people and the plaques were paid for by Americans.

after the *Sturmgruppe* devastation of the 100th BG on 11 September did not of course cause, as the two 1943 Schweinfurt raids had done, a suspension of 8th Air Force operations as the Luftwaffe and the Reich's leaders had hoped, or even make the now Mighty Eighth break its stride. The next day the 2nd BD went back to the Henschel works at Kassel and ten aircraft of the 445th were among them. Only one of those had taken part in the previous day's raid, *Patsy Girl*. It had another crew. As standard practice Allied propaganda leaflets intended to demoralise by their accurate information were dropped with the bombs. Walter Hassenpflug, whose parents would be killed in a USAAF raid within two months, remembers: 'All local youths of the Hitler Youth, which included me, were hastily called together to pick up the leaflets and burn them immediately. In the process we found an American airman who was hiding. He was turned over to the police. Later I learned he was Lt Frank J. Bertram.'[40] Many of the airmen shot down were still unaccounted for – indeed one evaded capture until 6 October. The onslaught on the 445th BG had been so complete it would remain throughout the rest of the war as the worst loss suffered by any heavy bomber Group.

It had also been a disaster for the German Air Force, a virtual suicide mission. But even the Luftwaffe could make its presence felt in the Kassel area the next day, both in the air and on the ground. Bombardier Bill Ethridge logged his first mission over the Reich with a sortie to the Merseburg/Leuna oil complex on 28 September. Ethridge was born in Baden-Baden, Illinois, and his grandparents on both sides had been German immigrants to the USA. He had been earning the good salary of $125 a week at the Lockheed Plant in Burbank, California when he applied for the Aviation Cadet programme in November 1942. 2/Lt Etheridge, who had married in training, had been in the UK for only eleven days when he found himself on the 447th BG battle order for Merseburg in a 'war-weary B-17F . . . [that] looked like a dog', he wrote after the war from notes he made at the time. 'A prior crew had it painted purple and added a 4F skeletal-faced hooded figure of the Grim Reaper complete with a scythe over his shoulder . . . She was called *The Uninvited*. What a great start! Because we were the newest crew on the mission to Merseburg we flew tail-end Charlie, a position the German fighters just loved.'[41]

The route to the target for the twenty-nine planes of the Group took them within a few miles of the defences of Kassel and 2/Lt Ethridge saw anti-aircraft fire for the first time, as he later vividly recorded.

> Someone had described the flak as being so heavy one could walk on it and that was no exaggeration. [It first appeared] as ink-black clouds with hellish-red centres then as they enveloped the forward moving aircraft they became hail storms full of jagged bits of metal . . . I must have jumped a foot when a piece of shrapnel broke through the nose and hit the bulkhead directly behind me. A searing pain knifed across the back of my neck and I could feel a trickle of blood between my leather helmet and coat collar. The wound turned out to be a deep scratch, but I still have the scar as a souvenir.'[42]

Soon after the Group began heading east from the Kassel area enemy fighters showed up in number and Ethridge's tail gunner called up on the Interfone:

> 'Two coming in from 6 o'clock low and looks like they are headed for us.' Within seconds 109s had passed the squadron. One B-17, the left-wing man for the leader, turned downward with smoke flowing from his right wing . . . three chutes. The escorts peeled off in pursuit . . . I watched in horror as one of our P-51s slid directly in front of an Me 109 that had apparently circled back in anticipation of the

247

exact manoeuvre our escort had executed . . . The German pilot immediately opened fire and our fighter friend spiralled down trailing smoke. We did not see a parachute.[43]

Over Leuna-Merseburg Ethridge followed his training and hit the bomb release switch on a count of three after the lead plane's ordnance fell away. 'My Nordern sight was right on as it clicked,' he wrote. 'We did photograph the target through the bombsight. After developing we were pleased to see our specific squadron's bombs had scored several direct hits. As our escort group turned away we were immediately picked up by a whole flock of [US] fighters.'[44]

Ethridge and the navigator had noticed a drop in the right wing on the return flight and the pilot had issued a 'don parachutes' order. The crew chief later inspected the interior of the mainplane and discovered a cannon shell had sheared part of a bracket and link pin joining the wing to the fuselage. 'The crew chief estimated that one semi-violent manoeuvre or a wind shear could have collapsed the wing,' the bombardier wrote. This and the hundred jagged shrapnel and bullet holes in the air frame condemned the B-17. 'The Uninvited had flown her last mission and was pulled away to the salvage yard to be scavenged for parts,' Ethridge recorded. The flak and fighters in the Kassel area had proved a traumatic introduction to operational flying and it was too much for one man aboard. 'He reported to Headquarters the next day, stated his decision and offered up his non-com rank. Subsequently he was demoted to private and was assigned to various non-flying tasks,' the bombardier wrote.[45]

The mixture of despair, exhilaration, fatigue, gusto, torment and triumph that was the daily routine on the 8th's airfields went on. The 100th BG had now held its 200th mission party in style after a B-17 had been despatched to pick up a share of what the Group navigator Major Harry Crosby described as a 'huge supply of whisky and vodka which had arrived in London'.[46] At Debach flight engineer Ernest Barton was now approaching and sweating out the final missions of his tour. On 30 September Barton boarded the B-17 *Reluctant Lassie* for his twenty-seventh mission, a transportation target. Over Germany as Lt Treece headed down the bomb run towards the marshalling yards at Bielefeld, *Reluctant Lassie*'s bomb doors were slowly winched open as were those of Treece's fellow 493rd BG pilot 2/Lt Edison LaFlame, flying above him. Both released as the leader's ordnance went down. It is possible that Barton, who would have been in the top turret, looked up at that moment. If so the image of LaFlame's ordnance leaving the bay was the last thing he ever saw. A bomb from the B-17 above struck *Reluctant Lassie* and both aircraft exploded. Only one crew member from each aircraft survived, neither Barton nor Treece among them. The next day sixteen more telegrams were on their way to homes across the Atlantic telling families that their son, husband or father would not be returning from the ETO.

In West Palm Beach, Florida, the Brainards had already been told for the second time in two months of the Secretary of War's regrets about one of their Air Force sons. The family, who had been so relieved to hear that Bill Brainard was a PoW, were plunged into deep anxiety again, this time for Newell. Kay Brainard had now completed her application to join the American Red Cross and was waiting to hear when she would be needed for training to go overseas. She would arrive in a country where bombers crashing and exploding were leaving physical scars on the landscape and sometimes in the very lives of the civilians who had welcomed America's friendly invasion.

11

'All hell broke loose'

The impact the American air forces made on the people of rural England could be direct, shocking and even explosive. Bombers particularly fell out of the sky on a regular basis, sometimes onto a village below. One in six of the 6,537 Fortresses and Liberators of the 8th Air Force lost in the ETO were destroyed in accidents. Airmen arriving in Britain in 1944 to begin their tours were already aware how easy it was to die without a shot being fired. In 1943 alone when many of them were training, 20,000 separate accidents were recorded at airbases in the United States, killing 5,603.[1] If it was easy to kill yourself in the warm, clear skies of home it was even more feasible in England where the weather could change in an instant.

The most tragic event of all occurred at the village of Freckleton, just east of USAAF Air Depot 2 at Warton, Lancashire. Two refurbished B-24s took off on test early on 23 August 1944 before being delivered to the 2nd BD. Soon afterwards their pilots were ordered '*You are to land immediately*' because a violent storm was about to pass through. By the time they arrived in the airfield circuit visibility had been significantly reduced by the driving rain, so severe it was causing flash floods in Southport and

'All hell broke loose'

Blackpool. Lt John Bloemendal, flying *Classy Chassis II*, was on final approach from the west to Runway 08 when he reported to Warton Tower that he would 'go around', thus aborting. Shortly afterwards, out of sight of the second aircraft, *Classy Chassis II* was apparently in a low-level steep bank when eyewitnesses saw it hit a tree top with its right wing tip, then the corner of a building, ripping the whole mainplane away. The fuselage of the 25-ton bomber continued, partly demolishing three houses and the Sad Sack Snack Bar, which had been opened to cater for American servicemen from the airbase, before crossing the Lytham Road. A part hit the infants' section of the Freckleton Holy Trinity School. Fuel from ruptured tanks spilled out. What happened next wiped out much of a generation of the village. William Banks, working at Freckleton Post Office, looked out to the west immediately after the crash. 'I saw the tail of the plane in the centre of the road in front of the school – it looked like a lorry,' he told USAAF investigators. 'Almost instantaneously the school, highway and plane burst into flames. This was preceded by a vivid flash of lightning at the most severe part of the thunderstorm.'[2]

Teachers and small children, aged four to six, many of whom had only begun school the day before, were engulfed in a sea of flame. Ruby Currell was one of the children who survived. 'I remember . . . all hell broke loose. I saw a girl fall over and I got under a desk,' she said. 'The morning was a bright one, assembly had finished and we were at our desks receiving instruction of the lesson we were to do that morning. Suddenly the sky went dark, so dark the lights in school had to be put on.'[3] Then as the rain lashed down and the thunder rolled the plane hit two classes. Although the rest of the school was still standing the older children had to be got out to safety quickly. On that desperate morning seven children and two teachers were pulled from the rubble of the infant classes, but as the hours and days passed, the teachers and four of the children lost their battle for life, their injuries too severe.

When the bodies were counted after the fire was finally extinguished and the mortally injured had succumbed, the death toll came to thirty-eight schoolchildren and six adults. In the Sad Sack Snack Bar, fourteen more adults were dead – seven Americans, four RAF personnel and three civilians. The three US airmen on the B-24, including Lt Bloemendal, were also killed. Ruby Currell suffered severe burns to her body, but while recovering in hospital she had a surprise visitor – Bing Crosby, the singer and film star, who was touring US bases in England. The official USAAF report into the crash, noting that many of the pilots coming to the UK commonly believed poor English weather was little more than showers, recommended that in future all US-trained pilots be emphatically warned of the dangers of British thunderstorms.

Two months later a sixteen-year-old boy was mortally wounded and eight aircrew killed instantly when a Flying Fortress of the 486th BG suffered an engine failure on take-off from Sudbury and tore the roof off a house. Major Smith and his family were asleep at Woodhall House Farm when Lt Clarence Herrmann turned his Fortress onto Runway 25 in the darkness and gunned his engines. But as he thundered down the concrete headed for Cologne at 0537 it became clear to onlookers the reverberating roar of No. 4 engine had now died. A minute later, as Lt Herrmann desperately tried to gain height, the aircraft hit the upper floor of the building just beyond the runway. Major Smith woke to hear his wife screaming and the upper floors of the house burning furiously. His daughters quickly appeared, but Raymond Smith was trapped in a blazing bedroom. His father managed to clear away debris and the teenager emerged. He was walking, but his face and hands were terribly burned.

As the family escaped, other aircraft of the 486th BG were roaring overhead at low level having just taken off in turn, their tail gunners looking down on the inferno below and the debris of what moments earlier had been a fully laden B-17 now strewn across a field. All of Herrmann's eight crew were dead, but he had been thrown clear, burned and with severe brain injuries. Raymond Smith died the next day. Both American and British authorities had been anxious to move on from the Freckleton disaster and now this particularly horrifying accident involved British Allies once more. When a B-17 came down on the village of Parham, Suffolk, a few weeks later, therefore, local newspapers were aware of the need to accentuate the positive – the fact that although there was considerable damage no civilians were killed.

Flt Officer James McQuire's aircraft *Gloria Ann* had growled and echoed down the main runway at nearby Framlingham in freezing fog headed for marshalling yards at Frankfurt. But just after lift-off the B-17 struck a row of trees. The aircraft, heavily laden with bombs and fuel, bounced off a railway line at Parham, demolished the village chapel, came to rest against a bank alongside the Parham–Framlingham railway then exploded. 'Visibility less than 200 yards. Flt Officer McGuire took off at 0834 hours,' the 390th BG control tower log recorded. 'His B-17 could not be seen from the tower and the duty officer noted that it sounded like a normal take-off. About a minute later flying control heard the explosion.'[4] The district newspaper related: 'The crew were killed instantly – inside the plane and [an]other being thrown some distance away. Yet not a single person in the village was seriously injured, although most of the houses were damaged. The gatekeeper of the local railway station, Mrs Snowling, was blown from her kitchen into another room, but as she termed it "gathered herself together" to reach the phone and warn an approaching train that the lines had been torn up.'[5]

There was no apparent logic to who would die and who would be saved as bombers plunged out of the sky onto English villages and countryside. Fate's death sentence pointed at random to both rich and poor, powerful and weak, the high and the low of society. In August, less than two weeks before the Freckleton disaster, the son of a former American ambassador and brother of a future President, was vaporised in the largest explosion in British skies in the Second World War. Lt Joe Kennedy had completed a tour of anti-submarine patrols from the US Navy airbase at Dunkeswell, Devon, when he volunteered for a series of secret missions known as the Aphrodite Project to the US Army Air Force and the Anvil Experiment to the US Navy. The theory was to load warweary Liberators and Fortresses with more than 21,000lbs of the British explosive Torpex – stuffed into the fuselage in hundreds of boxes between flight deck and bomb bay – have a pilot and co-pilot take off and point the aircraft in the general direction of the selected target then have them bale out over Britain after an accompanying plane had taken over radio control of what was in fact a huge flying bomb. It would be sixty years before air warfare by drone became operationally successful and then by unmanned aircraft from start to finish.

Kennedy – whose isolationist father Joseph had ended his ambassadorship to Britain in 1940 after it was revealed he believed the UK would soon be invaded – was the hope of the sixth such mission. The experiments so far had indicated he was part of little more than a suicide club. On the initial operation eight days earlier four stripped-down USAAF B-17s had lifted away with the purpose of taking out V-weapon sites. The first had spun out of control and crashed after the pilots baled out; the second went down at Sudbourne, Suffolk, killing the command pilot; the third tilted out of control and came down near Orford, by the coast, killing the co-pilot and exploding with such force it was spread over two acres. Only the final plane got as far as its target zone of Watten, north-east France, but even that crashed 1,500ft short. On 6 August three more B-17 flying bombs took off, all aimed at Watten. Just one got into enemy territory before it came down.

'All hell broke loose'

The other two went into the North Sea – the second of these making circuits around the unwitting naval base of Ipswich at 2,000ft for several minutes (its vast load of ordnance fully armed) as the crew of the mother aircraft desperately tried to correct its flight path. When they successfully did so it also went down into the water, but fortunately away from the coastline.

Now it was decided to try with a single B-17 against Heligoland. One of the crew was killed when his parachute failed to open on abandonment and later, almost predictably, the B-17 went into the sea. A mission to Heide, in Schleswig-Holstein, was little more promising. Three aircraft failed before the target was reached because of radio-control problems, though the fourth hit the ground near enough to cause significant damage and casualties.

It was time for the US Navy to be given its chance – in the shape of Lt Kennedy, whose father had such high hopes of him making President, and his co-pilot Lt Wilford Willy. By one of those strange coincidences of war, flying 300ft behind Kennedy was the son of the then current American President. Colonel Elliot Roosevelt was aboard a Mosquito from the 25th BG Photographic Wing he commanded, to observe the mission, aimed at blowing apart the vast Mimoyecques super-gun site in Pas-de-Calais from which Hitler had hoped to launch 6,000 shells a day on central London. In fact, unknown to the US Navy, the RAF's Dambusters squadron had already destroyed the super-gun capability, so the mission wasn't necessary at all. Kennedy and his co-pilot took off from Fersfield at 6.05pm and climbed over the golden wheatfields of Suffolk heading south-east for Framlingham. At Dresser's Cottage, Darsham, Michael Muttitt, a keen plane-spotter at nine, heard it coming. The stripped-down Liberator levelled out at 2,000ft, assembled with its escort including the radio-control master aircraft, turned north for Beccles and Kennedy took his hands off the column to let the radio mother ship fly the plane. The Liberator had completed one turn under radio control when the crude television camera in the nose was switched on to aid guidance in the final stage of the aircraft's flight. Two minutes later and eight minutes before Kennedy and Willy were due to bale out the bomber blew up. It was over New Delight Wood at Blythburgh, Suffolk. The huge blast immediately felled hundreds of trees as it rolled over them. An eyewitness described how where the drone had been there was now a yellow sun with smoke edges and flame shooting straight up and down from it like a pair of fireworks. In an instant, the centre had become a greenish-white cylinder of fire, flat at the top and squeezed into an hourglass-shape in the middle. Michael Muttit recorded his memories of that day in later life.

> I watched in horror as the lead aircraft exploded in a huge fireball. I vividly remember seeing burning wreckage falling earthwards while engines with propellers still turning, and leaving comet-like trails of smoke, continued along the direction of flight before plummeting down. A Ventura broke high to starboard and a Lightning spun away to port eventually to regain control at tree-top height over Blythburgh Hospital. While I watched spellbound, a terrific explosion reached Dresser's Cottage in the form of a loud double thunderclap.[6]

As the blast expanded in seconds at least sixty houses in Blythburgh and other homes in Walberswick, Thonington and Hinton were badly damaged. A total of 147 properties were affected, some up to fifteen miles away. Fortunately the only deaths on the ground were among farm animals.

In the air it was a different matter, Kennedy and Willy had simply vanished and Roosevelt's son also nearly died when the Mosquito he was flying in was thrown into a spin, the pilot recovering only a few feet from the ground. Young Mick Muttit was on the scene the next morning. The blast had occurred directly over his grandfather's house at Blythburgh Fen. 'Damage to property was widespread,' he recalled.

> Grandfather listed 'roof tiles dislodged, all ceilings down, walls cracked, glass blown out of windows'. Similar damage occurred at a second cottage nearby and at Aunt Ada West-gate's Shepherd's Cottage one mile north-east of the datum point . . . Most of the lighter wreckage had fallen directly below the point of detonation, where a fierce fire had burnt a large area of heath land. The heavier, engines, propellers, and main undercarriage assemblies were found over a mile to the north. A poignant reminder that lives had been lost was provided by the tattered fragments of parachute silk and cord entwined amongst brambles bordering the B1125 Westleton to Blythburgh road.[7]

The wreckage of Lt Kennedy's aircraft was scattered over an area three miles long and two miles wide. An investigation decided the aircraft had exploded because there had been no electrical shielding to prevent rogue electromagnetic transmissions opening up a solenoid which had set off a detonator. There were various theories about where the deadly transmissions had been made, including that they came from a tank crew in training below or from an unwitting radar establishment. The radar station had been sending out a continuous stream of signals in a bid to jam German V-weapon launchers.

Joseph Kennedy's planned political heir had disappeared and post-war the former ambassador began grooming his younger son Jack for the White House. We can only speculate what might have happened if by that chance of fate Joe and not Jack had become leader of the free world. How, for instance, would Joe have reacted in the Cuban missile crisis which brought the world to the edge of a nuclear war and was averted by the American President's superior brinkmanship?

Cpl Jack Feller, the USAAF control tower assistant whose own pilot brother had been lost in April, recalls the day he met the affable Lt Joe Kennedy just before he died.

One day in August, 1944 I was on duty in the control tower of the 493rd BG at Debach when an odd-looking B-24 landed and was parked near the tower. On the radio the pilot asked that an MP guard be put on the plane and no one was to go near it. A Captain McFarland, who had recently completed his missions at Debach, got out and came up to the control tower with a US Navy officer. The navy officer knew Lt Moore, who was duty officer in the tower. They were like home-town buddies greeting each other and soon Lt Moore started introducing the navy officer to the other men in the tower. He said, 'This is the ambassador's son, Joseph Kennedy' . . . The B-24 had no markings or numbers. It had no waist gun windows, no nose guns and in place of the top turret was an open cockpit. McFarland and Kennedy went to the Debach movie theater to watch a top secret movie with other technicians on guided missiles and remote control.[8]

The Aphrodite Project continued haphazardly throughout the late summer and autumn, two B-17s being directed in the general area of Berlin because precision Aphrodite attacks were an obvious failure. But like the others they failed to get anywhere near even a large target such as the Reich capital, one of them going down in the North Sea and the other in Sweden. The US Navy launched only one other Anvil mission after losing Lt Kennedy, an attempt to hit U-boat pens in Heligoland in September. The explosive-packed bomber flew into an island in error. The final USAAF radio-controlled mission took place on 1 January 1945 against Oldenburg, Germany. Both B-17s were shot down by flak before reaching their power station target. Finally on 27 January Carl Spaatz ended the whole sorry experiment, thereby averting the possibility of another disaster over the UK.

If some sections of Britain's population were at risk from the USAAF others were prepared to actually reach out into danger to save American flyers. They were members of the Air Sea Rescue Service provided by the RAF and Royal Navy. The USAAF bombers which plunged into the English landscape were weighed against a significant number ditching in the North Sea and English Channel as their crews struggled to bring their crippled machines home after a mission. Those airmen were almost entirely dependent on the host nation to save their lives.

The Air Ministry, who had learned much in the Battle of Britain, had agreed in September 1942 to provide air-sea rescue (ASR) services for the Americans via the RAF and Royal Navy, a welcome gesture as the 8th Air Force made its first tentative forays into mounting a bomber offensive. By that time the British had an efficient joined-up rescue structure linked by a communication network in which emergency calls from airmen in trouble deployed spotter aircraft within minutes to locate crews in their rubber dinghies, followed by speeding surface craft. But at first the USAAF was slow to grasp what was needed both in training its own airmen to prepare for ditching and in utilising the British services available to rescue them.

Most US flyers, for instance, had an entrenched view that it was better to bale out of a doomed aircraft over the sea rather than try to put it down in the water. This belief had some justification in Groups equipped with Liberators. The official wartime history of the USAAF recognises that the high-wing design of the B-24 severely reduced the chances of a crew surviving a ditching. 'In a forced landing at sea the fuselage had to absorb the whole impact, and often the bomb-bay doors would fly open and the plane would break in two, either just forward or aft of the wing roots,' it admits. But conversely: 'Flying Fortresses ditched well because of a rugged structure and a hydrodynamic shape that prevented porpoising or diving under the surface as the plane hit the water. Since the low midwing absorbed part of the initial shock and added buoyancy, an undamaged B-17 might float half an hour or more.'[9] The general sluggishness by the 8th AF in supplying personal rescue aids to its airmen similar to those issued to British flyers – which would include signal mirrors, sea-marker dyes, coloured smoke, and, where possible, a dinghy radio – together with inefficiency in coordination, meant that in the whole of 1943 only 28 per cent of 8th crews reported to be in distress over the sea were saved. Yet even two years earlier the RAF was rescuing a third of its own crews who had gone into the water.

A British Air Council memorandum dated 8 November 1943, pleading with the Admiralty for forty more Motor Torpedo Boats to be converted to rescue launches to add to the fifty already in use, reveals that in the nine-month period to October 4,320 Allied aircrew were involved in forced landing in home waters and 'a further substantial increase is expected in 1944'.[10] The 8th finally took appropriate action.

'Despite the tardiness and incompleteness of the AAF's efforts to provide its own emergency rescue squadrons, the record suggests that a growing awareness at AAF Headquarters of the importance of air-sea rescue paid good dividends,' the official USAAF history relates.[11] Those changes included appointing the 65th Fighter Wing to operate a rescue-control station at Saffron Walden in Essex specifically tasked with fixing the location of American aircraft in distress. In September 1943 VIII Bomber Command assigned one bomber per group to search along the routes of its missions on request from Air Sea Rescue. And now, exactly one year later, 90 per cent of AAF crews forced down at sea in the ETO after the surprisingly heavy casualties as the autumn of 1944 approached, were recovered. That efficiency would be maintained throughout the autumn and until the end of the bomber offensive, a collective total of 1,972 American airmen being saved by British and a few US rescue units in the waters around Great Britain by March 1945.

Where an aircraft ditched and at what time of year made an enormous difference to chances of survival. In a chart produced by the Air Ministry as the USAAF began to improve its record in ASR, 88 of 113 ditchings close inshore in the Channel and North Sea in the spring and summer of 1943 were shown to have ended in successful rescue compared to only 16 out of 114 further out in the same period. It was towards the end of that time frame that British ASR launches carried out the largest rescue in one day of USAAF personnel, 118 American bomber crewmen being pulled from the North Sea on 6 September 1943, after their aircraft ran out of fuel because they had been ordered to orbit assembly points for too long while a decision was made whether the weather was suitable for them to continue to Stuttgart. They would not have survived later in the year.[12] In the autumn and winter, if an airman depended on his life jacket to keep him alive in the water, death from hypothermia was rapid. It set in at only two degrees less than normal body temperature of 37 degrees centigrade. First came the shivering as the body attempted to maintain its core temperature by diverting blood to the internal organs. Within twenty to thirty minutes, depending on the amount of clothing and other factors such as weight, age and health, shivering would cease as there would be no more energy left in the body to keep it going. There would then be a rapid fall to 30 degrees where an airman would become disoriented, then unconscious.

If they didn't now drown because their life jackets had not proved efficient enough to keep their mouths above water, body temperature would continue to fall to 28 degrees where heart-beat irregularities would occur, finally ending in cessation of the heart muscle at 20 degrees. Even if the airman had made it to a dinghy his demise was only postponed, not prevented, his soaked clothing producing the onset of the same temperature losses as if he was in the water, but over a longer period.[13] Those sent out to search for a ditched bomber crew always knew they were in a race against time.

On 7 October 1944 a Flying Fortress of the 457th BG went down in the water returning from an oil industry target and Howard Roth, now commissioned, was tasked with looking for it in the heaving expanse of the grey North Sea. 'Another pilot and myself were sent out on air-sea rescue,' he remembers. 'They give the navigator a grid and we work this grid to see if we could spot the downed airmen who would be in a couple of yellow rafts. We must have worked the grid for a good hour, but then we spotted them and those guys were waving and the navigator called the position and we circled for another 45 minutes to an hour until the air-sea rescue boat located them and took them in. That made us feel good.'[14]

The day before, 2/Lt Bill Ethridge, the 447th BG bombardier wounded on a mission to Merseburg, ditched in the North Sea with the rest of 2/Lt Vladimir Mateyka's crew. They had been shocked to discover the objective for what was only their second operational sortie was Berlin. The 4th Combat Wing, of which the 447th BG was part, lost fourteen Flying Fortresses on the mission in a mass attack by German fighters, but it was anti-aircraft fire from the Reich capital's flak positions that doomed 2/Lt Mateyka's plane with hits on two engines and damage to gas tanks. He battled across Holland to keep the aircraft flying as it spewed fuel and all detachable equipment was thrown out to reduce weight, from guns to fire extinguishers. The B-17 stopped losing height, but as the crew crossed the Dutch coast all tanks showed empty and putting down in the North Sea became the only alternative. The pilots picked out a trough in the heaving, froth-flecked grey waves and made a perfect ditching. The rest of the crew were braced in the radio room. 'We exited one by one via the top hatch as soon as we hit the water. The exiting was orderly and surprisingly unhurried. The pilots had popped out the side hatches after hitting the water and a 10-man rubber raft was waiting on each wing,' Ethridge related. Eight of the crew had made it to the rubber dinghies, but then had to help the co-pilot, 2nd Lt Keith McCall, extricate the pilot who had a head wound after hitting the windshield on ditching. 'To our amazement the B-17 stayed afloat for an hour,' Ethridge continued. 'Three P-51s appeared and circled overhead almost immediately after we ditched, hopefully getting a fix on our position . . . Darkness settled . . . Occasionally an iceberg the size of a bathtub floated by . . . the waves were high and angry . . . about every third or fourth wave crashed the rafts, keeping them filled with water and causing violent seasickness . . . We had nothing to bail with except our hands . . . We had to fight against an overwhelming hopelessness.'[15]

But the British Air Sea Rescue services had now been alerted by the US 65th Fighter Wing at Saffron Walden and the next morning the RAF 280 Sqn, which was equipped with ration-packed, motorised airborne lifeboats slung beneath their twin-engined Warwick rescue aircraft – seaworthy craft which the USAAF would not adopt until the following spring – dropped the boat by parachute. 'It settled in the water less than 500ft from us and we cheered the accuracy,' the bombardier wrote. After the exhausted Americans reached the 20ft craft an Fw 190 appeared, chased the RAF plane into cloud and signalled the USAAF crew's position to its headquarters. The skipper of the RAF aircraft, P/O Hagg, would report back at RAF Beccles in Suffolk that as he left the area his rear gunner saw the survivors making 'a rather weak attempt to reach the boat. Apparently they had been weakened by fatigue and sickness and were suffering from chronic immersion, hypothermia. The wind and sea presented horrifying conditions.'[16] Underneath the lifeboat's hooped-tarpaulin weather-shielding the Americans began to recover, however. 'With the flush of anticipating a weekend in London we made short work of the biscuits and water. They were delicious,' Ethridge recorded. They chugged on hopefully towards England when at 1500 hours a Luftwaffe Dornier 24T flying boat appeared, circled and landed. 'They took us aboard slowly, searching for our side arms,' the bombardier wrote. 'Inside an officer said, "For you the war is over."'[17] The Allies had lost another battle to save a highly-trained bomber crew to fly and fight again. But rescue by a British launch cannot have been far from hand. The small craft of the Air Sea Rescue service carried enough fuel to stay away from their base for seventy-two hours if the cruising speed of 15mph wasn't exceeded from the twin 650hp engines.

In 1944 Arthur Hickingbottom was an eighteen-year-old crew member of Royal Navy Rescue Launch RML 512, part of the RN Coastal Forces base HMS Midge at Great Yarmouth. His rank was Stoker First Class, which meant he was the assistant mechanic in a total crew of sixteen comprising three engine room hands, the Captain (Don Mackintosh) and his First Lieutenant, the Coxswain, six seaman/gunners, two telegraphists and a sick-berth attendant. The rescue launch's geographic location meant it was usually called out for standby duties in the North Sea, covering the outbound and inbound routes of USAAF bombers after the details had been supplied from Saffron Walden to the Royal Navy and RAF when the 8th AF mission field order came in. 'It was difficult to know what you were going to finish up at,' Hickingbottom remembers. 'The Navy only told you what you needed to know.'

As engine room staff we only knew from the time we left harbour and what revs were called for that gave us roughly a distance we had sailed. We did work out that the three ships of our group were in line with the flight path, first one about ten miles off the English coast and next one halfway and the third one about ten miles off the Dutch coast. This was rotated each day. Where the rest of the flotilla was we never knew, it was like living in a bubble. Time at sea was mostly waiting around for something to happen or if sent on a search tracking backwards and forwards in the allotted area, assisted by US and RAF planes – after hours of searching often drawing a blank. The condition of the sea did not help as the North Sea could be very choppy and tide and wind had to be calculated accurately or you could be searching in the wrong area.[18]

The weather and sea state were often threatening – very daunting to the uninitiated, as the former stoker recalls.

One day our base at Gt Yarmouth was visited by two USAAF airmen who were sent to find out what the difficulties were on ASR patrols. We were chosen to take them aboard. As we were classed as sea-going ships we went out in all weathers. This day our waiting position was halfway to the Dutch coast and the forecast was not good. We had to be in position before the bombers flew over and then hang around until they returned, then we got the recall to base or a new position after it was established no aircraft had ditched in our area. As we had guests aboard we were to go straight back to base. The airmen reportedly said they found the experience interesting but not pleasant and would sooner be flying over Germany in flak.[19]

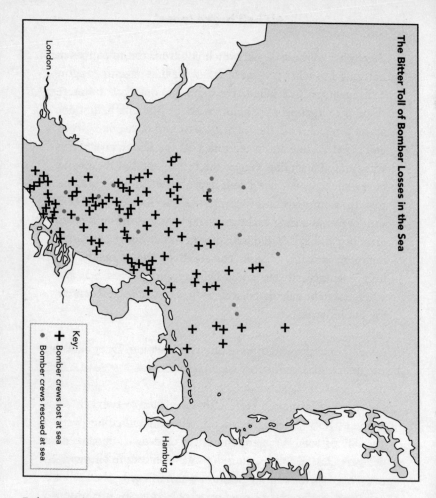

London.

Key:
+ Bomber crews lost at sea
• Bomber crews rescued at sea

Hamburg.

Each cross on the map represents a bomber crew, the great majority USAAF, lost in the North Sea in one six-month period. There are eighty-four, seven times more than the dot symbol for rescued crews. The chart, using figures to the end of September 1943, was prepared by the British Air Ministry in answer to what was seen as general tardiness by the 8th Air Force to adopt the lessons the RAF had learned in the Battle of Britain about saving airmen from drowning. A year later improvements that included a specific US rescue-control station at Saffron Walden and assigning one bomber from each 8th AF Group to search along the routes of its missions on request from Air Sea Rescue meant 90 per cent of AAF crews forced down at sea in the ETO were recovered – usually by RAF or RN special launches. By March 1945 a collective total of 1,972 American airmen had been saved by British and a few US rescue units in the waters around Great Britain.

It wasn't just the weather which could make the patrols dangerous. One day in 1944 the crew of RML 512 were returning from a fog-bound standing patrol off the Dutch coast when they came across elements of the *Kriegsmarine*.

By dawn the fog had turned into a fine mist and after about an hour's sailing time the sun started to break through and then to everyone's amazement three German E-boats came into view ahead of us. The action stations was sounded and everyone scuttled to their positions not knowing what to expect as each E-boat could outgun us at least six times over and we fully thought we would be blown out of the water. What a scare! But simply nothing happened. We sailed through their ranks one on the port side and two on the starboard side.[20]

Apart from taking on board survivors rescued by other craft there was an incident weeks later when the crew saved USAAF airmen from the waves directly. The B-24 *Mizry Merchant* of the 493rd BG ditched in the North Sea after flak damage to a gas tank and engine caused a massive fuel loss on the bomb run to Russelsheim's vehicle works. The crew of RML 512 had been on station thirty miles off the Suffolk coast waiting for more than three hours in the summer sunshine for the bombers of the 3rd BD to return. They had tuned into the emergency-band radio which all USAAF aircraft were now equipped with, as gunners stood by on the small craft looking out for German fighters. The launch's skipper Lt Don Mackintosh related years afterward:

Around noon, the first Mayday calls came over the radio – far away, faint and confused. Gradually they died away. We never found out why. Many possibilities went through our minds, some we preferred not to dwell on. However, on this occasion, there was one call that persisted, and grew stronger and clearer. Control headquarters ashore responded with course instructions that would take the casualty to a track where rescue craft would be most able to respond quickly should it have to ditch. Alternatively, the plane might remain airborne long enough for it to be guided to a friendly airfield. We could only await developments, and make our preparations should we be called into action.[21]

The Mayday calls continued as the main bomber force passed to the east of the lone launch, then one particular call increased to an 'almost overpowering' level on RML 512's radio set as Lt Mackintosh and his crew headed for the assumed flight path, as the skipper recalled.

I had only been on the move for a few minutes when a lookout shouted 'Aircraft Red Four Five'. There, to the north-east and clearly visible to the naked eye, were three specks against the sky, low over the water. Through binoculars these showed up as a B-24, with a P-47 on either side as escort. Nearer still, and it could be seen that the Liberator had no engine power and that the plane was on a long, low glide. It was simply the speed of the descent that enabled the pilot to keep his plane airborne for long enough to be able to make a successful touchdown . . . the plane eventually hit the water on an even keel, sending up a great wave of spray.[22]

The pilot, Lt Lyle Wikenhauser, had made an excellent landing in the sea, given the Liberator's characteristics, but it didn't stay afloat for long. Lt Mackintosh continued:

We were, by then, a little more than a mile away, and the plane had ditched right ahead of us. In the seconds it took the disturbed water to subside, the plane had disappeared, and in its place were men floating among the waves. Two men were clinging to a wheel, but there was no other wreckage. The plane's dinghy, which should have surfaced, had not done so. But for our being on the spot and able to take the survivors on board, they would have had to wait for a rescue boat to reach them, and shock and hypothermia would almost certainly have taken lives. It is a tribute to the Air Sea Rescue control ashore for their deployment of the rescue boats along the bombers' flight path, and the skill and courage of the Liberator pilot and crew in keeping airborne for long enough for us to be able to reach them so quickly. [One man was missing, however.]

Before we radioed details of the rescue to base, I took a last look at the apparently untroubled sea, and I saw, almost alongside, the body of an airman floating upright just beneath the surface. Our crew got a line around him and hauled him aboard, where our paramedic spent a long time trying resuscitation, but it was hopeless. Quick though the rescue had been this casualty must have been under water for all of fifteen minutes.[23]

The body was that of the plane's bombardier, 2/Lt Carl McClendon, who was in his position in the nose when the aircraft went down.

Down in the engine room young Arthur Hickingbottom looked through the portholes in short snatches as he tended the idling machinery. 'I remember seeing an airman clinging to some wreckage and I learned later that he would not let go to catch a line so our coxswain swam out with a line, tied it round the airman and to himself and they were both pulled to safety,' Hickingbottom says. 'I later saw McLendon's body respectfully covered with a tarpaulin placed on the deck aft of the sick berth.'[24] The launch's

White Ensign was lowered to half mast in tribute to the dead officer as the boat returned to Great Yarmouth.

Drowning was just one of the ways of dying the young US flyer could contemplate in his darker moments, trying to sleep in his cold Quonset hut after a mission. Other possibilities included being torn to pieces by flak or fighter shell; burning alive, pinned inside a blazing aircraft by centrifugal force as it spiralled faster and faster towards the earth; or simply drifting away into a sleep never to waken from as enemy action destroyed personal oxygen supply. But the death that seemed the cruellest was where one American airman killed another, simply by collision. It was an increasing danger as larger air fleets took to the sky and flying conditions worsened with the passing of summer.

AUTUMN

12

'Bodies were scattered all over the area'

The British weather came high in the list of bellyaching by the average American airman. The typical summer's day was described several times in print as rain in the morning, followed by more rain in the afternoon. There was even more to complain about now that the English autumn had arrived. The leaves might look pretty as they drifted slowly down in russet showers, red and pale yellow over country lanes, but it was also a period of the year when the mists rolled in from the North Sea, clamping the flat Suffolk and Norfolk countryside in a grey cocoon of damp which inevitably penetrated the soul. The weather was even being altered by the USAAF itself. Fleets containing well over 1,000 bombers with the same number of fighters were routine at this time and the trails in the sky of their passage caused condensation from their exhausts in the high cold air to turn the local sky white, thus blocking out any sunshine to those below and lowering the temperature even further.

Gathering such huge formations together over East Anglia in the created overcast was fraught with danger. Keeping the individual bombers tightly tucked together in their assembled Groups heading out over the North Sea above conflicting pockets of chill and even colder air was perilous too as pilots fought to control their bucking machines. Veterans of the 306th BG remember the mission to Hanover on 22 October 1944 as a particularly black day, without the intervention of the enemy, as 2/Lt Howard Roth recollects.

The mission was marred by two collisions involving our Group. The first came around noon when we were climbing over toward the Dutch coast. We were to bomb a foundry and at 12,000ft and in a slight climb Alyea [Lt Harry J. Alyea, from Michigan] was leading the high squadron. I was flying the right wing of the lead and we were making a slight turn to the left when one of the planes called him and asked what his air speed was because that pilot was indicating 140 and usually we were at 150. I was on the outside and I was at about 150 so I wasn't too concerned. I had a grandstand view of what happened next.

In formation you have the lead, the left wing and the right wing and the ship flying what we called the hole is in back and directly underneath down below, so it's not flying in the lead's turbulence. The hole ship slid ahead . . . and I think it created a kind of low-pressure vacuum because it looked to me that the hole plane was just sucked up into the lead ship. As soon as it hit, the lead ship went up and sharp-banked to the right and the wing came in contact with the center of the hole ship. The hole ship broke in half and I could see the waist gunners tumble out of the opening and about 12ft of the wing of the lead ship broke off and it spiralled down . . . Captain Joseph Mathis was the pilot of the hole ship. I was talking to him before take off and he had said this would be his last mission and he would be heading home to see his wife and two kids and he was really happy about it. It really affected me to think that now that would never happen. I told the navigator to call in air-sea rescue. He gave them the co-ordinates and they picked up Sgt Hastings Key, the sole survivor of Mathis's ship, within 45 minutes. He was shot down on a later mission and became a prisoner of war.[1]

Years later at a Group reunion Howard Roth had his photograph taken with Sgt Key, who later wrote across the print, 'Thanks for the radio call skipper.' Roth says: 'Key can thank the navigator for giving accurate coordinates to Brit Air Sea Rescue. To see 17 of your buddies die in full view I'll never forget.'[2]

The 306th bombardier Lt Andrew Vero, who had met the royal princesses at Thurleigh and was now approaching the end of his tour, had been scheduled to fly in Cptn Mathis's aircraft, but had switched places with another officer, 2/Lt Brill, who also was one mission short of going home. Lt Vero remembers:

Captain McKee, my original crew pilot, was trying to get all of the crew to finish together as we came up to our 34th mission. I was qualified to fly as a bombardier or DR [dead reckoning and short-range radar] navigator which made it easier for the scheduling officer to place me. The night before the mission to Hanover Ivan Brill, another bombardier, came to ask me a favor. He was in the room next to us and only needed one mission to go home. He had been waiting to fly it for months, but he had lost all his crew and had to wait for a spot. He had also just received a letter from home which had him very upset. He said he had talked to Operations and they said since I could fly as bombardier or navigator maybe I could switch with him. I said OK if the scheduling officer agreed and they put us both on the same mission. I didn't want to end up losing a chance to fly my own mission as this would be the 34th for me. As it turned out on the mission I was flying in the No. 2 aircraft in the squadron with Brown as the pilot.[3]

That chance switch made Lt Vero the sole survivor of his crew. Air Force records show Cptn McKee flew as co-pilot to Lt Alyea in the lead plane on the mission and was therefore killed. The rest of Lt Vero's crew with Brill were flying in the No. 4, plane, the other aircraft that went down, commanded by Cptn Mathis. The mission to Hanover continued without further loss, not one of the 171 aircraft of the 1st BD tasked with hitting the foundry being shot down, but it was not the end of witnessing sudden death in the air for the men of the 306th BG, as 2/Lt Roth describes.

Before we got back to base the ceiling was down to about 800ft. One squadron was approaching from the east and was well in sight when another squadron broke out of the gloom on the south side of Thurleigh. Reportedly both squadron leaders saw each other, were in radio contact and agreed that the west-bound group would climb and the north-bound group would descend. All went well until the last of the north-bound planes went up instead of down and collided with the tail-end plane of the west-bound group. There was a horrendous explosion and two crews totalling 17 men were killed. Bodies were scattered all over the area and one of the runways. Falling debris started several fires around the base and the incident caused great anguish among those who witnessed it. There was a picture taken of the collision . . . I went by the hospital and got a glimpse of the unloading of body parts out of the emergency vans. It was a horrendous scene all over the base. I completely blanked it out of my mind and still can't recall any details.[4]

2/Lt Walter Douglas, the ex-sergeant telephone maintenance supervisor, was now mid-way through his tour with the 305th

BG and nearly had it brought to an abrupt halt that day over Thurleigh as he headed for his home base of Chelveston in a haze at no more than 150ft.

> A B-17 suddenly appeared in front of us. We barely missed it. Then two B-17s hit head on to our left. Some aircraft were forced to dive and touched the tree tops. I decided to land at the base that was under my aircraft (Thurleigh). I just figured it would be best to get on the ground. Parts of two B-17s were scattered along the runway with bodies of the crews. I called my base and advised them that I was getting married the next day in London and to send some transport-ation. Somewhat to my surprise they did. So we left our aircraft at that base and got back by truck. I got married the next day to an English girl I had met on my first time in England.[5]

Lt Vero finished his tour a short time later and went back to the States. 'I sometimes feel like a ghost . . . ,' he says. 'Ivan Brill's request to switch places with me still haunts me.'[6]

Most 8th AF flyers experienced or at least saw a near-collision at some time in their tour. 2/Lt Roth remembers: 'We had to stay close in formation to stay in sight of the plane we were meant to. If we drifted out of sight we were in deep trouble.' Keeping that plane in view was a monumental task. 'Any pilot when you're up 8, 10, 12 hours on a mission and all you are doing is keeping your eye on the lead plane you are flying off of and keeping it close, you can't move your head for any large amount of time . . . Every once in a while I'd look ahead and you could see this stream of bombers, maybe two Groups, and sometimes you'd see a huge explosion which meant there was a direct hit on the bomb bay and of course there'd be nothing left.'[7]

It was only when an airman was back safely on the ground

that he had time to think about what he had seen. 'What was heartbreaking was when they [the quartermaster's staff] would come in the barracks and remove the personal effects of fallen comrades, including photos of their loved ones,' Roth says.[8]

Assembly was a particularly complex operation in which any tiny displacement by any aircraft in the assigned order of Groups, Wings or Air Divisions could throw out an entire schedule. F/Lt George Millington, the Beaufighter navigator at RAF Coltishall in Norfolk, shocked by drunk USAAF enlisted men in Norwich, was now impressed by how many aircraft the Americans had to gather together from the bases surrounding his own. 'They would rise like a swarm of insects to orbit . . . After about an hour when the airfields would have hundreds of circling aircraft over them they would all merge together in one vast swarm, perhaps a thousand aeroplanes moving out over the sea . . . It was very quiet after they had gone.'[9]

The harshest European winter in decades was now approaching and the individual collisions of October would be overshadowed by many more as conditions deteriorated. The elements of threes trying to find Group commanders in the murk over radio beacons would become disoriented, delaying Group assembly, which would then hold up Wing assembly. Sometimes Wings departed a Group short, with that unit desperately trying to catch up over the sea. Yet all Groups were supposed to be in train at exactly 150mph. If they didn't it caused a concertina effect where the further in the rear a Group was the further it got strung out and lost the protection of the rest, thus becoming a prime target for fighters. It was a daily recipe for disaster and collisions were frequent in the tussle to gain protection of the mass.

Lt Col. James Stewart concluded that 'the most complicated part' of the 8th Bomber Offensive 'was the assembly, getting together different Groups from numerous airfields situated all over East Anglia and lots of time in marginal weather, getting them into formation at one point at a certain time to arrive, so that each group had its own place.'[10] Eventually the leaders of the 8th Air Force came up with a plan. 'To cut down on mid-air collisions the bombardier had a red light and the tail gunner an amber light that they flashed in clouds,' recounted 2/Lt Douglas.[11]

The 8th mounted major missions on eighteen days in October leaving few periods for its crews to recover. What brief rest time they had was spent sleeping or leafing through magazines or newspapers in worn and split leather armchairs in the base Aero Club library or officers' quarters day room. There was little to be seen in *Stars and Stripes* or *Yank* magazine or *Air Force* – the official monthly journal of the USAAF – of the missions they were currently flying. By late 1944 the press corps at Supreme Allied HQ in France had 1,000 war correspondents filing three million words a day and the land war they wrote about was now dominant.[12] But for once in the US airman's newspapers and magazines there was a lot to be found about women, not just the pictures of Hollywood stars which would decorate hut walls, but about girls in the Army Air Force. The great contribution the women of America were making to the war was finally being fully recognised by the service press.

The October issue of *Air Force* had as its cover picture Lt Frances Sandstrom, one of the USAAF's flight nurses, who were known as 'Air WACs' to their male comrades. The reporter for the magazine admitted 'we were looking for someone very pretty' and spotted the girl from Air Transport Command taking a sightseeing trip in Manhattan. Lt Sandstrom – who like all flight nurses wore aircrew wings over the left pocket of her olive drab Ike jacket with an N where the shield of a pilot would be – was now on the transatlantic air evacuation run for wounded airmen and soldiers who were out of combat for good. But the USAAF magazine wanted to talk to her about her earlier experiences. Lt Sandstrom had been stationed at a 9th Air Force troop carrier base in England and watched with other nurses the C-47s take off for Normandy on the night before D-Day then waited anxiously for them to come home after they had dropped their paratroopers on the other side of the Channel. 'We knew most of the crews as we had been restricted to the base so long. I guess we nurses were like a cheering section at 0200 when they began coming back. As soon as we could see the number of a plane we'd yell, "There's Jack . . . there's Mike . . . there's Jimmy, hooray!" she said.' On D-Day plus nine Lt Sandstrom made her first flight to a casualty clearing station in the beachhead, the C-47 putting down at a newly completed metal-strip runway. 'The troops were fighting only three miles away and we could hear land mines exploding around us,' she said. 'About sundown we went back to the beach and picked up our patients, 16 litters and two ambulatory patients . . . They were dirty, right out of the foxholes . . . Each time I gave a man a drink, he smiled, or tried to, and thanked me as if I had done something very heroic and wonderful.' Since D-Day the girl from a Washington town called Opportunity had made five flights into France and thirteen Atlantic crossings.[13]

By October 1944 more than 150,000 women were serving in the US Armed Forces, abroad as well as at home, but the number would now remain fairly static and only weeks earlier *Stars and Stripes* had reported retrospectively: 'Recent sharp increases in WAC and WAVE enlistments have brought the strength of both women's military units to authorised quotas. The WACs had 77,000 members on active duty July 1st while WAVES had an enrolment of more than 70,000.'[14] The Women's Army Corps had also celebrated its second birthday with the anniversary of its members' first year of service in England. Figures were slightly outdated by October, but in May more than 4,000 had been on duty in the UK. Their numbers were now boosted by American girls already here. The *Stars and Stripes* issue for 16 October 1944 reported:

> Forty-three new WACs will be sworn into service in London today. They are all American citizens who have been working and living in Gt Britain. They form the second group of American gals in Britain to join the WAC, the first group, numbers 44, having come into service on Aug 31st. The new WACs include schoolteachers, officer workers, store and factory employees. Two sisters are among them, Patricia and Pamela Marmont, daughters of Percy Marmont, an actor of fame during the days of silent movies. Patricia* herself is an actress and delayed her entry into the service in order to complete a picture.[15]

Yank magazine had already displayed on its front cover a picture of Lois Konantz of St Paul, Minnesota, who had joined the WAC in London as a Pfc. The magazine said she had 'transferred from the Women's Auxiliary Air Force of the RAF where she'd been serving for almost three years' and she was shown wearing her WAAF uniform with a US steel helmet.[16]

Airmen on the combat stations of the 8th Air Force seldom saw a WAC. They were usually based at Wing or Bomber Command or Fighter Command headquarters, some of those at the latter base being employed as plotters moving symbols around a chart table to mark an aerial battle as the WAAF had done in the Battle of Britain. Those British girls had been known as the 'beauty chorus' and it seemed no accident that the WAC plotters

---

* Patricia would in fact appear in a 1949 comedy film about the WACs, *I Was a Male War Bride*, starring Cary Grant, and had a successful post-war career on British TV. Pamela was in the 1954 Noel Coward play *After the Ball* at London's Globe Theatre.

working alongside top brass were all good-lookers too. The only American women the young men who flew combat missions saw were Red Cross girls, of the kind Kay Brainard wanted to join, who gave out refreshments to crews as they entered briefing huts after a mission and ran the enlisted men's dances at base Aero Clubs twice a month. The American Red Cross had spread its appeal far and wide. Even General Spaatz's daughter Katherine, known as 'Tatty', was an ARC girl, helping to man a Clubmobile unit which visited East Anglian bomber bases handing out the coffee and sticky buns the 'doughnut girls' were famous for.

There were a few exceptions, however, to the WAC exclusion from combat bases. Cpl Grace Sharkey was one of them. Cpl Sharkey, who had assembled aircraft instruments at a Philadelphia plant before joining the WACs in March 1943, was one of a group of female Link Trainer instructors who had been sent to England in the summer of 1944 to hone the skills of pilots and navigators on the heavy bomber fields. S/Sgt Beryl Harris, of Colfax, Illinois, was another, helping to train flyers of the 306th BG at Thurleigh in automatic pilot procedure, 7,706 hours of instrument training being given to 1,120 combat pilots and navigators at the Bedfordshire base.

However, Cpl Sharkey's time in England was the most dramatic among the group. She was awarded a medal for an act of heroism when the bomber she was flying in crashed, the story being related in the army newspaper in November. She was said to be travelling as an 'observer' in a newly-modified B-24 from her base at Cheddington, Buckinghamshire, when it suddenly banked and lost height over the Biddulph area of Staffordshire, then struck a tree, the No. 3 engine bursting into flames as the aircraft ploughed into a field. 'The ship was blazing fiercely,' the story ran, under a headline of 'Icy-veined WAC Saves Crew'. Cpl Sharkey told the reporter:

'Smoke filled the interior and everyone seemed too stunned or injured to move. For a minute I thought we were trapped . . . The only way out seemed through the nose. I kicked out the Plexiglas and crawled through the opening. Some of the other crew members were stirring then and I helped them out. The navigator (Karl W. Ruthenbeck) was right behind me. The pilot and I helped the radio operator (T/Sgt Ralph A. Sandmeyer) – the last one out – just in time.' A few seconds after Grace and the crew had cleared the plane six explosions shook it. The pilot, Lt Tommie E. Leftwich, of Pine Bluff, Arkansas, said: 'She acted quickly when time was the difference between life and death.'[17]

Cpl Sharkey was nominated for the Soldier's Medal and the crew named their replacement aircraft *Lady Grace* after her.

Cpl Sharkey wasn't the only WAC in England to win a medal. S/Sgt Becky Sharp, a stenographer at the headquarters of the 2nd BD was photographed in November having a Bronze Star pinned on by General Kepner 'for meritorious achievement' assisting officers of the 2nd BD's part in the Invasion. 'She was the first WAC to be so honoured in the ETO and worked 16 hours a day,' the story ran.[18] Cpl Sharkey also wasn't the sole WAC to be honoured by having her name on a plane. In the new spirit of recognition for America's servicewomen *Stars and Stripes* began a competition in the autumn to find the most attractive WAC in the ETO. It had begun in early October with the GI paper publishing a picture of a good-looking girl soldier whom the newspaper staff dubbed 'ETO's Prettiest'. Airmen and GIs alike were quick to respond with letters detailing the charms of their own favourite all-American girl in the service and *Stars and Stripes* decided to make it a full-scale competition week by week with a prize at the end.

Ruby Newell was one of the early contenders, the front page

of the army newspaper reading: 'Below is a picture of WAC Ruby Newell, of Long Beach, Cal., submitted by the Joes and GI Janes of the 8th AF, 3rd Bomb Division, as their choice to bear the title "ETO's Prettiest WAC". Say her backers: "Our Ruby has blonde hair, blue eyes and dimples as well as all those other little characteristics of feminine pulchritude so pleasing to the eye. Ruby's picture, appearing in newspapers and magazines, has adorned GI barracks in the States, foxholes in the Pacific, Africa, Sicily, Italy and France."'[19]

By mid-November selection was down to the final seven. 'The girls arrived in London Saturday night and appear before judges Sunday morning,' a *Stars and Stripes* reporter wrote. 'Sunday afternoon they attend the Army–Navy football game at White City Stadium where attractions will be noted at half time. Monday night contestants and judges will attend Tommy Trinder's *Happy and Glorious* at the Palladium. They will be guests of honour at Rainbow Corner for the second anniversary (Sunday) dance.'[20] Tension was now high among the newspaper's GI readers and on 14 November Ruby Newell was announced the winner with her prize revealed as 'a portrait photograph by a well-known former Hollywood artist now with a serial number'. The officially recognised glamour girl in uniform said: 'I know I'm in for a lot of kidding when I get back to my base. I like to eat, the more the better, and for some reason thank heaven it doesn't show in my figure.'[21] Within weeks a B-17 of the 385th BG would be flying over Germany with *Ruby's Raiders* in honour of Cpl Ruby of the 3rd BD staff emblazoned across its nose, portrait included.

Not everybody in the United States approved of the competition or of nose art and pin-ups in general. After the German propaganda coup in the winter when shot-down bombardier Lt Ken Williams was pictured in German newspapers wearing a combat leather jacket with *'Murder Inc'* inscribed across the back, there had been a general clampdown on bomber nose art to ensure it wouldn't offend the top brass. But although there was less of it at this stage of the bomber offensive, it was considered so good for crew morale most Group commanders either actively encouraged it or wisely turned a blind eye. Not all nose art or jacket insignia showed a shapely pin-up. T/Sgt Frank Petrucci, a flight engineer with the 351st BG, now heading back to the States in the autumn at the end of his tour, remembers: 'The name of our aircraft was *Our Lady, Queen of Heaven*. She protected us. We got through our tour without a scratch. There were a lot of holes in the plane at times, but nobody got hurt. All our missions were memorable. When you get up at 2 o'clock in the morning and have to face German fighters and everything else it's kind of bad. One time coming back from Berlin I went and lay down. The first thing I heard was *kerpow!* Flak hit my guns and the ammunition chute and dropped down right by my feet. It was a big piece of shell and I've still got it today.'[22] The name on a plane's nose was seen as a talisman by its crew and just as there were all kinds of crews there were all kinds of names from the sacred, such as T/Sgt Petrucci's, to the profane *Mountain' Time* above a painting of a reclining, naked blonde on a B-24 of the 487th BG at Lavenham.

Then there were the pin-ups of beautiful, pneumatic, scantily clad blondes that were the speciality of the artist Alberto Varga for *Esquire* magazine. The wartime US Postmaster General Frank C. Walker tried to withdraw the magazine's second-class mailing privileges because of pressure from conservative groups and took his fight all the way to the Supreme Court where he lost, as moral codes shifted with the war. *Yank* magazine began printing the pin-ups of Varga's all-American girls, which increased the combat airman's longing to finish his tour and go home. Pin-up pictures adorned crew-room lockers from Alconbury to Wendling and some religious groups in the States expressed concern. As far back as February *Stars and Stripes* had alluded to the issue in a story datelined New York. 'Rabbi R. Brickner of Cleveland who has just returned from touring the ETO says American soldiers' favourite pin-up is a map of the United States,' it claimed.[23] One GI wrote in *Esquire*: 'The photos are clean and healthy and give us a good idea of what we are fighting for.' They may have given USAAF flyers an idea, but it wasn't necessarily about what they were fighting for.

Pin-ups of film stars were certainly a talking point on the bases and in the service magazines supplied to them. While the famous wartime picture of Hollywood's Betty Grable in a swim-suit showing her well-insured legs featured in many a USAAF field work station, the German-born screen idol Marlene Die-trich arrived in England in September for a series of USO shows. She was photographed in uniform 'displaying her famous gams [legs]', *Stars and Stripes* noted.[24] No wonder that the GI news-paper decided to get in on the act by organising its own beauty contest of pin-up girls in the service. But there were some who thought WACs should be taken more seriously and as the service-women themselves knew, their contribution to the war was not in doubt.

Rita M. Strobel Geibel was a USAAF WAC photographic technician at an 8th Air Force Reconnaissance Base Laboratory in High Wycombe, printing photographs of the results of the bomber offensive. 'The women were criticized, and you know a lot of it was nothing but garbage,' she remembers. 'There was a lot of conflict between the women and men' – though basic training for WACs was the same tough routine as male recruits underwent. 'We had to climb obstacles. We had to lie down in the mud. We practiced abandoning ship at New York . . . in case we sunk when we were going overseas. We did everything just like them [the men].'[25]

In England she found herself posted to photographic work even though she had had no training in it.

We [the lab] printed over two million prints in a month, and you know . . . it was history on a multi-printer. We had never seen these machines. They just put us on it, and we learned to use them . . . Sometimes we worked 24 hours, around the clock, with three shifts. [When] we'd come off a shift at eleven o'clock at night, we had to walk two miles up a hill from the lab in complete dark. We would just get settled down and all of a sudden those sirens would go off . . . You were so tired from working, and all you wanted was sleep. [But] we had to go out and stand in those foxholes until they called clear. We used to always say, 'I'd rather be in the hut and hit with them than be out in the open and hit with them.'[26]

The WAC kept churning out increasingly devastating USAAF strike photographs right to the end of the conflict in Europe.

Even by the autumn of 1944 America's leaders were so sure victory was only a matter of time preparations were already being made for the post-war world. The Servicemen's Readjustment Act, known as the GI Bill, had now been passed by Congress and forces publications gave many column inches to its finer points in September and October. Returning airmen and soldiers were guaranteed a year of unemployment pay as they adjusted to civilian life; low-interest loans to start a business; attractively priced mortgages and, crucially, the benefit that more than any other created an entrepreneurial, skilled citizenship who would propel the United States into a land of plenty in the 1950s – cash payments of tuition and living expenses to attend college, high school or vocational education, an opportunity 2.2 million veterans seized. A poster just issued in the autumn for pinning up in USAAF crew rooms showed a stunning, smiling *Rosie the Riveter* type – women now making up nearly 37 per cent of the US work force, a rise of 10 per cent from the pre-war level. She urged:

BLOOD AND FEARS

'That home-of-your-own may be just a dream now . . . but it's a dream that can come true if you'll save some of your hard-earned pay!' Sadly for many 8th AF flyers, as October turned to November dreams of home and beauty would end in ashes, the deadly flak of Merseburg scything through massed bombers cutting fuel lines and flesh with impassive equivalence.

13

'The greatest air battle of this war'

Albert Speer considered himself not only efficient, but a man who kept his promises to himself and to others. At the beginning of the Allied oil offensive he had told *Generalmajor* Adolf Gerlach that the one hundred heavy flak guns his 14 *Flakdivision* was equipped with to defend the synthetic fuel complex at Leuna-Merseburg and other refineries in the Leipzig area, would be increased beyond measure. The Reich Armaments Minister's underlings had squeezed the 100,000 forced foreign labourers used by the Krupps war material empire to churn out anti-aircraft guns and shells in prodigious numbers. Persuading such a workforce was not hard, they either worked or starved. There were also methods by which the Reich's own citizens could be spurred to maximum effort: for example, the threat of the *Arbeitserziehungslager*, Gestapo-run work-education camps for slackers to which hundreds were despatched each month. 'They did not lack much of the terrors of the concentration camps,' Walter Rohland, Deputy Chief of the Reich Iron Federation, revealed in post-war interrogation.[1]

Anti-aircraft gun and shell production was spread wide. The Škoda works in Pilsen, Czechoslovakia, one-time arsenal to the

Austro-Hungarian empire, produced thousands of 88mm flak guns which so far had proved beyond the capability of the Allied bomber fleets to limit, Pilsen itself being taken by General Patton's Third Army only three days before the end of the war in Europe. There was a further, geographic, aid to enable Speer to keep his pledge. The fact that there was much less of the Greater Reich to defend, now the Allies' ground forces had made such progress, helped to concentrate Germany's anti-aircraft defences around what was important. By the autumn of 1944 nothing had higher priority than its oil supplies and the greatest need of all was to protect the complex of Leuna, three miles from Merseburg's centre. Leuna produced not only fuel for the Luftwaffe, but other by-products of the synthetic process as well as its ersatz methanol, ammonia and nitric acid – chemicals for explosives, engine oil for tanks, rubber for truck wheels. A total of 35,000 people worked there night and day, 10,000 of them slave labourers, ensuring that no part of the synthetic chemical process was ruptured. Any break in the chain caused a product shortage that disrupted other industries too, right throughout the Reich.

Speer could now consider his promise to *Generalmajor* Gerlach to have been fulfilled. There were at this time 600 units of heavy flak ringing Leuna-Merseburg, a sensational increase from the considerable hundred guns of 88mm and even greater calibre that Gerlach had begun with in the early summer. All of the developing numbers of flak nests had taken a steady toll of the B-17s and B-24s returning to the complex. But the flak had not stopped destruction. In fact the last six missions by the 8th Air Force to the same target spelled out a message of continuing decline. Production had at first been halted for twenty-four hours; the next day there had been heavy damage again by bombs; repair work had then been disrupted by another accurate raid and that had been the story in the final three raids of September.

The *Ammoniakwerk Merseburg* plant at Leuna, which had been

producing 175,000 tons of aviation fuel in April was yielding only 7,000 tons six months later. From the autumn onwards the Luftwaffe was existing on its previously garnered, and now fast dwindling, reserves – at the start of October 180,000 tons compared with 580,000 tons at the beginning of May.[2]

Tactics on both sides of the battle for Leuna-Merseburg had also changed. At first the Americans had suffered considerably from radar-predicted flak, so the 8th AF had begun dropping huge amounts of the metallic-foil strips known as 'chaff' to jam the Würzburg radar sets. Then the Germans had turned to setting up box barrages to a point in the sky just before decision time on the bomb run, in a bid to spoil the Americans' aim. It was daunting indeed for a lead bombardier to see rows of black puffs unfolding ahead of and all around his fragile Perspex enclosure, so easily pierced by a deadly shard of shrapnel. But the bombs continued to fall with tolerable accuracy. The Wehrmacht diverted 7,000 of its skilled engineers to carry out continuing repairs to the plant and thousands of slave labourers were brought in to work under their direction, often carrying out urgent reconstruction and building concrete blast walls around essential machinery. The Gestapo arrived to bully.

On the evening of 1 November Albert Speer could perhaps consider, however, that his promise to *Generalmajor* Gerlach had at last paid dividends. Leuna-Merseburg had not been attacked since 7 October though other oil refineries had and it was easy in the fantasy world of the Nazi leadership to consider that the Americans had finally decided it was a target too costly to crack. In fact Carl Spaatz was about to launch his largest mission to the complex so far, 683 bombers of the 1st and 3rd BDs to unload on 75 acres of synthetic oil production. Further B-17s and B-24s would strike at the fuel targets of Castrop/Rauxel and Sterkrade as well as marshalling yards, putting 1,174 bombers aloft at one time, escorted by 968 fighters.

The young Americans now sleeping fitfully in England would witness scenes in that mission which would stay engraved on their memories for ever as Adolf Gerlach's flak battalions wreaked terrible damage to their Fortresses and Liberators and the Luftwaffe itself turned up in force at last to fight, scrambling 500 of the fighters *Reichsmarschall* Hermann Goering had been conserving for just such an air fleet. Whether they were on the battle order for Leuna-Merseburg or not, the combat airman of the 8th Air Force counting off their missions before they could return home were well aware already how tough the oil campaign was proving.

Lt Seymour Isaacs, a B-17 command pilot with the 34th BG at Mendlesham, flew his first sortie with his crew to an oil refinery in Hamburg on 25 October, eight days before the big Leuna-Merseburg mission. 'Flak took out our complete oxygen system and continued to disable the top turret, subsequently injuring the flight engineer, S/Sgt Oliver,' he remembers. 'The ball turret gunner Sgt Francisco Pereira passed out through lack of oxygen. All this required our seeking a lower altitude and returning to the UK alone, but we did eventually pick up a P-51 fighter escort. I found out much later it was flown by Captain Bud Peterson.'*[3]

How well the airmen slept the night before what has been called by some the greatest air battle over Germany depended to an extent what base they were on. The 91st BG was quartered at the brick-built former RAF station of Bassingbourn near Cambridge and conditions were very good indeed for the time. Lt John Howland, the PFF navigator, was based there for a few weeks before his tour ended. He had first flown into it on 20 April for the crew to be briefed to fly deputy lead with the 1st Combat

---

* The youthful Peterson was already an ace at the time and eventually was accorded 15 and one half victories with the 357th FG. He became a major at 21, the youngest in the whole USAAF.

Wing for what was supposed to be Merseburg. He recorded his impressions in his diary:

> Landed at Bassingbourn without problems and holed up in some Englishman's mansion that has been converted to a BOQ. Man, what a layout! Got out of the nicest bed that I've slept in for quite some time . . . Bathed and shaved like the landed gentry and after breakfast made our way to a briefing at 1045 hours.
>
> All kinds of brass is here. Secretary of State Ed Stettinus, General Jimmy Doolittle our top man in the 8th AF and many others. Also ran across Sam Newton and Bert Stiles, friends from Colorado College, who fly together out of Bassingbourn as pilot and co-pilot respectively . . . Had no problem meeting the assembly schedule and we were just ready to leave the base when a recall was issued and the mission scrubbed because of bad weather. We weren't scheduled to arrive home until 2117 hours. I never heard of any mission lasting till after 9 o'clock at night, but then this wasn't just any mission. Looking back it was all a big show of pomp and politics for the visiting dignitaries. I'll have to admit it was pretty impressive.[4]

Lt Howland flew back to his base at Chelveston, leaving behind his friend 2/Lt Stiles, who was making notes for a book about the bomber war.

Very few stations could measure up to the pre-war relative comfort of Bassingbourn. At Glatton, near Peterborough, home to the 457th BG, it was Quonset huts for all, 20ft wide and 30ft long, where single coke stoves failed to extend their heat more than a few feet across the cement floor. Enlisted members of several crews could share a hut, ranged in double bunks with only a couple of feet of shelf space above for personal possessions.

Officers' quarters were only slighter better, the corrugated iron huts being divided into shared rooms. S/Sgt John Briol shared his Quonset with other enlisted men at Glatton including fellow members of Lt John Welch's crew. They had painted 'Sack Time Hovel: Through these portals pass the world's tiredest mortals' over the door. On the night of 1 November Briol, from Freeport, Minnesota, which was later an inspiration for writer Garrison Keillor's Lake Wobegon stories of small-town life, was trying to get as much rest as he could before he climbed into his ball turret again tomorrow. S/Sgt Richard Gibbs, a gunner on the 749th Sqn of the 457th BG at the time, remembers Glatton as a place where new crews were simply ignored. 'It was just as if we were invisible. It did not take long for us to adjust and become just like the men that we had seen upon our arrival,' he wrote years later. 'I was to spend eight months in this squadron without knowing anyone who did not live in our hut. The crew was everything in our life. We worked with our crew and we played with our crew. No exceptions. Several other crews came to live in our hut along with us, but we stayed aloof from them. One crew came to our hut and was missing two days later. It simply did not pay to enlarge the friendship scene.'[5]

It was the same story at Rattlesden, the station of the 447th BG and across most of the 8th's bases including the 486th BG at Sudbury – stark cement and corrugated iron, hastily put together in the rough semblance of an aerodrome for the duration of the war where the comfort of home was a distant memory. S/Sgt John MacBride slept fitfully at Sudbury. The gunner was aware the morning's mission would be the crew's thirteenth. 'Had we believed in 13 being an unlucky number we would have been really frightened,' he wrote later. 'As it was we refused to call it our 13th mission, but titled it 12B instead.' At Deopham Green, near Attleborough, base of the 452nd BG, there was an added reason not to sleep: a plague of mice in the damp Quonset crew huts, finding shelter from the cold outside. Co-pilot 2/Lt Donald Smith, who would take part in the Merseburg missions in November, remembers he quickly learned to hang up all his clothes or the mice would eat holes even in his heavy topcoat.[6]

The call to briefing on 2 November was particularly bleak as the pre-dawn mist spread across the fields; the knowledge that the target was Merseburg made the atmosphere even chillier. A 'big show' for the brass as Lt Howland experienced would have been welcome indeed, instead of the rush of reality that was now the dreaded knowledge of Merseburg with its corridors of death-dealing flak. Yet at first the mission went without a hitch. Collisions during assembly could be expected in a maximum effort of such magnitude, but there were none until the air fleet had crossed the North Sea. Two Fortresses of the 447th BG touched in a turn and one went down immediately, the other making a crash-landing in Belgium.

The plan now began to unravel for some as the Groups flew on for eastern Germany across total overcast. It was the sixteenth mission for 2/Lt Dean Eakin of the 486th BG, one of those who had seen a comrade's B-17 wrecked and burning after hitting a farmhouse at Sudbury two weeks before. Eakin would not make it to Merseburg. Just before the Initial Point for the bomb run his plane lost power from one engine and the 2/Lt turned for home as the rest of the Group flew on, including the 486th's Flying Fortress named *Blue Streak* by the crew of 2/Lt David Paris. The navigator flying with them that day was Lt William Beeson, a veteran of thirty-one missions, who had been told before take-off at Sudbury this would be his last and he could go home.

S/Sgt John MacBride, left waist gunner in the 486th bomber of Lt Edward Unger, would have much to write up the next day in the combat diary he was keeping. 'This was the 100th mission for the 486th, so we felt as if we were making history that day,' he would begin. 'Got up at 3.30, briefed at 4.30 for an oil plant and took off at 7.15.'7 The crew had already had a taste of fame. When they arrived at Kearney, Nebraska, to pick up a Fortress to fly over to Britain to begin their tour they found a gleaming new aircraft decorated with the signatures and well wishes of Boeing workers. It was the 5,000th bomber to roll off the manufacturer's assembly line at Washington and some of the inscriptions the crew noted included proposals of marriage and phone numbers. During official ceremonies which included much photo-taking by the press the crew was presented with the *5 Grand* and set out for combat via Bangor, Maine. It was then found the effect of the paint used in writing all over the bomber caused a 5mph reduction in its cruise speed. The *5 Grand* crew flew on to Gander, Newfoundland, where after a few days' rest they took off for Nuts Corner, Ireland. There the razzamatazz ended. Another bomb group needed B-17s more badly than did the 486th, so the aircraft was transferred to the 96th BG and the crew had to continue their trip to England by ship, being assigned another bomber when they got to Sudbury. There was a constant supply of replacement Fortresses now crossing the Atlantic, but every effort was made to conserve: a B-17 flying with the 457th Group was made out of two salvaged aircraft, one half in the early olive drab, the other gleaming aluminium. It was named *Arf & Arf* by its crew in tribute to the popular British beer order of mild and bitter in the same glass.

The intimation that all would not go as planned for the bomber stream started to grow as the 457th BG reached the penultimate turn before the IP for the bomb run. The Glatton Group slowly deviated to the north away from the rest of the 1st BD. The Luftwaffe had now been alerted and ten *Gruppen* were rising to do battle. Much was expected of them by Goering, known throughout his air force as *Der Dicke* (the fat one). The *Reichsmarshall*, out of favour with Hitler for two years because Luftwaffe results had not matched its leader's much-vaunted promises, was now desperate to show the Führer his air force still counted. Less was expected by *General der Jagdflieger* Adolph Galland who was aware how inadequately trained were the young pilots of his fighter force because of fuel shortages. The few veterans left were also vanishing like fleeting shadows. If by their skill they managed to shoot down a Mustang pilot, they were immediately overwhelmed by two or three of his comrades, trained to fight together. Goering, who had not allowed the *Jagdflieger* to react in force since September, each week storing new fighters coming from the factories to build up his strength for the right occasion, was now prepared to waste the young lives of his under-trained men.

The black, death-dealing puffs of flak alley opened up on the Groups just after they turned onto the IP. The preponderance of heavy guns that Albert Speer had so assiduously supplied to 14 *Flakdivision* put up box barrages which arrived in the sky in train for the close-formation bombers to pass through in turn, shards of German iron pinging through thin American aluminium to find vital machinery and flesh. It was the heaviest concentration over Merseburg the USAAF had ever seen, nearly 500 bombers being hit, some lightly but others savagely as engines exploded, airframes shuddered from close blasts and snapped control wires whipped and sang inside fuselages. Stricken aircraft began to fall, spinning away faster and faster to the grey undercast, trailing orange fire. But none suffered a more spectacular demise than *Blue Streak* of the 486th BG. An 88mm shell exploded in the left main fuel tank of 2/Lt Paris's aircraft and the rear of the plane disintegrated in a furious belching of ragged blue and yellow flame. Others in the Group saw the whole of the front of the aircraft, where navigator Lt William Beeson had been working through what he had known would be his final mission before going home, also enveloped in a second and shattering explosion – the propellor from No. 2 engine jerking away. For a moment the whole mainplane was outlined against the clouds, the American star and bar insignia on the left wing clearly defined amid the inferno. Then it was gone, an image captured by an aircraft camera which remained forever burned in the memory of many who were there that day.

Paris's 486th comrade S/Sgt MacBride recorded within hours:

Our Group ran into 18 minutes of steady and accurate flak before, during and after Bombs Away. Looking out of my waist window I could see the exploding flak make black puff balls which formed a huge U in the sky as the radar controlled guns on the ground followed our formation around. When it came time for us to drop our bombs three of the 19 250 pounders hung up so we had to drop them later over a forest. The B-17 behind us got a direct hit just as bombs were released and blew up in mid-air. Several fellows were thought to have been seen baling out, but due to the suddenness of the explosion it was seriously doubted whether or not any escaped. We had four small holes in the plane plus having our antenna shot in half.[8]

Bombs gone the Fortresses thundered on for the rally point. It was now that the 457th, heading back to join the main stream after its navigation error – it had in fact bombed near Bernberg thirty miles away from the briefed target – was overwhelmed by the Luftwaffe. *Sturmbok* Fw 190s of II (Sturm)/JG4 and supporting Me 109s saw the Group outlined against the sky and came in ten abreast. 'There were enemy fighters galore,' S/Sgt John Briol recorded in his combat diary. 'I was blasting away at the nearest one as he was coming up on us. I saw his prop and cowling go flying away and part of his wing tip go sailing behind him. The ship behind him, I think I damaged. Our tail gunner was also on him. He turned away smoking. Then, like last time, our fighter escort was there and it seemed like there were planes falling everywhere. One Fortress exploded behind us. A man was thrown through the side.'[9]

S/Sgt Bert Sitek, ball turret gunner in the 457th crew of Lt Robert Kelly, told later: 'Everything happened pretty fast that day, as it usually does when the Germans offer any opposition. We had been off the bomb run about 10 minutes when vapor trails from fighters started to fill the sky. Friendly or enemy aircraft?, was the question in everyone's mind. But we soon learned the answer. There were Fw 190s and Me 109s forming for one of those wolf-pack attacks.' The sight of several German fighters swooping in tended to give a gunner a subjective view of the war and at first S/Sgt Sitek thought they were all headed his way.

But as they came closer, they lowered themselves for an attack on the low and lead boxes. Every one of them followed his course except the leader who must have liked the looks of one of the planes in our box. I got my sights on him from about 600 or 700 yards as he made his attack from 7 o'clock. I could almost see the bullets hit home. As he got closer I could feel his 20mm burst around me. At about 200 yards he seemed to stop dead. The ship rolled over and the pilot came out. A second later the plane burst into flames and broke into several pieces.[10]

With no escorts in sight the fighters pressed their attacks in close then split in different directions, bombers falling, smoking in their wake. The fighters came round for another assault from the rear, but by that time P-51s – alerted by radio calls for help – were on their way and for the next few minutes the sky was a confused maelstrom of flashing cannons, crews of blazing B-17s returning fire with their .50 MGs and inexperienced Luftwaffe pilots baling out as the Mustangs turned hunters into the hunted. At the end of it all, nine bombers had exploded or hit the ground, seven from one squadron. The attack over, the parade of battered B-17s flew westward. The last to leave the sky over the oil complex had been the 91st BG. A total of four of the Bassingbourn force, which had lost eight aircraft in a raid on nearby Leipzig in the summer, had gone down to the merciless flak of Merseburg, manned partly by schoolboys now that the Wehrmacht was claiming most able-bodied men.

A sixteen-year-old from Brunswick was among those teenagers, his education at the city's *gymnasium* temporarily suspended because of the war. He served on a flak nest equipped with dual 105mm guns, which he saw bring down at least eight bombers during the raids on the Leuna complex. 'On days where there was no air raid warning or military service, some lessons in the main core subjects were given in the mornings, so that – at least formally – our education was going on,' he recorded. In the heavy raid of 2 November he saw a B-17 blown apart by a flak hit on the bomb run. 'An aircraft door fell on the field in between our gun emplacements,' he wrote. 'Inside we found blood spatter and small scraps of meat. We laughed about it then. We were so callous as 16-year-olds.'[11]

It was the schoolboy's home city of Brunswick where the 486th BG crew of Lt Dean Eakin now found a suitable target after losing power from one engine on the way to Merseburg. The bombardier spotted a rail marshalling yard and subsequent reconnaissance photos of their bomb strike showed they had hit it dead on. They were commended by the Group commander for their achievement in striking a key target of opportunity.

The 91st BG, now down to thirty-two aircraft, turned for the rally point, but the lead plane made a crucial navigation error. Instead of heading due west it turned north-west by compass reading. The rest of the Group followed and gradually drew away from the stream in the overcast. Ominously German jets were seen spotting ahead, then the Luftwaffe pounced on the isolated Group near Hamburg just before 1pm. The *Sturmbok* Fw 190s of IV (Sturm)/JG 3 came in line abreast from the rear and within minutes the orderly procession of the 91st BG had been turned into a cruel kaleidoscope of falling Fortresses and zipping cannon in snapshots of horror. Attacks continued for twenty-five minutes as the Fortress formation continued without the protection of escort fighters, who were engaged with Me 262s and Me 163s elsewhere. As one B-17 was seen going straight down, burning like a torch from nose to tail, witnesses could only register that at least that crew's ordeal was over. 2/Lt Ed Gates in the co-pilot's seat of *Nine-O-Nine*, in the low three-plane element of the 323rd Sqn, wrote later: 'As we closed to formation on the squadron leader (both our wingmen were gone as was his left wingman) a Fw 190 came in beside us, dropped his gear for an instant and tried to shoot down our squadron lead B-17 without success ... we exchanged glances for an instant and I thought, he doesn't look any more evil than I do – and probably no older. I turned 21 six weeks later.'[12]

2/Lt Frank Farr, who had been drafted in as replacement navigator to the crew of Lt O. J. Snow of the 323rd Sqn, which lost five bombers on the mission, saw the fighters lining up then diving repeatedly through the formation at 25,000ft as he manned his machine gun in the nose of *Winged Victory*. In the process he was slightly wounded by 20mm fragments. 'The third pass hit our left wing tanks and set the wing afire. With no hope of putting out such a fire, our pilot ordered "bale out",' Lt Farr recorded. 'I didn't attempt to open the chute until I judged I had fallen to about 10,000 feet. When I pulled the rip cord, it failed to open – I can still see that bright red handle with a wire attached – and I was still falling. Reflexively, I clawed at the front of my chest-pack and succeeded in pulling out a piece of silk that the wind caught.' The chute now open, Lt Farr remembered the most intense quiet he had ever experienced as bits of burning aircraft fell around him. 'When I hit the ground, I was covered immediately by two men, one with a rifle, the other with a shotgun. My jacket was shredded by the 20mm cannon fragments, but only three tiny bits penetrated my shoulder.' Farr was motioned against a wall and thought he was going to be shot, but instead curious, not unfriendly, villagers arrived, including a teenage girl who admired his green nylon flight jacket so he gave it to her. After a couple of hours he was taken to a *Volkssturm* post. 'While I was there, a sympathetic soldier, several years older than I, took from his footlocker a cookie and gave it to me. He let me know that his mother, who lived in Hamburg, had made them. I was touched by his compassion, the more so because the 8th Air Force had bombed Hamburg relentlessly. The man told me he was a veteran of the fighting on the Eastern Front. When I offered to share a bite of chocolate from my flying suit, he refused. I thought he was telling me that I would need it.'[13]

Fw 190s and Me 109s accounted for six aircraft of the Group's 322nd Sqn, planes with happy-go-lucky names such as *Miss Slip Stream* and *Gal of My Dreams*. Seven more, which included those lost over the target, were missing from other squadrons. The thirteen empty hardstands at Bassingbourn left gaps in the flight line like missing molars in a busted jaw after the survivors had begun to touch down around 5pm, ground crews to the missing left staring into the skies, hoping irrationally that their charges would return.

Crew chiefs, who sweated out missions by the aircraft they knew intimately and the men who flew them almost as part of their family, kept going on unreasoning optimism. Occasionally it did pay off. Lt Lesley Hull of the 486th BG came home late from the Merseburg mission with only one engine giving full power and had to land at the RAF air-sea rescue field of Beccles, Suffolk. It was hours before his crew chief waiting by the hard stand at

Target precision: A Fortress tail gunner catches this image of a fellow crew from his Group leaving the airfield target area of St-Dizier-Robinson, the smoke rising behind them testimony to the accuracy of their attack. To the left, other aircraft of the Group come in to bomb, pursued by flak. (National Archives, Air 20-6251)

View back at the bases: Eyes anxiously scan the skies from the control tower at North Pickenham for the return of a mission by the 492nd BG. The 492nd had rapidly established a reputation as the 'Hard Luck Group' because of high losses. It was particularly badly mauled in the first *Sturmbok* attack of 7 July 1944, only six B-24s returning to the Norfolk base. A month later it was withdrawn from the daylight offensive. Since introduction to combat on 11 May it had suffered a total loss of fifty-one aircraft in sixty-four missions – a greater percentage attrition than any other unit in the 8th. (USAAF)

Briefing: Grim faces as crews of the 92nd BG see the curtain drawn back from the target map and wait to hear the details unfold of yet another mission in which they would be laying their lives on the line. (USAAF)

Debriefing: There was no more welcome sight as tired crews filed into the interrogation hut than that of the American Red Cross girls serving hot coffee and doughnuts. The ARC girl on the far left in this 96th BG picture from Snetterton Heath is Katharine 'Tatty' Spaatz, daughter of General Carl Spaatz, head of the USSTAF and the man with whom the buck stopped in the continuing bomber offensive. (USAAF)

A total of 623 bombers of all three 8th AF divisions were assigned in the Berlin raid of 8 March 1944 to eradicate the important VKF ball-bearing factory at Erkner in the Reich capital's suburbs. The result is seen by the huge pall of smoke spreading over Erkner itself from the factory (left). (USAAF)

A refinement of the Pointblank Directive called for priority in the spring by both the USAAF and RAF against the strongly defended German aircraft industry. It was extremely costly to the 8th AF, with 361 bombers shot down in April alone and forty-two brought back so badly damaged they never flew again. Here the Arniswalde aero-engine plant near Stettin is hit by Fortresses of the 94th BG. Four aircraft of the Group failed to return. (National Archives, Air 20-6251)

Leuna-Merseburg was the most feared of targets by 8th AF crews. The picture above from the ball turret of a B-17 on 2 November shows why as the sky is filled with bursting flak, a terrifying sight to a gunner hanging underneath his bomber protected by nothing but Perspex. But after twenty missions by the 8th in daylight and two by RAF Bomber Command at night, the flak battalions of the giant synthetic oil complex were finally defeated, as the picture below of the wrecked plant shows. It was taken the same month, by which time the 175,000 tons of aviation fuel the complex had been producing in April was down to just 7,000. That victory came at great cost, as the photographs on the facing page reveal. (USAAF)

This image of *Blue Streak* plunging in flames after suffering a direct hit from one of the 600 flak guns surrounding the oil complex of Leuna-Merseburg was imprinted for decades on the minds of comrades of the 486th BG. All the crew perished, including the navigator who had been told it would be his last mission before going home. (USAAF)

A young girl poses by the wreckage of a Flying Fortress shot up by flak over Merseburg in November 1944, having made a crash landing in France after falling 15,000 feet then being attacked by fighters.

Where worlds collide: GIs lean out of the windows of the ARC Club at Rainbow Corner and take in the view of London double-decker buses and those strange little taxis being directed along Piccadilly by a British bobby. The 'American Invasion' changed Britain for ever. (USAAF)

Glenn Miller was not the only entertainer by far to visit England in wartime and take a tour of the air bases. Film star James Cagney in USO uniform is showing airmen at a base Aero Club that warm British beer isn't so bad after all. (USAAF)

A British policeman looks on in the cold of an October Sunday morning as a USAAF officer combs through the wreckage of Lt Clarence Herrmann's B-17 burnt out in a meadow just beyond the 486th BG base at Sudbury. The plane's no. 4 engine had died on take-off for Cologne and Herrmann had clipped the roof of Woodhall House Farm over the bedroom of sixteen-year-old Clarence Smith then crashed. Hermann was thrown clear with severe head injuries, but the rest of his crew died as did the terribly burned English teenager the next day. (USAAF)

A total of seventeen airmen have just died minutes from home in this incident over the 306th BG base when the last plane in the squadron of another Group over-flying the runways in poor visibility at Thurleigh went up instead of down and collided with the tail end of the 306th formation. 2/Lt Howard Roth, returning with the 306th from Hannover, saw falling debris start several fires around the base and bodies were scattered throughout the area. (USAAF; courtesy of Howard Roth)

Many Englishmen and women who were children during the war remember the generosity of Americans far from their own families. Here children queue up at Podington to take a truck back to their villages after a Christmas party thrown by the 92nd BG, each carrying a gift, many of them large model aircraft. (USAAF)

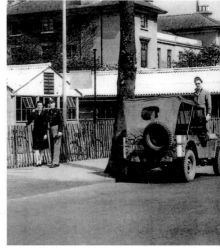

Girls from village England show American airmen how to jitterbug at this dance thrown by the 92nd BG. Most Groups had their own bands drawn from the wealth of talent in uniform and the 92nd was no exception. But more high-profile musicians usually played at dances in American Red Cross Clubs, such as this one at Bedford, where 2/Lt Howard Roth spotted Glenn Miller the night before he died. (Left USAAF; right courtesy of Howard Roth)

Sudbury would hear he was safe. The matter-of-fact tone in Lt Hull's combat diary cannot disguise the drama of his flight home.

> Lost No. 2 engine 20 minutes before target; salvoed bombs to stay in formation near Brunswick. Lost No. 1 engine 10 minutes before target, had to turn back at 25,000ft. Flew return course at 120mph, descending at 200–300ft/min; after two hours reached enemy coast [of Holland] at 8,500ft. Able to maintain 7,500ft at 120mph over Channel until 40 miles from England when No. 3 engine spouted oil and ran away. Feathered/unfeathered run-away for 10 minutes. Began losing altitude real fast, so threw out all ammo, flak suits, helmets, excess radio equipment and waist guns. Managed to level off at 6,000ft until No. 3 ran away again and oil pressure dropped to zero; feathered No. 3 over beach [of England] at 5,000ft. Sighted emergency field just inland; circled for landing, making downwind leg at 1,500ft. Made safe landing on No. 4 engine only.[14]

All four power plants of the B-17 had to be replaced and Hull was awarded the DFC for finally making it home on one engine.

After the horrors of the Merseburg mission there was a palpable sense of shock in the hard-hit Groups, the electricity of it passing right through the 8th Air Force. It had been hoped that the harsh losses of September and early October on oil targets had marked a turning point. *Stars and Stripes* spoke for many with its story the next day that the 'not-so-down-and-out Luftwaffe showed itself in strength yesterday'.[15] The 'Mail Call' section of *Yank* magazine, a considerable monitor of morale with its letters from GIs and airmen, replied to a mistaken belief by some that the Luftwaffe was finished with this missive from an unknown flyer of the 91st BG: 'Yet it seems the greatest air battle of this war took place on Nov 2. I for one wouldn't call a mission where eleven out of twelve 17's were knocked out in one pass, a "milk run." I saw just that happen.'[16]

But if it was a torment to the 8th Air Force the resulting profit and loss tally in war's ledger was an even bigger blow to the Luftwaffe. Flak and fighter leaders claimed to have shot down a total of eighty-two aircraft. It was in fact fifty-six, sixteen of which were fighters. But the Germans themselves lost 120 fighters with seventy pilots killed or missing and twenty-eight wounded. Four days later Luftwaffe staff officers had to appear before Hitler at his conference at the Eastern Front *Wolfsschanze* headquarters in Rastenburg and explain what had gone wrong. The Führer told them the 'miserable result' of what had long been intended as a planned serious blow to the 8th Air Force was 'most unsatisfactory'. He complained that he couldn't count on the fighters, which had eaten up labour and materials to pour out of the factories 'at the devil's own pace', to produce any kills. Even Hitler knew that the loss of so many aircraft was by now irreplaceable, made even more serious by the extinction of pilots. Less than two weeks later the Führer would face further evidence of the approaching end to his 1,000-year Reich when he was forced to quit the Wolf's Lair complex of bunkers because of the Russian advance.[17]

Conversely the Mighty Eighth was able to replace its crews and aircraft virtually overnight; two days after the slaughter of the Leuna-Merseburg mission more than 1,000 bombers attacked various oil and transportation targets in Western Germany for the loss of only five aircraft. Even when they went back to Leuna-Merseburg on the day Hitler was giving his Luftwaffe a roasting, only three Fortresses were lost from the 1st BD, though the flak damaged eighty-five more. The 3rd BD was meant to join in the attack, but bad weather led to a recall after they had entered German air space. The 180-degree turn that that necessitated for a whole air division inevitably brought its hair-raising moments in poor visibility. 2/Lt Donald Smith, co-pilot in the 452nd BG, had a healthy respect for flak. On his second mission he had been assigned as a replacement with another crew and as he settled himself into his seat in the cockpit 'the flight engineer thoughtfully got my attention', he wrote in a loose diary he made at the time. 'He pointed out a splintered hole in the wooden catwalk below, a patch riveted onto the metal seat under my left leg and another patch in the fuselage over my head, and explained that on the previous mission a piece of flak had come through that path and taken the co-pilot's leg off.'[18]

When the recall order came for the 3rd BD he found out how easy it was to be killed by comrades. 'Our Group started to turn,' he wrote. 'The Group behind us, offset to our left to avoid prop wash, did not hear the recall order. They continued to fly straight and ahead. Suddenly that Group flew right through ours, which was banked up in a left turn. Amazingly there were no mid-air collisions, but 80 planes were scattered all over the German sky. Everyone was looking for someone else to fly home with.'[19] Eventually 2/Lt Smith saw the white L in a black square on the tail of a B-17, the insignia of the 452nd, and fastened onto the plane. Others followed. But the dangers were not over for the returning division.

Over the North Sea one of the bombers of the 457th BG, which had been hit so badly on 2 November, went down in a collision. *Arf & Arf*, which had been patched together from two crashed Fortresses, was the aircraft – cut in two once more over the sea. S/Sgt George Crockett, in one of the other thirteen bombers the Group had scraped together for the mission after the Merseburg attrition, saw it happen, enlisted men who shared his hut at Glatton whisked away in a heartbeat. He wrote about the incident years later:

As we were returning over the coast, we were met with a flak barrage and flew through it without any apparent damage. We were flying above and to the left of Lt Elduff. I was the right waist gunner on Joe Coleman's crew *Rattle Snake Daddy*. Lt Furr's *Arf & Arf* was to the right and below Lt Elduff's *Bad Time Inc II*. As I looked down on Furr's plane, I waved to their left waist gunner, and he waved back. As I watched, they started edging closer and were climbing closer to our level. At the time I thought they were just tightening the formation, but they suddenly climbed up and under Lt Elduff and hit him. The next thing I saw was *Arf & Arf* in two parts plummeting towards the water.[20]

The formation was ordered to hold position as *Bad Time Inc II* made for an emergency landing in England, but Lt Coleman went down and dropped a rubber dinghy and Sgt Glen Wisdom, Lt Furr's tail gunner, made it to the dinghy and waved. 'As we left the area, there was a swarm of fighters circling over him and the flak started up again trying to reach them,' S/Sgt Crockett wrote. 'It was hard to return to our hut and find their bunks empty and their personal effects gone. A lot of us cried to ourselves that night. We were given a 48 hour leave and found ourselves drowning our sorrows in London.'[21]

Merseburg would feature three times more on the target list for the rest of the month. On the 21st the Luftwaffe air and ground forces claimed fourteen and another 205 came home displaying multiple flak holes. Four days later flak alone brought down eight bombers over Merseburg of the two complete air divisions despatched. First reports to Spaatz's headquarters at Bushy Park near Hampton Court Palace were that fifty-seven were missing until reports came in from the Continent of the bombers landing there, including 2/Lt Donald Smith's which had to go into an airfield at Brussels.[22]

On the last day of the month the 3rd BD sent 300 of its Fortresses to Leuna-Merseburg and lost seventeen as crews flew down a corridor of flak from the IP. No fewer than seven were from the 390th BG at Parham, five of them crashing or exploding after being hit by the AA fire and two being lost by collision. In a Pathfinder named *The Saint* claimed by flak with its crew was Lt Col. Louis Dolan, the Group Air Executive, one week away from his twenty-fifth birthday. Other, damaged aircraft had to land elsewhere, only twenty-two of the thirty-eight aircraft which had taken off from Parham returning to base.

Lt Dick Harris was the pilot of a B-17 flying just behind the Pathfinder aircraft in the lead squadron on the Group mission. Harris personally saw Dolan go down, together with two other 390th BG planes and three others so badly damaged they had to make emergency landings. He also witnessed the horror of a mid-air collision by people he knew and talked with. The flight until the formation approached the IP for Merseburg was deceptively uneventful, but then Harris's navigator, Flt Officer Wayne Wright, came on the intercom, telling the crew a problem in the PFF aircraft ahead meant the Group was 'nowhere near the IP', but at least thirty miles off course. The carefully selected course into the target to minimise where possible the danger from the numerous flak sites was now lost, as Lt Harris's vivid account describes.

There was nothing we could do about it. Like a herd of elephants we charged on from our imaginary IP, going onwards to destroy the Merseburg dragon. Flak was very strong in the entire area as we were probably exposed to Leipzig and Halle defences as well as Merseburg's. Soon the bomb bay doors were open and we were ready to let go. Wright was back on the intercom with a very agitated voice: 'We are 30 miles away'. Lt Chuck Curtis, our bombardier, reported that he could not see the target, but there was lots of smoke and broken clouds. What did we do? We charged on.

Flying in the slot we were directly under and slightly behind the Group lead aircraft. In that spot I watched him through my roof window. We were being bounced around by flak and turbulence as the lead plane started a sharp turn to the right and the deputy lead on his right wing started an equal turn to his left . . . Most of the planes began flying off as they started downward. I began a turn to my left, quickly trying to get out from under. Thank goodness for the skill of the fellow flying the aircraft on my left wing as they moved away just as fast, avoiding a collision. I think there was an explosion of the two planes. I wondered how any of us could possibly get through the flying debris.

As Harris tried to avoid the other aircraft flak burst into black, ragged clouds above him.

We watched as No. 1 and No. 4 engine instruments died and suddenly we felt severe vibration on No. 1. It was running wild and was in danger of tearing loose. With the help of the expert hand of co-pilot Lt Jock Jordan we were able to feather that propellor and finally had the same luck with No. 4. During that time I had managed to get No. 3 down to about 26 inches of manifold pressure, which made the vibrations reasonable. Dear engine No. 2 then, heroically, rose to the occasion in an almost unbelievable way. We set the throttle, prop pitch, supercharger and mixture at take off mode and left them like that until the engine's demise three hours later.

The bombardier dropped his bombs 'somewhere' and the crew now began their battle to try to make it home to Parham. 'We started unloading everything we could get out, radios, guns, bullets, clothes and finally the ball turret . . . We saw the planes losing altitude, saw several parachutes coming from which planes we couldn't tell. We saw one B-17 in a spin blow into a million pieces. It looked like charmed Merseburg/Leuna would win all the battles.'

Slowly the rest of the stream pulled away and the loneliness of a crew in peril with miles to fly to safety now filled the plane. As the plane sank gradually into denser air the rate of descent slowed. 'Engine No. 2 was purring and engine No. 3 was making some contribution,' Harris wrote. 'We had understood that Patton's Third Army was at Metz with the possibility of fuel and supplies for us and Wright gave us a course for there. We were flying at about 2,500ft in overcast with an airspeed of 105. We were losing both height and airspeed, but our hopes were still with us. We broke cloud to see that we were approaching a town too close to go around.'

Not surprisingly light flak now began to reach up from the town of Alzey, the tracer arcing slowly towards the bomber at first then zipping past. But not all: two shells hit the right wing and suddenly the B-17 was ablaze.

Now down to 1,700ft I gave the order to have the bomb bay doors opened and for the crew to bale out. At 1,500ft I checked the autopilot and headed for the bay. There I found our radio operator Sgt 'Dusty' Rhodes was straddling the open space on one side of the bay where he informed me he was not going to jump and would ride her down. Little did he know. I was able to get up to him on the catwalk and I leaned over to him as if I was about to let him in on a big military secret and I kicked one of his feet out from under him and down he went. A second or two later I was out of there. We were all captured that same night. Dusty made it fine.[23]

The 1st BD were also out over the oil refineries on 30 November, most of its Groups divided between Leuna-Merseburg and Zeiss. The 379th BG lost six aircraft on Zeiss, which had its own preponderance of flak sites, almost half of the total loss from the division that day. But Böhlen, another oil refinery near Leipzig, claimed others, including the 457th BG aircraft in which S/Sgt John J. Brio was the ball turret gunner. His pilot, Lt John Welch, had to crash-land in Belgium because of damage inflicted by the Böhlen gun sites. 'Our whole crew is safe,' Briol wrote in his diary.

Our target was on the other side of Germany, next to Leipzig. Then and there I never saw such horrible flak in my life. Fortresses started flaming, exploding and falling all around us. I was praying out loud again. Wham! And most of our No. 1 engine was blasted away. There were heavy thumps in the wings and gas started leaking. One rudder control was shot away. One of the oxygen tanks exploded. A big piece of flak came through the waist. One piece thudded against my ball turret but the guns saved me. Our radio was shot away and the G. Box burned out. Our flaps and landing gear control systems were shot away. We decided to crash land, because we figured we had a good chance. We came down in a field. The prop on No. 1 went flying.[24]

It wasn't just the deadly flak the youngsters of the 8th AF had to gird themselves to face as November came to a close; the *Sturmbok* of the Luftwaffe were much battered but still not out of the fight. Where they found a Group in a section of the bomber stream unescorted by fighters they could sweep in and inflict a savage blow within minutes. On 26 November that blow fell on the 491st BG, a Group that had lower than average losses since flying its first mission at the end of April and by the third week in November had not had one of its B-24s shot down for seven weeks. A mission to the Deurag-Nerag synthetic oil refinery of Misburg, twelve miles north-east of Hanover, would change all that.

The refinery had been chosen as the primary target of 243 Flying Fortresses of the 1st BD and they would go in first, but two Groups of the 2nd BD, equipped with Liberators, would bring up the rear. The first of them was the 445th BG, from which Kay Brainard's brother had gone missing on the disastrous Kassel raid, and the second was the 491st. The 3rd BD would also be out in force and between the three divisions three other targets had been selected – railway viaducts at Altenbeken and Bielefeld/Schildesche and marshalling yards at Hamm. The long stream of 1,073 bombers began crossing the Dutch coast shortly before 11am. On board one of the 1st BD Fortresses near the head of the stream was navigator 2/Lt Terry Messing, who had seen Glenn Miller and his orchestra play in London in the summer. Darting ahead and among the bombers were 668 fighters, nearly all Mustangs, and among those flyers was Lt Bert Stiles, the college companion of Lt John Howland. Stiles had now finished his tour as a co-pilot with the 91st BG, where he had made copious notes for a book he hoped to write. He had immediately volunteered for a second tour on fighters. Stiles had so far flown fifteen missions with the 339th FG from Fowlmere without a combat victory. But he had the satisfaction of knowing his air war book, which would be known as *Serenade to the Big Bird*, was finished.

As several Groups of Fortresses approached the navigation point of Dummer Lake, past Zwolle, forty-five minutes later three Luftwaffe jets began flying a parallel course in clear blue sky, establishing the strength and speed of the bombers. They arrived at a crucial point in the flight plan. Dummer Lake was where the stream was to split to attack the three different primary targets. Minutes later Luftwaffe radio transcripts beamed via the British code-breaking centre at Bletchley Park to US fighters in the air indicated bandits forty miles to the south, threatening the bombers heading towards Bielefeld and Hamm. The 356th FG, which had converted to the Mustang from Thunderbolts only six days before, went off to investigate and a flight leader spotted a force in fact coming from the east. 'I dropped my wing tanks and we met the e/a head on,' 2/Lt Rex Burden reported later at Martlesham Heath. 'We made a climbing right turn. We were then at approximately 24,000ft, the e/a were about 2,000ft below us in (two) gaggles of about 50 plus. There was a third top gaggle of 50 e/a at 28,000ft.'[25] Burden saw his leader destroy an Fw 190 as the wheeling, soaring Americans chased the enemy machines up to 39,000ft. Then Burden saw his chance to shoot down another and swooped on the Luftwaffe pilot's tail. 'I fired, scoring a concentration of strikes on the fuselage, where it is joined by the right wing and in the cockpit,' he said. 'The e/a slid down under me and my wing blanked it out. The destruction of this Fw 190 is confirmed by my flight leader.'[26]

The Misburg-bound bombers grumbled on, the fighter attack concentrating on the more southerly forces of the second and third bombardment divisions and being largely driven off. The B-17s and B-24s then flew past Hanover to the north-east in a deliberate feint to confuse the defenders into thinking Berlin was the target. As they did so crewmen aboard those bombers saw up to 200 enemy fighters to the south-east. With the exception of those Mustangs who had earlier been engaged and lost contact with other fighter Groups, the fighters now flew away from the Misburg force to take them on. Among the first to open fire was the 339th FG's 505th Sqn of which Lt Bert Stiles was part. His squadron mate, 2/Lt William Phillippi, flying as Green 3, said in his encounter report later that between 1245 and 1300 hours the squadron, including Stiles, encountered 40 to 60 Fw 190s flying in a very loose formation. 'Green leader, Lt Bundgaard, attacked an Fw 190 and got strikes all over him. The Jerry broke left and baled out. At this time another 190 attacked Green 2 from above and I broke into him observing strikes on his wing roots, fuselage and tail. As Jerry cut his throttle I overshot and broke to the left. Lt Loveless was firing and registering strikes on the e/a when I broke. The 190 rolled over, split-essed into the ground and exploded.'[27] Crucially Phillippi reported that the fight had taken place from '26,000ft to deck'. It is known that Stiles took on an Fw 190 in this action which whirled earthwards through thousands of feet and shot it down at low level. But almost immediately afterwards his own P-51 hit the ground, apparently as the ex-bomber pilot became a victim of target-fixation. Stiles, who had such hopes of becoming a famous author, was dead.*

The B-17s of the 1st BD had already arrived over the synthetic refinery at Misburg where they found flak defences of the strength Leuna-Merseburg had displayed. It was unfortunate that the carefully planned feint for the Misburg force guided them into a headwind, so that the bombers flew through the target at a groundspeed of 90mph, giving the flak nests ample time to register the height, course and speed. 2/Lt Terry Messing, with the 305th BG, recalls: 'We were hit by flak at exactly the same time that we dropped our bombs. We were a good target. We had to fly a steady course and the Germans knew our altitude. Flak exploded in our left wing and killed both engines on that side. We dropped 10,000ft right there.'[28] The aircraft commander, Lt Hank Smith, had brought the B-17 under control at 14,000ft, then it was hit again by flak and lost another engine.

The designed stratagem of the 2nd BD Misburg bombers had taken them west about ninety miles then they had made a turn towards the IP, which was at Wittingen, sixteen miles north-east

---

* In fact Bert Stiles's manuscript of his bomber tour did make him famous, albeit posthumously. *Serenade to the Big Bird* was published in London in 1947 and is now recognised as a classic of the air war, successive print runs lasting for decades.

of the target. Just before it was reached at 1226 the 355th FG spotted a large gaggle of Fw 190s coming towards the bombers at 10 o'clock low. Lt Charles Hauver, flying at 21,000ft, opened fire at 500 yards. 'The second burst showed strikes on the e/a with a good concentration of hits on the right wing,' he reported in his victory claim. 'The third and last burst from 300 yards hit the e/a squarely in the left side of [the] engine and cockpit. An explosion occurred and flames came out of the engine. The e/a went out of control at 17,000ft and headed straight down with flames coming out of it. I saw the canopy fly off.'[29]

The 491st and 445th were now going through Misburg without a cover of fighters as they were engaged to the north-east and south-east, but the low squadron of the 491st had unfortunately dropped all its bombs fifteen miles short of the target because a toggle switch had been knocked in error in the lead aircraft. Its need to cross the flak field of the oil refinery negated, the squadron then pulled away from Misburg to join the rest of the 491st at the rally point before Dummer Lake. The cohesion which made a Group effective in combined defence by its .50 machine guns was lost.

Fighters were already attacking the 445th BG on its bomb run and as ordnance began falling on the Misburg refinery from the 419th the *Sturmbok* of JG 301, equipped with Fw 190 A-8s and armoured A9s, swept in from the north-east to attack by standard line-abreast formation. The high squadron of the 491st BG as the last in trail was selected first, as bombs fell from the lead squadron. A later Distinguished Unit Citation for the Group described what happened next. 'The enemy fighters determinedly closed to point blank range and pressed their attack to within 100 yards of our aircraft. Successfully dropping their bombs on the target and defending itself to the last the entire squadron was wiped out while trying to rejoin the Group.'[30] The enemy aircraft then broke away individually and swung ahead of the two Groups, turning their attention to the 419th BG's middle low squadron. 'Using the same tactics they downed all but four Liberators from this squadron,' the citation read. 'Fighting desperately these four aircraft joined the lead squadron which had reduced airspeed to facilitate the rally and with their support held the hostile aircraft at bay until the friendly fighter support returned to drive off the attackers.'[31]

One by one the 419th BG machines had been knocked out, falling in flames leaving trails of greasy, streaming smoke across the cloud layer. Crewmen in the returning Liberators were later credited with seven Fw 190s destroyed, three probably destroyed and eleven damaged. These did not include those knocked down by the Group's devastated high squadron, some gunners sticking to their .50s to keep firing even though their burning planes were plunging from the sky without hope of recovery. At the same time as the 419th BG's low squadron was being methodically hacked to pieces, a squadron of the 445th BG just ahead was also being savaged, five of its eleven bombers falling away after single attacks. The airwaves connecting the B-24s with their own intended fighter cover, which had become separated, rang with anguished cries for assistance. As they had before, American boys were dying in great number above Europe for the sake of Europe, in a grisly tapestry of exploding cannon, lacerated flesh and searing fire.

It was more than fifty years before two of the crew of a 445th BG Liberator which made it home were able to describe the scene inside their own plane on its bomb run as up to a hundred enemy aircraft bored in, guns spitting red flame. Navigator Frank W. Federici and co-pilot Vincent Mazza were on the twenty-fifth mission of their tour. 'Our pilot, James A. Williams, was hit with a 20mm and killed instantly,' they wrote in 1996. 'The bullet went through his flak suit and embedded in his backpack parachute. The pilot slumped over the controls.' Mazza immediately took over with one hand while trying to hold the pilot back from the controls with the other to avoid a collision with other aircraft in the formation. He struggled because the dead pilot's flying boots were interfering with the rudder pedals, so the flight engineer Herbert Krieg got out of his turret to help.

The engineer saw the problem, but the co-pilot had to apply left rudder momentarily to free the boots (even though it meant turning into a B-24 on our left, then immediately applying right rudder to avoid a collision). The engineer freed the boots from the rudder controls. Our left wing almost touched the waist gunner on the B-24 on our left. The engineer strapped the pilot into his seat.

Then another wave of enemy fighters came in and a 20mm explosive shell knocked out the front turret, wounding the nose turret navigator and blowing out all of the lower Plexiglas in the nose below the turret and in front of the bombsight.

In turn, the bombardier (Leo Lewis) who had already synchronized the bombsight was knocked over and against the navigator, who in turn was knocked down onto the nose wheel doors. The bombardier's helmet and oxygen mask were knocked off and he was completely dazed. The navigator, Frank Federici, shook him and with sign language sent him back to the flight deck. The navigator called the radio operator, Carl Bally, and told him to watch for Leo Lewis or have Herbie Krieg attend to him. The flight engineer and radio operator shared their oxygen masks with the bombardier until another mask could be brought to him. The waist gunner, Eddie Goodgion, was called and asked to bring blankets and an oxygen mask for the bombardier whose ears and face were frost bitten. The tail gunner, Charles Bickett, had lost communication with the rest of the crew and was unaware of the situation.[32]

As the bombsight was already synchronised the navigator salvoed the bombs to ensure that they were released on target. After the bombs went down the navigator helped the wounded nose turret navigator, John Christainson, out of the turret. He was able to crawl back to mid-fuselage where the left waist gunner, Kenneth Brass, tended his wounded leg.

By then the Mustang escorts had responded to the carnage taking place in the target area. Cptn John Winder of the 353rd FG reported the Group had 'noticed two boxes of *unescorted* B-24s'. Though on the withdrawal and in the vicinity of Dummer Lake, they turned back. 'As we neared the box we observed e/a making stern attacks. I saw a lone 190 positioning for an attack, so I disregarded several that had headed for the deck and went after him,' Winder said. 'I fired one burst out of range to scare him off, but he continued his attack. I could not close sufficiently to knock him down before he made his attack and started his split S. After several turns I finally got in a good burst, observing hits all over the cockpit. He started smoking and spinning.'[33] Others saw the Fw 190's right wing come off before it hit the ground and exploded.

Lt Col. Harvey Henderson, a squadron commander with the 339th FG, shot down two Fw 190s that day in the various actions in which he was engaged. In his report of combat timed at 1300 hours south-east of Dummer Lake he said he saw four B-24s go down in flames before his own Group could arrive to help. The first Fw 190 he shot down broke off from an attack on a Liberator when he saw Colonel Henderson's Mustang closing in. 'I caught him with 30 degree deflection shot at about 15,000ft,' Henderson reported to Intelligence back at Fowlmere. 'He tried no other evasive action than to continue his dive and I gave him a second burst. I observed strikes on the wings and fuselage and the Jerry jettisoned his canopy and prepared to bale out. I fired again, saw strikes in the cockpit and the pilot rolled over the side but I did not see his chute open.'[34] Col. Henderson went on to say that: 'There were many 190s in the area, but I noticed that most of them were covered by P-51s.' In fact it would be a classic day for the 339th, whose pilots claimed no fewer than thirty-nine enemy aircraft. Col. Henderson had to chase his second victim for ten minutes in and out of cloud before getting strikes on the enemy's fuselage which sent him 'spinning down'.

By now the battered 445th BG and the remaining bombers of the 419th, fifteen fewer than had set out, were struggling to make it home. Aboard the bomber with its dead skipper now flown by co-pilot Vincent Mazza, the crew had had time to assess their chances. 'The navigator recognized that the co-pilot had gained complete control of the ship and since all four fans were working we were able to stay in formation for our mutual protection until we were out of enemy territory in spite of the cold air and wind-blast,' Federici and Mazza reported.[35]

The B-17 of 2/Lt Messing had already lost its battle trying to stay aloft on a single good engine. 'We kept trying to figure out "Can we make it, can we make it?" But the B-17 can't fly long on one engine and over Holland we got down to around 1,000ft where it's then getting too low so we baled out,' he said.[36] The teenaged tail gunner, S/Sgt Keith Hereford, who had been sure he would survive his tour, remembers:

On that last mission after we were hit the pilot came on the interphone and ordered, 'Come up to the waist.' When I got there there were four guys standing by the door and they pointed for me to bale out. Ooh, I didn't like that, so I got on the interphone and talked to the pilot and said, 'Is this it, do we have to bale out?' and he said, 'Get the hell out of here.' I was the first one to go and I think we were at about 1,200ft at that time. I went out head first and I waited until I had straightened up before pulling the rip cord because I didn't want to be head down when the chute opened. I was knocked out when I hit the ground. The wind was blowing and I could see a barbed wire fence and I wanted to get over that and I think my chin hit my knees. German soldiers had seen me land and I saw a truck go by with them on it. I crawled underneath a bush. My feet were sticking out I guess. I could hear the Germans come tramping down, then I heard 'Raus, bitte' and I turned around and I was looking up the barrel of a gun and I thought, 'Oh shit! He's going to pull the trigger.' I got up and I was captured.[37]

2/Lt Messing takes up the story:

All the crew got out. Two of the crew were picked up by the Dutch Underground and were taken over by Canadian troops some time before the war was over. I got a bum foot when I landed near a Dutch town. I was picked up right away by Dutch SS and they took me to this headquarters and as there was nowhere to sit and my foot hurt I sat on their leader's desk. It didn't go down too well, but I guess it kind of indicated how we Americans fought the war, cocky. Soon after I could hear anti-aircraft guns firing and they rushed me outside to see parts of a plane they had hit, come floating down. I heard afterwards it was probably a B-25, bombing a buzz-bomb base nearby. Later on three German soldiers came with Tommy guns and marched me ten or twelve blocks to some place. There was a Tommy gun on each side of me and one behind me. I felt kind of important, I rated three Nazis.[38]

Aboard his crippled Liberator Vincent Mazza was over Holland not far from the North Sea and was finally able to leave the formation for a lower altitude. But the navigator realised all his maps and charts were tangled in the control cables and ripped to pieces. As he was by now familiar with European pinpoints after so many missions Frank Federici gave compass headings from memory, the battered aircraft eventually making landfall at Great Yarmouth and returning to the circuit at Tibenham where the co-pilot made a landing by flying alongside another Liberator, thereby gauging his own airspeed and altitude. The co-pilot, navigator and bombardier all had to be treated for frostbite after stumbling out of the wrecked machine.

What remained of the savaged 491st BG came in to land at North Pickenham from 1600 hours onwards. The Group's 853rd Squadron had despatched nine Liberators. None came home. 'At first it never occurred to us that maybe our ships had gone down,' the squadron diarist wrote. 'But gradually after we had checked and rechecked with the tower, gradually we began to realise that such a thing could happen – that maybe it had happened. We fought the thought for a long time.' The Norfolk base was now firmly established among the flyers of the 2nd BD as not a place to complete a tour – its previous occupants, the 492nd, being switched to other duties after losing fifty-five Liberators and 520 men in eighty-nine days, fourteen of the bombers on an oil refinery mission to Politz in June.

As the battered bomber crews gulped their whisky-laden coffee at debriefing and the fighter jockeys filed their combat claims it was obvious that the guns of the 8th Air Force had inflicted another crushing defeat on the Luftwaffe. Goering had ordered more than 500 fighters aloft and American gunners and pursuit pilots claimed to have destroyed 114 of them. JG301 alone – which had engaged the 445th and 419th BG so successfully – lost forty of its pilots killed or wounded to the B-24s' gunners or the P-51s who came to the rescue. The cost had been thirty-four USAAF bombers out of the total stream of 1,073 on various targets, two-thirds from just two Groups of the 2nd BD. A total of 316 US airmen were missing, but the returned bombers also told a terrible tale of the individual savage price of war, bringing back the bodies of nineteen dead crewmen and thirteen wounded.

Federici and Mazza were able to attend the burial of their dead pilot James A. Williams at the American war cemetery at Madingley, Cambridgeshire, before the end of the week. By that time 2/Lt Messing was on his way to Luftwaffe interrogation, being picked up from a local Dutch jail where he had been kept for a few days. It was a bizarre and sometimes frightening journey.

A bus came along to take me and it went down the road awhile and then the engine died. The driver went out behind the bus and they were burning wood and the engine exploded the smoke from the wood. The bus would go another ten miles and he would have to stop again and fix the fire and we would go on again. Somewhere along the way we picked up my friend the pilot.

He and I spent the rest of our time as prisoners, less than seven months, together. They eventually put us prisoners in cattle cars and we were going down to Frankfurt for interrogation and we got to Münster where we had bombed the railroad yards a couple of months before. They had not got them repaired and we had to walk through Münster. Our guards had to protect us from the civilians. They were throwing rocks and sticks at us. The Germans were calling us *American terrorfliegers* at that time. They didn't know what Hitler was doing to British cities and thought we were bombing civilians. We didn't intentionally bomb civilians, but if there were people around the refinery they got hurt. We were taken on a regular train to Wetzlar [a satellite camp for Dulag Luft at Oberursel near Frankfurt]. Then we were transferred to prison camp at Barth on the Baltic and on the way there, on my twenty-first birthday, we went right through Berlin at night. I'll always remember where I was on my twenty-first birthday.[39]

The oil campaign would continue with lessening intensity right through to the following April, but Leuna-Merseburg, the most feared of its objectives, would only be attacked by the 8th Air Force twice more, in the first two weeks of December. Losses and flak damage were now on a steeply descending curve. RAF Bomber Command was by the winter adding its great weight in bomb tonnage to oil targets after Sir Charles Portal had ordered its leader Sir Arthur Harris to do so. It was the second time the Chief of the Air Staff had had to directly instruct his subordinate to join the Americans in the campaign which they rightly saw as a war winner. Harris considered refineries as 'panacea' targets not worth the bomb load compared to the industry within cities. Harris was right about many things, but was mightily wrong on this. And in fact when his Lancasters, with their much larger bomb bays than Flying Fortresses or Liberators, began visiting oil installations they caused lasting damage with their 4,000lb blockbuster bombs that the American air forces, whether from England or Italy, couldn't inflict.

The first Lancaster attack on Leuna-Merseburg, on the night of 6 December, made an enormous impression on the teenaged flak helper who had seen his battery bring down Fortresses a month before. He wrote that he had fallen into bed dead tired a few short hours earlier when in the middle of the night 'there came again alarm . . . I had that day just room service and wanted to go to bed. But I was one of the first on the gun and pulled the tarpaulin from it. On the way there, I heard a single plane in the air. This was the so-called "Pathfinder" which defined the route for the following.' Blockbusters and incendiary bombs tumbled from the Lancaster bomb bays. 'They hit the Leuna works and the town of Merseburg,' he continued. The American attacks had caused a shortage of shells which meant not every flak gun could be used.

> We received the command that we should bring up the ammunition of two guns, because *Ladehemmung* [blockage jam] had failed. So we left our artillery piece walls and ran to the other two guns. The individual anti-aircraft positions were surrounded by ramparts, to relieve the pressure on the ears from the pounding. Now, however, we felt that the more . . . I shouldered two shells and took this load back to our guns, while all around at a distance of a few kilometres new bombs exploded. Like lightning they flashed through me . . . We fired the last and then had to turn down the barrels and watch as the 'Christmas trees' (the slow-floating flares which the enemy used to illuminate) sank down, while the flames in Merseburg-Leuna works blazed in the sky . . . After this raid the Leuna works were so destroyed that (as we were later told) until the war ended full production could not be resumed.[40]

As autumn sharpened into winter the Luftwaffe was experiencing to a crippling degree the effects of the oil campaign. From Leuna-Merseburg alone the output in aviation fuel even by the end of September was down to 7,000 tons compared to 175,000 tons in April. It was the same story throughout the Greater Reich as three bomber air forces drained and torched supplies. The US 15th Air Force had had great success against the refineries at Ploeşti, Vienna and Budapest as well as synthetic petroleum plants in Silesia, Poland and Czechoslovakia as had the 8th Air Force against the targets General Spaatz had tasked it with, not just Leuna-Merseburg, but Politz, Ruhland and the crude oil refineries at Hamburg, Bremen and Hanover. Then there was Bomber Command of the RAF. Sir Arthur Harris's eventual response to his orders to make oil a priority had a devastating effect. Even though he had been tardy in the beginning, by the middle of September alone 11.7 per cent of his Command's total effort since the Invasion had been expended on denying the enemy their fuel supplies, 24,439 tons of bombs. This compared to 14.09 per cent in the same period (29,423 tons) on Harris's preferred choice, German towns and cities. The 8th Air Force expended 21.35 per cent of its bomber sorties (33,917 tons) against fuel supplies in this time frame.[41]

Not only was RAF Bomber Command therefore a considerable participant in the oil campaign, which some historians have denied, its heavier bomb load and great accuracy – now that all its bombers were fully equipped with the Mark III version of H2S ground-definition radar – created a more lasting effect than the 8th AF on oil installations, a necessary campaign of attrition that took thousands of American lives.

In more recent times it has become clearer why Harris was initially reluctant to attack oil targets and Spaatz so eager. From the middle of 1943 the then USAAF headquarters at Bushey Park had had good links with the British code-breaking centre at Bletchley Park, Buckinghamshire, where the Air Section in Hut 3 had been reading Luftwaffe signals for three years. This was without the need to be a member of the close circle who knew the Ultra secret, the cracking of the German Enigma code at Bletchley – a secret so important that if the German High Command had ever found out it was a secret no more the Enigma system would have been immediately transplanted.

From the day he took over as head of the USSTAF Spaatz had been getting distilled tactics reports from Hut 3, known as DISTAC, detailing strategic innovations by the Luftwaffe in the ebb and flow of the air war. Spaatz received his from US liaison officers at Bletchley, but Harris had been denied them because the route for RAF intelligence had been via the Air Ministry in Whitehall and incredibly for months they had not seen fit to forward them to Bomber Command headquarters at High Wycombe.

Eventually Harris's staff found out about them and intelligence links were vastly improved to aid raid planning. Spaatz so appreciated the DISTAC reports he would pay a personal visit to Bletchley Park in March, 1945.[42] Harris never went there. It is probable, therefore, that Spaatz even knew the Ultra secret itself while Harris didn't and the American commander was able to get a better overview of how denying the enemy his oil was winning the air war.

Only two years later Harris was moved to record in his personal testimony *Bomber Offensive* that he was 'altogether opposed' to being ordered by Portal to pinpoint oil targets from mid-1944 which he saw as a 'further diversion' from attacking German industrial cities, believing that success in the oil campaign 'was far from assured'. He agreed that it did of course succeed, but argued 'what the Allied strategists did was to bet on an outsider and it happened to win the race'.[43] It would be incredible today to find any historian describing the oil campaign's position in the field to war's winning post as 'an outsider'.

After inflicting such telling blows on the enemy it was unfortunate that the well-briefed Spaatz now had to pause in his main aim, defeated not by the Luftwaffe but by harsh weather conditions in Britain as snowstorms swept across the hills, followed by persistent freezing fog in the valleys. It was that icy weather grounding the air fleets which gave Field Marshall von Rundstedt the chance to launch Hitler's last gamble, a Panzer attack through the Ardennes towards Antwerp designed to split the American forces from the British and Canadians. It would be a bleak Christmas marred in particular by the tragic loss of two USAAF officers who had made an impact on British life in their own unique ways.

WINTER

14

'I bet our lives'

The depth of gloom that had now settled on the Groups mauled in the air battles of November was only matched by a depression west of Iceland which would limit the ambitions of General Spaatz for weeks. The cold front moving underneath warmer air meant big trouble for divisional commanders trying to assemble air fleets. This low pressure area moved south-east and then east over the UK in early December bringing Polar gales with blizzards in their wake.[1]

Transportation targets were the new priority as Albert Speer had dispersed much production away from the big cities that had attracted thousands of Allied bombers and on 2 December all three of the 8th Air Force's bombardment divisions were assigned to attacks on marshalling yards in Germany. But the 3rd BD had to recall all of its 160 aircraft heading for the Koblenz complex because of poor visibility. The weather was now the enemy's friend, and it was two days before USSTAF headquarters at Bushy Park was able to set the teleprinters to Groups chattering again as Spaatz seized a brief break in the conditions to despatch a force of more than 1,100 bombers. Its aim was to wreck seven marshalling yards to halt parts for the German war effort being moved around the country and so prevent completion of badly needed aircraft, tanks, artillery and U-boats. His determination to finish off the enemy from the air reached down to his crews, particularly those well into their tours and thus carrying valuable experience. The crew in which Lt Alfeo Brusetti was now a lead bombardier of the 832nd BS, 486th BG at Sudbury found they were called twice within days to fly a mission despite their hair-raising experiences on the first of them, on 30 November. That had been Mission 19 of their tour, to the ersatz oil plant at Lutzkendorf, which like all such targets was heavily defended, claiming two of Brusetti's Group, as he recorded.

I watched the Group right in front of us go through an especially heavy flak concentration and could see three of their planes on fire at one time. I was glad I could look into my bombsight for the rest of the run. As I looked up after 'bombs away' I saw a flash of 'snow' through the corner of my eye. It came from a piece of flak that came through the Plexiglas nose just as I started lifting my head up from the bombsight. The hole was at eye level. Our plane was hit several times. We pulled away from the target with our rudder controls shot away and no communication with the crew in the back of the plane. Our pilot, Lt Bereman, wanted a damage and crew report from there, so I hooked up my oxygen bottle and started back.

Everything OK until I entered the radio room which was also used by Lt [Rex] Tolliver, the radar operator, working behind his black drapes. I saw that a piece of flak had come in over the radio operator's desk and on through Lt Tolliver's drawn drapes. I anxiously pulled back the drapes and Lt Tolliver indicated a close call, pointing to the torn sleeve on his suit where the flak had gone through without actually hitting him. When I asked about Sgt Pentz, the radio operator, he pointed to the back of the plane. I went into the waist and found he was OK and manning one of the waist guns. He had moved there when he heard fighters were in the area and before the flak came through his room. Sgt Wall, the other gunner, showed me his flak helmet. It had a hole through the middle of it. I asked him how come he wasn't killed. He said he had it on the floor, resting his foot on it when the flak came through.

Our pilots, Lt Bereman and Lt Uzdrowski, did a great job of steering the plane by ailerons and engine thrust and got us back in one piece. On arrival over our base with our formation we informed the tower of our problem and that probably our brakes were also gone. They didn't want us to take the chance we might crash on landing so they told us to go to an emergency RAF field near the coast [Woodbridge] that was built for landing damaged planes. The runways were built extremely wide and long. It was just what we needed and we managed to come in OK. Our base sent over a truck for us and we were back by morning, exhausted, but grateful to be alive.[2]

Mission 20 for the crew was the marshalling yard at Giessen, north of Frankfurt. Being a squadron lead unit meant manning a radar-equipped aircraft designed to bomb through clouds – a method which would become the norm in this final winter of the war – and the following planes would release as its bombs left the racks. 'At the turn for the bomb run the Group would stay together or split up into its three squadrons following one another down the run and all bombing the leader's signal – a smoke bomb carried under the Lead's wing that was dropped along with the regular bombs,' Brusetti explained in post-conflict notes. 'Blind bombing required the use of both the radar scope and the bomb sight.'[3]

For Giessen a command pilot and an extra, pinpoint, navigator was added to the crew.

Our navigator, Lt [Bob] McCall, directed the formation by instruments while the second navigator, Lt Phillips, double checked our progress by visually checking positions on the ground. The best place for Phil to do this was from the bombardier's position, so I gave him my seat until the bomb run. I sat on an ammunition box looking out a small window in the side of the nose compartment. We did not expect any anti-aircraft fire until the run, so we were not wearing our heavy flak suits and helmets. Phil reported seeing a few flak bursts aimed at the formations ahead of us. I looked and figured these were only two or three guns firing and not worth putting my suit on for. McCall thought otherwise and asked for help as he tried to hurry into his. I stood up to give him a hand when I felt a jolt like being kicked in the leg by a horse. I knocked him over as I fell, with his flak suit landing on top of me. I next heard McCall shouting into the intercom, 'The bombardier's been killed, the bombardier's been killed.'

As soon as I could find the intercom button under all that mess I assured them that was not so. I knew I was hit in the right leg but didn't know how bad. It was a relief to find I could move it and then stand on it. No serious damage was done. I found the pant leg of my electric suit torn from the middle front to the middle back along the outside. My leg received a burn along this line. That piece of flak must have been spinning so that it went around the leg instead of into it . . . When I sat back down on the ammunition box and looked out of the window there was a big hole in the middle of it . . . I'm sure [the navigator, McCall] saved my life that day.[4]

The Giessen flak claimed two bombers, only one being lost on all the other targets combined in the marshalling yard raids.

The next day Spaatz had clear enough weather to order his 8th Air Force commander Jimmy Doolittle to call a mission to Berlin and Münster – from which three bombers failed to return – and on 6 December Doolittle was able to launch nearly 800 bombers on various objectives including Leuna-Merseburg, but then the weather closed in, turning to sleet driven by icy winds. It was another four days before Spaatz's East Anglian bomber crews were able to operate again and then not in great force. The USSTAF commander was itching to use his growing air fleets and on 11 December, with the promise of forty-eight hours of clear weather, he launched the largest mission of the war – 1,467 bombers of all three 8th AF Divisions escorted by 777 fighters. Their targets were marshalling yards and bridges in a joined-up plan to paralyse the German railway system. It didn't quite do that, but it did create chaos – the prime aim of the strategic bomber at this stage – and the Luftwaffe ground and air defences were only able to down five bombers and two fighters.

The following morning he was able to despatch more than 800 bombers to marshalling yards and again losses were minimal, only four being lost. It was what crews liked to call a 'milk run' and from the 100th BG the navigator of Lt Herman Streich's *Eager Beaver*, Lt Leon Schwartz, invited his family in Los Angeles to learn what combat flying was like in an hour-by-hour account from his aircraft, thus preserving those moments of a mission to Darmstadt for ever.

Dear Mom and Pa, I decided to write you a very unique letter today. I'm at 11,300ft at the present time. We are circling the English coast prior to departure to Germany on my 16th mission. I'm writing on a log because it's all I have to write on. We're starting to climb higher . . . Hands getting cold . . . Put on my gloves. We're at 13,000ft. I put on my oxygen mask. We level off at 18,000ft . . . We start climbing again and we are about to leave England . . . We are now over water and the crew test fire their guns . . . Sight of land ahead. We are now over the Continent. It's enemy territory. We put on our flak suits as we approach enemy territory . . . We have reached bombing altitude and stop climbing . . . The temperature is minus 38 degrees centigrade. Enemy fighters reported near target. Am over Germany and about to turn on the bomb run . . . We have dropped our bombs. I think we hit our aiming point . . . We start heading back. On the way back I don't usually work as hard as on the way out, but we are still over enemy territory so we must all be prepared just the same . . . They tell me today was easy, the enemy fighters did not materialise and there was no flak at the target . . . We have dropped down a couple of thousand feet and the sun is shining to the north. It's minus 35 . . . We are now back in friendly territory. We have been descending for almost an hour. We are down to 11,000ft and I can take off my oxygen mask. We have now left the Continent and back over water. Home soon. We have just crossed the coast of England . . . We are circling now to get the formation below the cloud . . . meanwhile I took my gun out of its receiver, eat a Kent bar of candy and smoked two cigarettes . . . After circling in fog for an hour and a half we are now ready to get out of the plane.[5]

It was a remarkably easy mission, particularly for the Darmstadt force. But one B-17 of the 497 that had set out to blast the marshalling yards had brought the war home in explosive fashion to those comrades who served the air war on the ground. Cpl Jack Feller, the clerk/orderly who had met Lt Joseph Kennedy in August, was at his post in the control tower of the 493rd BG at Debach when the commander of the *Devil's Own* called up while outbound over the North Sea. According to Cpl Feller:

> He said he had No. 1 engine on fire and needed to return for an emergency landing. The officer, Lt Moore, told him to land in the mud beside the runway, assuming it would be the other side of the runway to the control tower, but the aircraft landed right beside the tower wheels up and skidded along the mud.
>
> When it stopped I looked at the situation board and knew the Group had only been gone for an hour and 20 minutes and realised he still had his bombs on board. The crew were coming out from all sides and directions of the burning airplane. The co-pilot even came out of his side window. The fire truck started out, but we told them to stop. Lt Moore, in charge of the tower, called an emergency alert on the loudspeaker and we ran out of the back side of the building. I had just got out of the door when the bomb load exploded. Here came shrapnel through the air, little pieces of metal were falling all around and the explosion blew a tremendous hole right beside the runway and knocked the hangar doors down.[6]

Amazingly no one was seriously injured, but there now remained the problem of how to eventually land the rest of the Group. 'The black construction battalion who had built the base were still on the field and they had a bulldozer,' Cpl Feller remembers, 'so they were called out to scrape the metal off the runway into the hole made by the blast and get the big pieces out of the way, then volunteer crews were called out to clean up the concrete.'[7]

Most of the debris from *Devil's Own* went into the hole it had made. The bulldozer team were still finishing when the Group returned from bombing the marshalling yards at Darmstadt.

'They were calling over the radio when they were overhead and saw the area, asking "Was anybody killed?"' Feller recalls. 'They were startled to see such a mess.'[8] The returning B-17s were able to land on the damaged runway, but the control tower was out of action and the airfield circuit was being controlled by a hastily arranged emergency radio network. The clear-up operation was hampered by the weather. Later in the day blizzards struck the northern part of the UK and the temperature fell to an abnormally low level across the rest.[9]

On the 13th a wedge of high pressure crossing the country brought relief for a few hours. The 467th BG at Rackheath, near Norwich, had a big reputation for accurate bombing and the CO, Col. Albert Shower, was anxious that they keep it. He used that brief weather window to launch a practice mission to bring new crews up to the mark. 2/Lt Ed King, an aircraft commander with the 467th who had carried out his first operation on 2 December, had no indication of what was to come that day when he gunned his Liberator *Massillon Tiger* down the active runway at Rackheath and lifted it over the stark trees around the base. He described the memorable next few hours after the war.

It was one sunny day, when a sudden and vicious winter storm swept in over the British Isles and northern Europe like an express train. The practice mission having been called back, our formation headed out over the North Sea, looking for a way down through the solid cloud mass which was engulfing us. We were in the last squadron to turn and head down through the clouds, partly within a small canyon of clear space in that otherwise solid undercast. We broke out of the clouds a few hundred feet above the water, but as we proceeded toward the east coast of England, the cloud ceiling pushed us lower and lower, closer and closer to that icy sea.

Laval Beniot, our radio operator, God rest his soul, was plumbing our height above the water by measuring out the trailing radio antenna until he got a voltage drop! The cloud mass was now right on top of us. We appeared to be no more than 75 feet over the water when I decided that disaster was surely waiting for us just ahead and I opted to peel out of the formation and start climbing up into the cloud mass as we neared London. We climbed up and agonizingly up and around in that solid overcast until we finally broke out on top at about 22,000 feet. That climb on instruments proved to be the worst ordeal of my short flying career. I had at one point in that long climb suffered a complete loss of orientation, hope, and faith in my instruments, so that I was ready to just let go and let the plane take us into the North Sea or whatever was under us, but [co-pilot] Tom Elsen's encouraging voice got through to me and made me take hold again and come back fighting.[10]

For hours 2/Lt King flew up and down England's east coast searching for a hole in the overcast as the aircraft's fuel gauges declined towards zero. 'Finally one of the waist gunners screamed, "I see a light on the ground!"' the pilot remembers. 'I upended the *Massillon Tiger* and we spiralled down through that skinny little chimney until we broke out several hundred feet above the ground, practically on top of Rackheath. What a Navigator Ed Gore was. But we wouldn't have cared if we were over Germany!'[11]

The crew then found the runway was blanketed by snow and only one set of lights marking a single side of the hidden concrete was showing. 2/Lt King had no way of knowing which side it was as by now the tower radio was not answering. 'I bet our lives that the few runway lights were on the left side of the runway, and we went in,' the pilot recalls. The only way he could see through the frozen windscreen was by reaching through a side window with a wrench and scraping a '50 cents hole' in the ice.

> As I neared the depthless white sheet and began to flare out, my 50c hole rose up and looked at the black sky! The lights had passed from view, and the rudders were getting very mushy, and I rode the hell out of them, praying that it would not be a crash landing from 30 feet in the air. And then softly, gently, the nose came down and we realized that we were on the runway and rolling it out – the softest, smoothest landing I ever made in my life.[12]

In the train of 13 December's wedge of high pressure came local gales then more precipitation. It was particularly heavy in south-west Scotland – where it fell at 150 per cent of the average since records began in 1881 – and in Northern Ireland, mid-Wales and the West Riding of Yorkshire. But it was less than 50 per cent in the area from London to Cambridge and parts of Bedfordshire where many of the 1st BD airfields were. Instead there was an even more deadly problem for flyers – fog.[13]

The clampdown allowed squadron commanders to issue more leave passes and 2/Lt Howard Roth got one, so left the base at Thurleigh, Bedfordshire, with another B-17 commander he buddied with on nights out, Doug Schrack. The two friends headed to Bedford, the nearest large town, as Roth recounts.

> We got a three-day pass and signed in to stay at the American Red Cross Officers' Club. We went to the local pubs and had a few drinks and on December 14th we went back to the officers' club intending to hit the sack, but decided to go in the dining room and have a couple of drinks. I looked over at a table and told Doug, 'I think that's Glenn Miller.' I asked a waitress and she said, 'Yes, that's him.' I told Doug I was

going to ask Miller for his autograph. He said, 'You're stupid, you can't have a lieutenant asking a major for his autograph.' I thought about it for a while and said, 'I guess you're right.' Now I wish he'd kept his mouth shut. Holy smoke, think what that dated autograph would be worth today. When we left the dining room Glenn Miller was still there with his aide Lt Don Haynes. I believe he and Lt Haynes left in the morning about 9am. It's funny, that night I dreamt of a plane going down and right away I thought it was me. I told Doug. But it didn't foretell my future, it was another person's future.[14]

Less than twelve hours later Glenn Miller, who had relocated from London to Bedford with his Army Air Force band in the summer because of buzz bomb attacks on the capital, was dead. It was considered so potentially devastating to morale that the bandleader, whose music had beaten time with the war for British civilians and American soldiers and airmen alike, was gone that the USSTAF kept a clamp on the news, thus spawning a rash of theories how – and sometimes why – he died, ever since. But the most logical is simple enough to any flyer and that is the view the Air Force took. Miller, who had fourteen hit numbers in five years, had been playing at airbases and army camps in England for six months, but by December many of the GIs his band had entertained were now miles from Britain in foxholes facing the German army. The major planned to take his musicians to a new base on the Continent, starting with a Christmas concert on Allied Expeditionary Forces' radio from Paris for the front-line troops. As the weather turned foul and all flights were grounded, Miller fretted for days before the band's representative Doug Haynes was offered a lift with a US Army colonel in a Norseman which was due to leave RAF Twinwood Farm in Bedfordshire within twenty-four hours. Haynes was scheduled to make that flight, but when Miller heard it was due to take off he pulled rank, pushed Haynes onto the next flight and jumped at the chance to get to Paris as soon as possible.

As Haynes and Miller waited by the runway at Twinwood Farm for the Norseman to appear out of the mist on the afternoon of 14 December Haynes checked the huge thermometer at the side of the control tower. It read 34 degrees Fahrenheit, not far above freezing. Haynes noted in his diary later that as he helped Miller aboard the small plane he shouted, 'Good luck.' Miller, who would be in the sky in less than one minute, replied: 'Thanks Haynsie, we may need it.' The overcast was so low at the airfield on that dismal winter day that the plane, piloted by the combat-tour-expired Flt Officer John Morgan, disappeared almost as soon as its wheels left the ground. No trace of it or any of the men on board has been seen since. Bizarrely, Miller had had a premonition for weeks he would not survive the war. On 14 November Lt Haynes had noted during a visit to the American Red Cross Club in Bedford that Miller had told him he didn't think he would ever see his wife and son again. 'I know that sounds odd, but I've had that feeling for some time now,' Miller had said. 'You know the Miller luck has been phenomenal for the last five years and I don't want to be around when it changes.'[15]

There has been much conjecture about what happened to Glenn Miller, including the story by an ex-RAF navigator who claimed decades after the war that he saw the Norseman below him as bombs were jettisoned in the Channel from returning 3 Group Lancasters. They had been recalled from a raid on railway yards at Siegen, near Bonn, because thick cloud almost to the ground made even a GH-guided raid impossible. But W/O Ron Brown, a flight engineer with the RNZAF 75 Sqn, who was on the raid, remembers that the bombs were dropped miles away from the Channel:

We jettisoned our bombs set to safe in the pre-designated jettison area of the North Sea, from about 3,000ft. If the bombs
had been armed, dropping them from that height you would
have blown up your own aircraft. The bomb doors opened
and I doubt that the bomb aimer even saw the bombs falling away, the cloud was so thick. It's a nonsensical claim for
someone to make that they saw jettisoned bombs hit Glenn
Miller's Norseman flying at about 1,000ft because it wouldn't
have been possible to see anyone in that weather.[16]

Sgt Kenneth Turnham, a wireless operator on 115 Sqn, RAF,
began his tour on the day Glenn Miller was lost and also remembers the 'atrocious' conditions. 'The Siegen operation was just
like one of the old fogs in Manchester, you couldn't see a hand in
front of you,' he says. 'We were recalled and given a designated
area in the North Sea to jettison our bombs and that's where we
did. Nobody will ever know what happened to Glenn Miller, but
it's likely his aircraft iced up.'[17] Four years ago it was revealed that
Richard Anderton, a wartime civilian worker at Woodley airfield,
near Reading, kept a log of aircraft he saw each day and his note
for 15 December reads: '1 Norseman going ESE.'[18] The timing
is right for Miller's low-level flight and shows the direction as
heading to cross Brighton and over a narrow section of the Channel with much shipping, well away from the North Sea where
bombs might be jettisoned. Any pilot leaving Twinwood Farm
for the Continent would have to fly around London to avoid edgy
anti-aircraft gunners and a flight to the south-west near the Reading area would then enable an east-south-east track reducing the
time over water and avoiding Calais and Boulogne, still in enemy
hands and isolated by the Allies. An inquiry by the USSTAF in
fact concluded the Norseman's airframe had become encrusted
with ice and it had plunged into the sea.[19] As 2/Lt King had found
two days earlier, flying over the sea in low cloud was fraught with

danger when there was no horizon to fix on and it was therefore easy to fly straight into the water in error, without the added hazard of ice.

Miller's death made the swing music his band epitomised even more popular in Britain if that were possible. American Forces Radio provided a virtual non-stop evening programme of the sounds of Miller, Artie Shaw, Woody Herman and Benny Goodman. There were even films promoting swing bands of all levels of popularity. The movie *Swing Fever* featuring 'the old Professor of Swing' Kay Kyser, who liked to conduct his orchestra wearing an academic's mortarboard and gown, was just one of them screening in Britain in December. On and off the bases swing music was the vital sound for dances that winter. From Norwich to London there were few corners of eastern England where an airman couldn't find a dance on somewhere.

The day after Miller went missing the biggest, bloodiest battle fought by the US Army in the whole of the Second World War was launched through the forests of the Ardennes, where Germany had sprung her *blitzkrieg* attack at the start of the fighting in 1940. Hitler had been waiting since November for the kind of weather which would keep the Allied air fleets grounded, thus taking away the single most important advantage in the North West Europe campaign. Mid-December, with its freezing fog and low-lying clouds, would never provide a better opportunity. By the time the Battle of the Bulge, as it became known, had ended on 25 January, 610,000 American troops had been engaged, of which 89,000 were casualties including 19,000 killed. The Ardennes had been chosen because it was a weak point in the Allied line, a place where untried US divisions were sent and severely-tried divisions rested. For the Germans crucially it was where the British 21st Army Group and the US 1st and 9th Armies met. The Ardennes offensive was designed to split them – causing dissension at a fragile time for British and American relations – and head for the captured key port of Antwerp, which had only reopened in late November as a much-needed supply point for the over-extended Allied communication chain. It was because General Bernard Montgomery, leading the British 21st Army Group, and the head of the US 12th Army Group General Omar Bradley each claimed they were getting the short end of supplies that the dispute had begun.

Carl Spaatz would find he had a sudden new priority to bomb the German Panzer divisions into submission. But the weather could not be worse. Day after day as December marched on, Spaatz gazed out of the windows of his London office and watched the snow fall. His command of four air forces, the 8th, 12th, 15th and tactical 9th was now being officially recognised in the Allied press, somewhat belatedly, as head of the United States Strategic and Tactical Air Forces. Yet he had never felt more frustrated as his now mighty strength of fifty-eight bomber and fighter Groups in the 8th Air Force alone waited undisturbed on their airfields in East Anglia, frequent evening visits to adjoining village hostelries the only distraction.

At one of those hotels Combat Wing leader Brigadier General Frederick Castle was a welcome visitor. He was a friend of the landlord of the Swan at Lavenham, Suffolk, an archetypal half-timbered British pub in a picture-book village which had hardly changed in 500 years since the medieval wool trade made it among the twenty wealthiest settlements in England. Castle, who headed the 4th Bomb Wing at Rougham twelve miles away, liked to talk to landlord 'Robby' Robbins over a beer in the bar where the walls were covered with the signatures of servicemen including flyers from the 487th BG, just down the road. Recently the diminutive former businessman had added his name to those signatures.

Castle had an impeccable pedigree with the USSTAF as one of

the original seven officers brought over to England by General Eaker in 1942 to form what became the 8th Air Force in might and not just name. When he took command of the 94th BG his officers had thought him reserved, but Castle often ate post-combat meals in the enlisted men's mess, where flying clothing covered badges of rank. On 4 December, the day he won his brigadier's stars, smiling Red Cross girls at Rougham were pictured pinning them on him. Those civilians he met in the UK appreciated him too. He was a self-confessed anglophile and liked to walk the beguilingly pretty country lanes around Rougham, oak trees shading a quiet path to the heart of the base action, the green-painted control tower.

In nearby Bury St Edmunds there were the narrow winding streets to explore, passageways with high-pitched red-tiled roofs and both half-timbered and Georgian buildings, testimony to the ancient town's prosperity through the centuries. Castle enjoyed the patchwork and pageantry of England in equal measure. His many British friends ranged from regulars at the Swan to academics such as the Master of Trinity College, Cambridge.

But friends and promotion apart, Castle was a disappointed man in mid-December. Like most of the senior officers of the USSTAF he was straining at the leash to launch the bombers that could stop the German offensive in the Ardennes in its tracks. The weather had deteriorated further, however, turning to rain and widespread gales. Of the two divisions briefed to attack transportation targets on 16 December, the 1st BD had to abandon the mission over England in the atrocious conditions and of the 3rd BD only the 95th BG, the 490th and the 486th (part of Castle's three-Group Wing) made it through to Germany and bombed the Stuttgart and Bietingheim railway objectives. Two days later the 2nd BD and parts of other divisions were recalled from their missions to communication and tactical targets in Germany because of extensive cloud cover. The next day the effort was limited again as Spaatz tried to attack tactical targets in the Luxembourg and Koblenz areas to hold up the drive through the Ardennes.

However, bombardier Lt Alfeo Brusetti found that day that every cloud has a silver lining. 'On December 19th, about six months after I arrived in England my sister, Dee, and another army nurse were able to visit me at my base,' he recorded. 'Our squadron were not flying combat that day but we were scheduled for a training flight. We invited them to fly with us. It was against regulations, but everybody's eyes were conveniently turned the other way. We dropped our practice bombs and then just flew around . . . A nice adventure for all of us.' But days later Brusetti was writing to his sister: 'The fog rolled in the day after you left and hasn't budged since.'[20]

The clinging, freezing mist socked in the 8th Air Force until the 23rd. Morale began to dip among its aircrew. Christmas was coming, they were far from home and the weather meant they were no longer counting off missions which would take them back to the States any time soon. Young aircraft commander Howard Roth was missing his family and friends in Lockport, New York State, as Christmas approached. His quarters at Thurleigh could hardly be called home. 'Dingleberry Hall was the name of our barracks. It was a Quonset hut with small bedrooms on each end and to get into the bedroom you'd have to have a little seniority,' he recorded. 'Some of the guys who usually got those on occasion would take a spare uniform in town and bring in a gal through the gate. Of course they'd always arrive at night and they'd stay for a night or two.'

The cold was what occupied the minds of most of the hut's occupants.

My cot was about two places from the heater and a lot of my time was spent there during the winter. I was wondering how a small stove could heat that large Quonset hut, but I found out they placed a brick at the bottom of the grates and they had an oil line going to it. They got a fire going and then they started dripping oil, just a drop, drop, drop onto this brick until it was red hot and that would throw off enough heat for the whole barracks.

In Dingleberry Hall we decided to have some kind of a tree for the Christmas spirit. The American Forces airwaves started playing Christmas songs and everyone was blue, so my buddy and I scoured the farms around the area looking for some type of fir tree. We couldn't find any, so we settled on a 4ft or 5ft thorn apple bush and took that and set it up in the barracks and started decorating. We had one fellow that was quite adept at electrical appliances and he concocted a group of instrument bulbs he got over at the motor pool and wired them together and somehow got a transformer so we had our Christmas lights. For tinsel we used chaff, which was spread over targets before bomb runs to confuse German radar . . . for snow somewhere we got cotton balls.

And now for ornaments you wouldn't believe. We all got prophylactic kits whenever we wanted them. The enlisted men had to show a 'pro' kit before they went into town, a condom and some sort of ointment to ward off VD. So we got a bunch of kits and we inflated the condoms to ornament size and painted them different colours and hung them around the tree. The guys from around different barracks would stop in and really appreciated it. But the next day all the painted condoms were kind of wrinkly, suggesting leakage, and we were all a bit apprehensive about that.[21]

Others got a chance to visit London when bad weather grounded the bombers, clambering aboard packed trains in the early morning, stepping over guns and gas masks, then returning on the last night train, equally crowded, with the added discomfort of lighting painted blue which had not only kept the hunting Luftwaffe in the dark, but seat-searching American airmen too. Lt John Barry had arrived at Sudbury in early November as navigator in the 486th BG crew of Lt Wilbur 'Bud' Genz and shared Nissen Hut 19 with fellow officers. Barry, used to the bright lights of New York, had not been impressed with the entertainment on offer in rural Britain when he first arrived at the aircrew replacement centre at Stone, Staffordshire and went to a local dance. 'Cold, lousy band and girls who wouldn't have shamed Zazu Pitts,'* he recorded in the first pages of his tour diary. On 11 December he had been part of the largest mission of the war so far, but most of the bomb load had hung up. 'Took off at 0700, landed 14.15. Target: Koblenz. Our whole crew went along . . . brought five babies back. Marshalling yards. Got our first 48 hour pass tonight – expect to go to London tomorrow morn.'[22]

Wartime London in December had more than enough to offer for a young officer with money to spare. If he didn't want to stay at the American Red Cross Club at Rainbow Corner there were a variety of hotels willing and able to relieve a well-paid combat airman of his money at what he considered bargain prices. The Mascot in Baker Street was advertising '50 bright rooms with modern furniture, running water, telephones and gas fires' at five guineas for the whole week. It was easily affordable on a junior American officer's wages of approximately £15 a week with overseas allowance and flight pay, three times more than that of equivalent Pilot Officer aircrew in the RAF.[23] Meals could be taken in what had been the ballroom of the Grosvenor House hotel, now a gigantic mess hall for US officers because so many were working in central London or passing through. It could seat

---

* Zazu Pitts' lack of glamour typecast her as a worried spinster in several Hollywood films of the 1930s and '40s.

up to 3,000 at one time and served food with the same kind of rapidity that the specially built Ford plant outside Detroit was reportedly churning out B-24s, so the mess hall was nicknamed *Willow Run*. 'We hit London at noon, quiet subways, busy streets, good meals at crowded Grosvenor House, bomb ruins, Commandos, two-storey buses, good ale and Scotch,' Lt Barry recorded cryptically.

Fog or no fog General Spaatz managed to return his men to the war on 23 December with an attack in the rear of the battle area on seven objectives including marshalling yards and communication centres. The weather conditions at least kept the Luftwaffe on the ground and only one bomber was lost of 423 despatched. It came from one of Brigadier Castle's Groups, the 94th at Rougham. But if dangers from the enemy were few that day perils from nature itself were many. 2/Lt Walter Douglas, who had nearly hit another B-17 in haze over Thurleigh on 22 October, now had another opportunity to calculate how unlikely it would be he would see Christmas as he watched the mist settle over the 305th BG base at Chelveston. Despite the weather that day was clearly printed on his memory.

We were sure this mission would be cancelled. There was ice on the runway and ice-fog – 00 visibility. We were sitting in our ready tent waiting for the signal to call it off when they said 'Go'.

We were No. 1 for take off. A jeep with a big sodium light on the back led us to the first runway light. He turned his light off and said 'Good luck'. We tried braking to no avail so we charged down the runway, holding compass heading as best we could. As the co-pilot saw a runway light go by he pushed left rudder until I saw a light on my side. We did this until we felt a bump near the end of the runway (about 100ft left). We had about 90–100mph and I bounced the aircraft once and was about to bounce it again when the co-pilot pulled up the gear. I was waiting for the tree tops, but missed somehow.

The fog was about 100–150ft thick. When we popped up through it we were under another B-17 and had to duck back down again. Everything was then OK until on the bomb run in haze conditions. The Germans were firing ground to air rockets and AA, but above us some other Group dropped their bombs right through us. Miraculously no one was hit. When we got back to base we had to land on ice on a short runway, so we had to hit one brake then we slowed to about 50mph and ground-looped it to keep going off the end.[24]

The frustrated Spaatz was yearning for a break in the sky. He had been planning that if he couldn't mount several missions in the appalling weather then at the first opportunity he would launch a mighty, multi-pronged attack to help American infantry now being mauled by Panzers in the Battle of the Bulge. That opportunity came on Christmas Eve as a high pressure south of the British Isles turned north. Days of intense cold would follow after the 25th.[25] All 8th AF bomber and fighter Groups were told to prepare 'everything that will fly'. That would even include training aircraft. Nothing in the history of air warfare could be likened to the buzzing hive of activity at airfields from Alconbury to Wendling as Fortresses and Liberators followed one another down perimeter tracks, yellow-tipped propellors spinning arcs of faint colour in the dark while power plants barked and spluttered. The system of two crews for every bomber now being employed on the Groups meant nothing with four good engines would be left behind. A total of 2,046 bombers took off tasked with striking at thirty-one airfields and communication centres in Germany. This time the 8th Air Force's commanders were determined to seize air superiority again, prevent the Luftwaffe from flying and stop the German thrust by cutting off its supplies. The 467th BG put up sixty-two. The tenacious Group commander, Col. Albert Shower, took the 'everything will fly' order so seriously he even included the Group assembly ship. The black Liberator, the top and sides of its fuselage lurid with prominent yellow circles outlined in red, trailed the glittering aluminium shapes of the Group's other B-24s as the ship named *Pete the Pom Inspector*, a cartoon figure riding a painted bomb under the pilot's Plexiglas, went to war. But it was the 453rd BG at Old Buckenham where James Stewart was the Group Executive Officer that put up the most for the multi-missioned demonstration of America's industrial dynamism, with sixty-four Liberators heading for Germany. It took so long to assemble such a force into one long bomb train that some aircraft were crossing Felixstowe on the way out as others were coming back over the Wash, their task completed. And at the head of them all had been Brigadier General Fred Castle. His target had been an Fw 190 base at Babenhausen, between Darmstadt and Frankfurt, but Castle had never reached Germany. He had been shot down over liberated Belgium.

The thirty-six-year-old brigadier had called into the operations room of the 4th Bomb Wing at Rougham on the evening of 23 December after visiting other stations in his command. He had merely meant to announce he was back before going to bed. He had expected to find the Wing was stood down by bad weather, but was told it was likely they would take off. Then he discovered the 4th BW was leading the 3rd BD and the division was heading the whole 8th Air Force. He told the colonel assigned to lead the mission he would take it instead. 'This is the kind of thing they pay me for and this is what they would expect me to lead,' he said.[26] The next morning General Castle made his last trip to his beloved Lavenham, where he boarded *Treble Four* of the 487th BG who would point the way for the entire formation. Castle settled himself into the co-pilot's position, despatching Lt Claude Rowe to the tail, and the lead crew pilot Lt Robert W. Harriman fired up the engines to take off minutes later. Unknown to any in the van of the armada much of the 853-strong escort of Mustangs and Thunderbolts were delayed in leaving their own bases because of fog. General Castle's *Treble Four* was therefore alone out in front when the radioman T/Sgt Lawrence Swain called to report from Castle that the No. 1 engine was throwing oil and it was difficult to stay in formation. The 487th Group were already seventeen minutes late because of an unexpected wind shift. Castle then called over VHF that he was aborting because of the engine problem and, still over Allied-held territory, was handing over to his deputy.

A USSTAF report four days later details what happened next.

Three Me 109s were sighted and the General evidently decided to attempt to remain as leader. These e/a came through from 9 o'clock, but did not fire. The General could not maintain the lead, on account of mechanical difficulties, and aborted down and to the left. A single Me 109 made a pass from level and 2 o'clock, wounding Lt Bruno Procopio (the radar operator). Immediately afterward three Me 109s attacked from 3 o'clock level, setting No. 1 and No. 2 engines on fire. The pilot, Lt Harriman, gave the command to bale out. Lt Henry McCarty (navigator); T/Sgt Jeffers, engineer; and Capt Auer, pilotage navigator, baled out in that order. Lt Paul Biri (the bombardier) was preparing to bale out when the pilot appeared in the hatch and told him to wait for him, that he was unable to find his chute, and that they would both use Lt Biri's chute if he was unable to find his. Lt Biri waited at the open hatch and when the aircraft went into a violent spin, he was thrown out. Lt Biri estimates this was at 1,200 feet. Lt Biri opened his chute and hurt his leg in landing. Lt McArty [*sic*] made a delayed jump at 1236 and was uninjured. Both were picked up by American soldiers . . . Ground observers to whom Lt MacArty [*sic*] talked said the aircraft broke in half, hit a forest and set it on fire. Lt Biri stated that he did not believe the pilot or General Castle would have been able to leave the airplane after it began spinning.[27]

The 487th had been attacked by an Fw 190 *Sturmgruppe* force and covering Me 109s. After General Castle's plane was shot out of formation the Group's 836th Sqn, flying in the low rear position, was hit by the Fw 190s in standard *Sturmgruppe* line abreast and seven were shot down. The Deputy Mission Lead Captain Mayfield Shilling led the rest of the battered Group on into Germany where they bombed the assigned aerodrome target. Eyewitnesses reported that co-pilot Lt Claude Rowe, who had been given the role of tail gunner observer when Castle took his seat, was machine-gunned to death in the air by a Luftwaffe fighter after he baled out. But the official USSTAF report did not conclude this. A second stage of the investigation, dated 11 January 1945, which included a visit to the crash site, reported: 'Extensive blood stains in the tail gunner's position, .30 calibre and 20mm holes in the tail section and gunner's compartment indicate that the tail gunner was wounded while in the aircraft and not strafed as reported.' It also said there was evidence of a fire in the radio operator's compartment which would explain why the radioman T/Sgt Lawrence Swain fell to his death and was found without his parachute. His watch stopped at 1252. The radar operator Lt Bruno Procopio baled out and died of his wounds at a military hospital in Liège.

The USSTAF report then came to the conclusion which would result in the awarding of a posthumous Medal of Honor to General Castle.

From a physical investigation of the aircraft wreckage it can be pointed out with certainty that the General knowingly risked and paid with his life in not jettisoning the bombs, because of endangering friendly troops directly below, even though the aircraft was on fire and two engines were out of commission, plus being under intensive fighter attack. Through all of this he held the aircraft steady so the crew could safely bale out – if he had taken the evasive action the situation demanded, it would have jeopardized the crew while baling out. While holding the aircraft steady a 20mm exploded in the right wing Tokyo tank which in turn exploded and blew off the wing, throwing the aircraft into a violent right spin which caused the tail and fuselage section to shear off. The resultant forces of the spin were so great that the occupants of the cockpit (General Castle and Lt Harriman) were pinned inside.

Physical evidence and a dog tag showed that General Castle was in the aircraft when it crashed.[28] The waist gunner S/Sgt Hudson, the engineer T/Sgt Jeffers and the pilotage navigator Capt Auer survived with Lts Biri and McCarty. In the whole of that day's multi-pronged mission by 2,046 bombers only twelve had been lost. But eight of those had come from the 487th BG and unusually in the war the Luftwaffe had claimed one General.

It seemed nobody was exempt from death's scythe. Aces were even getting shot down by their own side. On Christmas Day, the day it was finally announced Glenn Miller was missing, Major George Preddy, who had claimed six Me 109s in one mission on 7 August, was returning from a patrol near Koblenz when he was hit by a US AA battery at Langerwehe near Aachen while chasing an Fw 190. Preddy, whose brother William would start flying combat with the 339th FG at Fowlmere within days and be killed on the Group's last mission, baled out but too low for his parachute to open. The former pre-war Barnstormer pilot had shot down a total of twenty-six German fighters since July 1943.

By then most of the rest of the 8th Air Force was remembering a more peaceful time when they lived at home with their families, enhanced by the fact it was a white Christmas after all, albeit from a heavy hoar frost.[29] Lt John Barry recorded in his diary at Sudbury: '25 December 1944. Merry Christmas. Quiet Christmas, but celebrate the birth of Christ under new, but contented surroundings. St Clair's party. Champagne from France.'[30] Jean St Clair was the Director of the American Red Cross Aero Club at Sudbury. Kay Brainard was about to set sail on the *Queen Mary* from New York to join her at the club in her first overseas appointment and begin a search for her missing Air Force brother Newell.

The 8th did fly a mission on Christmas Day. It was similar to the one the day before with nineteen different communication and rail bridges west of the Rhine, but small in comparison to the mission of the 24th, only 388 Liberators and Fortresses of the 2nd BD and 3rd BD hitting Germany for the loss of five. The 1st BD was not called on at all and many bombers were still on unfamiliar fields after landing away as the weather had closed in: Rougham for instance had 150 machines, RAF as well as USSTAF, which had landed in a hurry. At Polebrook crew chief S/Sgt Edgar Matlock recorded in his diary: 'There was little activity at our base. During the afternoon some combat personnel came back in trucks from the bases at which they landed yesterday . . . Christmas dinner was served in all of the Mess halls at the evening meal. There was turkey, dressing, cranberry sauce and most of the usual fixings.'[31]

It was strictly American food at the bases, which was a guarantee of excellence with no Brussels sprouts, a vegetable American airmen didn't understand and universally hated, even *Stars and Stripes* being stirred into warning: 'One of our spies reports the Brussels Sprouts season is rolling around again. As sure as death and taxes.'[32]

There had been the usual Christmas parties for children at all the airfields, airmen saving their sweet ration for Santa Claus to dispense. At Debach it was particularly hectic because crews of the 91st BG had had to put in there because of bad weather. Control room clerk Cpl Jack Feller remembers: 'As soon as the 91st BG crews were delivered to their aircraft our truck drivers went to pick up the children from towns and villages surrounding our base. About 300 English children were invited for a Christmas dinner and every one was given a gift. A turkey dinner with ice cream and an orange was a great treat for kids who had been in the war all of their life.'[33]

Paul Meen, who was eleven in 1944 living one mile away from the 100th BG's airfield, remembers: 'All the local children were taken to a party on the Thorpe Abbotts base. There was a lot better food there than what we had at home. There were trays of fudge on the table and we were afraid to take it because all children were brought up not to touch anything until they were told to.'[34] A party at Shipdham, Norfolk, was named Operation Reindeer. Wartime children described their amazement at 'coming into the Aladdin's cave ... Coloured lights, streamers, silver bells and a Christmas tree reaching up to the skies.'[35]

But good feeling and memories of Christmas past did not last long. It was almost as a presentiment that the airmen of the 8th discovered after the last of the turkey and sweets had been eaten that in wartime even nature itself in one-time sleepy Britain could provide its own rumbling spectaculars. On the night of 29/30 December there was an earth tremor and it extended for 200 miles from Carlisle to USSTAF country around Cromer. The quake hit at 1.35am, tipping some out of their beds. 'Buildings rocked in Manchester, Leeds, Bradford, Wakefield, Darlington, Sheffield, Retford and Spalding,' newspapers reported.[36]

It woke up airmen who had taken part in a multi-targeted

mission to communication centres and marshalling yards in northern Germany just hours before. Only four aircraft had failed to return from all three 8th Air Force divisions. Then finally on the last day of the old year young Americans far from home found themselves facing war in all its horror designed just for them. This time oil targets, dreaded for their flak defences, were on the list of objectives ranging from marshalling yards to bridges. A total of 1,327 bombers from all three 8th AF divisions would depart, but it was the 3rd BD tasked with the oil targets which took all the losses, twenty-six Fortresses going down. The mission had begun in the dark, so necessitated ascent on instruments. At Sudbury 2/Lt Virgil Raddatz had followed about half of the briefed crews into the air in *Nine Ten* when the inboard engine on his starboard wing caught fire. His co-pilot for the mission was right next to the fuel blazing in the blackness outside his window and had to bravely watch what happened next. Raddatz skimmed over the rooftops of Sudbury then managed to put down in a small field at nearby Little Cornard, skidding along into a tree. The crew rapidly evacuated the bomb-laden plane and once clear threw themselves down. The report by the airfield's Flying Control Officer John Rumisek the next day read: 'Suddenly *Nine Ten*'s co-pilot got up and began running wildly in circles. Screaming, he fell, threw up [vomited] and got up and began running again, members of the crew reported. [2/Lt Raddatz] was forced to chase his co-pilot and wrestle him to the ground, holding him until he quietened.'[37]

The remainder of the 486th BG and those who had taken off before the accident continued to their oil refinery target at Hamburg and returned safely, despite flak and fighters. But other Groups were badly hit. Co-pilot Lt Donald Smith, who took part in the Merseburg mission of 2 November with the 452nd BG, was among the force attacking Hamburg that day, in the front of the Group's Green Low squadron, as he later recorded.

The lead lost an engine and tried to keep up. The whole Group fell behind leaving them open to fighters. Suddenly I heard a scream, 'Green Low has bandits on its tail.' I switched to the other channel to tell the crew. I found out they already knew. Our own .50 cal machine guns began to chatter and I could see Fw 190s streak through our formation travelling at least 100mph faster than we were. Two waves hit us then silence . . . Glancus and my two wingmen were gone. Out of the corner of my eye I could see Money's plane pulling away to the left . . . I never learned what happened to our right wingman. He just disappeared. As we assessed damage we learned our waist gunner had a sliver in his forearm from an exploding shell and the plane had minor damage on one wing. The flight engineer was credited with a probable. Our crew members reported that Money's plane was on fire when it left the formation and it had blown up. They did not see any chutes. Such a sick feeling I had. The four officers in that plane had been sharing the same Nissen hut for four months and the bombardier, Francis Jones, was a Utah man and a very good friend. Francis had a two-year-old son.[38]

When Smith returned to the United States, his tour over, he learned Jones had in fact survived, baling out just as the B-17 blew up, damaging his hearing. The pilot Jack Money was still flying it when it exploded.

The 452nd BG lost five bombers that day, but the Group that suffered the most was the Bloody Hundredth from Thorpe Abbotts. Of the twenty-six bombers which failed to return from operations on 31 December, twelve were from the 100th – a bad day among many hard days the Group suffered that year. Lt Leon Schwartz, navigator in the Herman Streich crew, remembered that on the way in to Hamburg:

There was a captured B-17 in German markings flying a mile to our left giving our track, speed, and altitude to the flak gunners.

Nearing the target we were holding our breaths when just ahead of us a 100th plane was hit by a burst of flak. They immediately salvoed their bombs and plunged downward into another 100th B-17 in the formation and both went down in flames. We counted several chutes but it was obvious that many crew members failed to escape the doomed Fortresses. I don't know if I was aware at the time that the top plane was Floyd Henderson's with my friend Dick King along as substitute co-pilot. The bottom plane was Clifton Williams's whose navigator was my good buddy, Dick Williams.'[39]

Schwartz then felt something strike his flak suit and looked down to see 'a piece of shrapnel, still hot, on a part of my lap covered by my flak vest. I looked up and saw a good-sized hole in our plexiglass nose.'[40]

The flak continued into the bomb run, then the enemy fighters moved in. S/Sgt Paul Zak, ball turret gunner on Lt Harold Bucklew's *Silver Dollar*, damaged an Fw 190 which he saw go down in a shallow glide. 'The next thing I noticed was a lot of fighter planes falling in flames about a mile behind us,' he recorded after the war. 'I could hardly believe my eyes. The planes stopped falling after a while, but a few seconds later I saw another bunch of planes coming down, it seemed like all at one time . . . It reminded me of a bunch of burning matchsticks.'[41]

Lt Schwartz remembered: 'I watched what seemed an unreal scene, a spectacular movie, enthralled as I saw several of our attackers go into spins trailing columns of smoke, victims of our gunners. Three of our crew claimed to have hit a combined total of five Nazi fighters during the air battle.'[42] Planes from the 100th BG went down like swatted flies. Then as the B-17s exited German territory an event even more horrifyingly spectacular occurred. Lt Glenn Rojohn, commander of the *Little Skipper*, was closing the gap created by the demise of another 100th BG Fortress when his plane shuddered under a tremendous blow. The B-17 of his Thorpe Abbotts comrade, Lt William MacNab, had bounced upward and the top turret guns on MacNab's plane had jammed into the under fuselage of Rojohn's B-17, glueing the two huge aircraft together. The propellor of Rojohn's No. 1 engine had also dug into McNab's engine directly below causing a fire in that power plant. S/Sgt Zak, hanging in his turret below *Silver Dollar* immediately to the right, saw the whole drama unfold. 'They were flying as one plane, an unbelievable sight,' Zak related.[43] McNab's No. 2, 3 and 4 engines kept on running as did three of Rojohn's. After unsuccessfully trying to jerk the two aircraft apart by gunning his engines, the twenty-one-year-old skipper started a slow turn towards the German coast and told his crew to bale out. But his ball turret gunner was trapped and could not be freed. 'I called our navigator to give him the tail numbers of both aircraft,' Zak recalled. 'I also counted the chutes that came from both planes. All this time the two planes kept making a large circle to the left. Although we were flying away from them, I could see that the circles kept moving them towards land.'[44]

Six men baled out, Rojohn himself staying to battle with the controls as did his co-pilot, 2/Lt William Leek. The navigator, 2/Lt Robert Washington, swinging in his chute, saw the explosion as the two planes hit the ground still stuck together. But Rojohn and Leek walked away from the crash. As the two planes came to earth, at Tettens, near Wilhelmshaven, Rojohn's B-17 slid off the bottom aircraft, which immediately exploded. Alternately lifting up and slamming back into the grass, the remaining Fortress careened ahead, finally slowing when the left wing sliced through a wooden building. When Washington was captured by German soldiers he was taken to a truck and to his amazement there in the back were Rojohn and Leek. The plane's flight engineer, T/Sgt Orville Elkin, had his own remarkable escape, coming down ten miles out in the North Sea then being blown ashore by his parachute. The parachutes of two who had baled out of Rojohn's B-17 failed to open, but four who escaped from McNabb's plane drifted to earth safely.

The crew of *Silver Dollar* came home to Thorpe Abbotts where S/Sgt Zak was able to tell the amazing story at debriefing of what he had seen. The Herman Streich crew with navigator Lt Leon Schwartz aboard also returned unharmed to Thorpe Abbotts and Schwarz finished his tour in February to go home to his family in California. The sacrifices and hardships of 1944 were over. The dawn of final victory was spreading its comforting glow over the horizon. That New Year came in with a satisfying bang on most American bases. Lt Barry's diary entry from Sudbury reads: '31 December 1944. Payday. New Year's Eve. Flares, 45s, whistles and yells. Bring in the New Year. Got woke up at 1220 and was greeted by the boys. HAPPY NEW YEAR!'[45] The Germans had been stopped in the Ardennes and would soon begin the long retreat on all fronts. Crews who had survived their tours in the 8th Air Force were going home and others were arriving to complete the war. It was a better time to be an American airman than any since the 8th had launched its first heavy bomber raid in August 1942, lead by Paul Tibbets, who would help to swiftly end the Pacific war by dropping the first atom bomb on Japan. Losses by Americans in the skies of Europe were falling dramatically. The ascendancy of US power which would last into the next century was clear in the capitals of France, Italy and even England. Soon the American footprint would be evident in the German capital, but first they would help to ruin it and put the last nail in the coffin of German militarism.

15

'So cold tears came into my eyes'

It was a sure sign of that renewed optimism spreading from the rarified atmosphere at the peak of the USSTAF command structure to the 8th Air Force's East Anglian bases that missions in force were mounted on every day but five in the first three weeks of January. They were flown despite the intense frost, unusually heavy snow and even gales which airmen who had learned their craft in the sunny skies of Arizona, Georgia and Florida were now battling against. It was a surprise to the 8th's arriving new boys that they were expected to fly at all. Yet freezing morning after morning they found themselves in bleak and bitter Quonset huts being briefed for marshalling yards in towns across Germany; destruction of the Reich transportation structure had moved from tactically desirable to vitally necessary if the enemy was to be prevented from supplying and reinforcing the Ardennes front. The year had begun with the Luftwaffe's Operation *Bodenplatte*, an assault by hundreds of aircraft on Allied forward airfields on the Continent that wrecked or severely damaged more than 450 planes. The German loss was less, around 250 aircraft, a quarter to Mustangs and Thunderbolts the rest to artillery, including Germany's own who had not been alerted to *Bodenplatte*, absolute secrecy considered necessary to success. Germany's victory was pyrrhic. Its losses could not be made good and the net result was the Luftwaffe, though occasionally still able to sting viciously, was increasingly ineffective for the remainder of the war while conversely the fighter and bomber airfields of the Allies grew exponentially.

There were plenty of scare stories for the 8th's combat neo-phytes delivering the gleaming factory-fresh Fortresses and Liberators to hear from the experienced veterans coming to the end of their tours. S/Sgt John Day, a nineteen-year-old ball turret gunner from rural Maine, found his crew assigned to the 100th BG, replacements for airmen lost in the mauling the Group had received over Hamburg on the last day of 1944. He had already been told at the USSTAF replacement depot at Stone in Stafford-shire about the Bloody Hundredth's reputation as a hard-luck outfit, as he remembers.

As a beginner when you found out you were going to be sent to the Hundredth it was a little bit scary. We had been hear-ing these terrible stories about the 100th. When I arrived at Thorpe Abbotts I guess we got a little bit where guys were happy to tell us of the terrible things that had happened before.

The first couple of missions were in support of ground troops in the Battle of the Bulge. By the time I began there were P-51s escorting you all the way in and all the way out on every mission, so on my 25 missions we were attacked by German fighters less than half the time and even then often for only a few minutes because the P-51s would chase them away, so we were in much more danger from being shot down by flak than German fighters. The Luftwaffe was absolutely in decline at that time. On any given day we were hoping that the Germans wouldn't come up that day. The

Luftwaffe were having gasoline and personnel problems and the P-51s escorting us were all over us because their pilots figured they were far superior at that point to the Germans and their pilots all wanted to be aces. Those P-51 pilots had a different attitude, we just wanted to get over there and come back.

It was a very cold winter. We had electric suits and the model of aircraft we flew in was far superior to what the 8th Air Force had had earlier because problems the air force had had earlier had been recognised and corrected. I could adjust my electric suit in the ball turret but the problem was that a lot of heating cores are in the lower stomach and groin area of your suit whereas rolled up in the ball turret your back was against cold steel so your back got cold and you turned the heat up a bit on the rheostat. As a result your stomach would boil so you turned it down a little bit and then your back would get cold again, so you were always adjusting up or down.[1]

Not all were lucky enough to be flying in the latest model. S/Sgt Jerry Shulman, a college-educated New Jersey waist gunner with the Liberator-equipped 453rd BG, flew missions as 1945 began with a partly freshman crew because his aircraft commander became a lead pilot. He recalls:

How this pick-up crew was made up, they took a co-pilot who was a good man and made him number one, then they got a young green co-pilot from the U.S. He was the number two man. They got an engineer and radio man from a crew that broke up. I was the armorer, and they got three gunners from other crews. I flew three missions. But because we were such a new crew they gave us probably the oldest plane on the base. All of the newer planes had Plexiglas windows over the waist gun. In this plane, you opened a metal door the size of the newer Plexiglas windows with a little bit of window near the top. You tied it up and you had nothing but fresh air coming in at you . . . We were flying at 28,000 feet, the temperature was somewhere about 40 below zero. My hands were so cold I kept them between my legs. Tears came into my eyes.[2]

In the first month of 1945 the biggest danger to air crews was the weather. S/Sgt Richard Fredericksen, a top turret gunner with the 94th BG, was among the 779 crews taking part in strikes at German communication and rail targets on 6 January, a day of freezing north winds in which only one aircraft was lost to enemy action. But at Fredericksen's base of Rougham the temperature, which could leave lumps of ice in oil and fuel lines – causing critical blocking as they were sucked into carburettors, did for a B-17 bound for Ludwigshafen, as Fredericksen observed.

We had to stop behind a long line of Fortresses which were going thru the final run up. Already the first to be off had received the green light from the tower and was moving down the runway. As we watched, he failed to leave the runway properly and in a few seconds later we seen a flash of fire as he crashed beyond after striking a power line. We were all wondering why the bombs had not exploded when there came a terrible blast which jarred our ship and where the plane had crashed smoke and fire along with the small pieces of the plane flew several hundred feet in the air. Four airmen had escaped before the bombs exploded but the pilot who attempted to run was cut in two as he was blown by the blast thru a fence.[3]

Five were killed in the crash and three civilians injured.

General Spaatz moved his headquarters in January from London to Saint-Germain-en-Laye, west of Paris, where he considered he could keep a better eye on Continental weather conditions and the needs of the Allied armies. The demands for tactical support by his strategic bombers were constant. On the same day as the Luftwaffe's *Bodenplatte* was launched the Wehrmacht began Operation *Nordwind* against the sixty-eight-mile front of the US 7th Army, which had been forced to send troops to join in the Battle of the Bulge to the north. It was the Wehrmacht's last major offensive and it eventually cost the Americans more than 14,000 casualties in attack and counter-attack as the US 7th Army defended itself on three sides in the Vosges mountains of north-eastern France.

To prevent reinforcements or supplies arriving at either the Ardennes or Vosges fronts, Spaatz's bomber crews flew missions against a total of 234 separate targets in appalling conditions between the beginning of January and the 24th, when the weather finally defeated him as widespread freezing fog blanketed his East Anglian airbases. On most days more than 1,000 bombers were aloft and on some days he only lost two or three or even none at all to enemy action – for instance 619 Fortresses and Liberators being despatched to various marshalling yards in Germany on 15 January and all returning. However, crashes caused by bad weather were not counted in official records of mission loss totals as they occurred not in enemy territory but in England, at or near the bases.

How stressful operating in freezing fog and snow could be is revealed in the diary of the 493rd BG, which flew its 100th mission on 10 January. A party had already been held in anticipation a few days before in which fresh, clear ice had been provided for the plentiful supply of whisky and Coca-Cola by filling GI garbage cans with water and placing them in the bomb bays of

B-17s. 'They were flown around for about an hour locally at an altitude of over 10,000ft. The water froze and we had a large supply of very expensive ice,' Cpl Jack Feller, the control tower clerk remembers.[4]

In the early hours crews were briefed for the mission that would actually mark the Group's century. The proximity of the base at Debach, Suffolk, to the North Sea had often brought the worst of weather since operations began on D-Day itself. The conditions on 10 January were deadly, as the anonymous Group diarist wrote.

It had snowed immediately before take-off, making taxiing in the darkness even more tricky than usual, with the result that several aircraft got stuck off hardstands. After the first few planes were airborne Lt Butler's plane crashed and exploded two miles north of the field. Not long thereafter the perimeter collapsed beneath an aircraft just arriving at the take-off position on the only runway that could be used. Plans were immediately changed to taxi aircraft downwind on the runway in use, so that they could execute a 180 degree turn just before reaching the plane blocking the take-off position and start their take-off roll from there. Shortly after this plan was put into operation another plane had a tyre blow out on the runway.[5]

Despite the difficulties the Group despatched thirty aircraft and all crews returned safely to find four airmen had been killed in the plane which had crashed after take-off.

That day the crew of Lt Dean Eakin, who had bombed Brunswick's marshalling yards with such success after losing an engine on the big Merseburg strike, flew the final mission of their tour because they lost their skipper. They were leading the 486th BG from the IP to the rail yards of Karlsruhe when a flak burst took

10ft off the left wing and sent a splinter through the pilots' cabin. Lt Deakin slumped over the controls, his heart pierced by the shrapnel. The co-pilot, Lt Daniel Casey, brought the plane back to base on three engines. Most of the crew were three combat missions short of the total needed to finish their tour, but because they had flown several raids as lead they were given additional credit and their missions were declared complete.

The experienced were making way for the combat novices, being fed into the war machine in its furious final revolutions. S/Sgt Albert 'Bud' Porter, a twenty-four-year-old ball turret gunner from Elizabeth, New Jersey, was one. Porter had been trained as a radio man, but had been remustered to the tight ball turret because of his height of 5ft 7 inches. He hadn't been too keen to make the switch believing there had been some mistake when he reported to MacDill Field at Tampa, Florida to become part of a crew. 'The first time I saw a ball-turret was in a classroom at MacDill and we had an instructor who had flown combat, just come back,' he remembered. 'He said to us, "You're going to be in the safest spot on the airplane . . . the turret is armor plated, the only part of the airplane that is, and, secondly when you get over a target and the flak is coming up thick and heavy . . . you get the turret going around a circle, as fast as it would go . . . flak has a tendency to ricochet off a moving target."'[6]

Spaatz was still continuing his oil offensive as well as providing huge tactical support to US ground troops and on 17 January the third of his divisions, called from the start of the year 'air' rather than 'bombardment' divisions, split its forces between two refineries in Hamburg, the Rhenama and the Albrecht. It gave Bud Porter a chance to test the richochet theory, riding a ball turret with the 95th BG over one of those targets. It was the first of nine missions he would fly with his nineteen-year-old Texan pilot Lonnie McClintock before the war ended in Europe, as he related years later.

Nobody had ever shot at Mrs. Porter's little boy in his life and we're over Hamburg, Germany, and the flak is coming up thick and heavy. Honestly, I'm scared, you know, not knowing what to expect and, here I am, in this turret, all by myself, and thinking at that time, 'What am I doing here? What am I doing here?' So, I had the turret going around in a circle, as fast as it would go. Now, we got back okay and, we're being interrogated by a debriefing officer who wants to know how the mission went. The first question is addressed to me. He said, 'Porter, how was the bomb drop?' I said, 'Bomb drop? I don't know. I had the turret going around in a circle, as fast as it would go,' and he said, 'No, you're supposed to watch the bomb drop . . . You've got the best seat in the house,' and it's true, really. So, from then on, why, I paid attention to the bomb drop.[7]

On the crew's second mission over Germany a few days later their aircraft suffered major flak damage. Porter continues:

I had the turret in such a position, luckily, that I saw it happen. All of a sudden, there's a gigantic hole between Number One and Two engines in the wing and a shell had gone right straight through the wing and did not explode. If it had exploded, I wouldn't be here. Anyway, it knocked down One and Two engines and all the oil came out, hit the turret, and the plane started straight down. Now, I have never experienced anything like this in my life, but the vibration caused by the two engines that were knocked out, had what they called runaway props, they were spinning and causing such a vibration, it felt like the plane's going to tear itself apart. I thought that [it] was going to go any minute. Through the intercom, the pilot is screaming, 'Prepare to bale out, prepare to bale out.' Now, I came out of that turret like I was shot out of a cannon and I forgot all about the oxygen connections, the electrical connections. All I knew was, 'Hey, we're going down,' you know, and, now ... I didn't have room in the turret for a parachute. So, I put the parachute alongside the turret, so when I came out, I could grab it and put it on.

Well, when the plane started straight down, the chutes took off. So, when I came out of the turret, the chute wasn't there. I didn't have sense enough to try to tie it to the turret in some way. Right now, we're supposed to be a well-trained, well-disciplined crew; forget it. It was absolute [chaos] and I mean seriously, it was chaotic. We thought we were gone and our radio operator got so excited, he came out of the radio room and forgot his chute and saw this chute lying on the floor and grabbed it. It was mine. We had what we called chest chutes that hooked on the front, and they said to make sure that the ripcord handle is on the right-hand side, because, if it's on the left-hand side, when it opens, it will get all tangled up and wrap around you. [The waist gunner] he's on the floor. He's got it on wrong and he's trying to get it off and you've got to remember, we're in twenty-five, thirty below zero temperatures, gloves, you know. So, we dropped straight down 15,000 feet and you have no idea the pressure that a dive like that causes against the controls of the plane and ... it's awful to try to get [strength] enough to try to pull this doggone airplane out of its dive and, as Lonnie, our pilot, said, if it hadn't been for [co-pilot] Bob Cochran, who was a big guy and strong, if he had been as small as I was, we couldn't have pulled the plane out and, finally, [they] pulled it out of the dive, got it levelled.

Now, we only have two engines and we can't maintain altitude and, of course, we're out of the formation and you're always afraid; the Germans always looked for stragglers to knock off, and so, we were afraid of that and we couldn't stay in the air. [The pilot asked the navigator to get them to the nearest Allied airfield.] So, we came down in Brussels, in a half-baked landing, but made it okay. Now, we're all out of the airplane, thanking our lucky stars that we made it, and our bombardier had forgotten to lock his nose guns, which were supposed to be in locked position, pointing up to the sky. We're all around the nose with these .50-caliber machine guns over our heads. He got in the nose and lost his balance, fell up against the trigger switches and these two .50s took off and we hit the ground, like we thought we're going to get wiped out . . . He thought he wiped out the whole crew. So, then, when things got calmed down, I said, 'Okay, who took my parachute?' and the radio operator said, 'Oh, my God, Bud, I'm sorry, I did.' They flew a '17 over to pick us up. We got back the same night.[8]

Landing at airfields on the Continent which had lately been in German hands brought particular perils. Sgt Eldon Bevons, a 390th BG ball turret gunner, was on his sixth combat flight when his pilot was forced to land at a former Luftwaffe base in Laon, France, in January because of a bad oil leak. 'After getting out of the airplane our engineer stepped on a personnel mine and most of the crew was wounded,' he recorded. 'I was in the Laon field hospital for a few weeks.'[9]

The 390th were to suffer a heavy loss while Bevons was in hospital. On Sunday, 14 January 370 B-17s of the 3rd Air Division were sent to oil storage targets at Magdeburg and at Derben near Brandenburg. The Nazis still rated preserving the Reich's oil supplies as the highest priority and as both targets were on the route to Berlin it was clear the dwindling forces of the Luftwaffe based in the area would be called into play to defend it. To split the enemy's aerial resources, therefore, 187 Flying Fortresses of

1AD were assigned to bomb bridges over the Rhine at Cologne while 348 Liberators of 2AD hit oil targets near Brunswick. What happened in fact was that the Me 109s and Fw 190s were massed to attack the Derben and Magdeburg bombers. Only one of the Cologne force was shot down and the Liberators returned home intact. But after the raid there were nine gaps in the flight line of the 390th BG at Framlingham and at Lavenham, home of the 487th BG, there were four.

The Magdeburg bomber crews had been briefed to make a feint towards Berlin then cut back between Berlin and Branden-burg and unload over the Magdeburg synthetic oil refinery. Lt Andrew Norman, navigator to Cptn Jack Stanley, a lead pilot with the 487th BG, recorded in his diary within hours of returning: 'About 50 miles past Hamburg I saw four P-51s drop their tanks and peel off. One strafed a railroad, couldn't see the other three. About a minute after they went down the Luftwaffe jumped the 390th flying two minutes ahead of us. They got all nine of the low squadron in about a three minute fight.'[10] Cptn Stanley, a former flight instructor, who was leading the low squadron of the 487th BG, had a grandstand view of the enemy fighters going after the 390th. 'B-17s and fighters were going down in all directions, smok-ing, spinning, blowing up. It was fantastic,' he wrote in his own combat notes. 'You could see the gun fire from the bombers and enemy aircraft flashing red streaks across the zero cold sky. Kept praying that we wouldn't be next. Looked out again and enemy aircraft were still attacking Group ahead. The whole low squad-ron had been shot down and they were going after the high.'[11]

Cptn James Browning, leading a Flight of the 357th FG, was alerted by the sight of contrails at 12 o'clock and started climbing with the other Mustangs. At 27,000ft he saw 'planes exploding and spinning down in front of us'. The time was 1245 and he and his Flight were twenty-five miles north of Brandenburg. Browning saw an unengaged gaggle of twenty-five-plus Me 109s passing in front 5,000ft below and dived into the attack, his Flight following. 'I picked out a Me 109 on the right side and fired a burst observing a concentration of hits on the cockpit and engine. The e/a did a violent snap roll and then spun down completely out of control,' he related back at his Leiston base. Browning's wingman shot down another Messerschmitt which had got on Browning's tail and the captain then fired three or four bursts at an Me 109 which had appeared at short range in front of him and that also went into a spin. He then tacked onto a third Messerschmitt which was breaking right. The enemy pilot closed his throttle to make the Mustang overshoot, but Browning was already firing a long burst, 'raking the e/a the length of the fuselage to the engine with a good concentration of hits. The enemy e/a rolled over and went down out of control. The entire gaggle of enemy e/a had been broken up', he related to Intelligence.[12]

Browning had accounted for three of the enemy within minutes and the rest of his Group had had a similar field day with the inexperienced pilots of the Luftwaffe as the air battle continued. When they filed their mission encounter reports for Intelligence officers shivering in the mist rolling in from the North Sea at Leiston they claimed fifty-six outright victories and one shared for the loss of just three of their own, the largest number ever shot down by a Group on one mission.

In Cptn Stanley's Fortress Lt Norman watched as the air battle which had decimated the low squadron of the 390th BG continued afresh, as he recorded later in his combat diary.

Not 15 minutes after that scramble was over about 30 Fw 190s queued up about a half mile off our right wing. Before they could start in the P-51s hit them. Just before we turned, north of Brandenburg they hit the 390th high squadron. I could see the 20mm shells bursting throughout the formation. Four B-17s went down. In the two attacks I saw about

12 fighters go down, couldn't tell whether they were 51s or 190s. Our high lead lagged behind just before Brandenburg. He never came back – it is supposed that the fighters got him. When last seen he was behind us at about 18,000ft and in the target area.[13]

On the Magdeburg target itself 'bomb and flak was fairly intense', Cptn Stanley told Intelligence at Lavenham. 'We came in at Group formation and bombed on lead Group. Bombs fell short. As bombs fell away my engine No. 2 was shot out and we immediately feathered it. Kept on lead and No. 4 smoking badly. Babied it all the way back to England where I finally feathered it and made a two-engine landing.' There he learned that three in the high squadron of his Group had been seen going down near the target, including two aircrew on the first mission of their second tour.* He had 'quite a few holes' in his left wing and stabiliser from 'very accurate' flak.[14]

Lt Norman saw the effects of the flak hit on No. 2 engine 'right outside my window', then when No. 4 started running rough the mission Group leader 'thought it was about to catch on fire. Jack opened the cowl flaps and cut it back. We held the lead – otherwise we never would have kept up. I kept a course to Brussels available in case we needed it. The high squadron dropped on the marshalling yard at Osnabruck. At the Dutch coast we headed for home and had to feather No. 4.'[15]

Friedrich Kowalke, who had been a schoolboy flak helper at Magdeburg, had graduated aged seventeen to the Reich labour service and on 14 January was staying with his grandmother at Tangerhutte, about seventy-five miles west of Berlin, as the air battle unfolded above him. 'It was a beautiful winter day, then the

---

* It was later found that three bombers of the 487th had collided on the run in to Magdeburg and a fourth was missing after being attacked by fighters.

alarm was given. The 8th AF was on its way and as a former "observer" I did not want to stay in the air raid shelter,' he recorded. He saw some bombers approaching from the north in line astern, 'obviously heading for Magdeburg. Clearly visible was the chaff from the waist gunners with the foils gleaming in the sun. P-51s were making up the rear of the column. Shortly afterwards B-17 elements appeared in the east, flying a NW course. They were on their bomb run for the Derben oil storage depot. The bomb detonations we then heard were accompanied by violent ground shocks, due to the frosty weather. I saw an Fw 190 spinning to the ground, obviously a victim of P-51s.'[16]

The Luftwaffe fighter Kowalke saw in its final moments was just one of a total of eighty-nine enemy aircraft destroyed and claimed by the pilots of Mustangs which had accompanied the 3AD bombers to the Magdeburg and Derben oil targets. The US fighter groups lost only five. Once again a terrifying sudden onslaught on American air power by equally frightened German youngsters defending their homeland had proved another dying gasp in the death rattle of Goering's once mighty Luftwaffe. On the ground also the Wehrmacht's Ardennes offensive was now a retreat as fuel shortages caused by the combined American and British air forces' oil and transportation campaigns became starkly evident. Lt Col. Joachim Peiper's 1st SS Panzer Division, whose troops had carried out the massacre of American PoWs at Malmedy, abandoned the last of their fuel-starved tanks by mid-January and began the gradual trek on foot back to Germany. On 20 January French troops, soon to be joined by the US 3rd Infantry Division, began clearing the Colmar pocket in the Vosges mountains of central Alsace. By 25 January the Germans' shocking successes on the Western Front were over as Allied reinforcements arrived in the Vosges from the Ardennes, having forced the Germans back from Bastogne to their original start line to the east.

It was fortunate, therefore, that it had been no earlier that the severest winter weather of all arrived in Britain. Freezing conditions at Spaatz's heavy bomber bases in East Anglia became so extreme from 24 January that all missions were halted for four days. Mean temperature at Leeming, Yorkshire, in RAF bomber country was noted at minus 9 centigrade and there was heavy snow right down eastern England as well as fog.[17]

Every day but five since Christmas Day 8th AF crews had been called to halt in various ways Hitler's attempts to divide the Allies, deluded he could make a separate peace in the West. Lt William A. Roberts, co-pilot to Lt Lesley B. Hull of the 486th BG at Sudbury, flew nine missions in the first three weeks of January of his thirty-seven-mission tour, including a ten-hour flight to Mainz and back on the 13th after which he recorded in his combat diary: 'Lots of guns and heavy flak. Two planes ran together in the clouds ahead of us. Just missed one'; and his pilot Hull wrote in his own notes passed on to him: 'Had to circle at 5,000ft for 1.5 hours before landing due to low visibility at base. Landed OK after instrument let down and three passes at field.'[18] Lt John Barry, the navigator who had enjoyed champagne at the base's American Red Cross Aero Club Christmas party run by Club Director Jean St Clair, flew eight missions in the whole of the month, partly because he was switched to another crew midway through and by great good luck was able to take a three-day pass to London with his first crew and then two more with his second.

Red Cross girl Kay Brainard was now aboard the *Queen Mary* on the last stage of her journey to the adventure of a lifetime and her attempt to find news of her missing co-pilot brother. She had completed her four weeks' training in Washington DC in December, but her departure to the ETO had been delayed because replacements for GI casualties in the Battle of the Bulge took up all the spare bunk space in troop ships. She did not then know she was bound for the Sudbury airbase where she would assist Jean St

Clair in running the Aero Club for enlisted men. She would arrive in the wake of the air war making another lurch forward, this time to the Reich capital and its awesome flak defences.

The German army was by then in a purely defensive position, withdrawing in the west towards the Rhine and taking with it its 88mm artillery which bolstered the anti-aircraft defences of the Reich as Germany's front line was shortened. That flak would become the deadliest peril to the 8th Air Force bomber boys as the dangers of ice, snow and gales lessened with the unfolding of January into February. Carl Spaatz's Groups had mounted a prodigious campaign to contain the German army's ambitions in the Ardennes and Alsace-Lorraine, but the severe weather had prevented the USSTAF chief from using his mighty resources of both bombers and fighters to their true potential. Now Hap Arnold was putting pressure on him from Washington to finish off the European bombing campaign quickly so that resources could be transferred to the Pacific. Spaatz signalled his superiors on the other side of the Atlantic that the war against the Nazis was definitely being won, but was not over yet. Flak defending Germany's cities was 'plentiful, was accurate and too deadly' but fighters 'no longer stood in our way with the strength they once mustered'. It was the ferocity of this flak that airmen of the 8th would remember for decades to come.

16

'The birds were really flying. What a sight!'

Somewhere in England, Feb. 9th, 1945. Mother dear, My new address is 486th Bomb Group (H), APO 559, c/o Postmaster, New York, NY. At last I have my assignment and I'm on the job. I think I'm going to like it a lot. I'm on a bomber base, at an Aero Club. Got here last night. At present there are three girls here, but one of them is leaving, so there will be just Jean St. Claire and myself at the Club. Jean is the Club Director – a very cute gal and I think she'll be nice to work with.

So wrote Kay Brainard in the first of hundreds of letters which would encapsulate what it was like to be a bright and eager American girl in England amidst the urgency of war. In that first letter she set the scene for her new life.

It's no small job, as the club is quite large. We have a staff of English hired help who do all the real work – in the kitchens, cleaning, even bookkeeping. We gals just supervise and act as hostesses, girl-friend, mother, sister or whatever. We have a large dining area – a big lounge – a game room

– and a kitchen. And two offices and a library/reading room. All in Nissen huts strung together at odd angles. Our living quarters are not bad, but the cold is going to be something to contend with. We have only small coal stoves in our rooms, and it's not very warm. But maybe summer is coming ... Meantime I have long woolens to wear. It won't be too bad. We sleep with hot water bottles and bed sox!

... In a few moments I'm going out to 'meet the mission' and serve the returning airmen coffee and rolls and cakes. The birds were really flying today – what a sight to see! Had breakfast in bed this morning. There are some things about this job that are positively enticing. Have met scads of people from Florida.[1]

Not being privy to the Group commander's secrets, Kay Brainard had thought the mission had been to Berlin and noted that in her diary. The returning airmen the girl with the All-American smile was greeting for the first time were not in fact returning from Berlin, but from an attack on a munitions plant at Weimar. Enemy fighters had been seen in force, but P-51s had broken up their attack without loss to the Group. The Berlin raid had taken place six days before and a B-17 of the 486th BG was now lying in a Polish field beyond the Eastern Front. It and five others of the 1,000-plus B-17s that had set off to bomb the heart out of the Reich capital had taken that course east because crippling damage from Berlin's fearsome flak defences had meant their crews knew they would never make it home to England. Lt Arthur Ogle had been piloting the lead plane of the 486th with Major John Rex alongside as Command Pilot in the right-hand seat when flak disabled one engine on the bomb run and another as Ogle turned for home. A third quickly failed and Rex told Ogle to turn east over the Russian battle front. Less than two hours later Ogle and his crew were being greeted by Polish partisans as they evacuated their buckled B-17 after a wheels-up landing.

The raid on Berlin essentially marked a shift in policy by the USSTAF. America had begun its bombing campaign in Europe with the aim of making precision strikes against factories and other, small key targets and thus sparing civilian lives. Britain, its capital blitzed for fifty-seven consecutive nights from 7 September 1940, had already tried a daylight strategy and discovered painfully that its woefully under-armed bombers could not compete against the cannons of the Luftwaffe's Me 109s. It had therefore been forced into a nocturnal campaign if it was to take the battle to the enemy at all at a time when Churchill's soldiers and sailors were losing the war at various points of the compass. The protective cover of darkness also cloaked targets and it was as a result of a specially commissioned report to the War Cabinet – it was eventually proved that only five per cent of RAF bombers setting out in the first two years of war got within five miles of their objective – that there began a policy of carpet-bombing, destroying whole sections of cities to eradicate workers' homes and cut off their transport links, their gas and electricity supplies while at the same time destroying a few factories as well. The primary aim had been to strangle the Reich economy, but it also killed thousands of civilians, a fact Harris considered the Churchill government should be more honest about. This new raid on Berlin would not be the first time the Americans had struck at the centre of the Reich capital. The costly Berlin raid of 29 April 1944 had as its aiming point the Friedrichstrasse railway station because it was considered it controlled all east–west, north–south railway traffic through the city and therefore the movement of war material from the factories in the suburbs that the USSTAF had hit in March.

But by and large America's command structure had considered

they fought a more noble war than their Allies, until now. Spaatz's recent Transportation Campaign which had necessitated bombing marshalling yards in towns and cities had resulted in similar inaccuracies as RAF Bomber Command had found just before its leaders turned to saturation bombing. The appalling winter weather Spaatz's crews had had to cope with meant raids depended on the same blurred radar-marking the RAF had been carrying out at night and most bomb loads missed their targets, striking civilian housing and infrastructure in the attempt to find rail complexes and bridges. Throughout the entire war only about one in ten of the American bombers sent to Germany in fact bombed visually. A conference into the effectiveness of bombing and air force gunnery was held in Paris at the beginning of February attended by delegates from the 8th, 9th and 15th Air Forces. A subsequent report was made to Hap Arnold, Commander in Chief of the Army Air Forces in Washington, revealing that, 'During the last four months of 1944 our H2X bombing under conditions of 10/10 cloud had placed only 58 per cent of the bombs within five miles of the assigned aiming point.'[2] This had shades of the 1941 British Butt Report which had forced RAF Bomber Command into saturation bombing. The US European bomber offensive crews themselves were aware that the Norden-bombsight pickle-barrel accuracy that newspapers and broadcasters liked to boast of was an illusion. Most combat diaries reveal admissions of bombing short or wide which Washington and air force publicists chose to ignore.

The daylight campaign was always a struggle to balance accuracy against protection for the bombers by efficiently combining their firepower. The great 8th Air Force innovator Curtis LeMay had compromised by developing the staggered squadron and Group formation known as the Combat Box which combined with other boxes had allowed .50 MG cones of fire in a concentration over thousands of yards from each direction.

There was a flaw, however, in that the width of the box determined the same spread of bombs, hopefully of about 2,500ft. Average bombing accuracy throughout the war 'expressed as a circular error probable' was in fact approximately three-quarters of a mile. The problem of protecting the bombers without the consequent loss of bomb concentration beset the 8th Air Force to the final weeks of the conflict. In that last winter there had been a further private admission that pickle-barrel bombing was a myth in Europe. On an average mission only four aircraft in any thirty-six-plane Group by now had Norden bombsights – the lead, deputy lead and high and low squadron leads – and only twelve in total would have bombardiers, whose expensive training had been reduced to pressing the bomb-release gear when the leader's ordnance dropped away. The remaining twenty-four bombers would have 'toggliers', remustered gunners usually, who performed the same button-pressing task but without the glory of commissioned rank.

It was prosaic practicality therefore – a hard truth Sir Arthur Harris had been forced to accept for his own Command two years before – which persuaded General Spaatz to adopt a policy more in line with that of the RAF, particularly as the lessons of war had now produced greater accuracy in RAF bombing. When the British came up with Operation Thunderclap, therefore, General Spaatz was more willing than he had been to listen. The Thunderclap concept had been put forward by Churchill's Chief of the Air Staff, Sir Charles Portal, to other Allied chiefs in the late summer of 1944 as the Wehrmacht was in retreat. He suggested that a huge raid be launched against Berlin where it was expected to cause '220,000 casualties, 40 per cent of these may expect to be killed. It is suggested that such an attack, resulting in so many deaths, the great majority of which will be key personnel, cannot help but have a shattering effect on political and civilian morale all over Germany.'[3]

As the days shortened the Thunderclap idea was temporarily shelved, though Portal remained committed to the idea, his office promoting the similarly engendered Ruhr-targeted Operation Hurricane to Harris in October. Hurricane had been designed to achieve 90 per cent destruction of the Ruhr city areas attacked and to inflict heavy casualties that would break civilian morale. Eventually Thunderclap came up again in January as the Russians launched their new offensive in the East, which would eventually end in the street battle for Berlin. The Joint Intelligence Committee submitted a report to the War Cabinet on 21 January warning that the Russian offensive might well stall if the Germans, now marshalling their reserves – expected to amount to forty-two divisions within weeks – were able to position them on the Eastern Front swiftly, the critical time being mid-February.[4] Churchill then minuted his Air Minister Sir Archibald Sinclair asking 'whether Berlin, and no doubt other large cities in East Germany should not now be considered especially attractive targets'. Sinclair consulted with Portal who said attacks in support of the Russian advance should in certain circumstances have priority. In fact towards the end of January Portal had written to the Deputy Chief of the Air Staff Norman Bottomley urging that after other obligations had been fulfilled, 'We should use available effort in one big attack on Berlin and attacks on Dresden, Leipzig, Chemnitz, or any other cities where a severe blitz will not only cause confusion in the evacuation from the East, but will also hamper the movement of troops from the West.'[5] Bottomley, told of Churchill's minute, then wrote to Harris on 27 January spelling out that Portal considered it would not be right to mount a series of knock-out 'Thunderclap' blows solely to Berlin in the near future, but that subject to 'the overriding claims of oil and other approved target systems within the current directive' there should be a 'big attack on Berlin and related attacks on Dresden, Leipzig, Chemnitz'.[6]

The next day Bottomley and Spaatz agreed to send new target

priorities to the bomber divisions and RAF Groups. Top priority was oil targets, but immediately below was Berlin, Leipzig, Dresden and 'associated cities'. Third came 'communications' which were essentially transport centres; and finally jet aircraft and communications in the south of Germany. Oil targets required precision, not likely in the current winter weather in northern Europe, so when poor weather prevailed the British and Americans would attack targets in cities.[7] Both Bottomley and Spaatz knew that meant that if the weather would not allow the USSTAF to precisely attack oil plants, any raids on city targets would in fact be area attacks. The 'big attack on Berlin' fell to General Spaatz. There would be no doubt what he was signing up for: Portal's call in the summer for a raid on the Reich capital in which 110,000, 'the great majority of which will be key personnel', would be killed, being circulated to Allied Air Chiefs. Spaatz delegated it to General Doolittle, head of his 8th Air Force, to carry out a week later. It didn't sit well with the hero of the Tokyo raid.

Doolittle was aware, as all the bomber barons were, that the Casablanca Directive approved by the Combined Chiefs of Staff of the Western Allies in January 1943 and issued to the heads of the RAF and USAAF bomber commands, thus beginning the combined air offensive, had spelled out: 'Your Primary object will be the progressive destruction and dislocation of the German military, industrial, and economic system, and the undermining of the morale of the German people to a point where their capacity for armed resistance is fatally weakened . . .' It went on that Berlin should be a prime target when conditions existed 'suitable for attainment of specially valuable results unfavourable to the enemy morale or favourable to Russian morale.'

But so far the 8th had tried to hit particular targets rather than engaging in city-wide attacks which it was hoped would prove a blow to morale. It was the necessity to operate in appalling weather that had brought about the German civilian deaths in the winter Transportation Campaign. Now Doolittle considered he was being asked to target civilians per se, by launching hundreds of bombers nominally against the small target of the Templehof marshalling yards. The altitude required of 26,000ft to give his crews a chance in the flak would inevitably lead to wholesale destruction in the centre of the city in what would be the biggest raid of the war by the Allies on Berlin. The given reason for the attack was that the German 6th Panzer Army was believed to be moving through the city on their way to the Eastern Front and would be using Templehof.

Doolittle, as honourable as the medal ribbon he wore, was a soldier first and diplomat second and told Spaatz what he thought. 'There are no basically important strictly military targets in the designated area,' he signalled to his commander on 30 January. 'We will in what may be one of our last and best remembered operations, regardless of its effectiveness, violate the basic American principle of precision bombing of targets of strictly military significance for which our tactics were designed and our crews trained and indoctrinated.' Spaatz replied with ambiguity, but left no doubt that the attack would go ahead as ordered.[8]

Doolittle had also been concerned about using his B-24s on the raid which would mean them taking on the Berlin flak at 3,000ft lower than the Flying Fortresses could manage. He had good reason to worry about his Liberator crews. The three rings of gun sites around the city and the three huge flak towers in the centre itself had helped to establish a loss record for the 8th Air Force of sixty-nine bombers missing, on the Berlin industry raid of 6 March the previous year, one bomber in ten being shot down. The 8th commander therefore decided to leave his 2AD out of the Berlin mission and send its Liberators to Magdeburg oil and transportation targets among others. It left him with 1,003 Fortresses of the 1st and 3rd Air Divisions for the Reich capital.

'The birds were really flying. What a sight!'

By the pre-dawn of 3 February as the curtains were raised on the target at briefings from Thorpe Abbotts of 3AD to 1AD at Thurleigh, there was little doubt that the 8th Air Force was now in a different kind of war. The thirty-eight crews of the 100th BG who would be going were informed they would be bombing the railhead at Templehof in the centre of Berlin. They would lead the entire 3AD.

It was a different briefing at Nuthampstead in 1AD country, however. The 398th BG was told it was a 'demoralisation' mission to 'cause confusion and break morale'. Lt Chester Szarawarski, a command pilot with the 305th BG at Chelveston, who would be flying the last of his thirty-five missions, remembers: 'The aiming point was the peace monument right in the heart of the city, which was where the government buildings were. The government buildings and the Chancellery, the Reichstag whatever were right there.'[9] There was no doubt also in the mind of the diarist of the 367th Squadron of the 306th BG at Thurleigh, north of Nuthampstead, about why the raid was being mounted. 'The aiming points were concentrated in that part of the city where buildings which house the administration agencies of the German government were located,' he wrote. Somewhat erroneously he claimed the 'entire 8th Air Force' was throwing its weight 'against the disorganised and panicky city'. His fellow diarist with the Group's 423rd Squadron said crews 'cheered when they saw the target was Berlin'.[10]

As the young airmen had stumbled into breakfast less than an hour before, still wiping sleep from their eyes, they had heard the sound of more than 1,000 RAF Lancasters and Halifaxes returning from night raids on Wiesbaden, Wanne-Eickel and Karlsruhe. The previous night 122 Mosquitos of the Light Night Striking Force had each dropped 4,000lb bombs on the Reich capital. 'The roar of planes of the RAF filled the silent morning air,' the diarist recorded. It was because of that the crews voiced their approval

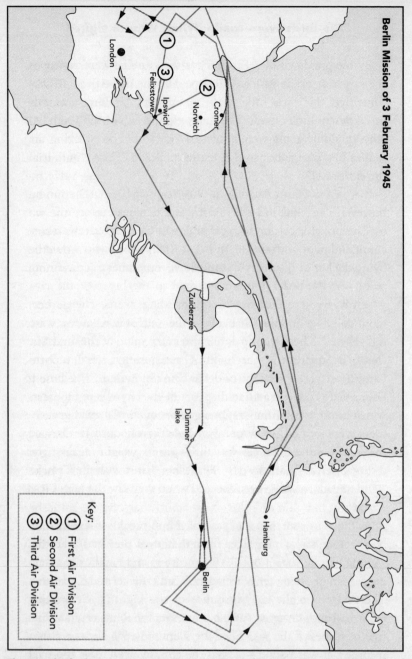

Key:
1 First Air Division
2 Second Air Division
3 Third Air Division

The route plan for the campaign-changing USAAF Berlin mission four months before the war's end, in which the British Chief of Air Staff estimated there could be 100,000 civilian casualties. The track out was almost straight from the Zuiderzee to Berlin, allowing for a dog leg for fighter escorts to join near the familiar pinpoint of Dümmer Lake. The route called for an exit rally point to the south east, an advantage to damaged aircraft, some of which went on to land behind Red Army lines.

of the target at briefing, he said. They 'cheered for the support being given to the RAF bombing and in aid of the great Russian offensive'. He went on: 'The aiming point in Berlin was the centre of the city, around which is located the Tiergarten, Air Ministry, Potsdammer Station and Friedrichstrasse Station and many other important government buildings.'[11] The enthusiastic diarist, who shared his role with two others, was a day out in his calculations of when the RAF had last been to Berlin, but he was as keen as most Army Air Force officers to see the war ended as quickly as possible by whatever means when he wrote: 'Bombing was at 1109 hours just as the people were recovering from the night mission by the RAF, or preparing for their noon meal.'[12]

In the briefing room at Thurleigh was a civilian. It had been considered so important that the 8th would now be laying waste to the centre of Berlin after previous attacks in March and May 1944 on factories in the outskirts, that a famous BBC reporter would be accompanying the men from the Bedfordshire base to describe to listeners gathered round their own peaceful domestic hearths the sight of the Reich capital being blasted and burned in daylight. Guy Byam had brought them the sound of battle many times before. In November 1940 he had survived the sinking of HMS *Jervis Bay*, sacrificed by her skipper to the German pocket battleship *Admiral Scheer* to save a convoy; flown with the RAF Lancaster film unit on the Tallboy bomb attack on the battleship *Tirpitz* on 15 September 1944; and dropped with the paratroopers at Arnhem two days later where he had been captured then escaped by knocking out his guard. Byam was a lucky man and he would be flying with an experienced crew in a lucky aircraft. *Rose of York*, the B-17 the future Queen of England had christened at Thurleigh in August 1944, had by now brought several airmen through their tours and had been bombed up for its sixty-third mission. Byam had seen the aircraft before. He had been the

BBC duty reporter covering its naming ceremony by Princess Elizabeth that August day. Today Byam would be flying with Lt Vernon Daley.

An hour later in the gloom of the ready tent by each aircraft's dispersal pan each crew member, bulky and cumbersome in their flying clothing, went through the routine of final personal preparations for flight as they waited for 'stations time', the signal to climb aboard. Pockets were patted for flight rations of Mars bars, pilots and co-pilots checked once more the Group formation flimsy showing their aircraft's aerial position, navigators counted off protractors, pencils and course and distance calculators, radiomen read again the list of codes. For many there was a strict, though unnecessary pattern to be followed before each mission. Airmen themselves called it superstition then. Today it is recognised by psychiatrists as obsessive compulsive disorder, induced by stress. There was a gut-wrenching, heart-squeezing tension to the brink of nausea as each contemplated what lay ahead. The breath burst out in rapid puffs in the freezing air. Then, bang on 0650, at last came the green flare arcing through the darkness, signalling the time to climb aboard. Now the real work of the day could begin.

In his officers' Nissen hut at Thurleigh Lt Howard Roth heard the splutter then choking roar of the engines of forty-one aircraft fifteen minutes later as their pilots got ready to nudge out of dispersal pans in the dark. The tour the young pilot had begun with an attack on a German oil refinery in August was now over and he was waiting for the posting within days to the 70th Replacement Depot, which would begin his journey back to Lockport, New York. His last mission had been to Mannheim in 'old 674', a great plane that took a lot of damage. When Roth's tour ended it was handed over to a Texas pilot and he was shot down on his first mission.

As the bombers of the two Air Divisions crept in line down perimeter tracks then turned onto active runways, some touched their lucky charms for the last time as they faced the final mission of their tour. At Glatton ball turret gunner S/Sgt Briol had been woken in the Nissen hut he shared named 'Sack Time Hovel' four hours before to eventually learn that the final sortie of his thirty-five-mission tour would be on the Reich capital. He had much to reflect on as Lt John Welch gunned his 457th BG Fortress down the concrete for Berlin, including seeing an airman 'thrown through the side' as a B-17 exploded behind his turret on the Merseburg raid of 2 November.

From Sudbury Lt Alfeo Brusetti, the bombardier who had taken his army nurse sister flying in his B-17 in December, was also on his way to Berlin as lead bombardier for the 832nd BS, 486th BG, with his usual skipper Capt Ron Bereman. He would write to Dee the next day: 'At last, after many false starts, and a lot of griping I got another mission in. And what a mission!! Read today's headlines and you'll know why I had a busy day yesterday. You'll never catch me asking for rough missions, but I was darn glad when I found out we were to lead our squadron in on Big B.'[13] Brusetti had four missions to complete to finish his tour, but, unknown to him, flying alongside him in the B-17 *Blue Grass Girl* of Lt Lewis Cloud were two of his former comrades now on their final mission before being returned to the States. One of them had arrived on the crew as a replacement after two ball turret gunners in succession had refused to fly in that position, the last being 'replaced by Sgt Jones, a combat veteran from the Pacific Theatre, a dependable gunner', the bombardier recorded in his combat diary. 'We lost him when the ball turret was replaced by a radar bombing instrument on our plane. We also lost our tail gunner, Sgt Frank Chrastka, at the same time when his position was used by a "formation coordinator" on lead ships. They were placed in a pool and flew when and wherever needed. On February 3rd,

1945, they were both flying their last mission in a plane that was flying on our left wing.'[14]

In the co-pilot's seat of the aircraft at the head of the whole 3AD was Major Robert Rosenthal, the 100th BG flyer whose final mission of his first tour had been the Berlin strike of nearly a year ago, on 8 March. The second tour he had immediately volunteered for had been cut short by a crash-landing in France coming back from Nuremburg in September, Rosenthal being hospitalised with a broken arm and internal injuries. He had returned to the 100th as commander of the 418th Bomb Sqn in December. The Berlin raid would be his fifty-second mission. S/Sgt John Day, the nineteen-year-old ball turret gunner who was one of the newest members of that squadron, remembers him as 'a warrior like General Patton or LeMay and we weren't at all sure that it was good to be there, but we adjusted in the end. You quickly form allegiance to the group and we were very happy. We thought the 418th was the best squadron.'[15]

In 1AD Lt Col. Marvin Lord was leading the 91st BG. The man who would normally be in the left-hand seat of the lead plane, the keen Major Immanuel Klette, was away on a short pass so his very experienced crew was taken by Lt Col. Lord, the Group Operations Officer, who had never been to Berlin and wanted to record it in his list of missions. Further back in the 1AD stream was the 398th BG. They were due to be ninth in line over the target. Just before the Initial Point where lead bombardiers took over their aircraft to fly straight and level on the bombsight, each Group began to close up, causing prop wash for those behind, which was why two pilots were needed to control each aircraft. Lt Perry Powell of the 398th's lead element fell back several hundred feet and he dropped the nose of his B-17 to avoid the turbulence. He then came too close to the low squadron and instinctively pulled back strongly on the control column, pitching his aircraft to 45 degrees. It proved too great a degree of stress for the fuselage of the heavily-laden B-17 and it broke in half beyond the ball turret. The front half of the aircraft then continued up and into Lt John McCormick's plane, slicing away the nose. The navigator fell out without a parachute. Only three chutes were seen from either aircraft. The rest of the Group flew on towards Berlin, trying to block from their minds what they had just witnessed.

Minutes later Berlin's terrifying flak defences of the strength General Spaatz had been thinking of when he warned Washington the air war was by no means over, began to exhibit their presence to the B-17 crews. They consisted of batteries of three converging rings of heavy flak. The first extended for forty miles around Berlin. Others picked up the glittering columns, picking off individuals and passing on the remainder all the way to the centre of the city where defence consisted of the bomb-proof flak towers, one in the Tiergarten, another in Friedrichshain, the third in Humbolthain park to the north, each equipped with 128mm, 105mm and 88mm guns. The 130ft-high concrete structures, which between them could accommodate 30,000 people, were designed to create a triangular protection of the government offices in the centre of Berlin. Once at the core of these circles of death the Flying Fortress crews had to sit and continue to take it as their machines proceeded straight and level out again through the rings to the Rally Point, pilots sweating as they fought to restrain bucking and jerking control columns.

It was as the seemingly innocent black puffs began to bloom and multiply around the droning B-17s that the parkland in the west of the Reich capital started to unfold, though some parts of the city were still cloud covered. 'Over Berlin the weather was CAVU to 10/10s cloud and the lead bombardier states the Tiergarten was visible for miles,' the enthusiastic diarist of the Thurleigh-based 423rd Bomb Squadron recorded.[16] Bombs from the leaders had already fallen as the 306th BG arrived and smoke was wreathing the red flashes of other ordnance now falling from the Fortresses. Each had carried a high explosive load, not incendiaries, to blast apart the concrete of government buildings and apartment houses in the centre of Berlin. But as gas pipes were severed, fires sprang up and soon a vast blaze was raging through Friedrichstadt, Luisenstadt and the central area of Mitte as well as the working-class district of Kreuzberg, slightly to the north. 'What a horrible thing to finish up on,' S/Sgt John Briol of the 457th BG wrote. 'I could see Berlin below, smoking and exploding from the first groups over the target. There were two tremendous explosions ahead of us as two Fortresses got hit and blew to bits right in front . . . Another got hit and went down in a steep dive. Half the men baled out and went floating down into the fire and smoke.'[17]

One of the first aircraft to be doomed was that of Lt Col. Marvin Lord. Just after bombs away a flak shell in the waist split the aircraft in two. As a lead crew eleven very experienced men were on board including a radio operator on his 79th mission and an engineer on his 81st. For the ball turret gunner, who had served in the Pacific, it was his 108th.[18] That random flak also brought down another skilled airman, who had beaten the odds so many times, 'Rosie' Rosenthal of the 100th BG. Major David Lyster, CO of the Group's 350th Bomb Squadron, known as 'Handlebar Hank' because of his RAF-style moustache, revealed: 'We were flying deputy lead to Rosie that day. We were leading the high Group and at the IP we saw Rosie get hit by flak and watched as he went down, counting parachutes. Rosie had seemed immortal.'[19]

An anonymous eyewitness report at the later 100th BG debriefing related that the aircraft may have been hit by a ground rocket. It was 'a few seconds before bombs away,' the airman said, though the aircraft continued on its run and dropped its bombs. 'Fire and dense smoke was seen in the fuselage and bomb bay, including the cockpit. The bomb bay doors closed and then reopened. The pilot opened his window and peeled gently off to the right, directing the deputy leader to take over on VHF and flew level for a few moments while six crew members baled out (three appeared to come from waist and or tail and three from the bomb bay). There was a small explosion in No. 3 engine nacelle and the a/c headed down, burning and beginning to spin when last seen at 15000ft.'[20]

Rosenthal was still aboard at that point, trying to control the aircraft as those members of the crew remaining alive baled. Then at 1,000ft he went out himself, his chute opening over the Russian lines where he was picked up by the Red Army together with three of his crew. Four more who had jumped earlier became PoWs including the pilot Cptn John Ernst, who had a leg amputated in a German hospital that night. One of the navigators aboard was killed as was the bombardier.

The Russian Vistula–Oder Offensive which had begun on 12 January had ended the day before the Berlin raid with the Red Army 300 miles further on at the banks of the Oder river only forty-five miles from Berlin. USSTAF crews had been told that of their four choices of making it to safety if their aircraft was badly damaged, heading for the Eastern Front, although the nearest option, was the least safe. They were warned of 'Russian attacks' on US aircraft seeking a haven over the front line and crews had been issued with a small square of silk carrying the Stars and Stripes and the Russian equivalent for 'I am American'. It was only in desperation, therefore, that crews headed east, but six were forced to take that option after being hit by flak over Berlin, one of them being that of Lt Arthur Ogle of the 486th BG. It would be weeks before Rosenthal or Ogle and his crew were back in England.

The Berlin flak claimed twenty-one Fortresses and another fifteen went down later. From 3AD the 100th BG lost three as did the 306th BG, all from the nine aircraft the 367th squadron had put up. 'Flak over the target was intensely accurate, tracking for about 12 minutes, but none of our 423rd planes were damaged,' the squadron diarist recorded.[21] But that of Lt George Luckett of the 367th received a direct hit. 'A burst of flak in the right wing tore off the wing,' his own squadron diarist related. 'Up to four chutes were reported from the plane before it disappeared in flames.'[22] Then flak started a fire in the No. 3 engine of Lt Roland Lissner's aircraft. The crew battled to put it out. Finally *Rose of York*, the Fortress Princess Elizabeth had named, was hit too. Lt Vernon Daley had one engine shot out over the Reich capital and a fuel tank punctured. He tried to keep up with the formation, but began to lag to the rear of the western-bound column.

Below the blaze in the city had reached such an intensity it would burn for four days, driven by a westerly wind, turning everything in its path to ash and only dying out when it reached waterways, wide streets or parkland. The aiming point of the Templehof rail yards had not been destroyed in the raid, but the Anhalter Bahnhof, from which many of Berlin's Jews had been transported to death camps, was left with most of its roof missing and the rest tottering dangerously, so no trains could run. Potsdammer Bahnhof, which had not functioned for months because of earlier bombing, had been hit again. The key German personnel Portal originally had in mind for Thunderclap were never specified but the raid did end the evil of a Nazi who had taken the lives of many citizens whose conscience would not allow them to support Hitler. Roland Freiser, who led the People's Court and enjoyed ranting at and ridiculing defendants in the dock before sentencing them to be beheaded, was dead, killed by a beam falling from the roof of his building blitzed by an anonymous American togglier.

The *Rose of York* was next heard of over the North Sea. The pilot of another returning B-17 near the Frisian Islands heard Daley report that his aircraft was damaged but he thought he could make it to England. Shortly afterwards the luck of the aircraft and that of reporter Guy Byam, who had escaped so often before, ran out. Nothing of the aircraft or its crew has ever been found. By that time the third 306th BG flak victim, the aircraft of Lt Roland Lissner, had diverted to neutral Sweden, the engine fire having been put out. The crew were unhurt apart from tail gunner Sgt George Beck who was hospitalised with a slight flak wound.

There was one further tragedy beginning over the sea, however. Lt Alfeo Brusetti had been unaware that two of his former comrades were in *Blue Grass Girl*, flying on the left wing of his own 486th BG aircraft. 'We were almost across the Channel when their plane caught fire,' he recorded. 'They were both killed. Only four people in the front half of the plane were able to bale out. We didn't know our old crew members were on that plane until after we landed. We knew they were flying their 35th and last mission that day, but we didn't know in which plane. All of us on the crew were devastated by this event.'[23]

An official USSTAF investigation into the strange accident was made within days, and reported:

The engineer, radio operator, waist gunner and ball turret gunner gathered in the radio compartment forward of the ball turret to congratulate each other on the expiration of their tour as most were on their last mission. A fire started in the ball turret area and quickly spread along the wooden floor. The pilot reported a fire on board and gradually turned the aircraft out of formation. The crew gradually began baling out. The engineer [T/Sgt Richard Warlick] was the first to leave, followed by the navigator, bombardier and co-pilot. The BTG [S/Sgt Johnny L. Jones] got out too low for his chute to open in time. Other aircraft in the flight reported the aircraft went into a steep turn, crashed to the ground, exploded and burned. Four of the nine-man crew – pilot, radio operator, waist gunner and the tail gunner

[S/Sgt Frank T. Chrastka] – were still in the aircraft when it struck.[24]

The aircraft came down at Reydon, near Southwold on the Suffolk coast, the blaze which doomed it believed to have been caused by a leaking oxygen line.

Meanwhile the fires were still burning in Berlin. Reich Propaganda Minster Josef Goebbels claimed between 20,000 and 25,000 civilians had died in a 'terror raid'. So extensive was the damage when reconnaissance pictures reached General Spaatz's headquarters showing one and a half miles of devastation in the central Mitte area, it seemed Goebbels' figures were right. It had after all been the biggest attack on Berlin of the war and the likelihood of a huge civilian toll was supported by initial crew reports such as those which spurred the chronicler of the 423rd Sqn of the 306th BG to write: 'Damage to all sections of the city was severe and smoke over the area gives evidence of many fires. Crew members stated that the entire centre of the city was on fire or smoking.'[25] Portal's original idea of Thunderclap had been of course to cause such a shocking loss of life that it would tip the ordinary German into giving up. In fact the death toll was 2,894, with 20,000 wounded. They were certainly ordinary enough, working men and tired housewives for the most part in areas such as Kreuzburg and elsewhere now short of homes for another 80,000 following the raid.

So many had survived because Berlin did not lack shelter space, the three flak towers guarding the city centre amply providing accommodation behind thick concrete. There was also some evidence that Portal and his followers were not entirely wrong that German morale could be finally and irrevocably cracked by bombing. Berlin correspondents of newspapers in neutral countries were often able to reveal the true story of what was happening among the German people, which gave the lie to Goebbels' propaganda of resolute forbearance. Even those from

Occupied countries made subtle notes. Danish correspondent Jacob Kronika published this account in 1945 of a conversation he heard between three women in a Berlin bunker as bombs rained down from the Flying Fortresses. One announced: 'We're getting cheated with our dead,' followed by agreement from a second who said: 'The same coffin is used for all funerals in the chapel. But there is no corpse in the coffin.' A third woman now added her information that the dead were all being cremated together at the Baumschulenweg crematorium, the ashes poured at random into urns and whoever wanted an urn could take one. 'If we don't count for anything in life then why should the dead?' said the second woman, quickly followed by the first with: 'Something must be done. There are limits.'[26] It was fortunate for the women they were overheard by a sympathetic newspaperman; a Gestapo informer would have led them before a court similar to Freiser's where they would have been sentenced to beheading as traitors.

Lt Chester Szarawarski returned safely to Chelveston from his momentous final mission. Reflecting on it years later he said:

> The Germans were bombing cities, they were attempting to destroy England, you saw evidence of that everywhere, wherever you travelled . . . I think we went to Merseburg about six times, we went to some others where there were synthetic oil plants, we were hitting marshalling yards, we were hitting on several occasions known factories and they knew what was being manufactured there . . . That one mission was to Berlin . . . well you couldn't feel too badly about it because it was where the government buildings were.[27]

Operation Thunderclap and its initial concept as an offensive to create chaos and break German morale had called for four German cities to be heavily blitzed. The next on the initial list after Berlin was Chemnitz and 437 bombers of 3AD duly unloaded on the city on 6 February. A conference in Malta between Roosevelt, Churchill and the Allied chiefs of staff two days before had decided synthetic oil still had the priority in the bombing war, but the second highest was 'Berlin, Leipzig and other associated cities where heavy attack will cause great confusion in civilian evacuation from the east and hamper reinforcements'.[28] In the initial planning of raids for 6 February Chemnitz had been selected as a secondary target should the total force of more than 1,300 Fortresses and Liberators have been unable to find their smaller, varied oil targets across Germany. The weather conditions over the industrial city were no better and a total of 800 tons of bombs went down on PFF radar marking on what was hoped was the marshalling yards, without flak or fighter interference. The Civic Hospital was among the buildings hit. The force then found itself battling a 130mph headwind. The target in south-eastern Germany had been at extreme range and returning bombers began to run out of fuel, putting down wherever crews could find as they descended through the cloud. Only half of the B-17s despatched by the 100th BG made it back to Thorpe Abbotts, for instance, and at least some bombers from most Groups had to land wherever they could in Belgium and northern France. It was the last memorable mission for Lt Alfeo Brusetti of the 486th BG.

We soon realized we didn't have enough gas to get back. Most of the planes did as we did and landed at the first airfield they saw. Over the next few days the 8th AF couldn't mount a major mission until these planes were refuelled and flown back to England. We landed on a small fighter strip in Charleroi, Belgium. The pilots there flew P-38s on photo reconnaissance missions. For a couple of days we managed to find something wrong with our plane, but then decided we'd better not find anything more wrong or they'd court martial us. I brought several bottles of champagne back with me, as did most of the others. One of the bottles I brought back to the States and when I got married in 1946 we opened it.[29]

It was the fourth mission for Brusetti's fellow Sudbury officer Lt Frank Ellersick, whose flight time was a record for the Group, 10 hours 58 minutes, before he managed to land at Lille. 'Two days of fun there,' his togglier, S/Sgt Chester Stanek, wrote in his combat diary. Stanek had found 10/10s cloud when he came to drop his bombs. 'Forgot to put bomb bay switches on and bombs hung up when I released toggle switch. Finally realized what was wrong and dropped bombs. Navigator Clyde Whitted had to kick out last bomb.'[30] There was little damage to Chemnitz, but Spaatz may have considered he had in part fulfilled his obligation. But there was now a third city which Churchill and the RAF considered should be subjected to a heavy attack to help the Russian offensive – Dresden.

The ancient Saxon capital was as different to the capital of the Reich when it came to putting civilians in harm's way as it was possible to be. Berlin was guarded by rings of flak only matched by those of vital oil targets such as Leuna-Merseburg. Dresden's flak defence would be described as 'neglible' by aircrew, because they had been removed to be used as anti-tank weapons on the Eastern Front seventy miles away.[31] Secondly, with its bomb-proof flak towers Berlin had a public central shelter system to rival any. But in Dresden the city authorities had woefully neglected the building of shelters except for themselves. Even the local SS commander, Martin Mutschmann, whose men had been used to construct a secure bunker in the garden of Dresden's Gauleiter, had been angry enough to fire off a protest to Heinrich Himmler in late 1943 reading: 'I do not think it right that such a bunker be installed in the Gauleiter's garden of all places, because the greater part of the population still has no access even to a properly constructed air raid shelter.'[32] If the uncertain weather of

February favoured the Allies, therefore, and the target could be marked visually and not by radar with its attendant inaccuracy, the damage and loss of life was likely to be extreme.

The USSTAF had been meant to be the first to bomb Dresden, where eight years later a US report calculated there had been 110 factories, with 50,000 workers toiling for the Nazi war effort. If they had done so, America's young airmen and not RAF Bomber Command might have suffered disapprobation – though as part of the pre-eminent post-war nation, not to the degree the English crews endured for decades. But Spaatz's men did not go first as had been intended for Shrove Tuesday, 13 February, to light up the city for the RAF crews following that night. The intended attack on marshalling yards of the ancient baroque city, known as the 'Florence of the North', was postponed because of the poor flying weather which had changed from the great freeze of January into gales and rainstorms in early February. On the 12th a depression which had been sitting off Ireland moved east bringing heavy rain then fog, which put paid to any plans Spaatz had for operating the next day.[33] It was, therefore, to the sound of RAF bomber squadrons returning from Dresden in the early hours of 14 February having efficiently created a firestorm that killed thousands, that USSTAF crews were alerted to playing their own part in Germany's Ash Wednesday.

The Flying Fortresses arrived over the still-burning city shortly after noon, but in the smoke and cloud covering Dresden only one Group, the 379th, was able to find its target. It was the Friedrichstadt marshalling yards to the west. Other Groups in the 316-bomber force recorded that their view was obscured by clouds so they bombed Dresden on radar. Victor Klemperer, a Jewish academic who had been warned only hours before the RAF attack that he was being deported to Auschwitz, was alerted to the new ordeal approaching as he made his way from a make-shift shelter by the banks of the Elbe. 'I heard the ugly hum of an aircraft above me coming rapidly closer and diving,' he recorded in his diary. 'I ran towards the wall [around the Jewish Quarter], threw myself to the ground, my head against the wall, my arm over my face. There was already an explosion and little bits of rubble trickled down on me. I lay there for a little while longer. I thought, "Just don't get killed now!" There were a few more distant explosions then there was silence.'[34]

Incendiaries and high explosive were widely dispersed over the city in the USSTAF raid. Weather conditions were now such that more than sixty aircraft became separated and bombed Prague sixty miles away in error while others struck Brüx and Pilsen, also in Czechoslovakia. The diary of the 369th squadron of the 306th BG reveals that 'bombing was on Dresden through 8/9ths cloud with no visual correction'. The records keeper added: 'There was no AA fire at the target, but the Group had meagre inaccurate tracking north of Kassel, at Chemnitz, north of Frankfurt and over the front lines. Three Fw 190s attacked a straggler from the low squadron, one flying over him, two under and each attacked other aircraft, seriously damaging two and wounding two crew members.' However, Sgt Edward Richards, top turret gunner in another B-17 of the squadron opened fire at 700 yards, closing to 100, forcing the aircraft to break away. 'The Fw went down in flames and broke up before reaching the clouds,' the diarist recorded. 'Captn Boylston Lewis left the formation shortly after the fighter attack in the Dresden-Chemnitz area. Lewis is reported to have made a 180 degree turn and headed east. One chute was seen.'[35] Lt Jack Henley, commanding another of the squadron's aircraft, called up on VHF to say he was low on fuel and heading for a field on the Continent. Like Captn Boylston and his crew he was never seen again. A total of five B-17s were missing after the Dresden raid, including one from the 379th BG, the only Group to find its target, shot down over the front lines on the way home. The next day American aircraft returned, 1AD being diverted from its primary target of the Böhlen synthetic oil plant because it was obscured by cloud and bombing Dresden instead. It failed to hit the Friedrichstadt marshalling yards and, as on the previous raid bombs were scattered over a wide area. But one stray bomb destroyed the guillotine in the courtyard of the prison in the Südvorstadt suburb in the south of the city where it is believed more than 1,000 people were executed in the course of the war for a range of offences from resisting the Nazis to defeatist talk. Another bomb destroyed the prison's north wall killing several prisoners but allowing others to escape.

According to the official German report *Tagesbefehl* (Order of the Day) No. 47 issued on 22 March the number of dead recovered by that date from all four raids, RAF and USSTAF, was 20,204 and the total number of deaths was expected to be about 25,000.[36] The Reich Propaganda Minister now saw a great opportunity. As Germany's cities had turned to ashes in this final phase of the air war and it was obvious the Luftwaffe was unable to keep its oft-repeated early promise that the homeland would not be bombed in the way they were bombing other nations, Goebbels had found himself in a dilemma. He could hardly cavil at the serious harm being done to Germany while still maintaining that it would be the final victor. However, after the Berlin raid of 3 February he had enlisted the unwitting aid provided by newspapers in neutral countries by claiming up to 25,000 had died. Now, in an increased attempt to force the Allies to call off the bomber offensive by appealing to the 'international court' of public opinion, he became even bolder after what had undoubtedly been a firestorm so horrific the whole world would be shocked. He had his agents simply multiply by ten the Dresden casualty figures and protest that a jewel of world architecture whose 'few' factories 'mainly manufactured toothpaste and baby powder', had been lost. As early as 25 February, a Reich Propaganda Ministry leaflet with photographs of two burned children was released under the title

Dresden – Massacre of Refugees, stating that 200,000 had died. By the end of March the Propaganda Ministry had made it precisely 202,040, which simply added a nought to the known *Tagesbefehl* figure. Goebbels' inventions would lead to serious questioning on both sides of the Atlantic into how the combined bomber offensive was being conducted, a furore that would last for decades lay ahead.

But there was no such equivocation for those at the sharp end of war. Their anxiety was to finish the conflict as quickly as possible and go home. On the bases those who cared for the combat airmen knew only excitement in the atmosphere of living for the day when a future was always uncertain.

That zest for life was exhibited by Kay Brainard at Sudbury as she met the men of the 486th BG coming back from Chemnitz on 14 February, which 3AD had bombed while the 1st Air Division was trying to find its targets at Dresden. She wrote in her diary:

This afternoon when we were providing coffee and sandwiches for the boys returning from their bombing mission, a sassy little lieutenant came up to me and said 'Aren't you Kay from W. Palm Beach?' I thought perhaps he was being a little fresh, so I just smiled, said yes, and kept on pouring coffee. Sort of ignoring him. As he turned to go, I caught a glimpse of disappointment in his face, so I called out, 'Why do you ask?' He said, 'Don't you remember me? I'm Dick Witt – I used to ride my bike to the travel bureau to deliver rail tickets to you . . .' That was quite a few years back, and he is now a Bombardier – with a mustache!* He knew both Bill and Newell – has only been in England since January.[37]

---

* 2/Lt Witt was later shot down in the B-17 commanded by Lt Billy Wood, who was seen with his chute on but apparently didn't survive. Witt was among those who did.

The previous day Kay had written to her mother:

> BE MY VALENTINE? Dearest mother, Things are progress-
> ing nicely, and I might say rapidly, inasmuch as I had a date
> with the CO (Lt Col. Glendon 'Jeep' Overing) of the field
> last night . . . One of the boys introduced me to him in the
> Officer's Mess the other night and I mentioned that I would
> like to see how the base operated sometime, so he said he'd
> see that I got a tour of inspection . . . He's young, very attrac-
> tive [and] a pilot! Yesterday afternoon he phoned and asked
> if I was still interested in seeing the base, I said I was, so he
> said he'd be by to pick me up, also Jean [St Clair], at 4.30.[38]

There then followed a tour complete with GI chauffeur of what
Kay described as 'off-limit offices where all the confidential work
goes on' and even a tour of a B-17. Later Col. Overing took Kay
to see a movie in Sudbury.

The rumblings of Operation Thunderclap would continue with
another heavy RAF raid on Chemnitz, but on 22 February there
was a further tectonic shift from the moral high ground with
which America had begun its European bombing war, when
Spaatz threw the weight of his air forces behind Operation Clarion. It had in fact been formulated at USSTAF headquarters in
December and called for 'a vast series of attacks by small groups
of planes coming in at low altitudes to bomb and strafe targets all
over Germany'.[39] The joint USSTAF/RAF series of strikes on the
German transportation system over two days was something of
an admission by Spaatz that his previous high-level attacks on key
German rail infrastructure since Christmas had achieved limited
success. This time forty-three targets of secondary value in the
Deutsche Reichsbahn were selected for simultaneous attack on one
day. Because they lacked the value to the Germans of marshalling

yards in bigger cities such as Leipzig or Berlin, flak defences were minimal, which meant the Fortresses and Liberators could bomb from lower altitudes, thus improving the strike pattern. The fact that the small-town stations and goods yards would be hit together, it was hoped, would cause a log-jam paralysis of an area of 30,000 square miles of railway lines.

However, it was in the second part of the plan where Spaatz put previous principles finally aside. The germ of Operation Clarion had been gestated by Major General Elwood Quesada the previous autumn. The head of the 9th AF had proposed sending 1,500 fighter bombers in pairs to attack bridges, railway stations, factories and residential areas to precipitate surrender. When the Clarion field orders finally came down the pilots of the Fighter Groups backing up the bombers found they had been given free range to sweep across the autobahns, country byways and hamlet lanes of Germany shooting anything that moved, as well as blasting rail traffic in transit. To fired-up fighter pilots let off the leash it gave them carte blanche to pulverise with their cannon the pace of rural civilian life from creaking farm carts to windmills. Many were told at briefings they were flying a mission to break German morale in the ensuing chaos across the Reich. Some senior Air Force figures had already protested. The head of the 15th AF, General Nathan Twining, requested Spaatz to think about how the public in America would react to the civilian deaths and Doolittle warned that Goebbels and his breed would use Clarion as justification for Nazi barbarism.[40] But the need to end the European war as quickly as possible was paramount and objections were overruled.

The plan only awaited two days of clear weather, to mop up on the second what had been missed on the first. On the night of 21 February the meteorologists reported the window was open. The next day 1,472 USSTAF heavy bombers supported by 862 fighters crossed into the Reich to begin their rippling, roaring wave of pounding, flashing, smoking devastation aimed at bringing movement to a halt and convincing the populace to stay under cover and stop assisting the war machine or die. The following day 1,274 bombers set off tasked with thirty transportation targets, some of them new and others that were being followed up to prevent emergency repairs. This time 704 fighters swept the fields and roadsides with their cannon. The strafing Thunderbolts of Spaatz's 9th Air Force on the Continent had also been fully engaged as had the RAF's 2nd Tactical Air Force. Nearly 9,000 aircraft, taking off from England, France, Holland, Belgium and Italy over two days had attacked railways, bridges and roads in an area bounded by Nuremburg, Hamburg and Berlin.

The 8th Air Force made an official film of Operation Clarion to show to both the chiefs in Washington and the GIs at base makeshift movie theatres in the ETO. In it Lt General Walter Todd, assistant chief of staff for 8th operations, said: 'We knew that if sufficient damage could be done in one, two, or three successive days the immediate destroying and paralysing that would follow such attacks would have a material effect on the fighting on all German fronts.'[41] And so it proved. From then until the end of the war the German rail system never recovered, any signs of movement over an increasingly circuitous supply system bringing a rapid response by the 8th in the north and the 15th AF in the south. In strictly military terms Operation Clarion had been a great success and for the cost of only eight US bombers and two fighters over two days. The way was now open for clearing of strong resistance in the Reichswald Forest and eventual crossing of the last barrier to the Fatherland itself, the Rhine.

Like all US service personnel in Europe Kay Brainard read the news and hoped for an early end to the war. It would mean the return of her PoW brother Bill and perhaps by then she could finally find out whether her other airman brother Newell was still alive. On 18 February she had paid a visit with Col. Overing and other officers to the Third Strategic Air Force Depot between Bury St Edmunds and Thetford, sitting 'with all the commanding officers of the nearby fields', and returned to find a letter from her mother. It seemed to indicate that the Air Force had confirmed there was no further news of Newell and official hope was therefore fading. She replied immediately: 'The news about Newell has upset me quite a bit, but I shall do as you are doing and keep telling myself he is all right. If I have an opportunity I am going to pay a visit to his former base sometime. I don't know yet where it is.'[42]

But two days later she was able to make a positive reply.

Col. Overing (Jeep) made a visit to 8th Air Force Headquarters yesterday on business, and while there he very kindly looked into the matter of our 'missing' Newell. He came up to me at dinner tonight to report, and this is what I learned: On that day [27 September 1944] a great number of ships were lost – 33 I think, and 22 of those were from Newell's Group. However, it is reported that a number of parachutes were seen, in fact, more than have since been reported 'prisoners'. Their records show that six of Newell's crew are still reported 'missing'. (Perhaps your news on the boys may be more up to date). Out of those lost that day, three boys (two gunners and a navigator) have returned thru underground help – but it took 4 months or more. Col. Overing also said that the report was that those planes that went down went down due to engines out – tails damaged enough to make it necessary to bail out, etc, but no planes exploded in air. In other words, he thought it all quite encouraging and thought it highly probable that some of those boys are being hidden out, or there is the possibility that he may be in a German hospital . . . I don't want to get your hopes up too high, or Lorraine's [Newell's young wife], but I'm just telling you what Jeep told me. He has arranged with the 8th Air Force Hqtrs to be notified at once if they receive further word . . . when I go to London I'm going to try to see if I can find out something about Bill. I am wondering if and when he is set free we can get together over here before they send him home.[43]

The first of Kay's leaves in the capital bursting with Americans would come as the 8th Air Force planned a series of constant, devastating blows against Hitler's Reich, terrible in their relentless tenacity. In February 1943 as the main RAF bomber offensive was in its infancy and that of the then USAAF was just beginning, Goebbels had made a speech at the *Sportspalast* in Berlin condemning the Jews for Germany's latest setbacks and asking the German people if they wanted 'total war'. He had been cheered to the rafters. Operations Thunderclap and Clarion had now shown the Nazis and those who had turned a blind eye to persecution of minorities what total war meant. In the next five weeks the destruction of Germany would reach its apogee. The RAF would drop more bombs in that period, 67,637 tons, than it had in total in the first thirty-four months of the war. Yet Spaatz's men, with their fleets of Fortresses and Liberators, their hordes of bomb-carrying whining Thunderbolts and their swarms of ground-strafing buzzing Mustangs would exceed even this in a crescendo of destruction.

17

'Sitting off my wing was an Me 109'

The days of the Third Reich were truly numbered, seventy-one in fact, when the USSTAF returned to Berlin on 26 February to provide additional aid to the Russians. That day Soviet troops had just forced the surrender of 12,000 German soldiers after the month-long siege of Poznań in Poland. All along the Eastern Front German positions were disintegrating to release an orgy of looting, rape and murder by a vengeful Red Army. In the west the roar of more than 1,200 bombers of all three 8th AF air divisions protected by 650 fighters filled the sky. Once more the Groups had to bomb through cloud, their aiming points Alexanderplatz station right in the centre, Schlesischer *U-bahn* station in crowded Kreuzburg, plus the Stettiner marshalling yards in the north-east of the city. As they departed another 80,000 people in Berlin were homeless. In a report printed in most US papers a news agency described it as the 'biggest air attack on Berlin' and there was no compunction about where the bombs were falling. 'US heavy bombers dropped 3,000 tons of explosives into the heart of the city during the noon hour today,' the report ran. 'More than 500,000 small incendiary bombs were showered upon the refugee-crowded capital with three railway stations as the main targets.'[1] The 91st BG bombed the Schlesischer station and this time Major Immanuel Klette, whose crew had been lost in the raid of 3 February, was there. 'Bombing was done by H2X methods with unobserved results,' the diary of his squadron, the 324th, reported. What was known was not impressive. 'A plot made from Scope photos showed bombs to have fallen *near* assigned MPIs,' the diarist related.[2]

After Operation Clarion the Reich's air defences were so disorganised, helped in part by the presence of many 'chaff ships' on the mission spreading the tinsel strips to fill radar screens, that although ninety bombers were damaged by flak only three were lost. Similarly the Luftwaffe was able to put up so few fighters that the Mustangs shot down only four, without loss or apparent damage to any US fighter Group.

The next night Mosquitos of the RAF would return to Berlin to maintain the round-the-clock pressure on Germany's leaders and rob the populace of sleep, to further erode morale. The two-man crews of the Light Night Striking Force called them 'siren tours' of the Reich. They, and the constant attacks by the USSTAF, certainly irritated Goebbels, whose own days left before his suicide after having his wife poison their six young children, were now sixty-two. Writing in his diary on the last day of February he detailed:

Over Reich territory 1,100 four-engined American bombers with strong fighter escort attacked transport installations at Halle and Leipzig. In the afternoon 150 British bombers with fighter escort attacked transportation targets in Dortmund, Castrop-Rauxel and Recklinghausen. Some 300 British bombers made a raid on Mainz. Flying from Italy, 600 four-engined American bombers attacked industrial and transport targets in the Augsburg area. Some 80 aircraft from this formation made a subsidiary attack on Salzburg

... During the night two harassing raids were on Berlin, in each case by some 70 Mosquitos ... The Soviets deployed a total of some 1,200 aircraft, the majority in the area of the offensive in Pomerania.[3]

Raids on Berlin by the Americans by day and the British by night would continue and in the final days of the war even the Red Air Force would bomb Berlin to complete the sum of 363 separate Allied air attacks, in which a total of 65,000 tons of explosives were dropped. When the bombing stopped Russian artillery took over, Colonel General Erastovich Berzarin boasting that 40,000 tons of shells were fired into the capital in two weeks.

It was clear no city in the Reich was any longer safe from cataclysmic air attack. The sight and sound of more than 1,000 US bombers heading outbound across the East Anglian coastline between Southwold and Cromer, followed an hour or so later by almost as many fighters, became a daily routine as March blew in and thoughts of the ice, snow and later torrential rain of the previous bitter two months faded to painful but distant memory. Kay Brainard found herself in a frenetic switchback of demanding duty and sheer excitement as she was caught up in the 'here today gone tomorrow' atmosphere of an operational base in what had become known as Little America. On 2 March as 1,100 bombers and 700 fighters of the air division she was part of were out over various German targets, including Dresden, she took to the sky herself.

Within twenty-four hours she was writing to her mother:

Yesterday was a great day for me! Jeep took me flying in a B-17. We planned to fly out and watch the mission come in across the Channel, but found that anti-aircraft on the coast were on the alert for any planes just flying around loose, so we couldn't do that. Instead we just flew all around this part of England. We went up to 8,000ft which was way above the clouds, but not high enough to require oxygen. It was the most beautiful sight I have ever seen. The sun was shining brightly up there, and it was like a sea of frothing white foam beneath us. I called Jeep on the interphone (at that time I was riding in the Plexiglas nose with the bombardier) and told him just to let me out, because I didn't think I'd ever get that close to Heaven again! . . . We landed shortly before the mission was due back, so I could rush over to the briefing block and be on hand to serve coffee and sandwiches to the boys returning. When we were flying I sat in the co-pilot's seat some of the time and Jeep let me do the flying for awhile. Really nothing to it . . . just a little push and pull! But what a maze of instruments on the panel in front of me. That was confusing! How they ever learn what they all mean is more than I can figure out.[4]

That day the 486th BG returned to Sudbury without loss, but eight hours of holding a bucking, jerking Fortress in its formation slot all the way to the borders of Czechoslovakia and back as gunners constantly searched for *Sturmboks* of German fighters looking for the vulnerable, left its mark. 'The boys really look worn out when they come in – parachute harnesses hanging on them – Mae Wests still on – brief cases in hand (navigators anyway),' Kay recorded. 'Their first stop is at the table where I hold forth. On days when they have bombing raids they have to get up anywhere from 2am to 4am for briefing – even tho they may not have all cleared the field until 10am. It's quite an ordeal for these youngsters.'[5]

Of a total air fleet of 1,890 only fourteen bombers and thirteen fighters were missing, but it had been a savage day for the 385th BG half an hour or so up the road at Great Ashfield and in the same combat wing as the Sudbury Group. They had lost four crews from just such a *Sturmbok* attack, adding to the shock of two lost the day before in a collision. The Group had been making a west–east track following 2AD towards Magdeburg when they split off with the rest of their division to head south-east towards the Ruhland oil refinery. It was shortly after 10am when they were bounced by twelve Fw 190s and three Me 109s, Fortresses falling away in flames almost immediately.

The 78th FG was twenty-eight miles from Ruhland escorting the bombers past the Luftwaffe airfield of Burg when someone called in fighters at six o'clock low. Lt Duncan McDuffie, who came from the small resort town of Aiken, South Carolina, where the dancing film star Fred Astaire had taken to spending his family holidays, was about to establish a remarkable tally. He swooped down on the enemy with the 78th's CO Col. John Landers leading and positioned to the rear of the German fighters as they flew a left-hand pattern climbing out of the airfield. 'Col. Landers was on the tail of one. I pursued one which broke to the left. We made a half turn when I gave him lead while he was in a gentle climb,' he reported to Intelligence at Duxford later. 'After a good "squirt" I saw generous hits on the canopy and engine. He flipped on his back and went down. I figured he'd been had so continued on in the turn and found myself on the tail of another a/c. This was a repeat of the first situation except the e/a was on fire when he went in. I was then at cloud level, so went beneath them and saw a 109 on the deck that apparently never saw me.'[6] The Mustang pilot hosed the Messerschmitt with his cannon and it burst into flames and hit the ground.

McDuffie's fourth target that day was more alert, evading into cloud as the American closed at 7,000ft. 'I followed, gained on him and fired a short burst. Hits showed and he dodged back for a cloud. I followed and got in another short burst when he headed for another cloud,' McDuffie recorded. This went on, his victim dodging in and out of cloud while the lieutenant scored hits until with one final burst, McDuffie saw the Me 109 slide off one wing in a steep dive. By that time the flak defences of the airfield the two had been fighting above opened up. 'I, feeling the e/a was done for and to avoid the flak, climbed through the clouds to rejoin Cargo leader,' the ace, who would soon see four new swastikas painted on the nose of his Mustang, reported.[7]

The 3AD arrived over Ruhland to find their oil refinery target was cloud covered, nearly all of them then making for the secondary, Dresden. The 2nd Air Division headed for an oil plant and a tank works at Magdeburg but also came under attack. Lt Ted Wheeler was flying his fifth mission as a crew commander with the 467th BG, as he later described.

Because of the near solid cloud cover over the target, we were briefed to bomb by H2X. Enemy fighters attacked the Group ahead of us but did not hit us at this time. It was a squadron of Me 109s and they used a frontal attack for openers. This was a tactic we had been briefed on, and is the ultimate game of 'Chicken' or 'Aerial Roulette'. The enemy planes flying in line abreast came in head on at the same altitude as the bomber formation. The closing speed is over 500mph and they start firing when within range. These enemy pilots know that the bombers will not waver, so they are reasonably sure they will not collide unless something goes wrong or they miscalculate. This is a devastating and terrifying thing to experience. As they approach they roll upside down while firing, and dive under the bomber formation, break off and come back to attack from all directions.

We could not see too much of what was happening because the lead group was some distance ahead and to our right. A couple of the bombers dropped out of the formation trailing smoke. As we approached the IP we could see flak coming up ahead of the lead squadron, and by the time all three squadrons had made the turn on to the bomb run the barrage became intense and very accurate. As our standard procedure required that we take no evasive action on this leg of our attack, we could not help but feel like the proverbial 'sitting ducks'. This was perhaps the most nerve wracking part of any mission . . . With great relief we released our bomb loads at 23,000ft, and still bracketed by bursting shells changed course and altitude to the rally point . . . Because of the clouds being socked in over the target we were unable to observe our hits.

We were headed for home, but it wasn't over yet. As we skirted the gun positions of the Hanover/Brunswick area we were attacked by another squadron of Me 109s . . . They were all around us like a pack of hornets, and appeared to be working in pairs. They hit our third (trailing) squadron on the first pass, and one of the planes, #117 piloted by Lt Reid, had an engine shot out . . . They were now straggling below and behind our formation and easy prey for the German fighters.

Fortunately our own fighter escort had rejoined us after the rally point and were now engaging the 109s in dog fights. Two Messerschmitts made a diving pass from 9 o'clock high and disappeared under us. At that instant the Plexiglas window beside my head shattered and our right hand manifold pressure gauge and the left side mixture control gauge disintegrated in a split second. My #1 engine was also hit, and there were several holes along the left wing. It was determined later that a single stray 20mm bullet had done the damage to the instrument panel, tore through the nose wheel compartment, and exited through the lower right of the nose section. Our tail gunner reported to me on the intercom that Lt Reid's plane was going down trailing a plume of dirty smoke.[8]

Lt Wheeler, being blasted by sub-zero winds coming through the shattered window, was handed a wool face mask to put on.

As I adjusted my oxygen mask and checked the pressure gauge I could hear some excited chatter on the intercom. Someone said, 'Gee, Look out to the left!' . . . There sitting about 40ft off my left wing was an Me 109. As I stared in shock the German pilot lowered his flaps and landing gear and just flew right along with us.

Two P-51s had 'corralled' him and his only safe way out was to slide into our formation. Our fighters could not fire at him and our gunners could not fire without hitting each other. For this to happen at all shows the high degree of excitement and confusion with these encounters. It seemed like a long time that the German plane hung there, but it was actually only a few minutes. Never again would I be this close to the enemy! Our eyes met as he looked from side to side. Everything seemed so vivid it was almost hypnotic. There was a number 8 just forward of the iron cross painted on the fuselage, and what looked like a yellow serpent on the nose. Suddenly the wheels and flaps retracted and the plane rolled upside down and disappeared below, the P-51s in pursuit. We never saw them again so do not know the outcome, but we were all rooting for the Luftwaffe pilot and hoped he got away. I thought he was not only daring to do what he did, but very clever. We theorized that he may have been out of ammunition or that his guns were jammed when the American fighters closed in on him.[9]

2/Lt Alvah Reid did not survive. Only four of the crew of the aircraft named *Ellswof Jr* managed to bale out in time before it crashed near Dorsten, Germany. The parachute of one failed to open.

The next night the Luftwaffe fighter arm made its last attack on the British mainland. It was no accident that it took place on the 2,000th night of the war. Goering, derided by Hitler and his fellow Nazis, had been reserving his *nachtjagd* for just such an occasion when much propaganda could be made of the fact that Germany could still cause mayhem over the British enemy homeland. As RAF Bomber Command flew back from oil and transportation targets, more than 200 night fighters followed the Lancasters and Halifaxes and caught them up in their circuits when runway lights came on for landing, destroying twenty-two. The Ju 88s cruised up and down eastern England shooting up any aircraft or airfield in sight, British or American. Kay Brainard's base at Sudbury was one of those which came under attack. She wrote to her mother:

> We had two alerts. One came in the middle of the Officers' Club dance, so Johnny [Lt Johnny Rumisek] and I took a jeep at intermission and rode to the tower where he and Rudy [Lt Allen Rutenburg], my two best friends outside of Jeep, work. We stayed there until the white or all-clear signal, listening to radio messages coming in, instructing people and cars to extinguish their lights. It was fascinating! Then just when we had finished up the evening of fun and following coffee and toasted cheese sandwiches in Jeep's quarters (Rudy, Johnny, a visiting General, and other guests were there too) another alert was sounded.
>
> I had just gotten to our quarters when they announced 'take cover'. Jean [St Clair] came into my room and asked if she could sit it out with me. It seems this one was a more

serious one. We could hear the planes overhead, but we were so well blacked-out they couldn't locate us. They did make a stab at strafing our ammunition dump, and we heard their guns going rat-a-tat-tat. Funny thing, tho – it didn't scare us as we thought it was our own guns shooting at the Jerry planes. Anyway we suffered no damage.[10]

The 8th was out in force every day as the weeks unfolded in March. The air fleets grew with each mission as more aircraft and crews arrived in England to finish the war and fewer were shot down. In the first week of March 1,200 bombers setting out was the norm, by the second that had increased to 1,400. The targets varied from marshalling yards to refineries, from airfields to chemical works. The teenaged ball turret gunner John Day was experienced enough that month to work out which targets would bring the peril he feared most, as he told the author:

The flak was more frightening to a gunner than a German fighter because when a fighter comes at you you shoot back and you're in it. He is probably more dangerous than the flak if he's coming at you, but you are involved, whereas when you are over a heavily defended target there is nothing else you can do except slink up in a little ball and hope the flak doesn't hit you.

During the briefing in the morning if you were going after a railroad yard or an airfield you didn't worry much because there wasn't going to be much flak, but if it was an oil target you knew you were going to have a bad day. We also hit the Zeiss plant where they made optical instruments and several industrial targets in Austria and Hungary. When the war was approaching its end the missions were longer than in the beginning because by the time I was flying France and Belgium had been liberated and we were flying well into Germany.[11]

In March Kay Brainard had her first leave in London, described in a letter home.

Jeep Overing decided to take a day or two off too, so we drove in in his car. That made it nice as I got to see some of the countryside. There are no places at all of just wooded or scrub land – every bit of land is utilized. Most of it culti- vated, or being used for cattle grazing land. It's really lovely – and so green! No bushes and stuff like that, just rolling hills of grass and the cutest haystacks – all stacked up like little huts. And lots of houses with those thatched roofs, just like a picture.

In London I stayed at a Red Cross Staff Club called Gloucester Place – originally a city townhouse owned by some well-to-do Englishman, letting us use it for the 'dura- tion'. And no charge, it's compliments of the Red Cross for us . . . with breakfast in bed! We went to see the wonderful musical, *Something in the Air* . . . and we also went to Madame Tussauds Wax Works. That is quite a place with wax figures of everyone of importance you can think of.[12]

A visit to the wax works on Marylebone Road, where even fig- ures of American Presidents were displayed, was a must at some time or other for non-flyers who didn't need the traditional al- ternatives London provided for those Americans trying to forget what they had seen in combat. The three-day passes of Cpl Jack Feller from the control tower at Debach were well used, including a visit to Madame Tussauds and Buckingham Palace. 'Then there was the Tower of London and St Paul's Cathedral,' he remem- bers. 'I also had a tour through Westminster Abbey.'[13]

But there was always the prospect of being hit by a V-2 rocket. They had been arriving at an average of three a day since 8 Sep- tember 1944, when the first had killed a three-year-old child in

Chiswick. There was no defence as the world entered this new age of aerial warfare of country-to-country ballistic missiles, where the sound of the explosion was weirdly followed by the boom of its supersonic descent through the stratosphere. The only hope was to overrun all of the occupied territory on the Continent where their mobile platforms could be parked for a suitable range. The final V-2 on central London fell in Tottenham Court Road on 25 March, killing eleven, the last of 2,754 civilians to die in the capital by rocket with another 6,523 injured. They had even been launched against Norwich, to curtail the 8th Air Force's own aerial offensive. A total of forty-three were targeted at the ancient city at the heart of US bomber country but because Britain had captured and turned German agents, who then gave false information about how accurate the rockets were, they did no damage to the 8th Air Force, the most effective being one which created a new bunker on the Royal Norwich Golf Course.

The conventional USSTAF offensive was conversely having a much more obvious effect, bringing about a rapidly increasing collapse of the Reich. It was to aid that descent into chaos that a raid was launched against Hanover on 14 March. Alexander Nazemetz, a nineteen-year-old waist gunner at Thorpe Abbotts, was nearing the end of his tour when he was briefed for the industrial city. One of his duties was to push out chaff on the bomb run to confuse German radar trying to establish the bombers' altitude, as he recounted after the war. 'I was on my haunches, just opposite the right waist position, and I heard the announcement of, 'Bombs away,' from the bombardier . . . I looked out the window, and I had to look up, right, and I saw the bombs coming down. I was hit immediately . . . [The flak] came right across from the left side.' That day Nazemetz was wearing a throat microphone for the first time because the mic in his oxygen mask had developed a fault through previous formation of ice crystals. The haphazard decision probably saved his life.

My tail-gunner began to call me, instantly, and . . . what I did, because I had worn this throat mic for the first time, because the other one wasn't working, I had to press to talk . . . The talk button was on the handle of my gun. I think I tried to say, 'I'm hit.' But, I didn't hear it, right. Meantime, it's funny, because I'm trying to recollect this, and I remember looking down, and I saw the throat mic on the floor, and I saw the brass springs, and I thought, 'Now, isn't that funny?' This is all happening in a split-second, mind you, and then, I realized that I had taken my hand away, and my glove was all bloody. So, I reconnected myself to the old mic, and I just said, 'I'm hit,' right, and then, I heard the conversation. The pilot told the radioman to go back and check on what happened to me.

So, he came back on an oxygen walk-around bottle. This was something that ran for fifteen or twenty minutes . . . He was a ruddy guy, and he was this big weight lifter. He took one look at me and turned pale. And, I couldn't see what happened to me, right. Now, I only had a high school education, but I know about jugular veins. I knew where vocal cords were and I was unable to talk . . . and he just went so pale . . . The blood just drained out of him, and I thought, 'Jesus, what happened to me?' And then, he disconnected me, and then, he was talking. Then, the bombardier came back, and he sprinkled sulfa on me, and he gave me what he called a half a syringe of morphine. I didn't hurt, so I didn't want it . . . I know that I told him through hand motions. I couldn't speak, so, I was really scared. I thought something happened to the vocal cords, and I told him not to shoot red, red flares upon landing to indicate wounded on board . . . If the crew chief could see that it was his airplane, he'd get scared, and he didn't want anybody on his crew to get hurt, and I asked him not to do it, and, would you believe, I saw the red, red flares go over . . . just as we were coming in. The pilot asked permission to leave the formation, so that he could come in first, okay, and so . . . immediately, we landed. The doctor was there, and he said to me, 'Did you spit up any blood?' and I said, 'No,' and then, I think he said, 'You were lucky.' . . . Outside, I heard a voice say, 'Hey, Doc, you need the stretcher?' . . . I spoke then, and I said, 'No, I can walk,' and I could walk . . . I was in the hospital for three weeks.[14]

In that time the rest of the crew flew two more missions to complete the thirty-five needed for a tour and Nazemetz was let off the two he needed, so he could go home with his comrades.

The next mission the 100th BG flew while Nazemetz was beginning his treatment in hospital was to the textile spinning plant at Plauen, near the Czech border, on 17 March. The initial target had been the Ruhland oil refinery, but cloud cover forced a change of plan. It was the fourteenth time S/Sgt John Day faced combat in his ball turret, he remembers.

We were told at the briefing we were going to fly a spare aircraft. It was a long mission we were flying and we lost an engine near the target and then we got a flak hit on one of the inboard engines as we turned off after dropping our bombs and that engine stopped and one of the wheels came down. We had to drop out of formation because we couldn't keep up with anybody. We flew away from the target by ourselves and as we headed back we threw everything out of the plane that we could lay our hands on, all the guns went out and all the guts of the plane. Finally after I got out we dropped the ball turret, kind of a defining moment.

The noise of the wind coming from that hole afterwards

would scare you to death. We were still losing altitude, but when we got down to around 8,000 or 9,000ft we found we could hold that height. A P-51 showed up. We found out later that he was also in big trouble and his intention was to follow us home . . . Then a couple of German jets arrived and made a couple of passes. This P-51 went and hid behind us while they went by. The jets didn't hurt us though and made off and then we finally landed at a fighter base near Brussels, hand-cranking the other wheel down. As we landed, the damaged wheel that had dropped down over the target slowly collapsed, spinning us off to the side of the runway . . . There were two other wrecked B-17s already down there and while we were waiting for someone to come our pilot, George Murasco, went over to one and the crew were standing around it. The nose of the airplane was all crushed and there was a dead guy squashed up in the nose.* The pilot of this smashed airplane told Lt Murasco, 'We don't know who that is, it's not one of our crew, we're all here.' Apparently the dead guy had come from another plane and smashed into the one which had already had its nose cracked up.[15]

The next day the 100th BG went to Berlin as part of a 1,300-strong force attacking tank plants and railway stations. Thirteen bombers were lost, three of them from Thorpe Abbotts, but another eleven had to land in territory held by the Red Army. One of those, the aircraft of Lt Merill Jensen, also came from the Bloody Hundredth. Jensen's navigator, Flt/Officer Richard

---

* The dead flyer was the radioman from a 490th Group Fortress which had been caught in prop wash and collided upwards with the nose and engines of the B-17 of Lt Robert Tannenberg before falling away in two halves. Tannenberg's navigator and togglier had to hurriedly move back to the centre section of the aircraft when the nose section was hit, unaware of the mangled torso.

Scroxton, kept a diary of what happened until they finally got back into the care of their own air force. 'Nearing the target of Berlin and in clear skies four Me 262s attacked the formation from the rear hidden by con trails scoring hits in at least 4 B-17s in the formation,' he wrote. 'This aircraft sustained damage to the wing tips and three engines. The B-17 eventually crash-landed near a town called Koscian where the crew met up with the Russians.'[16] On 20 March the crew were taken by truck to Poznań and put on a train, then followed more truck rides, the crew eventually reaching Poltava on 3 April and flying out to Italy.

Hitler and his staff were deep in their bunker beneath the Chancellery leading a troglodyte existence when the B-17s broke through the Berlin defences once more and as Lt Jensen's crew were on their way to the Poznań railhead the Führer was re-sponding to a memorandum from Armaments Minister Albert Speer. It spelled out that in 'four to eight weeks the final collapse of the German economy must be expected'. Hitler's answer was to decide the German people had failed him and to issue a decree ordering *Gauleiters* to destroy everything which could be of future use to his enemies. 'All industrial plants, all important electrical facilities, waterworks, gasworks . . . all food and clothing stores . . . all bridges, all railway installations, the postal system . . . also the waterways, all ships, all freight cars and all locomotives,' must be wrecked. The result, the Führer said, would be 'the creation of a traffic desert'.[17] Meanwhile his soldiers and airmen would be expected to fight to the end. Speer testified at his own sub-sequent trial in Nuremburg that he then went back to the Ruhr and induced all those he could not to carry out the 'scorched earth' order.[18] 'When [Hitler] saw himself doomed,' Speer said, 'he consciously desired to annihilate the German people.'[19] What had played a major part in turning Hitler's dreams to bitter ashes was the Allied bomber offensive.

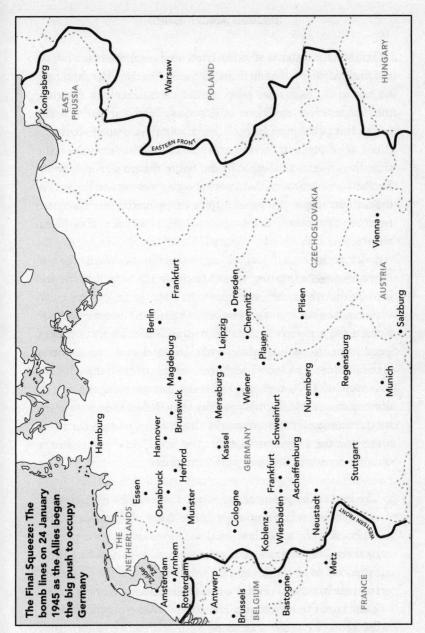

The Final Squeeze: The bomb lines on 24 January 1945 as the Allies began the big push to occupy Germany

EAST PRUSSIA
Konigsberg

POLAND
Warsaw

EASTERN FRONT

CZECHOSLOVAKIA

HUNGARY

AUSTRIA
Vienna
Salzburg

Frankfurt
Dresden
Berlin
Chemnitz
Pilsen
Magdeburg
Leipzig
Plauen
Brunswick
Merseburg
Wiener
Regensburg
Hamburg
Nuremberg
Munich
Hannover
Kassel
Herford
Schweinfurt
Osnabruck
Frankfurt
Stuttgart
Essen
Munster
Cologne
Wiesbaden
Aschaffenburg
Koblenz
Neustadt

THE NETHERLANDS

Zuider Zee
Arnhem
Metz
Amsterdam
Rotterdam
WESTERN FRONT
Antwerp
Bastogne
Brussels
BELGIUM

GERMANY
FRANCE

This map was issued by the US Army Information Branch for display at USAAF airfields, showing the front lines on 24 January 1945 as the Allies began the big ground offensive to occupy Germany: the Red Army from the East towards Berlin and Dresden; the Western Allies towards Cologne, Frankfurt, Stuttgart and Munich.

The state of utter destruction had now been reached to allow the final major land battle from the west. Cologne, the third largest city in Germany, had fallen to the US 1st Army on 5 March, the bridge across the Rhine at Remagen had been taken on the 7th and six battalions of American infantry had slipped across the Rhine at Oppenheim on the night of 23/24 March. At the same time the artillery onslaught in the battle Britain's Field Marshal Bernard Montgomery had been planning for weeks began 189 miles to the north. A total of 3,300 guns opened up on a German front of twenty-three miles across the Rhine either side of Wesel and the RAF completed the destruction of the city, having already reduced 97 per cent of its buildings to rubble over three nights in February. On the morning of 24 March the US 17th Airborne and British 6th Airborne divisions were dropped on the eastern bank.

During the last major paratroooper assault in Operation Market Garden the previous September many US aircraft had dropped supplies in the wrong place while being shot up by German ground forces. Lt Donald Jenkins, a navigator with the 44th BG lead crew of Lt Robert Seever, whose aircraft had been one of those damaged by machine-gun fire then, found they were given special training for the crossing of the Rhine, *Operation Varsity*, to make sure there were no mistakes this time. They were called to resupply at Wesel, the navigator remembers.

The lead crews practiced for about a week. We didn't know exactly what was going on until the day of the mission, but we knew it was a low-level, and we were leading a squadron by then. This was my pilot's last mission. We're leading the squadron and I think we were the only crew in our squadron that had ever been on a low-level mission before . . . we knew that the higher you are, the more these gunners on the ground can get a bead on you, and so, we knew that because we had been peppered with some small arms fire

on the Market Garden . . . my pilot got together with some
of the pilots that would be flying on our wing . . . 'As soon
as we drop our supplies,' he says, 'I'm going to push the
throttles forward, I'm going to push the wheel forward . . .
we're going to go right down as close to the deck as we can
go,' and he said, 'and I'm going to also turn tight. So, you
be ready for it and hang in there with me.' We practiced for
this particular mission for almost one week, practically every
day, that is, just the lead crews.[20]

On the actual mission the crew had cause to thank that tedious
training.

We did pilotage [navigating through landmarks], because we
were fairly close to the ground, the whole mission. As we
approached the Rhine and the IP we were at treetop level.
There was much evidence of the war near the Rhine. We
could not see the squadron ahead as we came upon the initial
point. The haze was very thick. [Our bombardier] guided us
down the bomb run. It was practically perfect. We dropped
exactly on the spot. In about fifteen seconds after dropping,
Bob racked it up into a fairly tight turn, so as to miss the
city of Wesel. Right after dropping, we again lost the slight
altitude in which we'd pulled up for dropping and he pushed
everything forward, so as to get the most speed. The whole
squadron followed us fairly well. We were hit by some small
arms fire, but no damage done . . . The other two squadrons
did not turn as soon or as sharp as we did. They received
more damage from small arms fire. Two ships crashed and
blew up. One fellow in another squadron fell out of the
bomb bays . . . the smoke was so thick, it was hard to see
almost, but it's really hazy from battle smoke. It was really
like seeing a newsreel of the battle. I mean, we're going 180

miles an hour, but you could take a quick look and you could see what was going on . . . So, anyway, one plane out in the outer edges of our squadron caught a bit of small arms fire, but most of us were in pretty good shape . . . Anyway, our squadron came through this with hardly a scratch.[21]

The training and the knowledge of an experienced lead pilot had paid off. The rest of 2AD's Groups did not do anything like as well. A total of fourteen Liberators went down to small-arms fire on the east bank of the Rhine, the highest 8th AF losses that day and eleven of them were from 14 Combat Wing, of which Lt Jenkins' Group was part. Looking back, Jenkins says, 'Both my pilot and I feel very proud of that mission.'[22]

Within a day of the Rhine crossing it was safe enough for Winston Churchill himself to go over by launch and inspect the ruins of what had once been Wesel. By the time another day had passed twelve newly constructed bridges were taking tanks, infantry and supplies across the river and the major British and American bridgeheads had linked up. The Ruhr west of the Rhine could now be sealed off, thereby ensuring most of Hitler's supplies of arms and ammunition, which had been reduced to a trickle by bombing, could go no further. A total of eighteen American divisions would be involved in the three-week mopping-up operation. That aim of encirclement had dictated much of the 8th Air Force effort in March. To support the Rhine crossing itself the 8th had flown a total of 1,747 bomber sorties, the Flying Fortresses isolating airfields in the Ruhr and the Liberators making supply drops to the airborne divisions. The fighter groups flew missions of support blasting everything in their path that moved, then landed back in England to rearm and took off for the front again. Some Groups made three trips.

As the armies of the Western Allies drove forward it became

apparent that bombing had reduced towns and cities east of the Rhine to acres of rubble, which could hide pockets of resistance. Interdiction, originally a term used in church circles for the debarring of someone from ecclesiastical privileges, was the new buzz word. Now for German civilians it meant a forbidding of the use of transport facilities by fighter sweep or bombing with what could be a Gomorrah-like result. On 15 March Spaatz's deputy chief of air staff, General David Schlatter, had written in his diary that the air force was repeatedly being asked by the army to bomb towns, many of them far from the actual fighting. He noted that it was Spaatz's policy to bomb 'a town as such' only when the army asked for it specifically. Spaatz was determined, he wrote, that a reputation for indiscriminate bombing would not be the post-war lot of his air forces.[23] But it was clear that in the determination to rapidly end the war Spaatz and Harris had responded massively to requests from the armies. One distinguished war correspondent, Chester Wilmot, wrote: 'In their enthusiasm to make sure of sealing off the battlefield the Allied Air Forces had put down on most of the interdiction targets three times the tonnage the army had asked for, and by so doing had aided the German rearguards.'[24]

The 8th Air Force dropped 75,323 tons of bombs on the Reich in March, its highest total of any month of the war. The 15th, whose targets were now mainly Austria and Southern Germany, dropped 30,265 tons. By comparison RAF Bomber Command, whose Lancasters had a bomb-carrying capacity almost twice that of a Fortress or Liberator, dropped 67,637 tons, 7,686 tons less than the 8th alone. Yet this had been a record monthly total for Harris's crews and was the same tonnage as the command had dropped collectively in the first thirty-four months of the war. The Mighty Eighth was undoubtedly now the master of the battlefield.

Even in the dark fantasy world of Joseph Goebbels' Propaganda Ministry the rays of reality were beginning to shed illumination.

On 25 March 25, after jeering at the trip across the Rhine Churchill had taken Goebbels had written: 'Somewhere we must bring
the enemy to a halt and it is of course disastrous that by all indica-
tions we have not succeeded in doing so on the Rhine. This again
is due to the enemy's catastrophic air superiority. He lays an area
he wishes to conquer so flat by massive air attack that resistance
is practically impossible.'[25] Churchill had promised an early peace,
creating what Goebbels called a 'real victory delirium' in both
Britain and America.

The knowledge that the war couldn't last long now had brought
a new urgency among some of the young and naïve in the United
States to get over to Europe before it finished. Cpl Jack Feller had
lately been transferred from the control tower at Debach to the
orderly room of the 55th FG at Warmingford, near Colchester,
when a young private came in and announced: 'I want to amend
my records.' He was asked why and he said he had used his brother's name to enlist because he was under-age. 'When asked how
old he was he said he was 15,' Feller remembers. 'A sergeant said
he would have to be court-martialled, but the officer said no, they
would just send him back and get him out of the army. "I don't
want to go home, I want to stay in the Air Corps," he said. He was
told he was going home, period. "Can I get a pass to London?"
he asked. "I've not been there yet." "Pack up your things and be
ready to go tomorrow," he was told. He began to cry and so the
chaplain came in to console him. The fifteen-year-old patriot just
wanted to serve his country.'[26]

The teenager wasn't the only one to lie about his age to find
adventure. A few months before S/Sgt John Millar had flown
thirty-five missions as a ball turret gunner with the 100th BG at
the age of seventeen. When he joined up in Indiana shortly after
his sixteenth birthday he avoided the need to show a birth certificate because his parents had signed a consent form. Millar, who
grew a moustache to look older, took part in six Berlin raids and

went home with a DFC after shooting down an Me 410. But the teenage aviator to beat them all was Sgt Desales Glover, a tall boy of 5ft 8 inches who joined the USAAF at fourteen. He graduated from gunnery school in the same class as Clark Gable and crossed the Atlantic to fly six missions with the 458th BG from Horsham St Faiths, near Norwich, including the Berlin raid of 6 March 1944, before his then age of sixteen was discovered and he was sent back to the States.

Others kept proving their courage again and again, refusing to quit and surviving against the odds. 'Rosie' Rosenthal was one of them, now returned to Thorpe Abbotts from Russia; Major Immanuel Klette whose crew had been lost on the early February Berlin strike was another. He was still flying to eventually make ninety-one missions with the 91st BG including its last. And then there was tail gunner M/Sgt Hewitt Dunn, incredibly on his fourth continuous tour at Framlingham. He had told *Stars and Stripes* in November: 'I want to go home just as much if not more than any fellow, but I can't until the fight here is finished.'[27] The fight *was* now nearly finished, but in April the final twitching of a dying Luftwaffe obeying an evil leader prepared to sacrifice his whole nation would ensure many young Americans who had expected to celebrate victory would not be going home after all to their anxiously waiting families.

SPRING

18

'Let the English celebrate'

It was a different air force now from the one which had greeted an English spring of a year ago. The men who had faced Goering's fighters and flak battalions then had met their foes head-on just beyond the peak of Luftwaffe power and the loss of men and machines in April 1944 had been the 8th's highest monthly total of the war. But as April 1945 opened General Doolittle's command was never stronger. He had 3,760 heavy bombers available, littering the landscape of his airfields throughout East Anglia, ready and waiting to finish the job.[1]

The resilient snowdrops and crocuses now peeking through hedgerows and garden plots tilled for vegetables in the enthusiasm of Dig for Victory campaigns seemed to reflect that American confidence that soon the bloodshed would be over and peace would peer shyly round the corner. The promise of those spring flowers touched the hearts of many, including Kay Brainard. 'We stopped in Sudbury and got lovely daffodils for the Aero Club,' she recorded about a visit to the tailors.[2] It was unusually warm and the temperature would hit 81 degrees Fahrenheit in the 1AD area south of Peterborough and in central London mid-month, where Americans and Britons alike strolled through the parks once more.³ There were hours of sunshine to savour after the clocks had been put forward, giving light in the evenings until 8pm. Who could not believe in concord as the English country-side prepared to show its true vernal glory. Easter Sunday fell on 1 April and Kay Brainard and Col. 'Jeep' Overing joined those praying for peace with a visit to lovely Lavenham.

'We travelled only a few miles to a church which is said to be the oldest in England,' she wrote to her mother. 'I couldn't get over the lack of similarity between an Easter service at home and here. Whether the war is the chief cause, or only partly, I don't know. However, no one looked dressed up, no corsages, no crowds, no Easter lilies . . . and not even Communion. But we felt better for having attended anyway.' Afterwards they drove to a nearby 'typ-ical English manor', to visit the British Colonel Hambro, a friend of the 486th BG commander, and toured the house and grounds, courtesy of the butler. Neither of them would ever realise it was the home of the head of the Special Operations Executive secret agent network they were inspecting. They then went on to lunch at The Swan in Lavenham, where the landlord 'Robby' Robbins had known the unfortunate General Frederick Castle. 'The meal was only fair, which is all you can expect with British rations – but The Swan is a hang-out for nice people in this area, and the man who owns the pub is a real character and everyone's best friend,' Kay related.⁴ In common with most Americans serving in England it was difficult for her to imagine how hard it had been to live for years in a country where food was rationed and every mouthful was precious. A couple of days earlier she had written home: 'If you eat out the menu seldom varies . . . It's either roast beef, or roast chicken (and not such hot chicken), with panned brown potatoes (they fry them in deep fat), Brussels sprouts (this never fails), rolls and no butter. If you want water you have to ask. A boy told me he was at a pub and asked for a drink of water and he got it, but had to pay a shilling.'⁵

'Let the English celebrate'

In the late afternoon of Easter Sunday she was back at work and in a different – American – world, where food was plentiful.

Had our Open House at the Aero Club and you wouldn't think it possible for boys to eat so much. We had 1,000 jam tarts, 800 rolls with spam, or crabmeat mixtures, and literally thousands of pieces of cake, with a dab of coloured sugar on top, resembling icing . . . using green, pink and lavender coloring to give an Eastery effect. We had the Colonel's staff over as guests and they brought along a visiting Col, who had to be shown all thru the club . . . At 8pm the band came over and we had more or less of a jam session, as there were only a handful of girls there. Some of the boys wanted to dance, tho – mostly jitterbugging – and I was worn down to a nub by evenings end . . .[6]

Lt Donald Jenkins, whose 44th BG crew had resupplied troops after the Rhine crossing, was also enjoying Easter Sunday – in Paris. His skipper, Lt Robert Seever, was tour-expired and while awaiting reassignment to the States had been asked to fly ground personnel on a trip to the French capital. Lt Jenkins went along as navigator with the engineer from the crew. When they landed one engine was running rough and they were told it would take until Monday to repair. The opportunity to see Paris was too good to miss. 'The Parisians were in a very festive mood, this [being] the first Easter Sunday in five years that they were not occupied, so, they were dressed in their finery . . . We got to bed about two o'clock in the morning,' Jenkins recalls. Back at Villacoublay Field later the B-24 was ready, but the weather had socked in the flight, so the engineer started passing round a bottle of brandy he had bought, believing the weather would not clear that day. It was a shock when they were told, 'You're cleared to take off right now.'

So, we go back to the aircraft and, oh, we were probably halfway through the bottle by that time . . . Of course, pilot Bob didn't have any more to drink. Some of the rest of us thought, 'Well, we're not driving this thing, right?' So, we passed the bottle around a little bit more, among the three of us. We took off and Bob was feeling pretty good, and we came down and buzzed the airfield . . . Wow, that made us feel good. So, then, we decided, 'Oh, let's go see the Eiffel Tower'. So, we take this big four-engine aircraft and make a pylon turn around the Eiffel Tower, and then, we headed for England, and, luckily, we got there uneventfully.[7]

It was just three days before the Liberator crews of 2AD felt the pain of war once more. Luftwaffe jet bases were the new target of the 8th's bombers and on 4 April six B-24s were lost on a mission to drop a long-held but little-used weapon by Doolittle of fragmentation bombs in quantity, designed to scythe shrapnel through aerodrome buildings and stationary planes, but an unsuspected danger to close-packed American formations themselves. Another seventy-six Liberators were damaged, mostly by flak over the airfields. T/Sgt Simon Liberman, a radioman on the 446th BG at Attlebridge, who had flown his first mission in mid-February, found his Group had been assigned to bombing the German airfield at Perleberg, north-west of Berlin. He recalls:

Before each flight you were told the type of opposition you might run into, and, I remember, it was near the end of the war, and we were, like, a diversionary group . . . they told us, when we flew to Perleberg, that we shouldn't have any real opposition, 'there are only women and children manning the artillery'. And that's where we got the most hits. We had more than 13 holes in the plane and the tail gunner caught a piece of flak in the sole of his shoe and felt heat there. He wasn't injured though, but, he did apply for a Purple Heart. I'm not sure whether he got it.[8]

On 7 April all three air divisions took off for a range of targets, half of them airfields, using the new bomb. The Sudbury-based 486th BG was among several assigned to the Kaltenkirchen airfield, near Hamburg, where Me 262s had been spotted parked in the forest alongside. Unknown to the mission planners they had been replaced that day by Arado Ar 234 jet bombers. There was no shortage of labour in manhandling the aircraft out of the trees and onto the one concrete runway. A constantly replaced starving work force provided by a camp for Russian PoWs and a sub-unit of the Neuengamme concentration camp was in huts by the airfield. A flak unit had recently moved in to protect the jets.

It was the twenty-first mission for togglier S/Sgt Chester Stanek, as he recorded in his mission diary.

Made a visual run on target at 25,000ft with temperature at −18 C. Target was supposed to be flak free, but we were caught in a beautiful tracking trap. Carried a bomb load of 38 fragmentation clusters with each cluster carrying six 20-pound independent bombs. On 'Bombs Away' rusted clusters separated immediately as they left the bomb bays. We were immediately below lead ship and several 20-pounders bounced off our wings as they fell free. Lt Center on our right wing was not so lucky. Several bombs flew back and hit his B-17 between his engines. All four burst into flames. Bale out order was given and we saw five chutes come out. The ship fell off on its right wing and blew up as it was spinning downward. Another B-17 went down in flames the same way about 10 minutes later. Saw one chute on fire with the airman trying to climb lines, or pulling on them to put out the fire. Clyde Whitted, our navigator, was hit in the leg by

a piece of shrapnel from the bombs. Fragmentation experiment considered a failure. Unlucky 100th hit by fighters
again. We were told 8th AF lost 14 planes shot down. Hell
of a mission.[9]

The fighters that had hit the 100th BG were involved in another
of those final gasps by an expiring Luftwaffe, which could inflict
such surprising damage. This was not the last flourish of Goering's airmen, but it was close to it. The once-mighty force was
now so short of fuel stocks and trained pilots that predetermined
ramming of its prey was seen as a tactic against the waves of
daylight bombing raids on the Reich. Oberst Hajo Herrmann, a
committed Nazi and an innovator of Luftwaffe tactics, organised
a special unit of 120 volunteers who would pilot stripped-down
Me 109 fighters to fly into a selected USSTAF air fleet, causing
such destruction it was presumed the Americans at least would
be forced to stop bombing for a while, as they had after the disastrous Schweinfurt missions of 1943. Such a breathing space,
it was considered, would allow the Luftwaffe to build up its Me
262 force unhindered, yet another example of the fantasy world
the Nazis were now living in and prepared to let others die for.
A written request for volunteers on 8 March from the head of
the Luftwaffe, Hermann Goering himself, promised 'immediate
flight training' and demanded: 'I call you to an operation from
which there is little possibility of returning.'[10]

Only some of the hastily assembled force of raw young recruits
were available as reports arrived in the late morning of 7 April of
more than 1,000 American bombers heading for Germany, but
it was decided to send them anyway on their pointless mission.
Their title of *Sonderkommando Elbe* was considerably grander than
the force itself, its pilots having had no more than ten days' flight
training. Hajo Herrmann was standing by in the *Fliegerkorps* operations room to control the operation. 'How would the men fight,

would their bravery compensate for their small numbers?' he wrote in a post-war account. 'As I watched the general situation map and saw the bombers coming closer I had to force myself to stay calm and to think of the operation cold-bloodedly.'[11]

The 100th BG were flying sixth in the bomber column when the thirteen novices in Me 109s, following their more experienced leader on a navigation beam he was receiving in his Fw 190, descended on the Fortresses out of the sun at 12.50pm just east of Dummer Lake, near Hanover. P-51s swooped down to spoil the ambush. The Bloody Hundredth, flying close formation, was then attacked for the next thirty-six minutes by single aircraft. 'The most oft-repeated tactic was an attack from nine o'clock high, passing through the formation and then making another pass from one to three o'clock, repeating several times,' a USSTAF mission critique stated.[12] 'Enemy aircraft opened fire from machine guns and 20mm cannon at about 500 yards and continued firing until out of formation. Crew reports e/a fanatically aggressive and attacked through heavy concentrations of fire from B-17s' guns.' The Me 109 pilots had been told to ram an engine, or the rudder of a B-17, but Herrmann had taken advice from the Luftwaffe research base at Rechlin and favoured a third alternative. 'The most effective, and at the same time, the safest method was to ram from above and astern against the trailing edge of the enemy's wings with airscrew rotating fully, acting as a circular saw,' he recorded. 'The impact would cause the wing to break off.'[13]

That is exactly what happened to the aircraft of 2/Lt Arthur Calder. Both the wing and the attacking Me 109 exploded and the remains of the B-17 spun down in flames. None of the crew survived. A second Messerschmitt rammed the B-17 of Lt William Howard, only six of the crew being able to escape. But another Messerschmitt went for the rear of *E-Z Goin'*, the Fortress of Lt Joe Martin. The fighter sheared off most of the rudder and the left horizontal stabiliser and made huge gashes in the fin forward of the rudder. It was some testimony to how well the B-17 was made that its skilful pilots were able to keep *E-Z Goin'* flying, despite an exhausting struggle with the controls for hours.

'Next day the Army Bulletin reported that 60 four-engined bombers had been brought down by ramming,' Herrmann related in his post-war account. In fact only seventeen had been lost by the 8th Air Force on all targets that day and only five by deliberate collision. 'I spoke with at least a dozen successful rammers, who had escaped by parachute. Most of them had been injured,' Herrmann related, adding that he then insisted that a much larger force of the pilots already trained for little else but collision be employed. 'The young men had scarcely any idea of what had been achieved,' he claimed.[14] In fact what they had achieved was small and their courage had been thrown away by a failed regime willing to sacrifice all for a battle already lost. The ramming tactic was not used again. The hastily trained youngsters now became ground troops, despatched south to what was hoped would prove to be an Alpine fortress.

E-Z Goin' finally made it home to Thorpe Abbotts. Ken Everett, a fourteen-year-old schoolboy, lived with his family half a mile away from the base in a house in line with one of the runways and what happened there on a daily basis had been part of his life for the past two years, listening to the engines start up for a mission as he lay in bed, sometimes seeing crashes on take-off, then, as he returned from school in the late afternoon, watching how many of the planes whose nose art and serial numbers he knew so well had come back. In the late afternoon of 7 April, he remembers, he was in the fields near his home when *E-Z Goin'* appeared, heading for the aerodrome.

Most of the tail had been taken away. On top of that the pilot had already lost one engine and soon after the collision the crew lost another engine. They managed to come home on two. To this day I don't know how they brought it back. I saw the aircraft fly very lopsided over the field. He couldn't get level, but the pilot managed to make a long circuit round and lined up. My great fear was that when he dropped down to land he would crash, but he got in safely and nobody was hurt. The tail gunner [S/Sgt Paul Gurling] didn't know until they landed exactly what had happened to the tail fin. He couldn't see back to it of course.[15]

An 8th AF intelligence report into the *Sonderkommando Elbe* attack noted that 'our losses were comparatively light while more than half the enemy force was destroyed or damaged' and concluded: 'From today's reaction it would appear that although the enemy is fighting a losing battle, the GAF is preparing to fight to a finish in a fanatical and suicidal manner.'[16]

That fanaticism was now evident in a rising tide of evil. SS men roamed the towns beyond the battle area with ropes in hand ready to hang from the nearest lamp post or tree any they saw as deserters. In the concentration camps that had not already been overrun, extermination increased instead of diminishing as Allied justice came closer. Two days after the fruitless, wicked waste of the *Sonderkommando Elbe* being sent into the air, Pastor Dietrich Bonhoeffer went to his death. Bonhoeffer, who had written, 'Silence in the face of evil is itself evil' and had practised what he preached by taking part in the July 1944 bomb plot against Hitler, was escorted naked from his cell at Flossenbürg concentration camp in Bavaria and hanged. It was on the direct orders of the Führer, who shortly before had come up briefly from his bunker in Berlin to award Iron Crosses to and to pinch the cheeks of thirteen-year-old members of the Hitler Youth, shortly to die pointlessly in battle at his bidding as he contemplated his own suicide. As the ecumenical Bonhoeffer, who had studied at a theological college in New York, walked to the gallows that morning he could hear the artillery of the Americans, who would liberate Flossenbürg two weeks later.

The countdown to victory was shortening rapidly, ushering in a new world where the structures of the old would be slowly rebuilt. Paradoxically freedoms in some quarters would be lessened, not increased – certainly in Britain as bureaucracy quickened its pace to advantage in the trudging wake of post-war austerity. While the war went on youngsters living near the bases of free-wheeling American flyers enjoyed a whirlwind of adventure. Lt Jenkins remembers his 44th BG offering local Scouts a ride in a B-24 'to foster good relations with the British people'. Lt Seever's crew were picked for the flight. 'We had maybe six Boy Scouts in the waist. My pilot's quite a joker. He's a very good flyer. We're up pretty high, and then, my pilot, Bob, put the plane in a dive and, of course, a power dive. You're like weightless. Everything that's loose starts to float. So, these Boy Scouts were floating in the air in the waist. I hooked my arm around a machine gun and I started pulling these kids down.' But there was a hole in the bottom of the fuselage from where the ball turret had lately been removed. It had been loosely covered by a piece of shaped wood. 'This ball-turret cover rose up in the air and there's this big six-foot hole there, and so, I got on the interphone and told Bob, "Hey, you know, sort of, like, this is fun and games, but we're liable to lose a kid" . . . because I'm trying to hang on to these kids, so that when he finally comes down . . . they're not over the hole . . . This cover is floating in the air and there's a great, big, gaping hole there.'[17] By the time Lt Seever had returned to straight and level flight a packed parachute had disappeared through the gap.

It didn't take boys long to realise the high-spirited Americans believed rules were made to be broken. Brian Ward had been born near what became the 493rd BG airfield at Debach and was sixteen in 1945. He remembers:

We had moved from Debach when they were building the base, to Woodbridge where I joined the Air Training Corps. I often cycled back to Debach because my aunt still lived there in a cottage almost within the airfield. I used to tell my dad, 'I'm going to see my aunt', but in fact I used to park my bike at the bottom of her garden and hop over the barbed wire fence to the Nissen huts where the aircrew were. I had a signed certificate from the ATC showing I had been trained in parachutes and the Americans being so hospitable said, 'Yes you can certainly have a flight in a B-17.' I had to produce my ATC flying log with my father's signature in. I used to go up to the control tower in my uniform and see one of the chaps in charge there and I would be told: 'Hang about boy and we'll get you a flight shortly.' There would be a B-17 going out to practise bombing or test an engine and a jeep would come along to pick me up and off I would go. I had seven flights in all. I was well aware that the plane I was flying in had probably bombed Germany the previous day and would possibly be bombing Germany again the next. I was allowed to sit in the gun turrets during flights. In my mind I shot down quite a lot of Messerschmitts.[18]

Despite the occasional vicious stings there was no doubt the air war was in its final stage. At Sudbury aircrew returning from the demanding daily ordeal of missions over Germany had been pleased to see an addition to the duo of Red Cross girls waiting with fresh coffee and doughnuts as they milled around waiting for debriefing. Jazz and swing enthusiasts had met her already. 'The lovely brunette who made a big hit at the Aero Club Jam Session last night was Mary Jo Wymond, the latest addition to our Red Cross staff,' wrote Kay Brainard and Jean St Clair in the weekly base bulletin on 11 April. 'Mary Jo, who just crossed the Atlantic three weeks ago, still finds the climate a bit chilly after her native Carpentaria, Calif. . . . Mary Jo has previously worked at the MGM Studios in filmland . . . Right now she is looking for a bicycle and a dog. Any help, fellas?'[19]

Two days later Sudbury and the other 8th Air Force airfields were in grief. President Roosevelt, elected to office for an unprecedented fourth term, was taking a short break in Warm Springs, Georgia, and having his portrait painted when he suffered a fatal stroke. 'We all deeply mourn the passing of our President,' Kay Brainard wrote to her mother. 'We have curtailed all activities at our Aero Club and so have all the Officers' Clubs and GI clubs on bases and in towns – thru Saturday noon.'[20]

Only a few days previously the Sudbury base had lost two of its Fortresses to flak on a mission to a jet airfield at Orianenburg and the 487th BG at Lavenham just down the road had lost four, a total of nineteen bombers from all three divisions failing to return. But it was never as bad again. Until late in the month the 8th regularly put up streams of more than 1,200 bombers on a variety of targets from airfields to marshalling yards and sometimes not one was shot down. Then on 25 April the crews of the USSTAF were called for what turned out to be their final mission from England. 2AD's Liberators drew marshalling yards in Austria and not a single B-24 was lost, but 1AD was not so fortunate. Its selected Groups were tasked with a journey all the way to Pilsen in Czechoslovakia to hit the Škoda works and a nearby airfield. The plant, which produced 88mm anti-aircraft guns and tanks, had been the subject of a disastrous RAF raid in April 1943 when Sir Arthur Harris's men had missed the works entirely because of poor Pathfinder marking, but devastated a mental institution instead, losing 11 per cent of the aircraft on the operation to the Luftwaffe. The American raid would be almost as chaotic.

The order to strike the Pilsen plant for the first time in two years came from General Eisenhower. Intelligence had already told him that patrols by Americans and Russians were likely to meet at any hour. As it was considered the Russians may not stop, despite demarcations being decided at the Yalta conference in February, a demonstration of Allied air power might help them to make up their minds. Destroying the hitherto untouched Pilsen complex would also prevent the Russians from carting away the stockpiled tanks and guns to build up the Red Army's arsenal in a post-war world. But the plant was within a built-up area and since the Dresden inquest Allied leaders were sensitive about civilian casualties.

In fact Winston Churchill had sent an amended memorandum to Harris on 1 April calling for an end to area bombing and reading in part: 'We must see to it that our attacks do not do more harm to ourselves in the long run than they do to the enemy's immediate war effort.'[21] RAF Bomber Command would therefore be bombing Hitler's fortress at Berchtesgaden on 25 April. The attack on Pilsen might turn out to be more controversial. The Škoda plant employed up to 40,000 men and women, most of them Czech, but others were slave labourers conscripted from conquered territories all over Europe. Many questions had been asked in Washington about Dresden after Goebbels' sleight of hand with fatality figures and the last thing the new President Harry S. Truman needed in the immediate post-war world was the Communists making their own capital from a mission by United States bombers alone, costing the lives of thousands of innocent workers. It was, therefore, decided to take the unusual step of warning the factory – and its defences – it was about to be blown apart. Mustangs were despatched on the 24th dropping leaflets over Pilsen, telling workers to stay away from the plant the next day.

The 307 crews of the eight bomb groups who would be making the 725-mile flight to the Škoda works were woken particularly early at the fields in the flat green triangle between Peterborough, Bedford and Cambridge. It was 2am as the CoQ enlisted men banged billet hut doors and called out, 'Breakfast now, briefing in an hour.' At those tense meetings the flyers of most Groups were told they were bombing Hitler's last arsenal, now that Field Marshal Model had lately surrendered his 325,000-strong army in the sealed-off Ruhr, a bigger capitulation than at Stalingrad. But others, including the 91st BG, were told they would be striking at Pilsen's own airfield, where eighty aircraft had been photographed, and at an Me 262 base at Prague. The attacks would be carried out simultaneously and visibility was expected to be good. It was stressed that in all cases bombing would be by visual identification to prevent civilian casualties. The stream would be led by the 389th BG and the 381st would bring up the rear. They would be behind the 91st BG from Bassingbourn, where the vigorous veteran Major 'Manny' Klette was in command of the 324th Sqn. The 324th would be the Group's low squadron with the major's *Klette's Wild Hares* in the lead.

As the Groups wheeled and climbed in the lightening skies over East Anglia beneath 10/10 cloud cover there were problems with division assembly, causing difficulties in station-keeping for the 91st; half an hour after crossing the Dutch coast, as the formation began its climb to bombing height, the 381st began to close up. An hour into the climb the 381st passed the 91st. Radio operators in the Bassingbourn Group at that time heard a BBC message as they individually swept across the tuning dials. They were alerted by the name Škoda. It had been sent to London from SHAEF HQ and it broadcast: 'Allied bombers are out in great strength today. Their destination is the Škoda works. Škoda workers, get out and stay out until the afternoon.' The inhabitants of Wesel on the eastern edge of the Rhine had been warned by Eisenhower some time before the river was crossed in force a month before that their town would be levelled, but this was the first time a heavily defended target had been alerted as the bombers were about to arrive. The crews of the flak guns around the works, whose abundance made infantry officer and future US Army historian Captain Charles MacDonald 'shudder' when his US 2nd Division liberated Pilsen two weeks later, were therefore standing by as the B-17s appeared in the west.

The lead bombardier discovered at the same time that the weather was not as promised, there was six-tenths cloud and the Škoda works was covered. It was decided to make a 360-degree turn over the target so that the Norden bombsight could be set up accordingly, the kind of news that sent a chill through every flak-conscious crew coming along behind. Making such a wide diversion inevitably caused difficulties of station-keeping in such a large force. Bombardier Leonard Streitfeld, on his 31st mission, recorded: 'This manoeuvre moved us from first to last place bringing up the rear of the 8th Air Force. As a result, this made our 398th Bomb Group the last ones to drop bombs by the 8th Air Force during WWII. On the first run there was moderate flak but on the second run the Germans were more precise with the flak, that was intense. There were seventy-eight anti-aircraft guns in range and we must have caught flak from all of them.'[22]

Pilots of the 91st, who would shortly be making a diversion to bomb the airfields and had found themselves reverted to the rear of the column on the climb, looked on a scene ahead quite unlike the ordered procession over the target they had expected, as squadrons orbited and planes hit by flak began to fall, trailing fire. With each pass the gunners below got more accurate and a total of six Fortresses were lost. By the time it became the turn of the 398th to bomb the range was established and two of the Nuthamstead aircraft fell away, parachutes opening in their wake, the last aircraft of fifty-eight the Group lost in the war. Six men died in Lt Allen Fergusen's *Godfather's Inc* and one in Lt Paul Coville's *Stinky Jr*.

'Every returning aircraft sustained battle damage – twenty-four major and fifteen, minor,' the mission report of the 303rd BG read. 'Five men in one crew were wounded. Many aircraft landed without gear or flaps. The end of the runway looked like a parking lot.'[23] One of the Group's Fortresses was hit by flak in its No. 3 engine immediately after the 'bombs away' call. The Fortress fell off to the right, almost straight down. Lt Warren Mauger ordered his crew to bail out, brought the plane almost level despite fire raging through the cockpit then went to exit through the nose hatch. Before he could do so the aircraft exploded and the pilot found himself tumbling over and over. He was eventually able to open his chute and landed with burns to his face and hands. He met a farmer who pointed in the direction of the battle front. Mauger met up with US troops ten days later, but three of his crew had been killed.

Two more aircraft damaged by flak collided near the battle lines on the way home, both from the 379th BG. Seven men from *Seattle Sue* and the tail gunner from *The Thumper* were killed. Another two Fortresses crash-landed on the Continent. A total of thirty-three US airmen were killed on this final daylight mission by the 8th Air Force. On the positive side nearly three-quarters of the Škoda plant was destroyed in the raid, twenty-eight buildings were flattened and thirty-three heavily damaged. That very day Hitler's Reich was also finally cut in two. Units of US General Hodges' First Army found soldiers from Marshal Konev's First Ukrainian Army at the Mulde river, at the Elbe, and near the north-western border of Czechoslovakia, in German territory. The US 97th Division also moved swiftly in the wake of the B-17 raid on the Škoda works, freeing Cheb, midway between Schweinfurt and Prague, and the first Czech city to be taken. The country Britain's Chamberlain government had refused to fight for in 1938 was now falling to the US Army and would soon be handed over to Russian occupation.

★

For a few days crews on the bomber bases expected to be called again, but no order came. More peaceful thoughts began to take root of a return to the familiar routines of civilian life. Most of the airfields had vegetable plots and it was to them that ground-pounders applied themselves as the pressure came off. The Red Cross bulletin at Sudbury recorded two new 'Victory gardens' and added: 'Victory is in the air and in the earth, as a good many Victory gardening Britons will affirm.'[24] S/Sgt Chester Stanek, gunner and togglier, completed his twenty-eighth mission on 21 April and it was obvious the Germans were beaten. 'Back to the Airfield at Ingoldstadt, Germany,' he recorded in his combat diary. 'Bad clouds/PFF all the way. Could hardly see the formation. I flew the ball turret, my original position while in the States, and had a great but bumpy ride. Swiss fighters came up to warn us away from the Swiss border.' From the virtually beaten Reich there was no flak, 'Not even in area near Munich.'[25]

Like everybody else at Sudbury S/Sgt Stanek was waiting day by day to hear that Germany had quit. It seemed ironic that after the promising start to April which had reached the eighties on the 18th, it was unusually chilly in the final few days of the month. 'Spring *was* wonderful, but winter is here again . . . It's been quite cold for several days now, and this morning the ground was covered with snow!' Kay Brainard wrote to her mother on the last day of April. 'We've cancelled the baseball game which was to be played this afternoon, and rumour has it we'll play ice hockey instead! . . . We keep expecting hourly to hear that Germany has surrendered.'[26]

A few days before Col. Overing had been transferred to Bury St Edmunds, eighteen miles away, as chief of staff of 4 Combat Wing, but Kay's invitation list to dances at different USSTAF airfields in the area was still full, being requested to attend four in one night. She had also taken a whirlwind forty-eight-hour pass to London with Col. Overing, which began with lunch at the

Grosvenor House, followed by shopping for records then Charles Street ARC Club 'for ice cream and chocolate sauce – only place in London you can get it!' followed by tea at the Senior Officers' Club, a Grosvenor House tea dance, dinner at the Lansdown and finally drinks at the Astor Club before the staff car took them back to East Anglia.[27]

There the All-American girl continued to cheer those she met, including patients at the nearby military hospital where Red Cross staff toured the wards handing out Coke and cakes. She told her mother: 'One boy said, "No thanks . . . I can't eat . . . but stand there at the end of the bed and smile at me!" [Later as I left] this boy called out to me, "Hey wait a minute". I hesitated and he said, "I just wanted to see you smile again".'[28]

In the first week in May Kay and 'Jeep' Overing went to Tintagel, Cornwall for a couple of days, staying at 'King's Arthur's Castle Hotel' and hiking and horse riding. They were driven down in the Colonel's official olive drab car, by his driver Eddie. Kay recorded in her diary on Monday, 7 May:

After dinner we decided to go for a ride and turned on the car radio just in time to hear the news broadcast and the marvellous announcement that THE WAR IN EUROPE IS OVER!!!! We quickly returned to the hotel and found the guests already celebrating the great news . . . We had some drinks in the bar with a happy group of English people – danced in the lounge to the Victrola – and finally to bed at midnight.

Tuesday, May 8th – officially VE Day (Victory Europe). After breakfast we packed up and departed from Tintagel . . . picked up Eddie. And drove on. Celebrations were going on in every town we drove thru . . . Red, white and blue flags strung *everywhere*. They must have stayed up all night doing it. Bonfires were being lit. Dogs, cats and children were all wearing red, white and blue hair-ribbons. Shop windows were full of red, white and blue merchandise . . . We stopped at a Red Cross Club in Andover to eat, because all shops were closed. It was a holiday. When Jeep dropped me off at the Aero Club a Victory dance was going full blast. He went on to Bury and Wing Hqtrs and I started dancing . . . It was a knock-down drag out affair, but everybody was happy and gay. It was 1.30am before I got to bed.[29]

On the bases the boys of the USSTAF found themselves slowly readjusting to the fact that there was going to be life ever after, after all. Many had been told that the streets of nearby towns were off-limits on VE-Day. 'They said, "This is an English [day]. Let the English celebrate for a day. Tomorrow, you can go to whatever you want, but, today, let them alone,"' ball turret gunner Albert Porter remembers. 'So we're on the base. We did what we usually always did when we couldn't get off the base, drank too much.' The flyers of his 95th BG at Horham and those of the other bomb groups had been issued with .45 automatics to protect themselves from German civilians if shot down. 'So at the end of the war, we all had these .45s and the guys had too much to drink. Every once in a while, you'd hear a shot. What they were doing, they were shooting holes through the Quonset hut roofs. That's what I remember about the day the war ended.'[30]

'VE-Day found comparatively few spontaneous outbursts of joy and enthusiasm among the men of the 487th BG,' the Group's chronicler recorded. 'It had been expected momentarily for some time. Moreover the knowledge that this was the end of one half of the war had its sobering effect.'[31]

T/Sgt Simon Liberman was one of the lucky ones, already off the base when the war finished. 'I happened to have a pass and I was in London and experienced the celebration,' he remembers. He saw the royal family come out on the balcony of Buckingham

Palace to greet the cheering crowds which stretched into Green Park. 'I was in that mass. I had a three-day pass, but, because of the celebration, all the trains and everything stopped running, and I couldn't get back to the base. The services extended all the passes for a couple of days . . . I remember sleeping and almost freezing to death in one of the parks in London, because I had run out of money.'[32]

Sgt William Epstein was a military policeman at the Elveden Hall headquarters of 3AD at Thetford and had been in England for more than two years. He admired the British for their stoicism under fire, particularly when he saw the blitzed area around St Paul's Cathedral, and considered a big part of the MPs' job was protecting the indigenous population. 'We made sure the soldiers were not interfering with any English people,' he remembers. 'We were an asset to the British police there, we worked close with them. We generally kept order.' On VE-Day it was considered more important than ever to make sure nobody among the high-spirited flyers of the 8th went a step too far, though that was difficult when apparently the whole of England had gone temporarily crazy, from merry-makers in the fountains of Trafalgar Square to lines of girls and GIs dancing the conga through the larger country towns. Sgt Epstein continues:

A couple of days before the Germans surrendered, we had heard that the Germans would surrender and they were waiting for terms and waiting for what to do. So, everybody was, naturally, expecting that and when the news finally came through that they were surrendering, and, unconditionally surrendering, I was at the base, at the camp, and that night I went to town. The English people took out the black-out curtains, they had a big bonfire. They were burning them and singing and dancing and shouting. One English woman wasn't happy that day. She had received a telegram from the war department. Her husband was killed. She received it that day of the celebration . . . But the English people were dancing, and singing, and shouting, and crying, and very emotional and American soldiers were glad, too. But then you started thinking about, 'When are we going to Japan?'[33]

S/Sgt Jerry Shulman had just begun his journey back to the States when peace came. The waist gunner who had found flying at altitude in the bitter cold of January almost unbearable had now been transferred from the 453rd BG at Old Buckenham to the 389th. On the night of 6 May he had returned to his comrades at Hethel after visiting friends to be told: '"We are leaving tomorrow morning. We are flying back to the States." I had bought a bicycle over there and I used to use it to go to town. I did not have time to send the bicycle off to my friends. Six o'clock the next morning, we flew up to Liverpool and the next day was VE day. We flew from there to Iceland.'[34]

The young men of the 8th Air Force who had created such a revolution in the British way of life were now departing with an efficiency so shocking in its alacrity it was difficult to comprehend. Group personnel of the 453rd BG left Old Buckenham as early as the day after VE-Day. The Fortresses of the 351st BG where Clark Gable had made his film *Combat America*, currently being shown at base movie theatres, were departing by 21 May, those of the 381st three days later, all yielding to the pressure General Spaatz had been getting from Washington to join the fight against Japan. They took all their equipment and rations or destroyed both. What to do with the ubiquitous bicycle, however, one of the few possessions of an airman which didn't belong to Uncle Sam, was a dilemma and not just for S/Sgt Shulman.

'When we left, a lot of guys wanted to take their bikes back with them,' gunner Albert Porter remembers. 'They wouldn't let you do that. So, I gave my bike to one of the girls.'[35] But most of the cycles were turned to scrap by US bulldozers, causing some resentment among villagers who desperately needed the pedal power they had given up, to be available for mobility of work now the war was over. The missing bikes were not the only void the Americans left. Village girls who hadn't already secured a life partner from the land of plenty and opportunity across the ocean, now never would. Hamlets which once had swung to the beat of the big bands and choked in the dust of roaring jeeps and trucks were backwaters once more, where the farmer's wagon might rumble its slow journey homeward to an evening of BBC classical records on the crackling wireless. The cry of 'Got any gum chum' was now frozen on the lips of children up and down the land.

'The Americans were suddenly gone,' Paul Meen, twelve years old when the Bloody Hundredth left nearby Thorpe Abbotts, remembers. 'Just after the war I used to bike up to the airfield to work the farmland and think about all that had happened there. Sometimes there would be a certain smell as you worked some ground where engine oil from the plane engines had been poured away in a ditch and it would all come back to me what had happened in that place. Norfolk was dead after the Americans went.'[36]

Their passing left an echo with the sound of the last of the fading engines. It resurrected the pain of parting from those who had disappeared years before.

19

'I can't get away from the things I've seen'

Many of the men who had fought their war in the skies of Europe came back to the United States by an unfamiliar medium, the ocean, where they were pitched and rolled for a week until the familiar skyscrapers of New York appeared on the horizon. It was a sight several airmen had not expected to see again and never thenceforth forgot.

S/Sgt Alexander Nazemetz, the nineteen-year-old waist gunner wounded on his last mission from Thorpe Abbotts in March, recalls landing at Staten Island on 13 May, Mother's Day.

We were still on the ship, and we were hanging over the sides, and they had sent out a little boat, with a band, and the girls, American girls, right. The buildings in downtown Manhattan had huge signs in their windows, 'Welcome Home'. When we passed the Statue of Liberty, there was absolute silence on the boat, absolute silence, until we got far enough away, but, it was amazing. There were 3,000 men on that ship, not a word was spoken. It was really quite inspiring.[1]

For many their return was a new birth, a chance to reap rewards from life. They would now make America the pre-eminent nation in the world and themselves prosperous.

But even at the very end there were still tragedies to be played out, a particularly bitter blow to waiting relatives who had been told their hero husband, son or father was coming home. In the rush to get men back hundreds were placed aboard returning bombers as passengers, a total of 2,500 aircraft, each with twenty men aboard refuelling at RAF Valley in North Wales before beginning the long flight across the Atlantic. On 8 June one of the last of the B-17s of the 351st BG took off from Polebrook piloted by Lt Howard Hibbard and as it approached Valley in poor visibility he asked for a compass heading to steer. The crew then flew the reciprocal course in error and hit high ground near Barmouth. All twenty men aboard were killed. On 28 July a B-25 flown by L/Col. William Smith who had lately returned from Europe where he had won a Distinguished Flying Cross, hit the seventy-ninth floor of the Empire State Building in New York in fog. Smith, his sole crew member and a sailor who was hitching a ride were all killed as were eleven office workers. Catherine O'Connor, an employee of the Catholic War Relief Conference, told reporters: 'The plane exploded within the building. There were five or six seconds – I was tottering on my feet trying to keep my balance – and three-quarters of the office was instantaneously consumed in this sheet of flame.'[2]

For those who had been told earlier in America's air war that their loved one was missing there was a seeping new sense of cruel reality, the knowledge that missing now meant friends or relatives would definitely not be returning as the last of the PoW camps were liberated. It was a slow, painful journey of acceptance for many. Kay Brainard had stayed on at Sudbury as she awaited transfer to a new posting on the Continent. Mother's Day cards were for sale at the Aero Club and Col. Overing had sent his own to Kay's parent, reading: 'Please let me try and take the places of William and Newell this Mother's Day and tell you I sincerely hope that the next will find them with you safe and sound again. I know it is hard, but be strong and confident in the perseverance of the 8th Air Force in our attempt to bring our Prisoner of War boys home as soon as possible. Your wonderful Kay is doing a splendid job here and is loved by everyone.'[3]

Two weeks later Kay Brainard wrote to her mother that she and Jeep Overing had driven to London for a last look at what had become *the* place to be for Americans, including a hometown girl from Florida. They had returned to his new base at Bury St Edmunds where they had lunch with his old friend, Col. Bobbie Burns. 'Bobbie excused himself for a few minutes, went to the airfield and took *Lil Shushy* [a P-51] up and gave us an impromptu buzzing and acrobatic show,' Kay wrote. 'He's a wonderful flyer. He later said he was working out his frustrations over Jeep and Bill Martin [the Lavenham Group commander] having to leave the ETO.'[4]

The age was now closing when an officer could take a fighter for a private flying display, simply on a whim. A new, more bureaucratic, season was beginning where rules and regulations became the priority. There was just time for keen English youth to seize the day for the last time. Brian Ward, who had regularly visited Debach, remembers one such incident.

Shortly after the war ended I was in the control tower looking for a flight and a pilot and another officer took me out to a Cessna at first, but that wouldn't start, so we all got in a B-17, these two officers and me and my pal from the ATC. We flew up to Thorpe Abbotts and were there all day. We came back in pouring rain and it was getting dark and I remember the more senior officer turning to the other and saying, 'We haven't got a navigator on board, have we? No problem we'll fly east and follow the coast down.' This they did and found the River Deben from the North Sea which brought them right in line for Debach airfield. We landed in low cloud and drizzle after a long day. My father, who was the sergeant in charge of the Debach Home Guard, was waiting for me as the jeep dropped me off at the control tower, with his bike propped against the wall showing he had been there a while. I got a verbal clip round the ear. He said, 'You're not coming up here again, your mother's been very worried.' [The young air cadet was not aware at the time that rule-breaking went all the way to the top.] I knew the pilot who had flown me was an officer of some distinction, but I didn't realise until later that he was the new CO of the Group, Lt Col. Shepler FitzGerald.[5]

Her own Colonel gone, Kay Brainard buried herself in the minutiae of the Red Cross, surrounded by GI olive drab, and worried about her own two brothers she last saw in uniform in 1944. One Thursday at the end of May she was in her quarters when there was a knock at the door. 'I said "come in" and in walked a GI . . .' she wrote to her mother. 'It took me a fraction of a second to recognize him, then I knew it was brother Bill! Gad, I never had such a shock in my life.'

Her enterprising radio operator sibling had asked a Red Cross girl as he was processed with other liberated PoWs through Le Havre if she could find out if his sister was in the Red Cross and if so where. Kay wrote excitedly:

Bill was able to get a flight over here. He phoned the base from Norwich where he landed and Mary Jo took the message – as I was in London seeing Jeep off. However, she kept it a secret from me, thinking the surprise would do me good. The first night he was here Mary Jo and I went to dinner at the officer's mess and several friends joined us at the table. After eating we went into the bar and had several drinks . . . the boys insisted on treating Bill, MJ and myself. [But over the celebrations loomed the shadow of the Brainards' missing brother.] I had to tell Bill about Newell. One of the first questions he asked was 'Where's Newell?' Sure hope we'll hear something on him too . . .'[6]

There was further excitement in the coming weeks. On 2 July Kay wrote home that she had been invited to a dance and party at wing headquarters to mark a big promotion. 'The new general is former Colonel Bobbie Burns . . . and what a great guy he is too,' she told her mother. 'The dance was a lot of fun, but I sure did miss Jeep.'[7]

Already, however, life in the ETO was providing new surprises for Kay. The Red Cross girl whose war had taken her into places and social strata she would never have dreamed of in West Palm Beach, found she was mixing with a movie star, making what would be an iconic film in post-war Britain, *A Matter of Life and Death*.

'Saturday night we were honoured in our little Nissen hut by having Kim Hunter, the movie actress spend the night with us,' Kay wrote. 'She is here in London making a picture with David Niven. She's a friend of our good friend Lt Rudy Rutenburg – he knew her before she went to Hollywood. She's very cute and very unaffected. We had tea together Saturday afternoon . . . Kim and I shared a room together, altho I didn't get in from the Wing dance until 4am. She was here all day Sunday too.'[8]

The bomb and fighter groups continued to depart the corners of Britain they had made their own. On 5 July it was the turn of the 486th at Sudbury, one of the last to leave. Kay and the other Red Cross girls were driven to the control caravan at the head of the active runway to wave to their friends taking flight, a familiar scene up and down East Anglia that spring and early summer.

> They took off at three minute intervals – 30 of them. Of course we knew most of the boys aboard them (10 crew members and 10 passengers), so they were shouting and making motions for us to come along too. And they'd throw kisses . . . All the boys who hadn't previously named their planes have done so now . . . to impresss the home folks when they land back in the States. Some of the names were *Impatient Virgin*, *Homesick Angel*, *Hitler's Night Mare*, *Sweetheart of the Skies*, *Winged Virgin*, *Kieffer's Kadets*, *Goin Home* [Bert Miller's plane] and *American Beauty* . . . and lots of others I can't remember now. Bert almost ran off the runway waving to us. When they had all left we went sadly to the mess hall and had real eggs for breakfast.[9]

The crews landed across the Atlantic in a different world to the one they had left. The old global order, exemplified by the British Empire, was gone, the sun finally having set on a class-bound way of life where Britannia ruled the waves which lapped the shores of large colonies it would soon be shedding at the behest of its ex-colony America.

Uncle Sam held the purse strings and the old country was virtually broke, having lost a third of its wealth paying for its survival in the war. A proportion of it had gone in reverse Lend-Lease to American forces, including £92 million on buildings alone erected in Britain for US airmen and soldiers.[10] But in September President Truman cancelled Lend-Lease and the British Labour Government had to seek help again from the United States. The White House extended a further $3.75 billion line of credit. It took sixty-one years before the debt and the interest on it was finally cleared. Rationing stayed in blitzed Britain for a decade along with the rubble.

In seizing Europe's skies for America the inheritors of new international power had learned what courage, tenacity and quick-witted wisdom they were capable of. Boys from poor farms and city ghettoes had become officers in the melting pot of conflict. They had literally travelled far in war's patchwork of experience, to timeless English villages; to a Communist dictatorship of Eastern Europe warped by totalitarianism, both Hitlerian and Stalinist; to the warm culture of Italy and egalitarianism of liberated France. They went to war as boys and came back as men of the world.

What they had learned in the process gave them a boundless confidence that had been stunted in their parents by the Great Depression in the decades before. The US Government showed them their thanks with the GI Bill. This now allowed once-poor boys to go to college. Combined with the tempering they had received in the forge of war it produced a well-educated, courageous graduate class in the late 1940s and early '50s with the entrepreneurial spirit to hold leadership of the world. To those of this class, who with their Allied comrades of the air had defeated the skill and bravery of the Luftwaffe, to allow Europe to be freed, anything was now possible.

For Germany's citizens nothing seemed achievable any more. They were finally rid of Hitler's tyranny, but living in cities which looked like the surface of the Moon. A total of 593,000 civilians had died in the combined US/RAF bomber offensive, including forced labourers from Occupied Europe, who did not have a priority for shelter space in the Reich, and the considerable number of civilians killed by Allied army shellfire, particularly in the taking of Berlin by the Russians. It compared with the 63,635 British civilian death toll from traditional German bombs and V-weapons. The 8th Air Force alone had dropped 714,000 tons of bombs from August 1942 to April 1945.[11] Yet none of this misery would have been visited on Germany without the fanaticism of Hitler and his cohorts. A German study in recent years revealed that he was advised in 1942, before the true awesome combined might of the American air forces and RAF Bomber Command was unleashed, that Germany could not win the war, but the dictator continued to exhort nothing less than total victory.[12]

2/Lt Martin Sherman, a non-flying radar operator with the 482nd BG, took one of the low-level aerial tours over Germany laid on straight after VE-Day to show those who served in the air force on the ground what all those bombs had achieved. 'We flew over Cologne, right over the thing, you know, where the bridges were knocked down, the whole area. The only thing left standing was Cologne cathedral,' he related decades later. 'We went to a town called Jülich. I'll never forget . . . The only thing standing was a chimney. Everything else, we could tell, people were walking and there was nothing higher than their waists, just rubble. Boy, I'll tell you, it gave you a feeling of power.'[13]

Kay Brainard was transferred to the German town of Wiesbaden as the summer ended and got a close, slow look at bomb damage through the windows of a bus which collected her party from Frankfurt station. She wrote her impressions in a letter home.

> During the drive (as well as from the train) we saw some of the work our boys did in Germany. Along the railroad as we came into Frankfort [*sic*] we saw miles and miles of bombed-out buildings, burned and wrecked trains, bridges broken in the middle etc. We knew it would be bad, but somehow you can't imagine *how* bad it is until you see for yourself. Frankfort is a shambles. Wiesbaden was never a primary objective, but what was called a 'secondary objective'. If for some reason they could not bomb their initial target, then they dropped their load on Wiesbaden . . . Or some

other secondary target. Weather often had a hand in their decision and they must have had a lot of bad weather, because Wiesbaden, to me, is a terrific mess. Germany has had it! Unbelievable . . . England, in comparison, had nothing. How the people of Germany stood the bombings as long as they did is more than I can understand. It must have been one long nightmare . . . The Occupation Forces are not going to stand short. Whatever is worth having, and left standing, in Germany now belongs to us! . . . The Germans who work for the Americans seem very servile.[14]

That perceived German eagerness to please also extended to a national amnesia about the existence of concentration camps, the true horror of which had been revealed as Allied troops swept through Germany in April. WAC Rita Strobel Geibel had also now been reassigned to Germany from her 8th Air Force photographic technician job at High Wycombe and with a female officer visited Dachau, oldest of the sprawl of camps across the Reich. Many years after the war she related what she had seen.

When I got there you wouldn't believe . . . they were still cleaning the camp up. And the smell, five miles before you even got there, you just couldn't believe. [They were taken into a room where 200 bodies had been removed.] There were blood stains, and it was just horrible in there. It looked like they had maybe scratched with their nails or something . . . They took everything from them, all their clothes and everything and just laid them in there, men, women, and children. They had the bones of these bodies ground up, pulverized, just like fertilizer. We came back from there . . . and there was a place where they had a very big stone. There was a brown rope hanging down . . . and on that they hung or shot them. There were blood stains all over the ground there. [There was also photographic evidence of Nazi brutality.] Well, you know when I first came home nobody wanted to see them [pictures of the prison camps]. They said they didn't believe it.[15]

Kay Brainard soon moved from Wiesbaden to an assignment at Aschaffenberg. She described it as 'a sad looking place, thanks to artillery attacks, plus bomb damage by the 8th Air Force. It's really a mess as it was a rail center and therefore a good target.'[16]

Before she left Sudbury she had celebrated VJ-Day with ground-based USSTAF personnel still on the base with GI maintenance units, riding into the centre of town on a truck. The scene was graphically described in a letter home. 'There is a huge statue of Thomas Gainsborough (the famous artist who was born in Sudbury) in the center of the square,' she wrote, 'and GIs, both American and English, were climbing all over poor Tom – putting their hats on his head – pouring a beer for him – wrapping flags around him.'

She joined up with some GIs and Red Cross girls and danced in the streets to music from a hurriedly rigged PA system.

It was lots of fun. We did the hokey-pokey [sic] and Knees Up Mother Brown – which are two favourite English dances. And just as foolish as the Yanks' jitterbugging. We finally caught one of the GI trucks back to the base about 1am. When we arrived at the Aero Club we found we had a huge bonfire in our front yard – almost. Someone (probably a celebrating Yank) had set fire to a big haystack in the field opposite.

When I came into the club yesterday morning, I asked Arthur (our storekeeper, who was in the British Merchant Marine for 20 years or so) if he had had a nice celebration. He said, 'No, Miss Kay, I went to church . . . somehow to me

it doesn't seem a time for celebrating . . . Thankfulness, yes –
but not a time to get all beered up and tearing around town!'
I agreed with him and said I was sure there were hundreds of
thousands of mothers throughout the world who wouldn't
feel in a celebrating mood either.[17]

There was finally a chance to tabulate the cost of war. More than
26,000 men were killed flying with the 8th Air Force. By comparison the toll among the 8th's comrades in the combined offensive,
RAF Bomber Command, was above 55,500, partial evidence that
equipping four-engined aircraft with .303 machine guns rather
than the longer-range and harder hitting .50s of the B-17 and B-24
was not a good idea. The RAF had dropped one million tons of
bombs in the course of the war, and like the 8th with its 700,000
tons in total, 80 per cent had been in the final 18 months. By 1944
the US Air Forces had 2.4 million flyers and support personnel.
At its peak in 1945 the 8th in England had 200,000 men. That
optimum strength was spread across a strike force of 2,800 heavy
bombers and 1,400 fighters between forty BGs and fifteen FGs.
Of the heavy bombers the 8th flew, 5,548 were lost in combat and
989 from other causes. The aircrew who took part in the offensive
from East Anglia won seventeen Medals of Honor, 220 Distinguished Service Crosses, 817 Silver Stars, 41,497 Distinguished
Flying Crosses and 2,972 Bronze Stars.

There was another medal 6,845 airmen of the 8th received, and
one that often testified to physical wounds received on combat
missions so severe, the pain might last for years. It was the Purple
Heart. There was also a further cost and that was on the psyche
of those who had taken part, for which there was no medal, only
in many cases a personal sense of shame.

As a man went through his tour and witnessed sights on a
regular basis his mind had never prepared him to see, his mental
defences of a sense of patriotism, unit pride, 'and his ability to

identify with his comrades', were brought into action to shelter him.[18] 'Among the most discernible [symptoms of emotional tension] were weight loss, aggressiveness, irritability, insomnia, excessive use of alcohol, startled reactions and even hypersexuality,' a 1943 report showed.[19] 'In addition to all these signs, it was not unusual by any means, for men to show other physical reactions to severe anxiety: Air sickness, headaches, backaches and various stomache ailments were not uncommon.' There could even be rare cases of paralysis, blindness and catatonia.[20] Out of every seven casualties among US Army *ground* troops on average one was killed, five were wounded and one was a psychiatric case. But the surprising result of statistical tabulations at the war's end was that the psychological damage among US aircrew displayed itself in fewer cases for treatment by the medical corps, not more. 'In fact despite their worsening states of health during their tours, aircrews were actually less inclined to report themselves sick. Most wanted to get through their missions,' a doctoral study showed.[21]

For a percentage, however, their experiences overwhelmed the personal well of courage every man has to a greater or lesser degree and their minds cracked under the strain. 'The experiences of one pilot illustrates this point remarkably well,' an Air Force psychiatrist wrote in a post-war volume.

On his tenth mission the plane in front of him exploded and what he took for a piece of debris flew back towards him. It turned out to be the body of one of the gunners, which hit directly in the number two propellor. The body was splattered over the windscreen and froze there. In order to see it was necessary for the pilot to borrow a knife from the engineer and scrape the windscreen. He had a momentary twinge of nausea, but the incident meant little to him. As he did not know the man the horrifying spectacle was at a psychological distance. It was two missions later, when his plane and crew suffered severe damage and he became intimately involved in the trauma, that the first incident was revived with its full traumatic meaning.[22]

In the spring of 1944 a report by the Office of the Air Surgeon on a survey of aircrew in the 8th, 9th, 12th and 15th Air Forces stated that four per cent of all aircrews entering heavy bombardment units were taken off flying status, at least temporarily, before the end of their tours. In the course of the 8th AF bombing offensive this would indicate about 4,000 being treated as emotional casualties at some time – less than one tenth of one per cent a month. But bottling up their emotions by the great majority came at a price. The emotional damage caused by the war was now being felt by US aircrew adjusting to civilian life. For some the knowledge of what they had witnessed and experienced was very close to the surface.

S/Sgt John Briol, who successfully finished his tour with the 457th BG in late February, found himself assigned to night guard duty at his Glatton base while awaiting a ship to take him home. The loneliness didn't help his state of mind. 'While I was walking my post, I was thinking of all sorts of things. I've seen too much happen,' he wrote in his diary before turning in. 'It's not much fun to see a riddled plane come back and see some poor guy's intestines splattered all over the inside and the rest of the crew crying like babies. When I have time on my hands it seems as if I can't get away from the things I've seen.'[23]

Alexander Nazemetz, the nineteen-year-old waist gunner wounded in mid-March, took the view that 'there was a certain amount of rehabilitation required by almost everyone who had seen combat, me included. When I came home . . . I don't know what you want to call it, [I felt] that nothing happened to me, even though I'd been through this experience. I remember that

I was not able to sit still. I dreamed about being in the war, but, I was always in the backyard watching the flak. I was down on the ground looking up. I would see the shoot[ing] going on, and then, I usually would wake up.'[24] Lt Don Ackerson, the 384th BG bombardier who baled out from his burning B-17 on his twenty-seventh mission in April 1944, was among those now returning from PoW camp, a place where he had relived many times the mission that brought him there. 'For months I couldn't close my eyes without baling out again and waking up completely terrified,' he says. 'This took years to overcome. I would dream of baling out with my chest pack parachute still in the plane. Or I would go to sleep and at that moment the plane engine noise would stop and I would wake up in shock.'[25]

Lt John Homan, a nineteen-year-old co-pilot with the 485th BG who came back to New York harbour two days before Christmas 1944, also admitted: 'After I was out of the service just for a short period, maybe a year or so after, I had some nightmares, especially revisiting some of the rougher missions.'[26] But S/Sgt Paul Dickerson, a twenty-one-year-old waist gunner in Lt Cecil Isom's *Patsy Girl*, one of only three bombers in the 445th BG to make it back to base from the disastrous Kassel mission of 27 September 1944 when a *Sturmbok* shot down 2/Lt Newell Brainard's Liberator and twenty-four others in six minutes, told a researcher: 'I think you just got busy and got on with your life. It was something you didn't want to remember.'[27]

So 1945 drew to a close. The final day of the year found Kay Brainard as director of the American Red Cross Club at Erlangen, Germany, and still hoping against hope for news of Newell. She had lately been seeking information from an air force medical officer. 'Had he been a hospital patient of any sort, [he] would have by this time been returned to the U.S.,' she wrote to her mother. 'Also, if Newell were a mental case, or amnesia, it would be very easy to identify him even if his dog tags, wallet etc were all missing . . . as the Army has fingerprint records on all soldiers.' She had begun the letter on a happier note. 'Happy New Year, last day of the year and what a year! Wouldn't have missed it for anything, and I'm happy to say the good days have certainly out-numbered the bad ones.'[28]

As 1946 opened the movie *A Matter of Life and Death* – with its female lead Kim Hunter whom Kay had entertained at Sudbury – was selected as the first Royal Command Film Performance. Its theme of limbo-like loss in which a baled-out pilot has to be judged by a celestial court whether he has been counted dead by mistake, struck a chord with many grieving families whose airman son, brother or husband had simply been declared 'missing' without further news. On both sides of the Atlantic mothers and sisters still hoped unreasonably that there had been some dreadful error in the records and Johnny would come marching home again.

But at the end of January Kay got what most would consider the final answer from the US Army. A letter marked HQ ETO, read: 'It is with deep regret that I inform you that our records indicate that 2/Lt Brainard has been officially determined dead as of 28 September 1945 by the War Department after no information has been received indicating any possibilities of survival.' The clinical assessment of what further concern the US military need show for one of its former airmen continued with: 'Details leading up to present status of 2/Lt Newell W. Brainard , 0-812929, unavail-able as his unit departed this Theater for the United States on the 28th May, 1945.'[29] The nagging need to know more continued with Kay for years.

Most of those who went home were happy to forget the war as they got on with building careers and raising a family. Among those airmen was James Stewart, who had gone from aviation cadet to Lieutenant Colonel in four years and flown his missions with the rest, being known as a 'regular guy' by those with whom he served. He returned to Hollywood, making the big US hit of

1946 *It's A Wonderful Life* in which this time a would-be guardian angel wins his wings by showing a citizen down on his luck how much he was needed. The movie appealed to the new values of servicemen anxious to put down roots as Joe Public. And so they did, going to college, marrying and buying their first home. It was decades later when the once young airman's now adult children started to ask about their service that the memorabilia came out of the attic and they began to remember that time in a different age when living for the day was paramount. Asked now why they volunteered to fly with the 8th Air Force and how they managed to continue despite the loss of comrades all around them, practically all will answer, without irony or false modesty: 'We had a job to do.' It was doing that job that put paid to Hitler and allowed three generations since to grow up in freedom. Many of their wives had their own experiences of hearing the sights and sounds of bombs and gunfire because they were Englishwomen who had grown up sheltering from the Luftwaffe. They were that post-war transatlantic phenomenon the GI bride.

There were more than 41,000 girls who married American servicemen in Britain during the war, producing 14,000 babies in the UK – and countless thousands more who became single parents after their GI lovers were killed or shipped Stateside. The free-spending, easy-going charm of lonely airmen far from home had proved irresistible to many an English maiden in blitzed and rationed Britain. But as their husbands were repatriated under Operation Magic Carpet they had to wait until the US Government had the last GI home.

The ban lasted until the end of 1945 and it was 26 January 1946 before the first ship to leave with the new emigrants set sail from Southampton. English newspapers flagged up the end of an era as they printed pictures captioned 'GI wives and babies waving goodbye to England from the SS *Argentina* exactly four years after the first US troops arrived in Britain'. The *Argentina* carried 626

US dependents, but it was quickly followed by the *Queen Mary*, which had established a reputation with its sister *Queen Elizabeth* for adaptable capacity to accommodate troops during the war, establishing a record on one run of 16,683 people on board. When soldiers weren't sleeping on deck or in echoing caverns of bunks six deep, they were queuing for meals served twice a day by cooks working in shifts. Then there was the gambling on both ships. USAAF man Joseph W. Zorzoli, who came over to England on the *Queen Elizabeth*, related years later: 'I had $17 in my pocket then I got involved in a blackjack game and before I realised we were passing the Statue of Liberty leaving the States I was already flat broke.'[30]

Now the Queens, known as the Grey Ghosts during the war, because of their 35-knot zig-zag course to outrun U-boats, their battleship-grey paintwork merging with Atlantic mists, had been rapidly refitted with cabins and nurseries for the nappy run to New York, high chairs in rows in the restaurants. That first peacetime January the *Queen Mary* alone shipped 12,886 GI brides to America and 10,000 to Canada. The crossing to reunite newlyweds was made at high speed and established another record, her fastest crossing ever of three days, 22 hours and 40 minutes. The fares were all taken care of by the US Government, although a very few brides had been allowed to pay their own passage while the war was still going on. Doreen Flowers sailed as a GI bride in October 1944 from Greenock to New York: 'The fare was £42,' she remembered. 'There were very few civilians on board but there were thousands of GIs, so the ship was very crowded. It was hard to walk on deck for the troops sitting on deck, gambling.'[31]

Most brides were met on shore by their mother-in-law and other members of their husband's family if he was still in the service. It could be a shock for both and often when the English girl arrived at her American family's home she discovered there was little of the Hollywood luxury that years of the silver screen had led her to expect. Sometimes girls from busy London found themselves living in the backwoods and took years to get over their homesickness. In a few cases GIs had frankly lied about their circumstances to catch a bride when chances at home were slim. Marriages quickly foundered as a result. As the last of the GI brides stepped ashore in New York in the coming months and their husbands left the service, it marked the end of an era in which the new world had come to save the civilisation of the old. There was only a brief time for reflection on the extraordinary change in society and the men and women who had been part of it.

Howard Roth's own war had taken him from a small-town high school to commanding a B-17 over Germany, witnessing a horrific collision over his base at Thurleigh in Bedfordshire and seeing the legendary Glenn Miller hours before he vanished for ever. He remembers:

Finally VJ Day came and the war was over so I was sent to Memphis, Tenn, and got discharge and took the train back to Buffalo. I was sitting in the train station waiting for my father to pick me up and he was a little late, and anyway I was thinking, two and a half years ago four of us, three buddies and myself, were in the same station waiting for a train to take us to Atlantic City for our basic training. Here, I'm back. Three of them got shot down. Dick O'Connor was a P-51 pilot shot down and killed while strafing targets in Germany; Joe Neden was a B-29 pilot who got shot down over Tokyo; Howard McIntyre was a navigator with the 8th Air Force who was shot down and became a prisoner of war. I must have a pretty busy Guardian Angel.[32]

The airfields such as Thurleigh and others throughout East Anglia where young men like Lt Roth took off and landed have now faded back into the farmland from which they sprang. Cracked concrete paths that once led to lines of Nissen hut billets today meander aimlessly into copses of full-grown chestnut, ash and elm, once saplings which divided those streets of Spartan homes for airmen. Roots now cover the rough rectangles of buildings, leaves rustling over the dread-filled dreams and echoing voices of those who once lived here and disappeared. But the young Americans who travelled so far to fight Europe's war and failed to return are not forgotten by those from both the city and the plough of England whose freedom they preserved.

Monuments to the US airmen who lived, sometimes briefly, in East Anglia during the war are found often in quiet corners including brass plaques in churches such as one in the medieval round-towered St Peter's at Holton, Suffolk, which reads: 'In memory of all the Americans who served in the cause of duty flying from the runways of Holton airfield', or that of another round-towered church, St Margaret's at Seething, Norfolk, which recognises in its churchyard the 448th BG 'and commemorates 350 men killed in action fighting for freedom'. Brigadier General Frederick Castle's name is now on the roll of honour in the fifteenth-century Lavenham Church together with 232 other US airmen, who died flying with the 487th in the Second World War. Other reminders are more public such as the bronze plaque which the 486th BG presented outside Sudbury Town Hall to its citizens in August 1945 for their 'fellowship, cooperation and understanding', remembering perhaps that the Suffolk town had a population of 7,000 people until the 2,000 or so Americans arrived. By the abbey in Bury St Edmunds is a dedicated rose garden funded by an American who served as a flyer in the area. Such memorials lie alongside the graves of Englishmen and women who died before America became a nation or in some cases before the Pilgrim Fathers had set forth.

But most impressive of all is the memorial America itself built, the USAAF Cemetery at Madingley, near Cambridge. Its thirty acres are laid out on rising ground so the visitor can see for miles across the arching semi-circles of 3,812 white stone crosses to the green layers beyond of the rich Cambridgeshire countryside stretching to the blue horizon's edge. Behind are the tablets to the missing and it is the sheer numbers of those who simply disappeared after taking off from their East Anglian bases that overwhelm the senses – 5,127 young Americans who came to free Europe from tyranny. The states from which they sprang to start that journey are carved into the stone beside each alphabetical roll-call. Farm boys from Indiana, Wisconsin and Idaho, many with German names, are remembered here alongside other sons of immigrants who formed the cities' teeming masses, young men of Italian and Irish heritage from New York and Boston. Nearly all are ordinary citizens who died before their potential could be recognised or achievements praised. They march from New Jersey's S/Sgt Frank J. Abbadessa, 95th BG to Pennsylvania's S/Sgt Bernard T. Zukosky, of the 386th. And somewhere in the middle is Lt Joseph Kennedy, united with the others in the democracy of death.

In recent years the memorials to such men have grown, not declined as the remains of airfields and control towers are preserved at last by the sons and daughters of the men and women who experienced the American invasion. The watch office at Debach remained derelict until local volunteers rescued it in 2002, creating a moving museum, and then expanded into other airfield buildings; volunteers at Thorpe Abbotts took over a derelict, windowless control tower with vegetation climbing the walls in 1977 to restore it in five years to how it looked in wartime when the Bloody Hundredth was establishing its hard-won death-or-glory reputation; Rougham, where the 94th BG operated has also had its central building brought back to life and reopened as a museum, the hum from units on an industrial estate beyond the trees redolent on a summer's day of the sounds of generators prior to start up of B-17 Wright Cyclones at lonely hardstands; Framlingham, from where M/Sgt Hewitt Dunn became the only man to fly one hundred missions with the 8th Air Force, now has not only a thriving museum, but an ex-veteran from the base who married a local girl and pops in to tell visitors what life was like when it could be measured in just days and weeks.

And the pubs where the airmen drank and caroused are there still, hanging on through the centuries despite the enormous social changes they have seen, not least in the past decade. The interior of The Dog at Grundisburgh is recognisable today as the hostelry, its walls imbued through time with the warmth of good fellowship, that S/Sgt Bob Arbib found that late summer wartime night when he and his fellow army engineers made their way down the lanes and tracks from the airfield at Debach they were building. But now it is the solid English middle-class who visit with their dogs, where seventy years ago black airmen gathered round the piano while the cartoonist Carl Giles tinkered with Broadway melodies. Outside the stream still flows gently through the village green as it had once so enchanted S/Sgt Arbib and his companions. It is not alone in standing as a testimony to the ghosts of those who came to save Britain. The White Hart at Great Yeldham, where a doomed New York gunner from the 381st BG convinced with his gifted mimicry visitor after visitor he was actually an Englishman hiding in the 8th Air Force, still welcomes the great-grandchildren of those who died flying from Ridgewell. The Buck just outside the technical site of the 446th BG at Flixton, near Bungay, which gave its name to the Bungay Buckeroos as the Group became known, remains solidly beside the quiet B1062; the one-roomed Nut Hatch in Bury St Edmunds, which boasted then and now to be the smallest pub in Britain, continues to spill its customers back from the bar onto the street, though now the uniform is sweater and jeans rather than badged and winged olive drab.

Evidence of the American air war conducted from England still surfaces occasionally. In 2012 an aviation archaeology group found the remnants of a Mustang which had crashed near Market Rasen on a training flight just after D-Day. The remains of its twenty-year-old pilot 2/Lt Charles Moritz, who had been in England only six weeks, were still inside, nearly seventy years on.[33] It wasn't quite so long for Kay Brainard before she got the answer she desperately needed about her missing Air Force brother Newell.

She had left for the States in April 1946, her Red Cross job over, though not before attending the Nuremburg trials where she saw Nazis from Goering to Speer, who had brought such pain into the life of her own and other families, arraigned. She, like many who saw them, was shocked by the banality of evil. 'Some of them look like bank tellers or department store clerks,' she told her mother. Unsurprisingly Kay's life was anything but ordinary. She married the cousin of her Red Cross co-worker Mary Jo Wymond, later divorcing then marrying again. She also became personal assistant to the American film star Douglas Fairbanks Jr, who had himself served in England during the Second World War. At his home she met David Niven, co-star in *A Matter of Life and Death* to the actress with whom she had shared her Sudbury quarters in 1945. There were other famous friends of her employer she greeted including Laurence Olivier, Joan Plowright and Princess Margaret. It was while working for Fairbanks in New York in 1990 that she was able to research the 445th BG's disastrous Kassel mission and was eventually sent a 118-page file marked 'Burial report'.

On page 80 she found out her brother had baled out near the village of Nentershausen after his Liberator was wrecked in the *Sturmbok* attack. He had a head injury and a nurse in the village bandaged it for him. Later he and another 445th BG flyer and two more who had come down in the nearby village of Suess were taken to a slave labour camp in Nentershausen and beaten up. They were then shot.

In 1948 there had been a trial of six Germans present in the camp that day, three of whom were hanged for their part in the murder of Newell Brainard and the others. Finally, there it was in black and white. The determined American girl, who had decided to join the wartime Red Cross to find out what had happened to her kid brother, had the answer at last. He had been murdered, hastily buried and subsequently reinterred in the Lorraine US cemetery at St Avold, France. It was forty-six years late. Kay died sixteen years afterwards.

Acknowledgements

I am particularly grateful to the following USAAF aircrew and other servicemen who participated in various direct ways in the preparation of this book. It is their unstinting help that made it all possible. Ranks are those when they left the service. All the flyers are recipients of the Air Medal, some with several clusters for repeated awards. Other decorations for gallantry, such as the Distinguished Flying Cross, are shown after the names of recipients: 34th BG: Lt Col. Seymour Isaacs. 91st BG: Col. Robert Morgan DFC with two clusters; Captn Frank Farr. 100th BG: S/Sgt John Day; T/Sgt Gordon Klehamer. 305th BG: 2/Lt Terry Messing; S/Sgt Keith Hereford. 306th BG: Lt Howard Roth; Captn Andrew Vero DFC. 339th FG: Major General Frank Gerard (deceased), Silver Star. 351st BG: T/Sgt Frank Petrucci. 357th FG: Col. Bud Anderson, Legion of Merit (twice), DFC with four clusters, Bronze Star, Croix de Guerre with Palm; Col. Jim Roughgarden DFC. 381st BG: Capt John Howland (deceased). 452nd BG: Capt Louis Hernandez (deceased). 486th BG: Lt Robert O'Boyle. 493rd BG: Cpl Jack Feller; T/Sgt Bill Toombs DFC. From the Royal Navy Rescue Launch 512 I am grateful for the help of Stoker 1st class Arthur Hickingbottom. From Air Chief Marshal Sir Arthur Harris's Bomber Command the following who allowed me to interview them contributed personal knowledge about aspects of the American flyer's war: 102 Sqn: Sgt Montague Clarke; 115 Sqn: P/O Ken Turnham; 158 Sqn: F/Lt Bob Farnbank; 218 Sqn: P/O Ron Brown; 408 (RCAF) Sqn: F/Sgt Laurie Godfrey; 630 Sqn: F/Sgt Bill Isaacs.

It would be remiss of me not to include here those who

Acknowledgements

through their personal diaries, letters and interviews left behind in museums and other research facilities and on the Internet and in Group records their accounts of their time in England during the Second World War so that other generations might benefit from the insight they provided into a unique period in history. They include: 100th BG: S/Sgt Alexander Nazemetz; Lt Edwin A. Stern; Sgt James A. Mack; S/Sgt Paul Zak; Lt Leon Schwartz. 305th BG: Lt Walter R. Douglas. 306th BG: S/Sgt Lee Eli Baar DFC; Sgt Calvin Brend; Lt Oscar Bourn. 384th BG: Lt Don Ackerson. 385th BG: 2/Lt Joel Punches. 392nd BG: 2/Lt Harry Thomas. 447th BG: 2nd Lt Bill Ethridge. 482nd BG: 2/Lt Martin Sherman. 485th BG: Lt John Homan. 486th BG: S/Sgt John MacBride; Lt Lesley Hull; S/Sgt Irving Saarima, by permission of his son John Saarima. 452nd BG: Lt Donald H. Smith, by permission of his daughter Susan Purves.

I am also grateful to the following civilian sources both in the UK and US, many of whom work tirelessly to ensure the memories of the Mighty Eighth are kept alive: Andy Wilkinson, 467th BG historian/researcher; Mick Hanou, 91st BG Memorial Association President; Mike Faley, 100th BG historian; Carol Batley, Ken Delve, Paul Meen, Brian Hopgood and Margaret Hopgood, all of the 100th BG Museum, Thorpe Abbotts; Darren Jelley and Brian Ward of the 493rd BG Museum, Debach; Dr Kevin Wilson, Secretary/Treasurer, 381st BG Memorial Association; Gerry Green of the 390th BG Memorial Museum, Parham; Douglas Brett, of the Duxford Fighter Collection; Peter Saunders of the Friends of Leiston Airfield; Leonard Aubert, nephew of Lt Leonard Coleman, of the 100th BG, for permission to use Lt Coleman's mission diary; Carole Bellis Hutchins for allowing me to use excerpts from the letters and diary entries of her mother, American Red Cross girl Kay Brainard; Becky and Joni Varner for permission to use the mission diary of T/Sgt Kirk Varner, of the 446th BG; Joe Ferris Jr of the 447th BG Association for permission to use 2/Lt William Davidson's account of his final mission; Christopher Montagna for allowing me to quote from the Merseburg account of S/Sgt Bert Sitek of the 457th BG; John F. Briol for permission to quote from the diary of his father S/Sgt John J. Briol, of the 457th BG; Linda A. Dewey of the Kassel Mission Memorial Society for allowing me to use excerpts from the interview with mission survivor S/Sgt Jack Laswell; Joe Dzenowagis Jr for permission to quote from Kassel Mission interviews carried out by his parents Joe and Helen; author Aaron Elson for contacts assistance concerning the disastrous 445th BG Kassel Mission; Debra D. Kujawa, of the 8th AF Historical Society for veteran quote assistance; Gordon Richards for his knowledge of the 8th AF and particularly the 306th BG, Thurleigh; Malcolm Osborn for sharing his knowledge of the 398th and 486th Bombardment Groups and of Americans at Bletchley Park. There are several people, both ex-USAAF and civilians, whose contribution, and often encouragement, was outstanding. They include Lt Howard Roth, Captn John Howland (deceased) and Sudbury resident Roley Anderson, also deceased, whose collection amassed over many years and now in the archives of the Sudbury Museum Trust, has added much to this book. I am also grateful to David Burnett, Secretary of Sudbury Museum Trust, who spent valuable time with me going through the Roley Andrews Collection. The staffs of other museums and archives also deserve thanks including those of the Pima Air and Space Museum, Tucson, Arizona; the Air Force Historical Research Agency, Maxwell Air Force Base, Alabama; the National Archives, Kew, London; the Imperial War Museum at Lambeth, London and Duxford, Cambridgeshire; the RAF Museum, Hendon, London; the Newspaper Library, Colindale, London; and Shawn Illingworth and Nic Molnar of Rutgers University Oral History Archives, New Jersey. I would also like to thank Alan Samson, publisher at Weidenfeld & Nicolson, whose patience and

Acknowledgements

encouragement over several years saw this transatlantic project at last reach completion, and my editors Paul Murphy, Simon Fox, Celia Hayley and John English.

After so many years it has been difficult sometimes to trace former air war participants or their families. If there is anyone I have missed out as a result I would ask that they contact my publishers so that proper acknowledgements can be made in future editions.

Notes

1: 'He had us dead to rights'

1 Unpublished manuscript quoted in Gerald Astor, *The Mighty Eighth*, p. 236.
2 Information from Roger A. Freeman, *The Mighty Eighth War Diary*, p. 183 and Internet sources.
3 Cptn John Howland's account, Imperial War Museum File 99/7/1.
4 Lt Don Ackerson's account, IWM 67/280/1.
5 IWM 99/7/1.
6 See Glenn Infield, *Big Week*, p. 57.
7 See Roger A. Freeman, *The Mighty Eighth*, p. 108.
8 USAAF Medal of Honor (MoH) citation for Lt Lawley, August 1944.
9 Ackerson, IWM 67/280/1.
10 Col. Spicer Encounter Report, Air Force Historical Research Agency, Maxwell AFB, Alabama.
11 Ibid.
12 Freeman, *Mighty Eighth War Diary*, p. 183.
13 392nd Bomb Group Association website.
14 Freeman, *Mighty Eighth War Diary*, p. 183.
15 USAAF MoH citation for Lt Lawley.
16 Freeman, *Mighty Eighth War Diary*, p. 183.
17 IWM 99/7/1.
18 See www.b24.net.
19 *392nd BGMA News*, August 1994.
20 Harry Thomas's account quoted in www.b24.net.
21 *New York Times*, 1 June 1999.
22 Freeman, *The Mighty Eighth*, p. 108.

23 National Archives, AIR 40-544.

24 *Stars and Stripes*, 21 February 1944.

25 *The Times*, 21 February 1944.

26 IWM 67/280/1.

27 National Archives, AIR 27-482.

28 Ilse McKee quoted in Kevin Wilson, *Men of Air*, p. 89.

29 Ibid., p. 90.

30 Wilson, *Men of Air*, p. 92.

31 Ibid.

32 *Behind the Wire* video, prepared for the Bomber Command Association by DD Videos, 1997.

2: 'Things are going to be tough from now on'

1 Personal Report to Commanding Officer, 100th BG.

2 Donald L. Miller, *Eighth Air Force*, p. 210, and other sources.

3 Freeman, *Mighty Eighth War Diary*, p. 126.

4 Joel Punches, *B-17F Flight Log*, http://www.94thinfdiv.com/pdf/b17f_flight_log.pdf.

5 Interview with author.

6 Miller, *Eighth Air Force*, p. 144.

7 Internet sources and Roger A. Freeman, *The Mighty Eighth War Manual*, p. 220.

8 *The Best from Yank*, British Library YD.2008.b.1478.

9 IWM 99/7/1.

10 Miller, *Eighth Air Force*, p. 245, and other sources.

11 *Daily Herald*, 4 January 1944.

12 Freeman, *Mighty Eighth War Manual*, p. 143.

13 Infield, *Big Week*, p. 49.

14 Wesley Frank Craven and James Lea Cate, *The Army Air Forces in World War II*, Vol. 3, p. 30.

15 Ibid., p. 356.

16 Addition to Punches, *B-17F Flight Log*, http://www.94thinfdiv.com/pdf/b17f_flight_log.pdf.

17 IWM 99/7/1.

18 IWM 67/280/1.

19 Sourced from 390th BG Memorial Air Museum, Parham, and *Time Team*, Channel 4.

20 *Stars and Stripes*, 22 February 1944.

21 *306th BG Echoes* newsletter, April 1989.

22 IWM 67/280/1.

23 Jesse Richard Pitts, *Return to Base*, p. 57.

24 IWM 67/280/1.

25 Ibid.

26 *306th BG Echoes* newsletter, April 1989.

27 Ibid.

28 Ibid.

29 Theo Boiten and Martin Bowman, *Battles with the Luftwaffe*, p. 101.

30 Ibid.

31 Sean Longden, *For the Victor the Spoils*, Arris Books, 2004.

32 Freeman, *The Mighty Eighth*, p. 110.

33 IWM 67/280/1.

34 Wilson, *Men of Air*, p. 214.

35 IWM 99/7/1.

36 IWM 67/280/1.

37 *306th BG Echoes* newsletter, July 1986, Vol II, No 3.

38 IWM 99/7/1.

39 Ibid.

40 *306th BG Echoes* newsletter, July 1986, Vol II, No 3.

41 Infield, *Big Week*, p. 108.

42 *306th BG Echoes* newsletter, July 1986, Vol II, No 3.

43 Ibid., p. 75.

44 Freeman, *The Mighty Eighth*, p. 112.

45 Statistics from Freeman, *Mighty Eighth War Manual*.

46 National Archives, PRO 24 WIM 44.

47 *The Best from Yank*, British Library YD.2008.b.14181; Saul Levitt article on Rosie's Riveters, p. 79.

3: 'A gasp of surprise and dread'

1 Wilson, *Men of Air*, p. 27.

2 Ibid., p. 50.

3 Written account by Lt Edwin A. Stern at 100th BG Museum, Thorpe Abbotts, courtesy of the 100th Bomb Group Foundation: www.100thbg.com.

4 Written account by Sgt James F. Mack, courtesy of the 100th Bomb Group Foundation: www.100thbg.com.

5 Stern written account, courtesy of the 100th Bomb Group Foundation: www.100thbg.com.

6 Mack written account, courtesy of the 100th Bomb Group Foundation: www.100thbg.com.

7 *Stars and Stripes*, 4 March 1944.

8 *Shepherd of the Seas* report by 65th Fighter Wing to General James Doolittle, March 1945.

9 *The Best from Yank*, British Library YD.2008.b.1478.

10 Ibid.

11 Ibid.

12 Encounter Report of Flt Officer Chuck Yeager, 357th FG, archived by Air Force Historical Research Agency, Maxwell AFB, Alabama.

13 *B-17s Over Berlin*, edited by Ian L. Hawkins, p. 148.

14 *Stars and Stripes*, 6 March 1944.

15 Ibid.

16 *The Best from Yank*, British Library YD.2008.b.1478.

17 Ibid.

18 Letter to his father from Lt Col. John Bennett. For a more detailed account see J. M. Bennett, *Letters From England*, p. 48. A reprint is available at the Tower Museum, Thorpe Abbotts, extracts courtesy of the 100th Bomb Group Foundation: www.100thbg.com.

19 For a more detailed description of the fatal step in the stream see Jeffrey Ethell and Alfred Price, *Target Berlin*, p. 42.

20 Alfred Price, *Skies of Fire: Dramatic Air Combat*, pp. 84–5.

21 Encounter Report of Lt Col. Glenn E. Duncan, 353rd FG, archived

by Air Force Historical Research Agency, Maxwell AFB, Alabama.

22 IWM 99/7/1.

23 Quoted in Robert Cowley (ed.), *No End Save Victory*, p. 273.

24 IWM 99/7/1.

25 Ibid.

26 Ibid.

27 Freeman, *The Mighty Eighth*, p. 115.

28 Price, *Skies of Fire*, pp. 84–5.

29 *Stars and Stripes*, 8 March 1944.

30 Pitts, *Return to Base*, p. 255.

31 Ethell and Price, *Target Berlin*, p. 103.

32 Ibid.

33 Encounter Report of Captn Glendon V. Davis, 357th FG, archived by Air Force Historical Research Agency, Maxwell AFB, Alabama.

34 *Stars and Stripes*, 8 March 1944.

35 Price, *Skies of Fire*, p. 91.

36 Ibid.

37 USAAF report quoted in Harold E. Jansen, *The History of the 446th BG*.

38 Ibid.

39 Letter to his father from Lt Col. John Bennett. For a more detailed account see J. M. Bennett, *Letters From England*, p. 48. A reprint is available at the Tower Museum, Thorpe Abbotts. Extracts courtesy of the 100th Bomb Group Foundation: www.100thbg.com.

40 *Stars and Stripes*, 8 March 1944.

4: 'What are those fools trying to do, kill all of us'

1 IWM 67/280/1.

2 Bennett, *Letters From England*, p. 49. Extracts courtesy of the 100th Bomb Group Foundation: www.100thbg.com.

3 Ibid., p. 50.

4 Interview by Shaun Illingworth, Rutgers Oral History Archives.

5 IWM 99/7/1.

6 Bennett, *Letters From England*, p. 51. Extracts courtesy of the 100th Bomb Group Foundation: www.100thbg.com.

7 USAAF records, archived by Air Force Historical Research Agency, Maxwell AFB, Alabama.

8 Bennett, *Letters From England*, p. 54. Extracts courtesy of the 100th Bomb Group Foundation: www.100thbg.com.

9 IWM 99/7/1.

10 *The Best from Yank*, British Library YD.2008.b.1478.

11 IWM 99/7/1.

12 *Stars and Stripes*, 9 March 1944.

13 IWM 99/7/1.

14 Alfred Price, *The Last Year of the Luftwaffe*, p. 47.

15 IWM 67/280/1.

16 *Stars and Stripes*, 10 March 1944.

5: 'Hiya Baby! Lovely day, isn't it?'

1 IWM 99/7/1.

2 Cptn John Howland's diary notes.

3 Robert Arbib, *Here We Are Together*, p. 10.

4 Ibid. p. 11.

5 IWM Sound Archive 16415/3/1-2-3.

6 Account to author.

7 Interview by Shaun Illingworth, Rutgers Oral History Archives.

8 Pitts, *Return to Base*, p. 177.

9 *Stars and Stripes*, 2 March 1944.

10 Helen D. Millgate, *Got Any Gum Chum?*, p. 76.

11 IWM Sound Archive 16415/3/1-2-3.

12 Account to author.

13 *Jump, Damn It, Jump!*, British Library YC.2007.a.14394.

14 Pamphlet by Army Services Division, Washington, 1943.

15 IWM file IWM 92/29/1.

16 Dan Brennan, *Never So Young Again*, p. 143.

17 John Costello, *Love, Sex & War*, p. 313.

18 Army Services Division, Washington, 1943.

19 Interview with author.

20 Interview with author.

21 Interview with author.

22 Ibid.

23 IWM 99/7/1.

24 Interview with author.

25 *Daily Telegraph*, 30 May 1944.

26 Major John M. Redding and Capt. Harold I. Leyshon, *Skyways to Berlin*.

27 *Sun*, April 1982.

28 Bud Hutton and Andy Rooney, *The Story of Tripes*.

29 Miller, *Eighth Air Force*, p. 138.

30 US Army Regulations 600-35, Section 12.

31 Costello, *Love, Sex & War*, p. 315.

32 *New York Times*, June 1943.

33 Evelyn Waugh quoted in Miller, *Eighth Air Force*, p. 223.

34 Wilson, *Men of Air*, p. 106.

35 Report of Psychiatric Study of Successful Air Crews, 11 October 1943, quoted in Colonel Mark K. Wells, *Courage and Air Warfare*, p. 68.

36 *Stars and Stripes*, 24 February 1944 (London edition).

37 Wilson, *Men of Air*, p. 106.

38 Juliet Gardiner, *Over Here*, p. 122.

39 Ibid.

40 Jansen, *History of the 446th BG*.

41 Notice from Sudbury Museum Trust: www.sudburysuffolk.co.uk/heritage.

42 Quoted in Gardiner, *Over Here*, p. 122.

43 *Stars and Stripes*, 4 March 1944 (British edition).

44 Ibid.

45 *Mustang Pilot*, p. 46.

46 Margaret Mead, *The American Troops and the British Community*.

47 Millgate, *Got Any Gum Chum?*, p. 32.

Notes

6: 'Up and down the streets people jeered and spat at me'

1 Figures compiled from list of missions in Freeman, *Mighty Eighth War Diary*.

2 Statistics from Martin Middlebrook and Chris Everitt, *The Bomber Command War Diaries*, p. 488.

3 IWM 67/280/1.

4 Miller, *Eighth Air Force*, p. 316.

5 Freeman, *The Mighty Eighth*, p. 282.

6 Robert Arbib, *Here We Are Together*, p. 50.

7 Ibid, p. 50.

8 Statistics from Miller, *Eighth Air Force*, p. 45.

9 Interview with author.

10 Account in 493rd BG Memorial Museum.

11 Interview with author.

12 Interview by Shaun Illingworth, Rutgers Oral History Archives.

13 Miller, *Eighth Air Force*, p. 340.

14 IWM 67/280/1.

15 Combat diary of Lt Leonard F. Coleman, courtesy of Leonard Aubert and the 100th Bomb Group Foundation: www.100thbg.com.

16 Transcript by John P. Blair of Davidson recording for 447th BG Association archives: www.447bg.com.

17 Ibid.

18 Ibid.

19 Ibid.

20 S/Sgt James V. Murphy, Report 4467, 4592, Missing Air Crew Reports, 1942–47, Record Group 92, National Archives, Washington, DC.

21 Hilary St George Saunders, *Royal Air Force 1939–45*, Vol. III, p. 87.

22 Craven and Cate, *The Army Air Forces in WWII*, Vol. 3, p. 153.

23 Ibid.

24 Ibid., p. 154.

25 Ibid.

26 Interview with author.

27 'The Right Plane and the Right Pilot', personal unpublished document by S/Sgt Irving Saarima in the Roley Andrews Collection, Sudbury Museum Trust, via David Burnett.

28 Interview with author.

29 www.bbc.co.uk/ww2peopleswar.

30 Interview with author.

31 Col. Clarence E. 'Bud' Anderson with Joseph P. Hamelin, *To Fly and Fight: Memoirs of a Triple Ace*: www.cebudanderson.com.

32 Ibid.

33 Ibid.

34 Ibid.

35 Freeman, *Mighty Eighth War Diary*, p. 251.

36 Account via Andy Wilkinson, researcher/historian 467th BG: http: www.the467tharchive.org.

37 Statistics from Miller, *Eighth Air Force*, p. 294.

7: 'Invasion! No longer just a gleam in the General's eye'

1 Interview with author.

2 IWM 99/7/1.

3 Arthur Bove, *First Over Germany: A Story of the 306th BG* (IWM – 18 (73)).

4 *306th BG Echoes, 1975–2000*, p. 935.

5 381st BG War Diary, transcribed from microfilm by Dave Osborne, quoted by permission of Dr Kevin Wilson.

6 IWM Sound Archive 16415/3/1-2-3.

7 *The Best of War Stories*, 8th AF Historical Society, pp. 35–6.

8 Ibid.

9 Interview by Shaun Illingworth, Rutgers Oral History Archives.

10 'The Right Plane and the Right Pilot', personal unpublished document by S/Sgt Irving Saarima in the Roley Andrews Collection, Sudbury Museum Trust, via David Burnett.

Notes

11 Unpublished document in the Roley Andrews Collection, Sudbury Museum Trust, via David Burnett.

12 Charles C. Huff, *The War Years 1942–1945*, privately published autobiography, Sudbury Museum Trust, via David Burnett.

13 Interview with author.

14 Combat diary of Lt Leonard F. Coleman, courtesy of Leonard Aubert and the 100th Bomb Group Foundation: www.100thbg.com.

15 Bove, *First Over Germany*.

16 Craven and Cate, *The Army Air Forces in World War II*, Vol. 3.

17 Statistical Control Division HQ AAAF Allied v Axis air strength report, quoted in Dwight D. Eisenhower, *Crusade in Europe*, p. 484.

18 *Gesamtübersicht über die durchschnittliche einsatzbereitschaft der flieg verbande, mai 1944*, File AH B6, Air Ministry, London, now Ministry of Defence.

19 *Observer* newspaper, 9 May 2004.

20 Ibid.

21 S/Sgt Saarima, 'The Right Plane and the Right Pilot'.

22 IWM 99/7/1.

23 Diary of 533rd Sqn, 381st BG, quoted by permission of Dr Kevin Wilson.

24 Interview by Shaun Illingworth, Rutgers Oral History Archives.

25 Ibid.

26 *306th BG Echoes, 1975–2000*.

27 Combat diary of Lt Leonard F. Coleman, courtesy of Leonard Aubert and the 100th Bomb Group Foundation: www.100thbg.com.

28 Diary of Kirk Varner, by permission of Becky and Joni Varner.

29 Interview with author.

30 *306th BG Echoes, 1975–2000*, p. 935.

31 *The Best of War Stories*, 8th AF Historical Society, pp. 35–6.

32 Unpublished document in the Roley Andrews Collection, Sudbury Museum Trust, via David Burnett.

33 Roley Andrews Collection, Sudbury Museum Trust.

34 Ibid.

35 IWM 99/7/1.
36 *D-Day Attack by the 8th AF*, privately commissioned DVD by John Howland.
37 Addition to Punches, *B-17F Flight Log*, Internet.
38 Craven and Cate, *The Army Air Forces in World War II*, Vol. 3, p. 190.
39 Interview with author.

8: 'An Me 109 came at me head on. I was terrified'

1 'My Experiences in the ETO', by T/Sgt Ernest Barton, privately published autobiography, Roley Andrews Collection, Sudbury Museum Trust, via David Burnett.
2 Interview with author.
3 PW and X Detachment Military Intelligence Service Report for the Adjutant General's Office, 31 August 1944.
4 Combat diary of Lt Leonard F. Coleman, courtesy of Leonard Aubert and the 100th Bomb Group Foundation: www.100thbg.com.
5 Hawkins (ed.), *B-17s Over Berlin*, p. 193.
6 S/Sgt Greenwood's account in 100th Bomb Group Foundation website, www.100thbg.com, used by permission of Michael P. Faley, 100th BG historian.
7 Ibid.
8 Interview with author.
9 PW and X Detachment Military Intelligence Service Report for the Adjutant General's Office, 31 August 1944.
10 Interview with author.
11 Combat diary of Lt Leonard F. Coleman.
12 Ibid.
13 *Stars and Stripes*, 7 July 1944.
14 Interview with author.
15 *Stars and Stripes*, 28 July 1944.
16 Combat diary of Lt Leonard F. Coleman.
17 *Stars and Stripes*, 14 August 1944.

18 Wilson, *Men of Air*, p. 374.

19 'My Experiences in the ETO', by T/Sgt Ernest Barton, privately published autobiography, Sudbury Museum Trust, via David Burnett.

20 Ibid.

9: 'Couldn't sleep. Kept seeing ships exploding'

1 *Stars and Stripes*, 7 August 1944.

2 Ibid.

3 Analysis by Dr Peter W. Becker in *Air University Review*, July–August 1981.

4 Spaatz Collection, Library of Congress, Manuscript Division.

5 Final Minutes of a Meeting held on Saturday, March 25, to Discuss the Bombing Policy in the Period Before Overlord, Spaatz Collection, Box 14.

6 Combat diary of Lt Leonard F. Coleman, courtesy of Leonard Aubert and the 100th Bomb Group Foundation: www.100thbg.com.

7 Ibid.

8 Ibid.

9 91st BG Dailies of the 324th Squadron 1944. Transcribed by Andy Caswell and scanned by Mike Banta; Internet.

10 Combat diary of Lt Leonard F. Coleman.

11 Alfred Price, *The Last Year of the Luftwaffe*, p. 91.

12 Combat diary of Lt Leonard F. Coleman.

13 Ibid.

14 Letter to Leonard Aubert from Col. Charles J. Gutekunst, 29 August 2005.

15 IWM Sound Archive 16415/3/1-2-3.

16 *Stars and Stripes*, 8 July 1944.

17 Ibid.

18 Account to author.

19 *306th BG Echoes* newsletter, April 1987.

20 Howard Roth's Veterans History Project (unpublished).
21 Ibid.
22 Ibid.
23 Ibid.
24 Interview with author.
25 IWM 61/127/1.
26 Ibid.
27 'My Experiences in the ETO', by T/Sgt Ernest Barton, privately published autobiography, Roley Andrews Collection, Sudbury Museum Trust, via David Burnett.
28 Ibid.
29 Account in files from Roley Andrews Collection, Sudbury Museum Trust, via David Burnett.
30 Interview with author.
31 Interview with author.
32 Interview with author.
33 Juliet Gardiner, *Over Here: The GIs in Wartime Britain*.
34 Ibid.

10: 'Some were blazing and some were blown to bits'

1 *Warplanes of the Third Reich*, p. 634.
2 Freeman, *The Mighty Eighth*, p. 184.
3 Heinz Knoke, *I Flew for the Fuhrer*, p. 177.
4 Price, *The Last Year of the Luftwaffe*, p. 91.
5 Knoke, *I Flew for the Fuhrer*, p. 178.
6 2/Lt Warren L. Soden, 100th BG, courtesy of the 100th Bomb Group Foundation: www.100thbg.com.
7 Ibid.
8 Interview with author, 1989.
9 Encounter Report of 2/Lt F. R. Gerard, 339th FG, archived by Air Force Historical Research Agency, Maxwell AFB, Alabama.
10 Howard Roth's Veterans History Project.

11 'My Experiences in the ETO', by T/Sgt Ernest Barton, privately published autobiography, Roley Andrews Collection, Sudbury Museum Trust, via David Burnett.

12 Interview with author.

13 Howard Roth's Veterans History Project.

14 Harry H. Crosby, *A Wing and a Prayer*, p. 288.

15 Interview with author.

16 T/Sgt Barton, 'My Experiences in the ETO'.

17 Ibid.

18 'The Right Plane and the Right Pilot', personal unpublished document by S/Sgt Irving Saarima in the Roley Andrews Collection, Sudbury Museum Trust, via David Burnett.

19 Ibid.

20 Interview with author.

21 Ibid.

22 S/Sgt Saarima, 'The Right Plane and the Right Pilot'.

23 Details and Contents of Stories told by bomber crews flying in and out of Sudbury airfield during early 1944 through to the end of August 1945, Roley Andrews Collection, Sudbury Museum Trust, via David Burnett.

24 Ibid.

25 Howard Roth's Veterans History Project.

26 IWM Sound Archive 2889, Thames TV, 1972.

27 Lt Bertram interview by Aaron Elson reproduced in his book *9 Lives: An Oral History*.

28 Mike Jones article quoting extracts from a publication issued by the Kassel Mission Historical Society. See www.rafb24.com.

29 Helen and Joe Dzenowagis, *The Dayton Tapes*, Vol. 1, 2nd Air Division Memorial Library, Norwich, quoted by permission of Joe Dzenowagis Jr.

30 Helen and Joe Dzenowagis, *The Kassel Tapes*, July 1991, 2nd Air Division Memorial Library, Norwich, quoted by permission of Joe Dzenowagis Jr.

31 Mike Jones article quoting extracts from a publication issued by the Kassel Mission Historical Society. See www.rafb24.com.

32 Interview with S/Sgt Jack Laswell, quoted by permission of the Kassel Mission Historical Society.

33 Encounter Report of Lt William Beyer, 361st FG, archived by Air Force Historical Research Agency, Maxwell AFB, Alabama.

34 Ibid.

35 Ibid.

36 Ibid.

37 Helen and Joe Dzenowagis, *The Kassel Tapes*, July 1991.

38 Mike Jones article quoting extracts from a publication issued by the Kassel Mission Historical Society. See www.rafb24.com.

39 Helen and Joe Dzenowagis, *The Dayton Tapes*.

40 Mike Jones article quoting extracts from a publication issued by the Kassel Mission Historical Society. See www.rafb24.com.

41 'Time Out: Remembrances of WWII from the Diary of an ex-PoW', IWM 99/43/1.

42 Ibid.

43 Ibid.

44 Ibid.

45 Ibid.

46 Crosby, *A Wing and a Prayer*, p. 288.

11: 'All hell broke loose'

1 Miller, *Eighth Air Force*, p. 166.

2 USAAF Aircraft Mishap Report obtained post-war by Lancashire Aircraft Investigation Team.

3 BBC TV, *Inside Out*, 26 January 2007.

4 Tower log, 390th BG Memorial Museum.

5 *Suffolk Chronicle and Mercury*, 29 December 1944.

6 Michael Muttit, 'Witness to the first Kennedy tragedy' and 'Joe Kennedy Junior's last mission' in Alan Mackley (ed.), *The Poaching Priors of Blythburgh*, 2002, pp. 52–5.

7 Ibid.

8 Letter to author from Jack Feller, June 2011.

9 Craven and Cate, *The Army Air Forces in World War II*.

10 National Archives, ADM 1/16201.

11 Craven and Cate, *The Army Air Forces in World War II*.

12 ASR Exhibition, Norfolk and Suffolk Aviation Museum, Bungay.

13 Analysis of how initial survivors of a disaster at sea eventually die, Titanic Experience Exhibition, Cobh, Co. Cork.

14 Howard Roth's Veterans History Project.

15 'Time Out: Remembrances of WWII from the Diary of an ex-PoW', IWM 99/43/1.

16 Operational Record Book of 280 Sqn.

17 'Time Out: Remembrances of WWII from the Diary of an ex-PoW', IWM 99/43/1.

18 Account to author.

19 Ibid.

20 Ibid.

21 Account by Lt Don Mackintosh, via Darren R. Jelley, of the 493rd BG Museum, Debach.

22 Ibid.

23 Ibid.

24 Account to author.

12: 'Bodies were scattered all over the area'

1 Howarth Roth's Veterans History Project.

2 Ibid.

3 Account to author.

4 Howarth Roth's Veterans History Project.

5 IWM 61/127/1.

6 Account to author.

7 Howarth Roth's Veterans History Project.

8 Ibid.

9 IWM 92/29/1.

10 IWM Sound Archive 2889, Thames TV, 1972.

11 IWM 61/127/1.

12 War Correspondent Exhibition, IWM North, 2011.

13 *Air Force*, October 1944.

14 *Stars and Stripes*, 2 August 1944.

15 *Stars and Stripes*, 16 October 1944.

16 *Yank*, 25 August 1944.

17 *Stars and Stripes*, 16 November 1944.

18 *Stars and Stripes*, 20 November 1944.

19 *Stars and Stripes*, 12 October 1944.

20 *Stars and Stripes*, 12 November 1944.

21 *Stars and Stripes*, 14 November 1944.

22 Interview with author.

23 *Stars and Stripes*, 21 February 1944.

24 *Stars and Stripes*, 26 September 1944.

25 Extract from 8th Air Force Historical Society oral history interview by Julie Croft, in James Clements (ed.), *Silent Heroes Among Us*.

26 Ibid.

13: 'The greatest air battle of this war'

1 Speer Papers, FD3063/49, Department of Documents, Imperial War Museum.

2 Reich production figures from captured German documents, quoted in Price, *The Last Year of the Luftwaffe*, p. 96.

3 Account to author.

4 Diary of Captain John W. Howland, IWM 99/7/1.

5 Wartime Memories Project, www.wartimememoriesproject.com.

6 'From the Right-Hand Seat of a B-17', IWM 97/22/1.

7 Combat diary of S/Sgt MacBride, Roley Andrews Collection, Sudbury Museum Trust, via David Burnett.

8 Ibid.

9 John J. Briol, 'Diary of a B-17 Ball Turret Gunner', quoted by permission of Marcella Briol and John F. Briol.

10 Quoted in Christopher P. Montagna, *Brightwood Boys*.

11 'Memories of Merseburg-Leuna 1944', www.luther-in-bs.de (inactive).

12 Memories of Lt Edward Gates, deceased.

13 For a fuller account see Frank Farr, *PoW: A Kriegie's Story*.

14 War diary of Lt Lesley B. Hull, Roley Andrews Collection, Sudbury Museum Trust, via David Burnett.

15 *Stars and Stripes*, 3 November 1944.

16 *Yank*, 4 December 1944.

17 See Price, *The Last Year of the Luftwaffe*, p. 110, for a full transcript of Hitler's dressing down.

18 Donald H. Smith, 'From the Right-Hand Seat of a B-17: A B-17 Co-pilot's Story of his WWII Experiences', 1995, IWM 97/22/1.

19 Ibid.

20 457th Association Newsletter, June 1991.

21 Ibid.

22 'From the Right-Hand Seat of a B-17', IWM 97/22/1.

23 Display account at 390th BG Museum, Parham.

24 Briol, 'Diary of a B-17 Ball Turret Gunner'.

25 Personal Combat Report, 2/Lt Rex Burden, USAAF Field Order 564A.

26 Ibid.

27 Encounter Report of 2/Lt William Phillippi, Historical Research Agency, Maxwell AFB, Alabama.

28 Interview with author.

29 Encounter Report, 354 Sqn, 355th FG.

30 Presidential citation for 491st BG, USAAF records.

31 Ibid.

32 2nd Air Division Association Journal, 1996.

33 Encounter Report, Cptn Winder.

34 Encounter Report, Lt Col. Henderson.

35 2nd Air Division Association Journal, 1996.

36 Interview with author.

37 Interview with author.

38 Interview with author.

39 Ibid.

40 'Memories of Merseburg-Leuna 1944', www.luther-in-bs.de (inactive).

41 National Archives, AIR 41/56.

42 BMP Reports by the German Air Section, p. 32.

43 Sir Arthur Harris, *Bomber Offensive*, p. 220.

14: 'I bet our lives'

1 Air Ministry Meteorogical Office Report for December 1944: www.metoffice.gov.uk/learning/library.

2 Account in files of Roley Andrews Collection, Sudbury Museum Trust, via David Burnett.

3 Ibid.

4 Ibid.

5 Lt Leon Schwartz, 100th BG, exhibit in Tower Museum, Thorpe Abbotts, courtesy of the 100th Bomb Group Foundation: www.100thbg.com.

6 Interview with author.

7 Ibid.

8 Ibid.

9 Air Ministry Meteorogical Office Report for December 1944.

10 2/Lt King's account via Andy Wilkinson, researcher/historian 467th BG: http:www.the467tharchive.org.

11 Ibid.

12 Ibid.

13 Air Ministry Meteorogical Office Report for December 1944.

14 Interview with author.

15 Quoted in Kevin Wilson, *Daily Express*, 10 December 2004.

16 Interview with author.

17 Interview with author.

18 *Daily Telegraph*, 7 January 2012.

19 *Lincolnshire Echo*, 14 December 1944.

20 Typewritten transcript of diary in files of Roley Andrews Collection, Sudbury Museum Trust, via David Burnett.

Notes

21 Howard Roth's Veterans History Project.
22 Typewritten transcript of diary in files of Roley Andrews Collection, Sudbury Museum Trust, via David Burnett.
23 *The Times*, 4 December 1944.
24 IWM 61/127/1.
25 Air Ministry Meteorogical Office Report for December 1944.
26 Quoted in interview with Col. Nicholas Perkins, 4th Wing Chief of Staff, in Freeman, *Mighty Eighth War Diary*, p. 403.
27 Report of Disappearance of Brigadier General Frederick W. Castle, investigation held at 4th BW HQ, Bury St Edmunds.
28 Ibid.
29 Air Ministry Meteorogical Office Report for December 1944.
30 Transcript of Lt John Barry's diary in files of Roley Andrews Collection, Sudbury Museum Trust, via David Burnett.
31 Freeman, *Mighty Eighth War Diary*, p. 405.
32 *Stars and Stripes*, 6 October 1944.
33 Interview with author.
34 Interview with author.
35 Gardiner, *Over Here*, p. 137.
36 *Yorkshire Evening Press*, 30 December 1944.
37 Extract from the draft document 'The Last Day of a B-17' as told by the crew of *Nine Ten* to Ken Keller, Roley Andrews Collection, Sudbury Museum Trust.
38 Donald H. Smith, 'From the Right-Hand Seat of a B-17: A B-17 Co-pilot's Story of his WWII Experiences', 1995, IWM 97/22/1.
39 Lt Leon Schwartz, 100th BG, courtesy of the 100th Bomb Group Foundation: www.100thbg.com.
40 Ibid.
41 S/Sgt Paul Zak, 100th BG, courtesy of the 100th Bomb Group Foundation: www.100thbg.com.
42 Lt Leon Schwartz, 100th BG, courtesy of the 100th Bomb Group Foundation: www.100thbg.com.
43 S/Sgt Paul Zak, 100th BG, courtesy of the 100th Bomb Group Foundation: www.100thbg.com.
44 Ibid.

45 Transcript of Lt John Barry's diary in files of Roley Andrews Collection, Sudbury Museum Trust, via David Burnett.

15: 'So cold tears came into my eyes'

1 Interview with author.
2 Interview by G. Kurt Piehler and Mark Weiner, Rutgers Oral History Archives.
3 'Crosses of Iron', journal of S/Sgt Richard A. Fredericksen, Wartime Memories Project.
4 Interview with author.
5 493rd BG records, quoted in Freeman, *Mighty Eighth War Diary*, p. 421.
6 Interview by Sandra Stewart Holyoak, Rutgers Oral History Archives.
7 Ibid.
8 Ibid.
9 Eldon Bevons' open letter to grandchildren: www.8thafhsoregon.com.
10 Lt Andrew Norman's combat diary, contributed by another crew member to www.487thbg.org.
11 Jack Fishman Stanley's Flight Log, January 1945–April 1945, transcribed by Laura D. Stanley: www.487thbg.org.
12 Encounter Report of Cptn James Browning, 357th FG, archived by Air Force Historical Research Agency, Maxwell AFB, Alabama.
13 Lt Andrew Norman's combat diary.
14 Jack Fishman Stanley's Flight Log.
15 Lt Andrew Norman's combat diary.
16 Summary of Bombing of the German city of Magdeburg by Friedrich J. Kowalke, Roley Andrews Collection, Sudbury Museum Trust.
17 Air Ministry Meteorogical Office Report for January 1945: www.metoffice.gov.uk/learning/library.

18 Combat diary of Lt Roberts, supplied to Roley Andrews Collection, Sudbury Museum Trust, by son Bill Roberts, via David Burnett.

16: 'The birds were really flying. What a sight!'

1 Katherine Brainard Hutchins, 'The Experiences of One American Red Cross Girl in World War II – As told through letters to her mother', Sudbury Museum Trust via David Burnett.
2 Quoted in Charles W. McArthur, *Operations Analysis in the US Army 8th Air Force in World War II.*
3 Norman Longmate, *Bombers: The RAF Offensive Against Germany*, p. 331.
4 National Archives, CAB 81/93.
5 Dudley Saward, *'Bomber' Harris*, p. 282.
6 Ibid., p. 284.
7 Ronald Schaffer, *Wings of Judgement*, p. 95.
8 Richard G. Davis, 'Operation "Thunderclap": The US Army Air Forces and the bombing of Berlin', *Journal of Strategic Studies*, Vol. 14, No. 1 (1991).
9 Interview by Kurt Piehler and Andrew Zappo, Rutgers Oral History Archives.
10 Monthly diary, February 1945, 423rd Sqn, 306th BG.
11 Ibid.
12 Ibid.
13 Account in files of Roley Andrews Collection, Sudbury Museum Trust, via David Burnett.
14 Ibid.
15 Interview with author.
16 Monthly diary, February 1945, 423rd Sqn, 306th BG.
17 John J. Briol, 'Diary of a B-17 Ball Turret Gunner', quoted by permission of Marcella Briol and John F. Briol.
18 Freeman, *Mighty Eighth War Diary*, p. 499.
19 See www.100thbg.com.

20 MACR 12046, USSTAF records.

21 Monthly diary, February 1945, 423rd Sqn, 306th BG.

22 Monthly diary, February 1945, 367th Sqn, 306th BG.

23 Account in files of Roley Andrews Collection, Sudbury Museum Trust, via David Burnett.

24 Reports of Aircraft Accidents, this copy belonging to Capt John Rumisek, flight control officer, 486th BG, 6 February 1945.

25 Monthly diary, February 1945, 423rd Sqn, 306th BG.

26 Jacob Kronika, *Berlins Undergang* (Copenhagen: Hagerup,1945), quoted in Jorg Friedrich, *The Fire*, p. 321.

27 Interview by Kurt Piehler and Andrew Zappo, Rutgers Oral History Archives.

28 McArthur, *Operations Analysis in the US Army 8th Air Force in World War II*.

29 Account in files of Roley Andrews Collection, Sudbury Museum Trust, via David Burnett.

30 Typewritten transcript of diary in files of Roley Andrews Collection, Sudbury Museum Trust, via David Burnett.

31 National Archives, NRR 837, AIR 14-3412.

32 Götz Bergander, *Dresden im Luftkreig*, p. 99.

33 Air Ministry Meteorogical Office Report for February 1945: www.metoffice.gov.uk/learning/library.

34 23 (=43) 5 (Klemperer, Victor) –2 99/2125, IWM Department of Documents.

35 Monthly diary, February 1945, 369th Sqn, 306th BG.

36 Frederick Taylor, *Dresden*, p. 412.

37 Katherine Brainard Hutchins, *The Experiences of One American Red Cross Girl in World War II: As Told Through Letters to Her Mother*, Sudbury Museum Trust, via David Burnett.

38 Ibid.

39 File 670.430-3, Feb 1945, Albert F. Simpson Historical Research Center, Maxwell Air Force Base, Alabama, quoted in Schaffer, *Wings of Judgement*, p. 90.

40 Schaffer, *Wings of Judgement*, p. 91.

41 *Operation Clarion*, 8th Air Force film unit.

42 Katherine Brainard Hutchins, *The Experiences of One American Red Cross Girl in World War II: As Told Through Letters to Her Mother*, Sudbury Museum Trust, via David Burnett.

43 Ibid.

17: 'Sitting off my wing was an Me 109'

1 Associated Press, dateline London, 26 February 1945.

2 8th AF Historical Society: www.8thadhs.com.

3 *The Goebbels Diaries*, p. 5.

4 Katherine Brainard Hutchins, *The Experiences of One American Red Cross Girl in World War II: As Told Through Letters to Her Mother*, Sudbury Museum Trust, via David Burnett.

5 Ibid.

6 Encounter Report of Lt Duncan McDuffie, archived by Air Force Historical Research Agency, Maxwell AFB, Alabama.

7 Ibid.

8 Account via Andy Wilkinson, researcher/historian 467th BG: http: www.the467tharchive.org.

9 Ibid.

10 Katherine Brainard Hutchins, *The Experiences of One American Red Cross Girl in World War II: As Told Through Letters to Her Mother*, Sudbury Museum Trust, via David Burnett.

11 Interview with author.

12 Katherine Brainard Hutchins, *The Experiences of One American Red Cross Girl in World War II: As Told Through Letters to Her Mother*, Sudbury Museum Trust, via David Burnett.

13 Interview with author.

14 Rutgers Oral History Archives.

15 Interview with author.

16 Flt Officer Richard Scroxton, 100th BG, exhibit in Tower Museum, Thorpe Abbotts, courtesy of the 100th Bomb Group Foundation: www.100thbg.com.

17 Chester Wilmot, *The Struggle for Europe*, p. 679.

18 *Nuremburg Trial Proceedings*, Part xvii, pp. 34–6.

19 Quoted in Wilmot, *The Struggle for Europe*, p. 679.

20 Interview by Shaun Illingworth, Rutgers Oral History Archives.

21 Ibid.

22 Ibid.

23 Schaffer, *Wings of Judgement*, p. 102.

24 Wilmot, *The Struggle for Europe*, p. 683.

25 *The Goebbels Diaries*, p. 236.

26 Interview with author.

27 *Stars and Stripes*, November 1944.

18: 'Let the English celebrate'

1 Statistics from Roger Freeman, *The US Strategic Bomber*.

2 Katherine Brainard Hutchins, *The Experiences of One American Red Cross Girl in World War II: As Told Through Letters to Her Mother*, Sudbury Museum Trust, via David Burnett.

3 Air Ministry Meteorogical Office Report for April 1945: www.metoffice.gov.uk/learning/library.

4 Katherine Brainard Hutchins, *The Experiences of One American Red Cross Girl in World War II: As Told Through Letters to Her Mother*, Sudbury Museum Trust, via David Burnett.

5 Ibid.

6 Ibid.

7 Interview by Shaun Illingworth, Rutgers Oral History Archives.

8 Interview by Shaun Illingworth and Jennifer Esposito, Rutgers Oral History Archives.

9 Mission diary of S/Sgt Chester R. Stanek, Roley Andrews Collection, Sudbury Museum Trust, via David Burnett.

10 Document shown and quoted in Adrian Weir, *The Last Flight of the Luftwaffe*, p. 46.

11 Hajo Herrmann, *Eagle's Wings*, p. 257.

12 3AD Report, USSTAF records, Maxwell AFB, Alabama.

13 Herrmann, *Eagle's Wings*, p. 254.

14 Herrmann, *Eagle's Wings*, p. 257.

15 Interview with author.

16 8th AF Intops Summary No 342, Re 7 April 1945, USSTAF Records.

17 Interview by Shaun Illingworth, Rutgers Oral History Archives.

18 Interview with author.

19 486th BG base bulletin, Wednesday, 11 April 1945.

20 Katherine Brainard Hutchins, *The Experiences of One American Red Cross Girl in World War II: As Told Through Letters to Her Mother*, Sudbury Museum Trust, via David Burnett.

21 Saward, *'Bomber' Harris*, p. 294.

22 Leonard Streitfeld, *Hell from Heaven*, Chapter 35: www.hellfromheaven.com.

23 303rd Bomb Group website: http://www.303rdbg.com.

24 486th BG Red Cross bulletin, April 1945.

25 'Missions flown over Germany by the crew of *Goin' Jessie* from Jan 1945 to April 1945', Sudbury Museum Trust.

26 Katherine Brainard Hutchins, *The Experiences of One American Red Cross Girl in World War II: As Told Through Letters to Her Mother*, Sudbury Museum Trust, via David Burnett.

27 Ibid.

28 Ibid.

29 Ibid.

30 Interview by Sandra Stewart Holyoak, Rutgers Oral History Archives.

31 The History of the 487th Bombardment Group, IWM 18 (73). 226 (487 Bombardment Group) 5).

32 Interview by Sandra Stewart Holyoak, Rutgers Oral History Archives.

33 Interview by Sean D. Harvey and Sandra Stewart Holyoak, Rutgers Oral History Archives.

34 Interview by G. Kurt Peihler and Mark Weiner, Rutgers Oral History Archives.

35 Interview by Sandra Stewart Holyoak, Rutgers Oral History Archives.

36 Interview with author.

19: 'I can't get away from the things I've seen'

1 Rutgers Oral History Archives.
2 About.com 20th century history: http://history1900s.about.com/od/1940s/a/empirecrash.htm.
3 Card in Katherine Brainard Hutchins file, Sudbury Museum Trust.
4 Katherine Brainard Hutchins, *The Experiences of One American Red Cross Girl in World War II: As Told Through Letters to Her Mother*, Sudbury Museum Trust, via David Burnett.
5 Interview with author.
6 Katherine Brainard Hutchins, *The Experiences of One American Red Cross Girl in World War II: As Told Through Letters to Her Mother*, Sudbury Museum Trust, via David Burnett.
7 Ibid.
8 Ibid.
9 Ibid.
10 *Daily Telegraph*, 12 November 1943.
11 Roger Freeman, *The US Strategic Bomber*, p. 155.
12 *The German Reich and the Second World War*, quoted in the *Daily Telegraph*, 19 July 2008.
13 Interview by Kurt Piehler and Rich Colton, Rutgers Oral History Archives.
14 Katherine Brainard Hutchins, *The Experiences of One American Red Cross Girl in World War II: As Told Through Letters to Her Mother*, Sudbury Museum Trust, via David Burnett.
15 Oral history session by Julie Croft. See Clements (ed.), *Silent Heroes Among Us*.
16 Katherine Brainard Hutchins, *The Experiences of One American Red Cross Girl in World War II: As Told Through Letters to Her Mother*, Sudbury Museum Trust, via David Burnett.
17 Ibid.
18 See 8th AF Report of Medical Activity, 8th AF 1940–1944, Air Force Historical Research Agency, Maxwell AFB, Alabama, 520 7411-10.

Notes

19 Office of Air Surgeon *Report of Psychiatric Study of Successful Air Crews*, 11 October 1943, AFHRA, quoted in Mark K. Wells, *Courage and Air Warfare*, p. 68.

20 See National Archives, Air 2/6252 and Richard A. Gabriel, *Military Psychiatry*, New York, Greenwood Press, 1986, quoted in Wells, *Courage and Air Warfare*, p. 70.

21 Wells, *Courage and Air Warfare*, p. 70.

22 Douglas D. Bond, *The Love and Fear of Flying*, p. 100–1.

23 Diary of John J. Briol, quoted by permission of Marcella Briol and John F. Briol.

24 Interview by Kurt Piehler and Kevin McGuire, Rutgers Oral History Archives.

25 IWM 67/280/1.

26 Interview by Shaun Illingworth, Rutgers Oral History Archives.

27 'The Dayton Tapes', Volume 1, 2nd AD Memorial Library, Norwich NL00087435.

28 Katherine Brainard Hutchins, *The Experiences of One American Red Cross Girl in World War II: As Told Through Letters to Her Mother*, Sudbury Museum Trust, via David Burnett.

29 Letter in Katherine Brainard Hutchins file, Sudbury Museum Trust.

30 Lounge display, *Queen Mary 2*.

31 Bulkhead display, *Queen Mary 2*.

32 Howard Roth's Veterans History Project.

33 *Calendar News*, Yorkshire Television, 12 May 2012.

Glossary

A/A Anti-Aircraft shell fire

A/C Aircraft

AD Air Division

AP Aiming point

ASI Air Speed Indicator

ASR Air Sea Rescue

BD Bombardment Division

Big Friends US combat fighter pilots' name for B-17s and B-24s

Butterfly bomb Early German cluster bomb, dropped in numbers when carriers burst apart on release from aircraft, causing the thin metal outer shell to spring open like a butterfly's wings, thus arming the ordnance. Many of these anti-personnel weapons were designed to explode if moved on the ground or picked up by the curious and surviving examples of the thousands dropped remain dangerous today.

BOQ Bachelor officers' quarters

BTC Bomb through cloud, relying on a radar scan

CAVU Aviation meteorological acronym meaning 'ceiling and visibility unlimited', which in practice meant ten miles or more

C47 Twin-engined multi-purpose aircraft, known as the Dakota in Britain

Chaff Metallised paper producing spurious responses on Luftwaffe radar. The RAF, who first used it, coded it *Window*.

CoQ Charge of Quarters, the enlisted man – usually a sergeant – who noisily wakened crews in their billets for the day's mission

ETA Estimated time of arrival

ETO European Theatre of Operations

DD Duplex drive, D-Day's swimming tanks

Glossary

DF Direction finding radio equipment

DFC Distinguished Flying Cross

DR Dead reckoning (navigation)

DUC Distinguished Unit Citation, later known as a Presidential Citation

E/A Enemy aircraft

Experten A recognised Luftwaffe ace with five or more confirmed victories

Feldwebel Sergeant in the Wehrmacht or Luftwaffe

FFI French forces of the interior, the Resistance

Flak Short for *flugabaehrkanone* (anti-aircraft fire)

FO Field order, the instructions for a mission issued from 8th AF headquarters by teleprinter to Groups

F/O Flight Officer

FTR Failed To Return, the final verdict on an operational bomber

FIDO Runway fog dispersal system using burning petrol

Fw 190 Focke-Wulf single-engined fighter; armoured versions led *Sturmbok* attacks

GCA Ground-controlled approach system for landing aircraft

Gee Airborne device receiving signals from one master and two slave radio stations by which a navigator was able to plot his exact course on a grid

H2X Radar scanner carried underneath bombers supplying features of terrain below to operator inside

ILS Instrument landing system

IP The navigational position where the straight and level bomb run to the target began

Jager Fighter aircraft or aircrew. The command structure was in staffels of nine aircraft, three staffels making a gruppe, three gruppe making a *geschwader*. In abbreviated form the Third Group of the First Fighter Geschwader would be III/JG 1.

Ju 88 Twin-engined multi-purpose Junkers aircraft, used as a bomber and night fighter

Kriegsgefangene German term for Prisoner of War

Little Friends American bomber crew name for US fighter escorts

LMF Lack of moral fibre, the harsh judgement made by the RAF on those who felt unable to continue operational flying. Their files were stamped.

Me 109 Single-engined Messerschmitt day fighter

Me 110 Twin-engined Messerschmitt fighter, more often used at night

Me 210 Improved version of the 110, superseded by the 410 which had increased speed and range

Mickey USAAF colloquial name for the ground-sweeping radar H2X

Mayday International radio distress call, originating pre-war

MPI Mean Point of Impact, the assigned target for a particular bomber Group and also the plotted result

OKW (*Oberkommando der Wehrmacht*) High command of Germany's armed forces

Pfc Private first class

PR Photographic reconnaissance

Purple Heart Corner Position of the last plane in the lowest right-hand corner of a formation

PX Post Exchange. A base commissary where US airmen could buy canned goods and other products including cigarettes at cut rates.

Rally Point The map reference over which Groups turned and assembled for the course home

R and R Rest and recreation, usually known as 'flak leave', a week in an English country house taken over by the USAAF for the duration and designed to restore shattered nerves or simply remove exhaustion

RNZAF Royal New Zealand Air Force

S2 A Group staff officer, usually a lieutenant, responsible for operations, security and acquiring and disseminating intelligence, who had a staff of his own, usually non-commissioned

S/E Single-engined aircraft

S/Sgt Staff Sergeant

Sortie One operational flight by a single aircraft

Sqn Squadron

T/Sgt Technical Sergeant

Glossary

TI Target indicator

USO United Services Organisation, set up in 1941 to entertain American troops overseas with shows often including Hollywood celebrities. Also organised local leaves for troops.

U/S Unserviceable

USAAC United States Army Air Corps, the military aviation service of the US Army until expansion into the USAAF in June 1941

USAAF The army air forces in all theatres of war under the absolute control of General Hap Arnold in Washington. They remained part of the United States Army until the independent United States Air Force came into being in September 1947.

USSTAF The United States Strategic and Tactical Air Forces was the title of the unified command under Lt Gen. Carl Spaatz at Bushy Park, West London, formed from the nucleus of VIII Bomber Command of the 8th Air Force in February 1944. It gave him control of air operations by the 8th AF, the ETO-based 9th Air Force (which with its ground-strafing fighters supplied much of the tactical element), and the 12th and 15th Air Forces in the Mediterranean.

VHF Very High Frequency, radio for inter-aircraft communication

Bibliography

ADDISON, Paul, *Now the War Is Over: A Social History of Britain 1945* (Jonathan Cape, 1985)

ALLING, Charles, *A Mighty Fortress: Lead Bomber over Europe*, edited by Elizabeth Alling Hildt (Casemate, 2002)

ALANBROOKE, Field Marshal Lord, *War Diaries 1939–1945*, edited by Alex Danchev and Daniel Todman (Weidenfeld & Nicolson, 2001)

ANDREAS-FRIEDRICH, Ruth, *Berlin Underground* (Latimer House, 1948)

ARBIB, Robert, *Here We Are Together* (Longmans, Green and Co., 1946)

ASTOR, Gerald, *The Mighty Eighth* (Dell Publishing, 1998)

BARDUA, Heinz, *Stuttgart in Luftkrieg 1939–45* (Klett Verlag, 1985)

BECK, Earl R., *Under the Bombs: German Home Front, 1942–1945* (University Press of Kentucky, 1986)

BEEVOR, Antony, *D-Day* (Penguin Group, 2009)

BENNETT, J. M., *Letters from England* (San Antonio, 1945)

BOITEN, Theo, and Bowman, Martin, *Battles with the Luftwaffe: The Bomber Campaign against Germany 1942–45* (HarperCollins, 2001)

BOND, Douglas D., *The Love and Fear of Flying* (New York International Universities Press, 1952)

BOVE, Arthur P., *First Over Germany: A Story of the 306th BG* (Newsfoto Publishing Co., 1946)

BRAYLEY, Martin, *The USAAF Airman: Service & Survival 1941–45* (The Crowood Press, 2007)

BRENNAN, Dan, *Never So Young Again* (George Allen & Unwin, 1944)

BRET, David, *Clark Gable: Tormented Star* (JR Books, 2007)

BROOKS, Geoffrey, *Hitler's Terror Weapons: From V-1 to Vimana* (Leo Cooper, 2002)

BUNGAY, Stephen, *The Most Dangerous Enemy* (Aurum Press, 2000)

Bibliography

CARRINGTON, Charles, *A Soldier at Bomber Command* (Leo Cooper, 1987)

CHORLEY, W. R., *Bomber Command Losses, 1944* (Midland Counties Publications, 1997)

CHORLEY, W. R., *Bomber Command Losses, 1945* (Midland Counties Publications, 1998)

COSTELLO, John, *Love, Sex & War: Changing Values 1939–45* (Collins, 1985)

COWLEY, Robert (ed.), *No End Save Victory* (Cassell and Co., 2002)

CRANE, Conrad C., *Bombs, Cities and Civilians: American Airpower and Strategy in World War II* (University Press of Kansas, 1993)

CRAVEN, Frank, and Cate, James Lea, *The Army Air Forces in World War II* (Office of Air History, Washington, 1983)

CROFT, Julie, WAC interview, in James Clements (ed.), *Silent Heroes Among Us*, 8th Air Force compilation (New Horizon Publishing, 1996)

CROSBY, Harry H., *A Wing and a Prayer* (Robson Books, 2004)

DEAN, Sir Maurice, *The RAF and Two World Wars* (Cassell, 1979)

DORR, Robert F., *Mission to Berlin* (Zenith Press, 2011)

ELLIS, L. F., *Victory in the West* (London, 1962)

ELSON, Aaron, *9 Lives: An Oral History* (Chi Chi Press, 1999)

ETHELL, Jeffrey, and Price, Alfred, *Target Berlin. Mission 250: 6 March 1944* (Jane's, London, 1981)

FARR, Frank, *P.O.W.: A Kriegie's Story* (AuthorHouse, 2004)

FEST, Joachim, *Speer: The Final Verdict* (Alexander Fest Verlag, 1999)

FISCHER, Josef, *Köln 1939–45* (J. P. Bachem, 1970)

FORSBERG, Franklin S., *The Best From Yank* (E.P. Dutton and Co., 1945).

FOOT, M. R. D., and Langley, J. M., *MI9: Escape and Evasion 1939–1945* (Bodley Head, 1979)

FREEMAN, Roger A., *The Mighty Eighth* (Macdonald and Jane's, 1970)

FREEMAN, Roger A., *The Mighty Eighth in Colour* (Arms and Armour Press, 1992)

FREEMAN, Roger A., with Alan Crouchman and Vic Maslen, *The Mighty Eighth War Diary* (Jane's Publishing, London, 1981)

FREEMAN, Roger A., *The Mighty Eighth War Manual* (Cassell & Co., 2001)

FREEMAN, Roger A., *The US Strategic Bomber* (Macdonald and Janes, London, 1975)

FRIEDRICH, Jorg, *The Fire: The Bombing of Germany 1940–1945* (Columbia University Press, 2006)

GARDINER, Juliet, *Over Here: The GIs in Wartime Britain* (Collins and Brown, 1992)

GILBERT, Sir Martin, *The Day the War Ended: VE-Day 1945 in Europe and Around the World* (HarperCollins, 1995)

GREEN, William, *The Warplanes of the Third Reich* (Doubleday and Co., New York, 1972)

HAINES, William Wister, *Command Decision* (Cassell and Co., 1948)

HARRIS, Sir Arthur, *Bomber Offensive* (Collins, 1947)

HASSEL, Fey von, *A Mother's War* (John Murray, 1990)

HAWKINS, Desmond, editor and compiler, *War Report: From D-Day to VE-Day* (BBC Books, 1994)

HAWKINS, Ian L. (ed.), *B-17s Over Berlin: Personal Stories from the 95th Bomb Group (H)* (Potomac Books, 2005)

HERRMANN, Hajo, *Eagle's Wings* (Guild Publishing, 1991)

HORSTMANN, Lali, *Nothing for Tears* (Weidenfeld & Nicolson, 1953)

HUTTON, Bud, and Rooney, Andy, *The Story of Tripes* (J. J. Little and Ives Company, New York, 1946)

INFIELD, Glenn, *Big Week* (Pinnacle Books, 1974)

JANSEN, Harold E., *The History of the 446th BG* (British Library, YA.1991.b.424)

JENKINS, Roy, *Churchill* (Macmillan, 2001)

JOHNEN, Wilhelm, *Duel Under the Stars* (William Kimber and Co., 1957)

KARDORFF, Ursula von, *Diary of a Nightmare* (Rupert Hart-Davis, 1965)

KLEMPERER, Victor, *To the Bitter End: The Diaries of Victor Klemperer 1942–45*, abridged and translated by Martin Chalmers (Phoenix, 2000)

KNOKE, Heinz, *I Flew for the Fuhrer* (Evans Bros, 1953)

Bibliography

LOGAN, Edward, *Jump, Damn It, Jump! Memoir of a Downed B17 Pilot in WWII* (McFarland and Co., 2006)

LONG, Vera A. Cracknell, *From Britain With Love: WW2 Pilgrim Brides Sail to America* (Denecroft Publishing, 1988)

LONGDEN, Sean, *For the Victor the Spoils* (Arris Books, 2004)

LONGMATE, Norman, *Bombers: The RAF Offensive Against Germany 1939–45* (Arrow Books, 1986)

LONGMATE, Norman, *The GIs: Americans in Britain, 1942–45* (Hutchinson, 1975)

MACKLEY, Alan (ed.), *The Poaching Priors of Blythburgh* (Blythburgh Society, 2002)

MCKEE, Alexander, *Dresden 1945: The Devil's Tinderbox* (Souvenir Press, 1982)

MCKEE, Ilse, *Tomorrow the World* (J.M. Dent & Sons, 1960)

MCCOLLUM, John W. (ed.), *The Best War Stories of the National Capital Area Chapter, 8th Eighth AF Air Force Historical Society* (National Capital Area Chapter, 8th Air Force Historical Society, 1996)

MEAD, Margaret, *The American Troops and the British Community* (Hutchinson, London, 1944)

MIDDLEBROOK, Martin, and Everitt, Chris, *The Bomber Command War Diaries* (Viking, 1985)

MILLER, Donald L., *Eighth Air Force* (Aurum Press, London, 2007)

MILLGATE, Helen D., *Got Any Gum Chum?* (Sutton Publishing, 2001)

MONTAGNA, Christopher, *Brightwood Boys: The History of the Men from the North End of Springfield, Massachusetts, During World War II* (Lulu Publishers, 2011)

MOOREHEAD, Alan, *Eclipse* (Hamish Hamilton, 1945)

OVERY, Richard, *The Air War 1939–45* (Europa Publications, 1980)

OVERY, Richard, *Bomber Command, 1939–45* (HarperCollins, 1997)

OVERY, Richard, *Why the Allies Won* (Jonathan Cape, 1995)

PITTS, Jesse Richard, *Return to Base: Memoirs of a B-17 Co-pilot, Kimbolton, England, 1943–1944* (Tempus Publishing, 2006)

POWERS, Thomas, *Heisenberg's War: The Secret History of the German Bomb* (Jonathan Cape, 1993)

PRICE, Alfred, *Skies of Fire: Dramatic Air Combat* (Cassell & Co., 2002)

PRICE, Alfred, *The Last Year of the Luftwaffe: May 1944 to May 1945* (Greenhill Books, 2001)

REDDING, Major John M., and Leyshon, Capt. Harold I., *Skyways to Berlin: With the American Fliers in England* (Bobbs-Merrill, 1943)

REYNOLDS, David, *Rich Relations: The American Occupation of Britain 1942–1945* (Phoenix Press, 2000)

RICHARDS, Denis, *Royal Air Force 1939–45. Volume I: The Fight at Odds* (Her Majesty's Stationery Office, 1953)

RICHARDS, Denis, *The Hardest Victory* (Hodder & Stoughton, 1994)

RICHARDS, Denis and Saunders, Hilary St G., *Royal Air Force 1939–45. Volume II: The Fight Avails* (Her Majesty's Stationery Office, 1954)

ROWBOTHAM, Tom, *Varga* (Magna Books, 1993)

RUMPF, Hans, *The Bombing of Germany* (Frederick Muller, 1961)

SAUNDERS, Hilary St G., *Royal Air Force 1939–45. Volume III: The Fight is Won* (Her Majesty's Stationery Office, 1954)

SAWARD, Dudley, *'Bomber' Harris: The Authorised Biography* (Cassell, 1984)

SCHAFFER, Ronald, *Wings of Judgement: American Bombing in World War II* (Oxford University Press, 1985)

SHERIDAN, Dorothy (ed.), *Wartime Women: A Mass-Observation Anthology 1937–45* (Phoenix Press, 2000)

SPEER, Albert, *Inside the Third Reich* (Weidenfeld & Nicolson, 1970)

STILES, Bert, *Serenade to the Big Bird* (Bantam Books, London, 1984)

STREITFELD, Leonard, *Hell From Heaven* (www.hellfromheaven.com)

STUBBINGTON, John, *BMP Reports by the German Air Section* (Bletchley Park Trust, 2012)

TAYLOR, Frederick, *Dresden: Tuesday 13 February 1945* (Bloomsbury Publishing, 2004)

TERRAINE, John, *The Right of the Line* (Hodder & Stoughton, 1985)

TREVOR-ROPER, Hugh (ed.), *The Goebbels Diaries: The Last Days* (Secker & Warburg, 1978)

TURNER, Richard E., *Mustang Pilot* (William Kimber, London, 1969)

VASSILTCHIKOV, Marie, *Berlin Diaries 1940–1945* (Alfred A. Knopf, New York, 1987)

Bibliography

WALLER, Maureen, *London, 1945: Life in the Debris of War* (John Murray, 2004)

WEIR, Adrian, *The Last Flight of the Luftwaffe* (Cassell, 2013)

WELLS, Mark K., *Courage and Air Warfare: The Allied Aircrew Experience in the Second World War* (Frank Cass, London, 1995)

WHITING, Charles (ed.), *The Home Front: Germany* (Time Life Books, 1982)

WILMOT, Chester, *The Struggle for Europe* (Collins, 1952)

WILSON, Kevin, *Men of Air: The Doomed Youth of Bomber Command* (Weidenfeld & Nicolson, 2007)

WINFIELD, Pamela, *Sentimental Journey: The Story of the GI Brides* (Constable, 1984)

WINFIELD, Pamela, *Bye Bye Baby: The story of the Children the GIs Left Behind* (Bloomsbury, 1992)

Index

INDEX

INDEX

INDEX

Big Week, 7, 13, 25–6, 32, 38, 42, 50–2,
    55, 57, 59, 61–5, 211, 215
  marks turning point, 61–3
  and RAF support, 55, 59, 61, 64
  survivors, 96, 202
Biri, Lt Paul, 351–3
Bishop of Chelmsford, 127
Black Thursday, 29, 32, 35, 52
Blackpool, 231–2, 251
Blainville, 152
Blakeslee, Colonel Don, 189, 192
Bletchley Park, 311, 324–5
Bloemendal, Lt John, 251–2
Blogger, Colonel Jacob, 172
Blythburgh accident, 256–7
Böhlen fuel complex, 214, 221, 310,
    402
Bonhoeffer, Pastor Dietrich, 443–4
Bottisham, 139–40, 153, 237, 242
Bottomley, Norman, 382–3
Bourn, Lt Oscar, 57–61
Bove, S/Sgt Arthur, 167, 171
Bowden, Lt W. W. 'Woody', 171,
    228
Bowman, Colonel Harold, 10–11
Boxted, 52, 67, 118–19, 132
Boy Scouts, 444
Bradley, General Omar, 195–6, 343
Brainard, 2/Lt Newell, 219, 235–6,
    238
  capture, 478–9
  goes missing over Kassel, 241, 249,
    311, 403, 406–8, 459, 461, 470–1
Brainard, Kay, 219, 235, 249, 282, 354
  and Bill Brainard's return, 459–61
  goes flying, 411–12
  and Luftwaffe attack on Sudbury,
    417–18
  and search for Newell Brainard,
    470–1, 478–9

and Sudbury base, 375–8, 403–4,
    406–8, 411–13, 417–19, 435–7,
    445–6, 451–3, 458–60, 471
  transferred to Germany, 464–6, 470
  and VE-Day, 452–3
Brainard, T/Sgt William, 219, 235,
    249, 403, 406
  returns from imprisonment,
    459–61
Brandenburg, 370–3
Brashares, Lt Joseph, 177
Brass, Kenneth, 317
Braswell, Ralph, 21
Bremen, 26, 93, 97, 324
Brend, S/Sgt Calvin, 44, 46–7
Brennan, T/Sgt Dan, 116
Brent, S/Sgt Landon, 16–19
Brereton, General Louis, 36
Brett, Douglas and Dennis, 120–1
Brickner, Rabbi R., 286
Brill, 2/Lt Ivan, 275–7
Briol, S/Sgt John J., 294, 298, 310, 389,
    392, 469
British War Cabinet, 62, 379, 382
Bronze Stars, 283, 467
Brown, W/O Ron, 340–1
Browning, Cptn James, 371–3
Brunswick, 5–6, 13, 15, 35, 39, 42, 69,
    82, 101, 142, 186, 236, 300, 303,
    366, 371, 415
Brusetti, Dee, 216–17, 345
Brusetti, Lt Alfeo, 216–17, 234, 330–1,
    345
  and Berlin raids, 389, 395, 398–9
Brussels, 152, 229–30, 306, 370, 373,
    423
Brussels sprouts, 354, 436
Brüx, 401
Buckingham Palace, 102n, 453–4
Bucklew, Lt Harold, 358

INDEX

INDEX

INDEX

Eisenhower, General Dwight D., 36,
  130, 134
  and Oil Plan, 201–2
  and Pilsen raid, 446–8
  and Transportation Plan, 150–1
Elduff, Lt, 306
Elizabeth, Princess, 208–10, 388, 394
Elizabeth, Queen, 208
Elkin, T/Sgt Orville, 360
Ellersick, Lt Frank, 399
Elsen, Tom, 337
Elsterwerda, 187, 189
Elveden Hall, 95, 454
Empire State Building, aircraft crashes
  into, 458
Epinal, 153
Erkner, 65, 74, 96, 98, 100
Erlangen, 470
Ernst, Cptn John, 393
Esquire magazine, 285–6
Etampes-Mondesir, 154
Ethridge, 2/Lt Bill, 246–8, 262–4
Euger, Charlie, 175
Everett, Ken, 442
Everett, Lt Orville, 223–4
Everitt, Tony, 122

Fairbanks, Douglas, Jr, 478
Falaise, 178
Farmer, Sgt Arnold, 84
Farr, 2/Lt Frank, 301
Federici, Frank W., 315–16, 318, 320–1
Feller, Cpl, Jack, 139–40, 153, 165, 183,
  258, 355, 419, 430
  and *Devil's Own* explosion, 334–6
  and party ice, 365–6
Feller, Cptn Charles, 139, 153–4
Fergusen, Lt Allen, 449
Fersfield, 255
Finsterwalde, 240

FitzGerald, Lt Col. Shepler, 460
flak defences
  eventual depletion, 410
  increased effectiveness, 136, 138,
  376
  over Berlin, 85, 96, 144, 378, 384,
  391, 393–4, 399
  over Dresden, 399
  over Leuna-Merseburg, 289–90,
  292, 297, 304, 307, 313, 323, 399
Flare Path, 206
Flossenbürg concentration camp,
  443–4
Flowers, Doreen, 473
flying bomb aircraft, 254–8
Foggia, 39, 193
Fowlmere, 225, 311, 353
Foy, Lt Robert, 67
Framlingham, 253, 255, 371, 431, 477
Frankfurt, 4, 149, 253, 321–2, 331, 350,
  401, 464
Freckleton disaster, 250–4
Fredericksen, S/Sgt Richard, 364
Freiser, Roland, 394, 397
French Resistance, 60–1, 157
Freya radar stations, 77
Furr, Lt, 306
Fürth, 56, 59

Gabay, S/Sgt John, 75, 77, 82
Gable, Clark, 107, 124, 431, 455
Gainsborough, Thomas, 466
Gaire, Paul G., 47
Galland, General der Jagdflieger
  Adolf, 50, 52, 65, 102, 297
Gardner, Peter, 157
Gates, 2/Lt Ed, 301
Gee system, 167, 174–5
Genshagen, 75, 86
Genz, Lt Wilbur 'Bud', 347

INDEX

INDEX

INDEX

INDEX

INDEX

INDEX

INDEX

INDEX

INDEX

INDEX

INDEX

INDEX